Christian Love

Bernard V. Brady

Georgetown University Press
Washington, D.C.

Georgetown Univeristy Press, Washington, D.C.
© 2003 by Georgetown University Press. All rights reserved.
Printed in the United States of America

10 9 8 7 6 5 4 3 2 1   2003

This volume printed on acid-free offset book paper.

Library of Congress Cataloging-in-Publication Data

Brady, Bernard V. (Bernard Vincent), 1957–
   Christian love / Bernard V. Brady
      p.   cm.
Includes bibliographical references and index.
   ISBN 0-87840-894-0 (alk. paper)
   1. Love—Religious aspects—Christianity—History of doctrines.   I. Title.
BV4639   .B72 2003
241′.4—dc21   2002015256

To
Cynthia, Mark, Patrick, Edward, Ellen, and Nora

For when we ask how good a man is, we do not ask what he believes or what he hopes for, but what he loves.

Augustine, *Enchiridian*

Contents

Preface

I love, therefore I am. Loving seems entirely natural and being loved seems wonderfully good. When we love great things or when we love greatly, we feel most alive. We make friends. We marry. We live in families. We feel a connection, however distant, with others. We work. We dedicate ourselves to ideals. We love, therefore we are.

Loving and existence are dramatically and emphatically tied together for the Christian. At least they ought to be. Christian faith attests to a God described as love, and holds that God demands that we love. God models love particularly and most intensely through the life, teachings, and death of Jesus. By nature we love; by faith we must love.

This book presents the occasion to think about love, ourselves as lovers, and what we love. It is an attempt to gather interesting and important voices from the Christian theological tradition and to hear what they have to say about love. A significant feature of the book is that it contains a pluralism of views (including several authors who do not appreciate this pluralism!). The first two chapters survey the biblical material on love. Then the following eight chapters take us through the relevant history of Christian thought. These views can be read as sincere appropriations and interpretations of the biblical themes. The pluralism evident here is not unbounded, however. It is circumscribed by the words of the Bible.

The first chapter surveys stories and sayings about love in the Old Testament. I use the term "Old Testament" instead of "Hebrew Scriptures" because I use the deuterocanonical writings, which are recognized as Scripture in the Roman and Orthodox Catholic traditions, but not in the Jewish tradition. The second chapter reviews the dominant themes of love in the New Testament. The third chapter explores the many writings of St. Augustine (354–428) on love. The next three chapters examine different understandings of love in the Medieval Ages. The fourth chapter focuses on the tradition of mystical love for God. It considers the theology of Bernard of Clairvaux (1090–1153), Hadewijch (dates unknown, her written work is dated around 1220), and Julian of Norwich

(1342–1416). Chapter 5 shifts from the monastery and convent to the courts of the lords and ladies; it addresses the phenomenon of courtly love that occurred approximately 1100–1400. The chapter also narrates the famous love story of Heloise and Abelard of the early 1100s. Chapter 6 describes the theology of love, caritas, from Thomas Aquinas (1224–1274). Chapter 7 presents Martin Luther's (1483–1546) theology of love. Luther's theology forms the foundation for the Protestant writers discussed in the eighth chapter, Soren Kierkegaard (1813–1855), Anders Nygren (1890–1977), and Reinhold Niebuhr (1892–1971). These authors argue for a strict and exclusive interpretation of Christian love. Chapter 9 describes the work and writing of three love "activists"—Martin Luther King, Jr., Mother Teresa, and Pope John Paul II. Chapter 10 reviews the work of several contemporary Christian theologians. Themes in this chapter include the experience of love, social consequences of love, and mutuality. The final chapter pulls together themes from various authors in the book to offer a conceptualization of Christian love.

I take all of these texts (I will reserve judgment for the time being on those in the final chapter) to be "classic" texts, in the sense that their message is enduring. They are interesting to read not only because they played an important role in history, but also because they still can have meaning for us today. There is a certain timeless quality to these writings. These texts offer "possibilities of meaning and truth"[1] that can contrast with the way we usually think about love. If we take these texts seriously we are challenged to reconsider and develop our own views.

Several themes recur in the book. One cannot speak of Christian love without some notion of self-sacrifice or service to the neighbor. Yet Christian love also entails relationships with others and particularly with God. Trying to bring these two ideas together is complicated. How does one love God? What ought one actually love when one loves one's neighbor? Should we love others because they are children of God, or for some other explicitly theological reason? Or should we love them because of their unique features? Ought we to love different things in different people?

A word of introduction concerns the language of the authors included in the book. The majority of the texts were written before the current movement away from the exclusiveness and presumptuousness of using the word man to refer to men and women. I have not taken the liberty to change the original language of our authors. I hope this will not be an insurmountable hurdle and that the reader can read with a generosity of spirit.

As you read, compare your experience to that of our authors. Think about the times you have been loved most deeply and when you have loved the most deeply. Think about what loving and being loved does to you. Think about whom and what you love and about the qualities of true love. Think about how Christian faith ought to inform all of these questions. Note, however, the serious limitation of this book. Bernard of Clairvaux reminds us that thinking about love is not sufficient. As you read about love, always bear in mind that thinking about love is not a substitution for loving. Bernard writes, "We must remember that love reveals itself, not by words or phrases, but by action and experience. It is Love which speaks here, and if anyone wishes to understand it, let him first love."[2]

Acknowledgments and Permissions

I owe a deeply felt "thank you" to many people. Thanks first to my colleagues, past and present, who helped me to follow leads, who proofread chapters, and who corrected my mistaken views, particularly Catherine Cory, Michael Hollerich, Shirley Jordon, Anne King, Shawn Madigan, Corrine Patton, David Penchansky, Mary Reichardt, Gerald Schlabach, William Stevenson, and Paul Wojda. Thanks as well to the anonymous readers provided by Georgetown University Press. Thanks to Richard Brown, director of Georgetown University Press, for his guidance, patience, and support. The Faculty Development Center of the University of St. Thomas, as well as the Aquinas Foundation, provided summer stipends for which I am extremely grateful. Thanks to James Gustafson for giving me this problem in graduate school. Thanks also to my loving wife Cynthia, who on more than one occasion had to pull me out of drifting thought about Augustine's view of love when I should have been thinking about more important things, including the car in front of me.

I also wish to thank the publishers for permitting me to quote extensively from the following copyrighted works:

Scripture quotations from the New Revised Standard Version of the Bible with the Apocryphal/Deuterocanonical Books. Copyright 1989 by the Division of Christian Education of the National Council of the Churches of Christ in the USA. Used by permission. All rights reserved.

From *Eighty-Three Different Questions* by Augustine. Trans. David Mosher. *Fathers of the Church*, vol. 70 (Washington, D.C.: The Catholic University of America Press, 1982). Used by permission. All rights reserved.

From *Sermons on Various Subjects*, by Augustine. Trans. Edmund Hill (Hyde Park, NY: New City Press, 1995). *The Works of Saint Augustine: A Translation for the 21st Century*, ed. John Rotelle. Used by permission. All rights reserved.

From *On the Morals of the Catholic Church*, by Augustine. In *St. Augustine: The Writing against the Manicheans and against the Donatists*, ed. Philip Schaff (Grand Rapids, MI: Eerdmans Publishing Company, 1983). Vol. 4 of *The Nicene and Post-Nicene Fathers of the Christian Church*. Used by permission. All rights reserved.

From *The Confessions,* by Augustine. Trans. Maria Boulding (Hyde Park, NY: New City Press, 1997). *The Works of Saint Augustine: A Translation for the 21st Century*, ed. John Rotelle. Used by permission. All rights reserved.

On the Song of Songs I, by Bernard of Clairvaux. Trans. Kilian Walsh (Kalamazoo, MI: Cistercian Publications, 1971). Used by permission. All rights reserved.

On Loving God, by Bernard of Clairvaux. Trans. Emero Steigman (Kalamazoo, MI: Cistercian Publications, 1995). Used by permission. All rights reserved.

On the Song of Songs IV, by Bernard of Clairvaux. Trans. Irene Edmonds (Kalamazoo, MI: Cistercian Publications, 1980). Used by permission. All rights reserved.

"The French Scholar-Lover: Heloise," by Betty Radice. *Medieval Women Writers*, trans. Katharina Wilson (Athens, GA: The University of Georgia Press, 1984). Used by permission. All rights reserved.

The Art of Courtly Love, by Andreas Capellanus. Trans. John Parry (New York: Frederick Ungar Publishing Co., 1959). The Continuum International Publishing Group. Reprinted with the permission of the publisher.

Luther's Works, by Martin Luther. Trans. Jaroslav Pelikan. Vols. 21, 24, 25, 27. Copyright 1964 by Concordia Publishing House. Reproduced with permission under license number 01 7-54A.

Reprinted from *Luther's Works*, vol. 51, by Martin Luther, ed. John Doberstein. Copyright 1959 by Fortress Press. Used by permission of Augsburg Fortress.

Works of Love, by Soren Kierkegaard. Trans Howard Hong. English language copyright 1962 by Howard Hong. Reprinted by permission of HarperCollins Publishers, Inc.

Reprinted from *Love and Justice*, by Reinhold Niebuhr. Ed. D. B. Robertson. Used by permission of Westminster John Knox Press.

Letter to Families, by Pope John Paul II (Washington, D.C.: United States Catholic Conference, 1994). Used by permission of Liberia Editrice Vaticana.

Love: A Fruit Always in Season, by Mother Teresa. Ed. Dorothy Hunt (San Francisco: Ignatius Press, 1987). Used with permission of Ignatius Press.

"Walk for Freedom" from *Experiment in Love*, by Martin Luther King. Reprinted by arrangement with the Estate of Martin Luther King, Jr., c/o Writers House as agent for the proprietor. Copyright 1963 by Martin Luther King, Jr. Copyright renewed 1993 by Coretta Scott King.

A Theology of Liberation, by Gustavo Gutierrez (Maryknoll, NY: Orbis Books, 1993). Used with permission of Orbis Press.

The Mind and Heart of Love, by Martin D'Arcy (New York: Henry Holt and Co., 1947). The publisher has made every effort to secure permission for the use of this copyrighted material.

On Christian Doctrine, by Saint Augustine, translated and with an introduction by D. W. Robertson, Jr. (Indianapolis, IN: Bobbs-Merrill, 1958). The publisher has made every effort to secure permission for the use of this copyrighted material.

The Experience of Love, by Jules Toner (Washington, DC: Corpus Books, 1968). The publisher has made every effort to secure permission for the use of this copyrighted material.

Love in the Old Testament: God's Love and Human Loves

'Aheb and Hesed

Where you go, I will go; where you lodge, I will lodge; your people shall be my people, and your God my God. Where you die, I will die—there will I be buried.

—Ruth

In the Old Testament there are several words translated into English as "love." The two primary words are 'aheb and hesed. 'Aheb is the more general of the two. This word has roots in the marriage relationship and thus has connotations of desiring and experiencing.[1] Usage of the term is, however, quite broad. While it is often used to express the romantic attraction between persons it is also used to describe general feelings of attachment between persons in families, friendships, and even political loyalties. 'Aheb is used to describe love between persons, God's love for people, people's love for God, and love for nonpersonal things. It presupposes a concrete inner disposition based on experience and includes a "conscious action in behalf of the person who is loved or the thing that is preferred."[2] 'Aheb suggests direct practical assistance to others. It demands the concrete acts of love and personal responsibility necessary for the maintenance of relationships and the community.[3]

Hesed, on the other hand, is more limited in its meaning but more frequent in its use. According to biblical scholar Katherine Dobb Sakenfeld, hesed has several characteristics.[4] First, hesed is always used in reference to people, never to things. Second, hesed is used within established relationships. Third, hesed in its most basic form refers to an action that "preserves or promotes life." Hesed is expressed by acts of "intervention on behalf of someone suffering misfortune or distress."[5] There is no accurate English translation of hesed. Biblical translators have used love, loving kindness, mercy, steadfast love, devotion, faithfulness, and loyalty for this Hebrew word.[6] Sakenfeld describes four features of an act of *hesed*. First, she writes, there exists a situation of distress. A person needs the help of another. Second, the situation is desperate. Third, the situation is such that there is only one who is able to help. Fourth, the help offered comes from the free decision of the other.[7]

In this first section on love in the Old Testament we have several testimonies to God's *hesed*. In these passages we see both statements about God and God's love as well as the implication that humans ought to do the same as God does. *Hesed* is the model and indeed the foundation of human love. Experiencing God's *hesed* compels people to live *hesed*. Sakenfeld writes, "From an Old Testament point of view any human loyalty, kindness, love or mercy is rooted ultimately in the loyalty, kindness, love and mercy of God."[8] H. J. Zobel writes, "God's kindness towards an individual places that individual in a new relationship with his neighbor. . . . Thus hesed shapes not only the relationship of Yahweh with human beings, but also that of human beings among themselves."[9]

The book of Ruth is an interesting starting point for the exploration of love in the Old Testament. The story is about faithful love. Alice Laffey writes, "The characters' relationships with one another evidence a fidelity which is grounded in the firm conviction that Yahweh will be faithful to his covenant people."[10] These characters illustrate both *'aheb* and *hesed*. The central relationship in the book is between Ruth and her mother-in-law Naomi. We read that both women have lost their husbands, and they share the grief they have in common. Naomi's grief is compounded, as she has lost both her sons as well. Naomi and her family had been living in the land of Moab for some time. Her sons married Moabite (foreign) women. After the death of her sons, Naomi decides to return to her native land of Judah. Her widowed daughters-in-law, Ruth and Orpah, want to stay with her, but Naomi bids them to remain. If they stay in their native land, she reasons, they might be able to marry again and start a family. Ruth refuses to let Naomi go it alone. She commits herself to stay with Naomi. At this point in the story Ruth utters her famous words of committed love. "Where you go, I will go; where you lodge, I will lodge; your people shall be my people, and your God, my God. Where you die, I will die—there will I be buried" (Ruth 1:16–17). Ruth's fidelity to Naomi is *hesed*.

The two women face hard times when they return to Judah. With the death of their husbands, Naomi and Ruth are left in poverty. There is no social security, or welfare, or indeed job opportunities for women (outside perhaps being a slave). They manage to survive by taking grain from that which is left over from others' fields. Biblical law requires that farmers must leave a part of their harvest for the poor to gather (see Lev. 19:9–10, 23:22; Deut. 24:19–22). Ruth labors for herself and for Naomi, taking food from the field owned by a man named Boaz, a distant relation. As Boaz enters the story, we see another form of love. Boaz allows Ruth to pick from the margins of his field. This is not necessarily because he loves her, but because he wishes to follow God's law.

The object of Boaz's love is God, or more directly, God's law. For Boaz and his contemporaries, following the law was the primary way one could know and follow the invisible, transcendent God. The law described the people's responsibility to the God who created them, saved them, and sustained them. It was what God required them to do. Deuteronomy states, "See, I have set before you today life and prosperity, death and adversity. If you obey the commandments of the Lord your God that I am commanding you today, by loving the Lord your God, walking in his ways, and observing his commandments, decrees and ordinances, then you shall live" (30:15–16). Perhaps Psalm 119 captures the love that directed Boaz's life. The Psalmist proclaims, "Oh, how I love your law! It is my meditation all day long" (119:7) and "I find my delight in your commandments, because I love them. I revere your commandments which I love, and will meditate on your statutes" (119:47–48).

The law of the Old Testament requires more than merely allowing the poor to glean from your fields. It also commands love of neighbor. Deuteronomy 10:17–19, for example, states, "For the Lord your God is God of gods and Lord of Lords, the great God, mighty and awesome . . . who executes justice for the orphan and the widow and who loves strangers, providing them with food and clothing. You shall also love the stranger, for you were strangers in the land of Egypt." The book of Leviticus likewise states, "You shall not take vengeance or bear a grudge against any of your people; but you shall love your neighbor as your self: I am the Lord" (Lev. 19:18). Leviticus also states, "When an alien resides with you in your land, you shall not oppress the alien. The alien who resides with you shall be to you as the citizen among you; you shall love the alien as yourself, for you were aliens in the land of Egypt: I am the Lord your God" (Lev. 19:33–34).

The lives of Ruth, Naomi, and Boaz illustrate faithfulness expressed in direct actions. These actions, as well as the convictions backing them, reflect their confidence in God and give the reader a sense of what God's love is like. Here is the story of Ruth.

Chapter 1: In the days when the judges ruled, there was a famine in the land, and a certain man of Bethlehem in Judah went to live in the country of Moab, he and his wife and two sons. The name of the man was Elimelech and the name of his wife Naomi, and the names of his two sons were Mahlon and Chilion; they were Ephrathites from Bethlehem in Judah.

They went into the country of Moab and remained there. But Elimelech, the husband of Naomi, died, and she was left with her two sons. These took Moabite wives; the name of the one was Orpah and the name of the other Ruth. When they had lived there about ten years, both Mahlon and Chilion also died, so that the woman was left without her two sons and her husband.

Then she started to return with her daughters-in-law from the country of Moab, for she had heard in the country of Moab that the Lord had considered his people and given them food. So she set out from the place where she had been living, she and her two daughters-in-law, and they went on their way to go back to the land of Judah. But Naomi said to her two daughters-in-law, "Go back each of you to your mother's house. May the Lord deal kindly with you, as you have dealt with the dead and with me. The Lord grant that you may find security, each of you in the house of your husband." Then she kissed them, and they wept aloud. They said to her, "No, we will return with you to your people." But Naomi said, "Turn back, my daughters, why will you go with me? Do I still have sons in my womb that they may become your husbands? Turn back, my daughters, go your way, for I am too old to have a husband. Even if I thought there was hope for me, even if I should have a husband tonight and bear sons, would you then wait until they were grown? Would you then refrain from marrying? No, my daughters, it has been far more bitter for me than for you, because the hand of the Lord has turned against me." Then they wept aloud again. Orpah kissed her mother-in-law, but Ruth clung to her.

So she said, "See, your sister-in-law has gone back to her people and to her gods; return after your sister-in-law." But Ruth said, "Do not press me to leave you or to turn back from following you! Where you go, I will go; where you lodge, I will lodge; your people shall be my people, and your God my God. Where you die, I will die—there will I be buried. May the Lord do thus and so to me, and more as well, if even death parts me from you!" When Naomi saw that she was determined to go with her, she said no more to her.

So the two of them went on until they came to Bethlehem. When they came to Bethlehem, the whole town was stirred because of them; and the women said, "Is this Naomi?" She said to them, "Call me no longer Naomi, call me Mara, for the Almighty has dealt bitterly with me. I went away full, but the Lord has brought me back empty; why call me Naomi when the Lord has dealt harshly with me, and the Almighty has brought calamity upon me?"

So Naomi returned together with Ruth the Moabite, her daughter-in-law, who came back with her from the country of Moab. They came to Bethlehem at the beginning of the barley harvest.

Chapter 2: Now Naomi had a kinsman on her husband's side, a prominent rich man, of the family of Elimelech, whose name was Boaz. And Ruth the Moabite said to Naomi, "Let me go to the field and glean among the ears of grain, behind someone in whose sight I may find favor." She said to her, "Go, my daughter." So she went. She came and gleaned in the field behind the reapers. As it happened, she came to the part of the field belonging to Boaz, who was of the family of Elimelech. Just then Boaz came from Bethlehem. He said to the reapers, "The Lord be with you." They answered, "The Lord bless you." Then Boaz said to his servant who was in charge of the reapers, "To whom does this young woman belong?" The servant who was in charge of the reapers answered, "She is the Moabite who came back with Naomi from the country of Moab. She said, 'Please, let me glean and gather among the sheaves behind the reapers.' So she came, and she has been on her feet from early this morning until now, without resting even for a moment."

Then Boaz said to Ruth, "Now listen, my daughter, do not go to glean in another field or leave this one, but keep close to my young women. Keep your eyes on the field that is being reaped, and follow behind them. I have ordered the young men not to bother you. If you get thirsty, go to the vessels and drink from what the young men have drawn." Then she fell prostrate, with her face to the ground, and said to him, "Why have I found favor in your sight, that you should take notice of me, when I am a foreigner?" But Boaz answered her, "All that you have done for your mother-in-law since the death of your husband has been fully told me, and how you left your father and mother and your native land and came to a people that you did not know before. May the Lord reward you for your deeds, and may you have a full reward from the Lord, the God of Israel, under whose wings you have come for refuge!" Then she said, "May I continue to find favor in your sight, my Lord, for you have comforted me and spoken kindly to your servant, even though I am not one of your servants."

At mealtime Boaz said to her, "Come here, and eat some of this bread, and dip your morsel in the sour wine." So she sat beside the reapers, and he heaped up for her some parched grain. She ate until she was satisfied, and she had some left over. When she got up to glean, Boaz instructed his young men, "Let her glean even among the standing sheaves, and do not reproach her. You must also pull out some handfuls for her from the bundles, and leave them for her to glean, and do not rebuke her."

So she gleaned in the field until evening. Then she beat out what she had gleaned, and it was about an ephah of barley. She picked it up and came into the town, and her mother-in-law saw how much she had gleaned. Then she took out and gave her what was left over after she herself had been satisfied. Her mother-in-law said to her, "Where did you glean today? And where have you worked? Blessed be the man who took notice of you." So she told her mother-in-law with whom she had worked, and said, "The name of the man with whom I worked today is Boaz." Then Naomi said to her daughter-in-law, "Blessed be he by the Lord, whose kindness has not forsaken the living or the dead!" Naomi also said to her, "The man is a relative of ours, one of our nearest kin." Then Ruth the Moabite said, "He even said to me, 'Stay close by my servants, until they have finished all my harvest.'" Naomi said to Ruth, her daughter-in-law, "It is better, my daughter, that you go out with his young women, otherwise you might be bothered in another field." So she stayed close to the young women of Boaz, gleaning until the end of the barley and wheat harvests; and she lived with her mother-in-law.

Chapter 3: Naomi her mother-in-law said to her, "My daughter, I need to seek some security for you, so that it may be well with you. Now here is our kinsman Boaz, with whose young women you have been working. See, he is winnowing barley tonight at the threshing floor. Now wash and anoint yourself, and put on your best clothes and go down to the threshing floor; but do not make yourself known to the man until he has finished eating and drinking. When he lies down, observe the place where he lies; then, go and uncover his feet and lie down; and he will tell you what to do." She said to her, "All that you tell me I will do."

So she went down to the threshing floor and did just as her mother-in-law had instructed her. When Boaz had eaten and drunk, and he was in a contented mood, he went to lie down at the end of the heap of grain. Then she came stealthily and uncovered his feet, and lay down. At midnight the man was startled, and turned over, and there, lying at his feet, was a woman! He said, "Who are you?" And she answered, "I am Ruth, your servant; spread your cloak over your servant, for you are next-of-kin." He said, "May you be blessed by the Lord, my daughter; this last instance of your loyalty is better than the first; you have not gone after young men, whether poor or rich. And now, my daughter, do not be afraid, I will do for you all that you ask, for all the assembly of my people know that you are a worthy woman. But now, though it is true that I am a near kinsman, there is another kinsman more closely related than I. Remain this night, and in the morning, if he will act as next-of-kin for you, good; let him do it. If he is not willing to act as next-of-kin for you, then, as the Lord lives, I will act as next-of-kin for you. Lie down until the morning."

So she lay at his feet until morning, but got up before one person could recognize another; for he said, "It must not be known that the woman came to the threshing floor." Then he said, "Bring the cloak you are wearing and hold it out." So she held it, and he measured out six measures of barley, and put it on her back; then he went into the city. She came to her mother-in-law, who said, "How did things go with you, my daughter?" Then she told her all that the man had done for her, saying, "He gave me these six measures of barley, for he said, 'Do not go back to your mother-in-law empty-handed.' "She replied, "Wait, my daughter, until you learn how the matter turns out, for the man will not rest, but will settle the matter today."

Chapter 4: No sooner had Boaz gone up to the gate and sat down there than the next-of-kin, of whom Boaz had spoken, came passing by. So Boaz said, "Come over, friend; sit down here." And he went over and sat down. Then Boaz took ten men of the elders of the city, and said, "Sit down here"; so they sat down. He then said to the next-of-kin, "Naomi, who has come back from the country of Moab, is selling the parcel of land that belonged to our kinsman Elimelech. So I thought I would tell you of it, and say: Buy it in the presence of those sitting here, and in the presence of the elders of my people. If you will redeem it, redeem it; but if you will not, tell me, so that I may know; for there is no one prior to you to redeem it, and I come after you." So he said, "I will redeem it." Then Boaz said, "The day you acquire the field from the hand of Naomi, you are also acquiring Ruth the Moabite, the widow of the dead man, to maintain the dead man's name on his inheritance." At this, the next-of-kin said, "I cannot redeem it for myself without damaging my own inheritance. Take my right of redemption yourself, for I cannot redeem it."

Now this was the custom in former times in Israel concerning redeeming and exchanging: to confirm a transaction, the one took off a sandal and gave it to the other; this was the manner of attesting in Israel. So when the next-of-kin said to Boaz, "Acquire it for yourself," he took off his sandal. Then Boaz said to the elders and all the people, "Today you are witnesses that I have acquired from the hand of Naomi all that belonged to Elimelech and all that belonged to Chilion and Mahlon. I have also acquired Ruth the Moabite, the wife of Mahlon, to be my wife, to maintain the dead man's name on his inheritance, in order that the name of the dead may not be cut off from his kindred and from the gate of his native place; today you are witnesses." Then all the people who were at the gate, along with the elders, said, "We are witnesses. May the Lord make the woman who is coming into your house like Rachel and Leah, who together built up the house of Israel. May you produce children in Ephrathah and bestow a name in Bethlehem; and, through the children that the Lord will give you by this young woman, may your house be like the house of Perez, whom Tamar bore to Judah."

So Boaz took Ruth and she became his wife. When they came together, the Lord made her conceive, and she bore a son. Then the women said to Naomi, "Blessed be the Lord, who has not left you this day without next-of-kin; and may his name be renowned in Israel! He shall be to you a restorer of life and a nourisher of your old age; for your daughter-in-law who loves you, who is more to you than seven sons, has borne him." Then Naomi took the child and laid him in her bosom, and became his nurse. The women of the neighborhood gave him a name, saying, "A son has been born to Naomi." They named him Obed; he became the father of Jesse, the father of David.

Now these are the descendants of Perez: Perez became the father of Hezron, Hezron of Ram, Ram of Amminadab, Amminadab of Nahshon, Nahshon of Salmon, Salmon of Boaz, Boaz of Obed, Obed of Jesse, and Jesse of David.

Hesed is faithful, committed love expressed in concrete actions. There are many places in the Old Testament where the *hesed* of God is directly proclaimed. The story of Moses receiving the covenant is but one example. After Moses receives and ratifies the covenant with God (Exod. 19–31), he returns to the people who, in his absence, set up an idol, the golden calf. In a fit of anger, Moses destroys the tablets of the covenant. After a time, God renews the covenant with Moses with the proclamation: "The Lord, the Lord, a God merciful and gracious, slow to anger, and abounding in steadfast love and faithfulness, keeping steadfast love for the thousandth generation" (Exod. 34:6–7).

God's *hesed* is described and celebrated in the Psalms. Psalm 36:5–10 and Psalm 89:1–2, for example, describe God's *hesed* in dramatic terms. God's love is as great as a mountain, as rich as a feast, and indeed it cannot be limited to things of the earth. It has been shown over time and will last forever.

PSALM 36: 5–10

Your steadfast love, O Lord, extends to the heavens,
>   your faithfulness to the clouds.
Your righteousness is like the mighty mountains,
>   your judgments are like the great deep;
>   you save humans and animals alike, O Lord.
How precious is your steadfast love, O God!
All people may take refuge in the shadow of your wings.
They feast on the abundance of your house,
>   and you give them drink from the river of your delights.
For with you is the fountain of life;
>   in your light we see light.
O continue your steadfast love to those who know you,
>   and your salvation to the upright of heart!

PSALM 89:1–2

I will sing of your steadfast love, O Lord, forever;
>   with my mouth I will proclaim your faithfulness to all generations.
I declare that your steadfast love is established forever;
>   your faithfulness is as firm as the heavens.

Psalm 136 is a beautiful song of thanksgiving narrating the human and eternal history of God's *hesed*.

PSALM 136

O give thanks to the Lord, for he is good,
>   for his steadfast love endures forever.
O give thanks to the God of gods,
>   for his steadfast love endures forever.
O give thanks to the Lord of lords,
>   for his steadfast love endures forever;
who alone does great wonders,
>   for his steadfast love endures forever;
who by understanding made the heavens,
>   for his steadfast love endures forever;
who spread out the earth on the waters,
>   for his steadfast love endures forever;
who made the great lights,
>   for his steadfast love endures forever;

the sun to rule over the day,
> for his steadfast love endures forever;

the moon and stars to rule over the night,
> for his steadfast love endures forever;

who struck Egypt through their firstborn,
> for his steadfast love endures forever;

and brought Israel out from among them,
> for his steadfast love endures forever;

with a strong hand and an outstretched arm,
> for his steadfast love endures forever;

who divided the Red Sea in two,
> for his steadfast love endures forever;

and made Israel pass through the midst of it,
> for his steadfast love endures forever;

but overthrew Pharaoh and his army in the Red Sea,
> for his steadfast love endures forever;

who led his people through the wilderness,
> for his steadfast love endures forever;

who struck down great kings,
> for his steadfast love endures forever;

and killed famous kings,
> for his steadfast love endures forever;

Sihon, king of the Amorites,
> for his steadfast love endures forever;

and Og, king of Bashan,
> for his steadfast love endures forever;

and gave their land as a heritage,
> for his steadfast love endures forever;

a heritage to his servant Israel,
> for his steadfast love endures forever.

It is he who remembered us in our low estate,
> for his steadfast love endures forever;

and rescued us from our foes,
> for his steadfast love endures forever;

who gives food to all flesh,
> for his steadfast love endures forever.

O give thanks to the God of heaven,
> for his steadfast love endures forever.

In the Hebrew Scriptures, *hesed* may be part of one's blessing or good wishes to another, for example, "May the Lord show steadfast love and faithfulness to you" (2 Sam. 15: 20).

A powerful description of *hesed* is found in the book of Hosea. Hosea was a prophet who lived eight centuries before Jesus. The times in which he lived were troubled. His people, Israel, had abandoned God for the gods, called Baal, of the neighboring country Canaan. The Canaanite religion was characterized by a fertility cult and ritual prostitution. Hosea describes this religion as harlotry. He believed that "Israel had forsaken its true lover to give itself to the Baals."[11] The nation was unfaithful to the God who led them out of slavery and who made them a nation. The striking piece in this story is that the troubled relationship between God and Israel is symbolized in the relationship that Hosea has with his wife, Gomer. Gomer is described as a harlot, as is the competing foreign religion itself, and she most likely participated in the cultic fertility rituals. By every right, Hosea ought to divorce her. This is the story of a love that is steadfast in the face of unfaithfulness. Hosea "knows beyond any doubt that Yahweh's love is unchanging no matter how the partner breaks the faith."[12]

The following excerpt is Hosea chapter 4. This chapter is Hosea's passionate and dramatic indictment against the people. Note the strong language the prophet uses to describe Israel's sins (which are being compared to Gomer's).

HOSEA CHAPTER 4

Hear the word of the Lord,
    O people of Israel;
    for the Lord has an indictment against the inhabitants of
        the land.
There is no faithfulness or loyalty,
    and no knowledge of God in the land.
Swearing, lying, and murder,
    and stealing and adultery break out;
    bloodshed follows bloodshed.
Therefore the land mourns,
    and all who live in it languish;
together with the wild animals
    and the birds of the air,
    even the fish of the sea are perishing.
Yet let no one contend,
    and let none accuse,

for with you is my contention, O priest.
You shall stumble by day;
 the prophet also shall stumble with you by night,
 and I will destroy your mother.
My people are destroyed for lack of knowledge;
 because you have rejected knowledge,
 I reject you from being a priest to me.
And since you have forgotten the law of your God,
 I also will forget your children.
The more they increased,
 the more they sinned against me;
 they changed their glory into shame.
They feed on the sin of my people;
 they are greedy for their iniquity.
And it shall be like people, like priest;
 I will punish them for their ways,
 and repay them for their deeds.
They shall eat, but not be satisfied;
 they shall play the whore, but not multiply;
because they have forsaken the Lord
 to devote themselves to whoredom.
Wine and new wine
 take away the understanding.
My people consult a piece of wood,
 and their divining rod gives them oracles.
For a spirit of whoredom has led them astray,
 and they have played the whore, forsaking their God.
They sacrifice on the tops of the mountains,
 and make offerings upon the hills,
under oak, poplar, and terebinth,
 because their shade is good.
Therefore your daughters play the whore,
 and your daughters-in-law commit adultery.
I will not punish your daughters when they play the whore,
 nor your daughters-in-law when they commit adultery;
for the men themselves go aside with whores,
 and sacrifice with temple prostitutes;
thus a people without understanding comes to ruin.

Though you play the whore, O Israel,
>> do not let Judah become guilty.
Do not enter into Gilgal,
>> or go up to Beth-aven,
>> and do not swear, "As the Lord lives."
Like a stubborn heifer,
>> Israel is stubborn;
can the Lord now feed them
>> like a lamb in a broad pasture?
Ephraim is joined to idols—
>> let him alone.
When their drinking is ended, they indulge in sexual orgies;
>> they love lewdness more than their glory.
A wind has wrapped them in its wings,
>> and they shall be ashamed because of their altars.

What should be the punishment for these sins, these crimes? How will God respond? The text that follows, God's response, has been described by prominent biblical scholars as "one of the high points of the Old Testament revelation of God's nature."[13] The passage describes God's love for Israel, Israel's rejection of that love, and God's enduring commitment to Israel. Punishment is called for, but this is not the final word. Hosea forthrightly describes God's freely given passionate response as *hesed*. The enduring love of a parent is used as an analogy to describe God's love. God is like a loving parent who feeds his children, embraces them, teaches them to walk, and leads them in the bond of love. "I was to them like those who lift infants to their cheeks. I bent down to them and fed them" (11:4).

HOSEA 11:1–9
When Israel was a child, I loved him,
>> and out of Egypt I called my son.
The more I called them,
>> the more they went from me;
they kept sacrificing to the Baals,
>> and offering incense to idols.
Yet it was I who taught Ephraim to walk,
>> I took them up in my arms;
>> but they did not know that I healed them.

I led them with cords of human kindness,
  with bands of love.
I was to them like those
  who lift infants to their cheeks.
  I bent down to them and fed them.
They shall return to the land of Egypt,
  and Assyria shall be their king,
  because they have refused to return to me.
The sword rages in their cities,
  it consumes their oracle-priests,
  and devours because of their schemes.
My people are bent on turning away from me.
  To the Most High they call,
  but he does not raise them up at all.
How can I give you up, Ephraim?
  How can I hand you over, O Israel?
How can I make you like Admah?
  How can I treat you like Zeboiim?
My heart recoils within me;
  my compassion grows warm and tender.
I will not execute my fierce anger;
  I will not again destroy Ephraim;
for I am God and no mortal,
  the Holy One in your midst,
  and I will not come in wrath.

Hosea 14:1–2, 4–9
Return, O Israel, to the Lord your God,
  for you have stumbled because of your iniquity.
Take words with you
  and return to the Lord;
say to him,
  "Take away all guilt;
accept that which is good. . . ."
I will heal their disloyalty;
  I will love them freely,
  for my anger has turned from them.
I will be like the dew to Israel;
  he shall blossom like the lily,
  he shall strike root like the forests of Lebanon.

His shoots shall spread out;
>
> his beauty shall be like the olive tree,
>
> and his fragrance like that of Lebanon.

They shall again live beneath my shadow,
>
> they shall flourish as a garden;

they shall blossom like the vine,
>
> their fragrance shall be like the wine of Lebanon.

O Ephraim, what have I to do with idols?
>
> It is I who answer and look after you.

I am like an evergreen cypress;
>
> your faithfulness comes from me.

Those who are wise understand these things;
>
> those who are discerning know them.

For the ways of the Lord are right,
>
> and the upright walk in them,
>
> but transgressors stumble in them.

Another powerful narrative of God's *hesed* and, in this case, an inadequate human response, is the short story of the prophet Jonah. Jonah is sent by God to preach repentance to Nineveh, the great capital city of Assyria, and enemy of Israel. Knowing the historical context is important here, for within a relatively short period several nations had oppressed Israel. Nineveh was one of them. For Jonah and his people, "Ninevah represents all that is hateful, repugnant, and cruel."[14] Jonah, understandably, has no interest in the salvation of these people and thus does not follow God's wishes. He heads off, instead, in another direction. The boat he is on meets with terrible weather and the sailors, upon hearing that Jonah is fleeing his God, surmise that this God is causing the terrible weather. They throw Jonah overboard to save themselves. Jonah is miraculously rescued by a fish and returned to the point where he got on the boat. God again sends him to Nineveh. Jonah finally goes and preaches a coming disaster if the people do not repent. Much to the readers' surprise (and indeed Jonah's!), the people do repent. Thus God does not bring about the calamity he promised to Nineveh.

The author of the book describes Jonah as being displeased and angry about this chain of events. We see then that disobedience is not Jonah's biggest crime. The "reason for his flight was that he did not want to see the Assyrians spared by a gracious God."[15] Jonah is something of a bigot. He says to God, "That is why I fled to Tarshish at the beginning; for I knew that you are a gracious God and merciful, slow to anger, and abounding in steadfast love, and ready to relent from punishing" (Jonah 4:2).

The story ends with a wonderful image, Jonah contentedly sitting under a bush that protects him from the harsh sun. God, however, sends a worm to kill the bush and Jonah thus loses his comfortable place. He becomes whiny and angry. The book concludes with these words from God: "You are concerned about the bush, for which you did not labor and which you did not grow; it came into being in a night and perished in a night. And should I not be concerned about Nineveh, that great city, in which there are more than a hundred and twenty thousand persons who do not know their right hand from their left, and also many animals" (4:10–11)?

Friendship

I am distressed for you, my brother Jonathan; greatly beloved were you to me; your love to me was wonderful, passing the love of women.

—2 Samuel

David (Ruth's great-grandson) is perhaps the most well-known personality of the Old Testament. His rise from harp player in the king's court to the greatest political leader of Israel (he was king from 1000–961 B.C.E.) is marked by both military achievements and moral blunder. His story, with its political twists and turns, mirrors our contemporary political world. Jonathan was the firstborn son of King Saul, the king who employed David as court harpist. I Samuel tells the story of how King Saul fell out of favor with the Lord and how subsequently the prophet Samuel was led by God to anoint David king. A natural rivalry then set up between David, the anointed one, and Jonathan, the heir to the throne. The rivalry, however, never occurred. David and Jonathan became very close friends. Their friendship rested on mutual interests. They were both young, aggressive men. They shared leadership styles and military prowess. They both, moreover, experienced death threats from the emotionally volatile and perhaps mentally ill King Saul. The story here picks up after David killed Goliath, the giant soldier of the Philistines, Israel's deadly enemy. The author repeats several times that David was loved, indeed loved by many people. No matter how much others loved David, however, Jonathan loved him more. Indeed he loved David "as he loved his own life" (1 Sam. 20:17).

The themes of fidelity, action, and affections come through in this story as they did in the previous stories. The story of David and Jonathan also illustrates another characteristic of love. Namely, love transforms those who love and those who are loved. Corrine Carvalho describes how the friendship between David and Jonathan changes both men, particularly Jonathan. In the beginning of the narrative, she notes, Jonathan is "willful, rebellious and irresponsible."[16] With his commitment to David, his whole attitude toward life is altered. By the end of this story, we have a man willing to give all for another. He becomes a person of moral character, responsible to God, and to his people. Love does this to people. When we make friends, Edward Vacek writes, "we transcend our individual, private needs and interests. We join ourselves to something beyond ourselves."[17]

1 Samuel 18–20

Chapter 18: When David had finished speaking to Saul, the soul of Jonathan was bound to the soul of David, and Jonathan loved him as his own soul. Saul took him that day and would not let him return to his father's house. Then Jonathan made a covenant with David, because he loved him as his own soul. Jonathan stripped himself of the robe that he was wearing, and gave it to David, and his armor, and even his sword and his bow and his belt. David went out and was successful wherever Saul sent him; as a result, Saul set him over the army. And all the people, even the servants of Saul, approved.

As they were coming home, when David returned from killing the Philistine, the women came out of all the towns of Israel, singing and dancing, to meet King Saul, with tambourines, with songs of joy, and with musical instruments. And the women sang to one another as they made merry, "Saul has killed his thousands, and David his ten thousands." Saul was very angry, for this saying displeased him. He said, "They have ascribed to David ten thousands, and to me they have ascribed thousands; what more can he have but the kingdom?" So Saul eyed David from that day on.

The next day an evil spirit from God rushed upon Saul, and he raved within his house, while David was playing the lyre, as he did day by day. Saul had his spear in his hand; and Saul threw the spear, for he thought, "I will pin David to the wall." But David eluded him twice.

Saul was afraid of David, because the Lord was with him but had departed from Saul. So Saul removed him from his presence, and made him a commander of a thousand; and David marched out and came in, leading the army. David had success in all his undertakings; for the Lord was with him. When Saul saw that he had great success, he stood in awe of him. But all Israel and Judah loved David; for it was he who marched out and came in leading them.

Then Saul said to David, "Here is my elder daughter Merab; I will give her to you as a wife; only be valiant for me and fight the Lord's battles." For Saul thought, "I will not raise a hand against him; let the Philistines deal

with him." David said to Saul, "Who am I and who are my kinsfolk, my
father's family in Israel, that I should be son-in-law to the king?" But at the
time when Saul's daughter Merab should have been given to David, she
was given to Adriel the Meholathite as a wife. Now Saul's daughter Michal
loved David. Saul was told, and the thing pleased him. Saul thought, "Let
me give her to him that she may be a snare for him and that the hand of
the Philistines may be against him." Therefore Saul said to David a second time, "You shall now be my son-in-law." Saul commanded his servants,
"Speak to David in private and say, 'See, the king is delighted with you,
and all his servants love you; now then, become the king's son-in-law.'"
So Saul's servants reported these words to David in private. And David said,
"Does it seem to you a little thing to become the king's son-in-law, seeing
that I am a poor man and of no repute?" The servants of Saul told him,
"This is what David said." Then Saul said, "Thus shall you say to David,
'The king desires no marriage present except a hundred foreskins of the
Philistines, that he may be avenged on the king's enemies.'" Now Saul
planned to make David fall by the hand of the Philistines. When his servants told David these words, David was well pleased to be the king's son-
in-law. Before the time had expired, David rose and went, along with his
men, and killed one hundred of the Philistines; and David brought their
foreskins, which were given in full number to the king, that he might become the king's son-in-law. Saul gave him his daughter Michal as a wife.
But when Saul realized that the Lord was with David, and that Saul's
daughter Michal loved him, Saul was still more afraid of David. So Saul
was David's enemy from that time forward.

Then the commanders of the Philistines came out to battle; and as
often as they came out, David had more success than all the servants of
Saul, so that his fame became very great.

Chapter 19: Saul spoke with his son Jonathan and with all his servants about
killing David. But Saul's son Jonathan took great delight in David.
Jonathan told David, "My father Saul is trying to kill you; therefore be on
guard tomorrow morning; stay in a secret place and hide yourself. I will go
out and stand beside my father in the field where you are, and I will speak
to my father about you; if I learn anything I will tell you." Jonathan spoke
well of David to his father Saul, saying to him, "The king should not sin
against his servant David, because he has not sinned against you, and because his deeds have been of good service to you; for he took his life in his
hand when he attacked the Philistine, and the Lord brought about a great

victory for all Israel. You saw it, and rejoiced; why then will you sin against an innocent person by killing David without cause?" Saul heeded the voice of Jonathan; Saul swore, "As the Lord lives, he shall not be put to death." So Jonathan called David and related all these things to him. Jonathan then brought David to Saul, and he was in his presence as before.

Again there was war, and David went out to fight the Philistines. He launched a heavy attack on them, so that they fled before him. Then an evil spirit from the Lord came upon Saul, as he sat in his house with his spear in his hand, while David was playing music. Saul sought to pin David to the wall with the spear; but he eluded Saul, so that he struck the spear into the wall. David fled and escaped that night.

Saul sent messengers to David's house to keep watch over him, planning to kill him in the morning. David's wife Michal told him, "If you do not save your life tonight, tomorrow you will be killed." So Michal let David down through the window; he fled away and escaped. Michal took an idol and laid it on the bed; she put a net of goats' hair on its head, and covered it with the clothes. When Saul sent messengers to take David, she said, "He is sick." Then Saul sent the messengers to see David for themselves. He said, "Bring him up to me in the bed, that I may kill him." When the messengers came in, the idol was in the bed, with the covering of goats' hair on its head. Saul said to Michal, "Why have you deceived me like this, and let my enemy go, so that he has escaped?" Michal answered Saul, "He said to me, 'Let me go; why should I kill you?'"

Now David fled and escaped; he came to Samuel at Ramah, and told him all that Saul had done to him. He and Samuel went and settled at Naioth. Saul was told, "David is at Naioth in Ramah." Then Saul sent messengers to take David. When they saw the company of the prophets in a frenzy, with Samuel standing in charge of them, the spirit of God came upon the messengers of Saul, and they also fell into a prophetic frenzy. When Saul was told, he sent other messengers, and they also fell into a frenzy. Saul sent messengers again the third time, and they also fell into a frenzy. Then he himself went to Ramah. He came to the great well that is in Secu; he asked, "Where are Samuel and David?" And someone said, "They are at Naioth in Ramah." He went there, toward Naioth in Ramah; and the spirit of God came upon him. As he was going, he fell into a prophetic frenzy, until he came to Naioth in Ramah. He too stripped off his clothes, and he too fell into a frenzy before Samuel. He lay naked all that day and all that night. Therefore it is said, "Is Saul also among the prophets?"

Chapter 20: David fled from Naioth in Ramah. He came before Jonathan and said, "What have I done? What is my guilt? And what is my sin against your father that he is trying to take my life?" He said to him, "Far from it! You shall not die. My father does nothing either great or small without disclosing it to me; and why should my father hide this from me? Never!" But David also swore, "Your father knows well that you like me; and he thinks, 'Do not let Jonathan know this, or he will be grieved.' But truly, as the Lord lives and as you yourself live, there is but a step between me and death." Then Jonathan said to David, "Whatever you say, I will do for you." David said to Jonathan, "Tomorrow is the new moon, and I should not fail to sit with the king at the meal; but let me go, so that I may hide in the field until the third evening. If your father misses me at all, then say, 'David earnestly asked leave of me to run to Bethlehem his city; for there is a yearly sacrifice there for all the family.' If he says, 'Good!' it will be well with your servant; but if he is angry, then know that evil has been determined by him. Therefore deal kindly with your servant, for you have brought your servant into a sacred covenant with you. But if there is guilt in me, kill me yourself; why should you bring me to your father?" Jonathan said, "Far be it from you! If I knew that it was decided by my father that evil should come upon you, would I not tell you?" Then David said to Jonathan, "Who will tell me if your father answers you harshly?" Jonathan replied to David, "Come, let us go out into the field." So they both went out into the field.

Jonathan said to David, "By the Lord, the God of Israel! When I have sounded out my father, about this time tomorrow, or on the third day, if he is well disposed toward David, shall I not then send and disclose it to you? But if my father intends to do you harm, the Lord do so to Jonathan, and more also, if I do not disclose it to you, and send you away, so that you may go in safety. May the Lord be with you, as he has been with my father. If I am still alive, show me the faithful love of the Lord; but if I die, never cut off your faithful love from my house, even if the Lord were to cut off every one of the enemies of David from the face of the earth." Thus Jonathan made a covenant with the house of David, saying, "May the Lord seek out the enemies of David." Jonathan made David swear again by his love for him; for he loved him as he loved his own life.

Jonathan said to him, "Tomorrow is the new moon; you will be missed, because your place will be empty. On the day after tomorrow, you shall go a long way down; go to the place where you hid yourself earlier, and remain beside the stone there. I will shoot three arrows to the side of it, as though I shot at a mark. Then I will send the boy, saying, 'Go, find the arrows.' If I say to the boy, 'Look, the arrows are on this side of you, collect them,' then you are to come, for, as the Lord lives, it is safe for you and there is no danger. But if I say to the young man, 'Look, the arrows are beyond you,' then go; for the Lord has sent you away. As for the matter about which you and I have spoken, the Lord is witness between you and me forever."

So David hid himself in the field. When the new moon came, the king sat at the feast to eat. The king sat upon his seat, as at other times, upon the seat by the wall. Jonathan stood, while Abner sat by Saul's side; but David's place was empty.

Saul did not say anything that day; for he thought, "Something has befallen him; he is not clean, surely he is not clean." But on the second day, the day after the new moon, David's place was empty. And Saul said to his son Jonathan, "Why has the son of Jesse not come to the feast, either yesterday or today?" Jonathan answered Saul, "David earnestly asked leave of me to go to Bethlehem; he said, 'Let me go; for our family is holding a sacrifice in the city, and my brother has commanded me to be there. So now, if I have found favor in your sight, let me get away, and see my brothers.' For this reason he has not come to the king's table."

Then Saul's anger was kindled against Jonathan. He said to him, "You son of a perverse, rebellious woman! Do I not know that you have chosen the son of Jesse to your own shame, and to the shame of your mother's nakedness? For as long as the son of Jesse lives upon the earth, neither you nor your kingdom shall be established. Now send and bring him to me, for he shall surely die." Then Jonathan answered his father Saul, "Why should he be put to death? What has he done?" But Saul threw his spear at him to strike him; so Jonathan knew that it was the decision of his father to put David to death. Jonathan rose from the table in fierce anger and ate no food on the second day of the month, for he was grieved for David, and because his father had disgraced him.

In the morning Jonathan went out into the field to the appointment with David, and with him was a little boy. He said to the boy, "Run and find the arrows that I shoot." As the boy ran, he shot an arrow beyond him. When the boy came to the place where Jonathan's arrow had fallen, Jonathan called after the boy and said, "Is the arrow not beyond you?" Jonathan called after the boy, "Hurry, be quick, do not linger." So Jonathan's boy gathered up the arrows and came to his master. But the boy knew nothing; only Jonathan and David knew the arrangement. Jonathan gave his weapons to the boy and said to him, "Go and carry them to the city." As soon as the boy had gone, David rose from beside the stone heap and prostrated himself with his face to the ground. He bowed three times, and they kissed each other, and wept with each other; David wept the more. Then Jonathan said to David, "Go in peace, since both of us have sworn in the name of the Lord, saying, 'The Lord shall be between me and you, and between my descendants and your descendants, forever.'" He got up and left; and Jonathan went into the city.

David is on the run, hiding from Saul, when he is told of the fateful battle in the mountains of Gilboa where the Philistines kill Saul and all his sons. When David hears the news, he offers the following elegy. Note how David describes Saul positively, as well as the words he uses to speak of his friendship with Jonathan.

2 Samuel 1:17-27

David intoned this lamentation over Saul and his son Jonathan. (He ordered that The Song of the Bow be taught to the people of Judah; it is written in the Book of Jashar.) He said: Your glory, O Israel, lies slain upon your high places! How the mighty have fallen! Tell it not in Gath, proclaim it not in the streets of Ashkelon; or the daughters of the Philistines will rejoice, the daughters of the uncircumcised will exult.

You mountains of Gilboa, let there be no dew or rain upon you, nor bounteous fields! For there the shield of the mighty was defiled, the shield of Saul, anointed with oil no more.

From the blood of the slain, from the fat of the mighty, the bow of Jonathan did not turn back, nor the sword of Saul return empty.

Saul and Jonathan, beloved and lovely! In life and in death they were not divided; they were swifter than eagles, they were stronger than lions.

O daughters of Israel, weep over Saul, who clothed you with crimson, in luxury, who put ornaments of gold on your apparel.

How the mighty have fallen in the midst of the battle! Jonathan lies slain upon your high places. I am distressed for you, my brother Jonathan; greatly beloved were you to me; your love to me was wonderful, passing the love of women.

How the mighty have fallen, and the weapons of war perished!

The friendship between David and Jonathan lasts beyond Jonathan's death. David remains faithful to Jonathan by protecting Jonathan's son. Sakenfeld writes, "Jonathan does *hesed* for David by informing him of Saul's murderous plans; David does *hesed* for Jonathan after Jonathan's death by bringing Jonathan's son Meribaal [Mephibosheth] back from exile to live at the royal court."[18]

2 Samuel 9:1–13

David asked, "Is there still anyone left of the house of Saul to whom I may show kindness for Jonathan's sake?" Now there was a servant of the house of Saul whose name was Ziba, and he was summoned to David. The king said to him, "Are you Ziba?" And he said, "At your service!" The king said, "Is there anyone remaining of the house of Saul to whom I may show the kindness of God?" Ziba said to the king, "There remains a son of Jonathan; he is crippled in his feet." The king said to him, "Where is he?" Ziba said to the king, "He is in the house of Machir son of Ammiel, at Lo-debar." Then King David sent and brought him from the house of Machir son of Ammiel, at Lo-debar. Mephibosheth son of Jonathan son of Saul came to David, and fell on his face and did obeisance. David said, "Mephibosheth!" He answered, "I am your servant." David said to him, "Do not be afraid, for I will show you kindness for the sake of your father Jonathan; I will restore to you all the land of your grandfather Saul, and you yourself shall eat at my table always." He did obeisance and said, "What is your servant, that you should look upon a dead dog such as I?"

Then the king summoned Saul's servant Ziba, and said to him, "All that belonged to Saul and to all his house I have given to your master's grandson. You and your sons and your servants shall till the land for him, and shall bring in the produce, so that your master's grandson may have food to eat; but your master's grandson Mephibosheth shall always eat at my table." Now Ziba had fifteen sons and twenty servants. Then Ziba said to the king, "According to all that my lord the king commands his servant, so your servant will do." Mephibosheth ate at David's table, like one of the king's sons. Mephibosheth had a young son whose name was Mica. And all who lived in Ziba's house became Mephibosheth's servants. Mephibosheth lived in Jerusalem, for he always ate at the king's table. Now he was lame in both his feet.

As friendship is an important element of everyday life, it is not surprising to find proverbs and moral sayings about it in Wisdom literature. There are five books in the Old Testament classified as "Wisdom literature": Proverbs, Job, Ecclesiastes, Sirach, and Wisdom. The general concern of Wisdom Literature is practical knowledge. Wisdom is, simply put, knowledge about life and how to live the good life. Wisdom literature has two primary purposes. It first presents insight about "how to get along in life" from reflection on common experience and observation of how the world works. It also preserves and passes on the tradition of "insights from previous generations of sages and elders" for instruction of the young.[19] Although wisdom sayings often take the form of action guides, they are not laws. They are intended to form the moral vision or character of the listener.[20]

The book of Proverbs offers the following advice on friendship:

—"One who forgives an affront fosters friendship, but one who dwells on disputes will alienate a friend" (17:9).

—"A friend loves at all times, and kinsfolk are born to share adversity" (17:17).

—"Some friends play at friendship but a true friend sticks closer than one's nearest kin" (18:24).

—"Wealth brings many friends, but the poor are left friendless" (19:4).

—"Many seek the favor of the generous, and everyone is a friend to a giver of gifts. If the poor are hated even by their kin, how much more are they shunned by their friends! When they call after them, they are not there" (19:6–7).

The longest biblical passage on friendship in the Old Testament is found in the book of Sirach, sometimes called Ecclesiasticus. Sirach, like Proverbs, intends to pass on Jewish tradition and cultural expectations from one generation to the next. Its author, Ben Sirach, was a teacher and the book is essentially an accumulation of his class notes.[21] Here are his thoughts on friendship.

Sirach 6:5–17
Pleasant speech multiplies friends,
    and a gracious tongue multiplies courtesies.
Let those who are friendly with you be many,
    but let your advisers be one in a thousand.
When you gain friends, gain them through testing,
    and do not trust them hastily.
For there are friends who are such when it suits them,
    but they will not stand by you in time of trouble.
And there are friends who change into enemies,
    and tell of the quarrel to your disgrace.

And there are friends who sit at your table,
    but they will not stand by you in time of trouble.
When you are prosperous, they become your second self,
    and lord it over your servants;
but if you are brought low, they turn against you,
    and hide themselves from you.
Keep away from your enemies,
    and be on guard with your friends.
Faithful friends are a sturdy shelter:
    whoever finds one has found a treasure.
Faithful friends are beyond price;
    no amount can balance their worth.
Faithful friends are life-saving medicine;
    and those who fear the Lord will find them.
Those who fear the Lord direct their friendship aright,
    for as they are, so are their neighbors also.

Sirach 9:10
Do not abandon old friends,
    for new ones cannot equal them.
A new friend is like new wine;
    when it has aged, you can drink it with pleasure.

Sirach 12:8–9.
A friend is not known in prosperity,
    nor is an enemy hidden in adversity.
One's enemies are friendly when one prospers,
    but in adversity even one's friend disappears.

Sirach 22:19–22, 25–26.
One who pricks the eye brings tears,
    and one who pricks the heart makes clear its feelings.
One who throws a stone at birds scares them away,
    and one who reviles a friend destroys a friendship.
Even if you draw your sword against a friend,
    do not despair, for there is a way back.
If you open your mouth against your friend,
    do not worry, for reconciliation is possible.

But as for reviling, arrogance, disclosure of secrets, or a treacherous
    blow—
    in these cases any friend will take to flight. . . .
I am not ashamed to shelter a friend,
    and I will not hide from him.
But if harm should come to me because of him,
    whoever hears of it will beware of him.

A final comment on friendship in the Old Testament comes from Job. Job is the paradigmatic example of the good person who suffers. The book of Job examines the role of faith in the face of suffering. Job is an outstanding person who is overcome with terrible misfortune. As his friends gather around him to counsel him, they soon come to the belief that Job must deserve his suffering. They think Job's misfortune is God's punishment for his sins. Thus they encourage Job to admit his guilt and repent. Job does not give in; he knows he is innocent. In the following passage he claims his suffering is magnified by the fact that his friends, who should have compassion for him and console him in his misery, are unsympathetic. They act more like his enemies than his friends.[22] He thus protests:

Job 6:11-21
What is my strength, that I should wait?
    And what is my end, that I should be patient?
Is my strength the strength of stones,
    or is my flesh bronze?
In truth I have no help in me,
    and any resource is driven from me.
Those who withhold kindness from a friend
    forsake the fear of the Almighty.
My companions are treacherous like a torrent-bed,
    like freshets that pass away,
that run dark with ice,
    turbid with melting snow.
In time of heat they disappear;
    when it is hot, they vanish from their place.
The caravans turn aside from their course;
    they go up into the waste, and perish.
The caravans of Tema look,
    the travelers of Sheba hope.
They are disappointed because they were confident;
    they come there and are confounded.

Such you have now become to me;
  you see my calamity, and are afraid.

Romantic Love

Three things are too wonderful for me; four I do not understand; the way of an eagle in the sky, the way of a snake on a rock, the way of a ship on the high seas, and the way of a man with a girl.

—Song of Solomon

The Song of Solomon (also known as the Song of Songs or the Canticle of Canticles) is a series of poems written back and forth between a man and a woman, both of whom remain anonymous, with an occasional verse by the "Daughters of Jerusalem." What makes the text so intriguing is that the poems are love poems, indeed erotic love poems, in which the couple celebrates their intense feelings for each other. There is no direct reference to God in this biblical book. "The reader searches in vain for any proclamation of religious insight and truth, or for an exposition or understanding of the people of God or indeed of the world of God."[23] The Song is not an abstract discussion of love. It is rather a dramatic and overwhelmingly positive presentation of human sexual love in its physical and emotional aspects. The reader is placed in a privileged position so as to hear the yearning and feel the pleasure these two lovers take in each other. The woman, for example, proclaims, "Let him kiss me with the kisses of his mouth!" (1:2) She says that she is "faint with love" (2:5, 5:8) and calls after her lover. She teases him and speaks descriptively of his physical characteristics. At the end of one such poetic statement she says, "This is my beloved and this is my friend" (5:16). The man too, is smitten with impassioned love. He refers to the woman he loves as his "perfect one," his "only one" (6:9) who has "ravished" his heart (4:9). He speaks longingly and at great length of his beloved's beauty.

Roland Murphy writes that the Song invites readers "to appreciate the qualities of tenderness, joy, sensual intimacy, reciprocal longing and mutual esteem, all of which are socially desirable and beautifully mysterious dimensions of human sexual love."[24] Othmar Keel likewise comments,

> The basis of love in the Song is not a vague genital lust but great admiration of the beloved partner, who seems unapproachable in his or her radiance—distant on inaccessible mountains, hidden in locked gardens, painfully longed for and sought. The lovers mutually experience one another as so beautiful, so radiant, so magnificent that every discovery, every approach, every possession of the other can be experienced only as unfathomable gift, never taken for granted.[25]

Throughout most of the Christian and Jewish traditions, the Song of Solomon was not read as Murphy and Keel suggest. The dominant historical view is that the book was to be interpreted allegorically: that is to say, that the text is not really about the love between a man and a woman. An allegorical interpretation holds that there is a deeper meaning to the text than what literally appears to the reader. In this case, the man in the Song of Solomon, often referred to as the "Bridegroom," is to be interpreted as Jesus, and the woman, often referred to as the "Bride," is to be understood as the Church or the individual soul. In the Jewish tradition, the man was God and the woman was the Jewish people. We will see an excellent example of an allegorical interpretation of the Song in chapter 4 of this book.

An allegorical interpretation of the Song is not unwarranted. Several times in the Old Testament we read of God's relationship with the people described in terms of the love between a man and a woman. The Hosea text discussed earlier is but one example. Perhaps the most striking use of this imagery is found in Ezekiel chapter 16. Here we read about God's love for the people of Jerusalem. Jerusalem is depicted as an abandoned infant girl left to die, a case of what we today would call "female infanticide." God will not let her die, indeed he cares for her and ultimately "marries" her. The text reads:

> Ezekiel 16:6–8, 13–14
> As you lay in your blood, I said to you, "Live! And grow up like a plant of the field." You grew up and became tall and arrived at full womanhood; your breasts were formed, and your hair grown; yet you were naked and bare. I passed by you again and looked on you; you were at the age for love. I spread the edge of my cloak over you, and covered your nakedness: I pledged myself to you and entered into a covenant with you, says the Lord God, and you became mine. . . . You grew exceedingly beautiful, fit to be a queen. Your fame spread among the nations on account of your beauty, for it was perfect because of my splendor that I had bestowed on you, says the Lord God.

While the allegorical interpretation of the Song has been the dominant view in history, the broad consensus of contemporary biblical scholars, however, favors a non-allegorical interpretation. Murphy, for example, concludes that the Song is about "human sexual fulfillment, fervently sought and consummated in reciprocal love between woman and man."[26]

Another interesting characteristic in the Song is the role that the woman plays in the text. The book was written in a culture dominated by men, indeed the identity of the woman was tied to the man in her life, and yet the woman in the Song has at least as many lines as the man. Moreover, she appears very nontraditional as she seeks out her love and initiates encounters. Although the references to nature, especially certain fruits and animals, are quite foreign to the modern reader, the format of the poems, giving equal voice to man and woman, is strikingly contemporary. Marcia Falk argues that the nonsexist attitude of the Song is part of its enduring power.[27]

SONG OF SOLOMON

Chapter 1: The Song of Songs, which is Solomon's.

THE WOMAN

Let him kiss me with the kisses of his mouth! For your love is better than wine, your anointing oils are fragrant, your name is perfume poured out; therefore the maidens love you. Draw me after you, let us make haste. The king has brought me into his chambers. We will exult and rejoice in you; we will extol your love more than wine; rightly do they love you. I am black and beautiful, O daughters of Jerusalem, like the tents of Kedar, like the curtains of Solomon. Do not gaze at me because I am dark, because the sun has gazed on me. My mother's sons were angry with me; they made me keeper of the vineyards, but my own vineyard I have not kept! Tell me, you whom my soul loves, where you pasture your flock, where you make it lie down at noon; for why should I be like one who is veiled beside the flocks of your companions?

THE MAN

If you do not know, O fairest among women, follow the tracks of the flock, and pasture your kids beside the shepherds' tents. I compare you, my love, to a mare among Pharaoh's chariots. Your cheeks are comely with ornaments, your neck with strings of jewels. We will make you ornaments of gold, studded with silver.

THE WOMAN

While the king was on his couch, my nard gave forth its fragrance. My beloved is to me a bag of myrrh that lies between my breasts. My beloved is to me a cluster of henna blossoms in the vineyards of En-gedi.

THE MAN

Ah, you are beautiful, my love; ah, you are beautiful; your eyes are doves.

THE WOMAN

Ah, you are beautiful, my beloved, truly lovely. Our couch is green; the beams of our house are cedar, our rafters are pine.

☙ ❧

Chapter 2: I am a rose of Sharon, a lily of the valleys. As a lily among brambles, so is my love among maidens. As an apple tree among the trees of the wood, so is my beloved among young men. With great delight I sat in his shadow, and his fruit was sweet to my taste. He brought me to the banqueting house, and his intention toward me was love. Sustain me with raisins, refresh me with apples; for I am faint with love. O that his left hand were under my head, and that his right hand embraced me! I adjure you, O daughters of Jerusalem, by the gazelles or the wild does: do not stir up or awaken love until it is ready! The voice of my beloved! Look, he comes, leaping upon the mountains, bounding over the hills. My beloved is like a gazelle or a young stag. Look, there he stands behind our wall, gazing in at the windows, looking through the lattice. My beloved speaks and says to me: "Arise, my love, my fair one, and come away; for now the winter is past, the rain is over and gone. The flowers appear on the earth; the time of singing has come, and the voice of the turtledove is heard in our land. The fig tree puts forth its figs, and the vines are in blossom; they give forth fragrance. Arise, my love, my fair one, and come away.

THE MAN

O my dove, in the clefts of the rock, in the covert of the cliff, let me see your face, let me hear your voice; for your voice is sweet, and your face is lovely.

THE WOMAN

Catch us the foxes, the little foxes, that ruin the vineyards—for our vineyards are in blossom." My beloved is mine and I am his; he pastures his flock among the lilies. Until the day breathes and the shadows flee, turn, my beloved, be like a gazelle or a young stag on the cleft mountains.

☙ ❧

Chapter 3: Upon my bed at night I sought him whom my soul loves; I sought him, but found him not; I called him, but he gave no answer. "I will rise now and go about the city, in the streets and in the squares; I will seek him whom my soul loves." I sought him, but found him not. The sentinels found me, as they went about in the city. "Have you seen him whom my soul loves?" Scarcely had I passed them, when I found him whom my soul loves. I held him, and would not let him go until I brought him into my mother's house, and into the chamber of her that conceived me.

THE MAN

I adjure you, O daughters of Jerusalem, by the gazelles or the wild does: do not stir up or awaken love until it is ready! What is that coming up from the wilderness, like a column of smoke, perfumed with myrrh and frankincense, with all the fragrant powders of the merchant? Look, it is the litter of Solomon! Around it are sixty mighty men of the mighty men of Israel, all equipped with swords and expert in war, each with his sword at his thigh because of alarms by night. King Solomon made himself a palanquin from the wood of Lebanon. He made its posts of silver, its back of gold, its seat of purple; its interior was inlaid with love. Daughters of Jerusalem, come out. Look, O daughters of Zion, at King Solomon, at the crown with which his mother crowned him on the day of his wedding, on the day of the gladness of his heart.

૨૪ ૨ૂ

Chapter 4: How beautiful you are, my love, how very beautiful! Your eyes are doves behind your veil. Your hair is like a flock of goats, moving down the slopes of Gilead. Your teeth are like a flock of shorn ewes that have come up from the washing, all of which bear twins, and not one among them is bereaved. Your lips are like a crimson thread, and your mouth is lovely. Your cheeks are like halves of a pomegranate behind your veil. Your neck is like the tower of David, built in courses; on it hang a thousand bucklers, all of them shields of warriors. Your two breasts are like two fawns, twins of a gazelle, that feed among the lilies. Until the day breathes and the shadows flee, I will hasten to the mountain of myrrh and the hill of frankincense. You are altogether beautiful, my love; there is no flaw in you. Come with me from Lebanon, my bride; come with me from Lebanon. Depart from the peak of Amana, from the peak of Senir and Hermon, from the dens of lions, from the mountains of leopards. You have ravished my heart, my sister, my bride! you have ravished my heart with a glance of your eyes, with one jewel of your necklace. How sweet is your love, my sister, my bride! how much better is your love than wine, and the fragrance of your oils than any spice! Your lips distill nectar, my bride; honey and milk are under your tongue; the scent of your garments is like the scent of Lebanon. A garden locked is my sister, my bride, a garden locked, a fountain sealed. Your channel is an orchard of pomegranates with all choicest fruits, henna with nard, nard and saffron, calamus and cinnamon, with all trees of frankincense, myrrh and aloes, with all chief spices—a garden fountain, a well of living water, and flowing streams from Lebanon.

THE WOMAN

Awake, O north wind, and come, O south wind! Blow upon my garden that its fragrance may be wafted abroad. Let my beloved come to his garden, and eat its choicest fruits.

❧ ☙

THE MAN

Chapter 5: I come to my garden, my sister, my bride; I gather my myrrh with my spice, I eat my honeycomb with my honey, I drink my wine with my milk. Eat, friends, drink, and be drunk with love.

THE WOMAN

I slept, but my heart was awake. Listen! my beloved is knocking. "Open to me, my sister, my love, my dove, my perfect one; for my head is wet with dew, my locks with the drops of the night." I had put off my garment; how could I put it on again? I had bathed my feet; how could I soil them? My beloved thrust his hand into the opening, and my inmost being yearned for him. I arose to open to my beloved, and my hands dripped with myrrh, my fingers with liquid myrrh, upon the handles of the bolt. I opened to my beloved, but my beloved had turned and was gone. My soul failed me when he spoke. I sought him, but did not find him; I called him, but he gave no answer. Making their rounds in the city the sentinels found me; they beat me, they wounded me, they took away my mantle, those sentinels of the walls. I adjure you, O daughters of Jerusalem, if you find my beloved, tell him this: I am faint with love.

THE CHORUS

What is your beloved more than another beloved, O fairest among women? What is your beloved more than another beloved, that you thus adjure us?

THE WOMAN

My beloved is all radiant and ruddy, distinguished among ten thousand. His head is the finest gold; his locks are wavy, black as a raven. His eyes are like doves beside springs of water, bathed in milk, fitly set. His cheeks are like beds of spices, yielding fragrance. His lips are lilies, distilling liquid myrrh. His arms are rounded gold, set with jewels. His body is ivory work, encrusted with sapphires. His legs are alabaster columns, set upon bases of gold. His appearance is like Lebanon, choice as the cedars. His speech is most sweet, and he is altogether desirable. This is my beloved and this is my friend, O daughters of Jerusalem.

~ ~

THE CHORUS

Chapter 6: Where has your beloved gone, O fairest among women? Which way has your beloved turned, that we may seek him with you?

THE WOMAN

My beloved has gone down to his garden, to the beds of spices, to pasture his flock in the gardens, and to gather lilies. I am my beloved's and my beloved is mine; he pastures his flock among the lilies. You are beautiful as Tirzah, my love, comely as Jerusalem, terrible as an army with banners. Turn away your eyes from me, for they overwhelm me! Your hair is like a flock of goats, moving down the slopes of Gilead. Your teeth are like a flock of ewes, that have come up from the washing; all of them bear twins, and not one among them is bereaved. Your cheeks are like halves of a pomegranate behind your veil.

THE MAN

There are sixty queens and eighty concubines, and maidens without number. My dove, my perfect one, is the only one, the darling of her mother, flawless to her that bore her. The maidens saw her and called her happy; the queens and concubines also, and they praised her.

THE WOMAN

"Who is this that looks forth like the dawn, fair as the moon, bright as the sun, terrible as an army with banners?" I went down to the nut orchard, to look at the blossoms of the valley, to see whether the vines had budded, whether the pomegranates were in bloom. Before I was aware, my fancy set me in a chariot beside my prince.

THE CHORUS

Return, return, O Shulammite! Return, return, that we may look upon you.

THE MAN

Why should you look upon the Shulammite, as upon a dance before two armies?

ꗊ ꗊ

Chapter 7: How graceful are your feet in sandals, O queenly maiden! Your rounded thighs are like jewels, the work of a master hand. Your navel is a rounded bowl that never lacks mixed wine. Your belly is a heap of wheat, encircled with lilies. Your two breasts are like two fawns, twins of a gazelle. Your neck is like an ivory tower. Your eyes are pools in Heshbon, by the gate of Bath-rabbim. Your nose is like a tower of Lebanon, overlooking Damascus. Your head crowns you like Carmel, and your flowing locks are like purple; a king is held captive in the tresses. How fair and pleasant you are, O loved one, delectable maiden! You are stately as a palm tree, and your breasts are like its clusters. I say I will climb the palm tree and lay hold of its branches. Oh, may your breasts be like clusters of the vine, and the scent of your breath like apples, and your kisses like the best wine that goes down smoothly, gliding over lips and teeth.

THE WOMAN

I am my beloved's, and his desire is for me. Come, my beloved, let us go forth into the fields, and lodge in the villages; let us go out early to the vineyards, and see whether the vines have budded, whether the grape blossoms have opened and the pomegranates are in bloom. There I will give you my love. The mandrakes give forth fragrance, and over our doors are all choice fruits, new as well as old, which I have laid up for you, O my beloved.

ꗊ ꗊ

Chapter 8: O that you were like a brother to me, who nursed at my mother's breast! If I met you outside, I would kiss you, and no one would despise me. I would lead you and bring you into the house of my mother, and into the chamber of the one who bore me. I would give you spiced wine to drink, the juice of my pomegranates. O that his left hand were under my head, and that his right hand embraced me! I adjure you, O daughters of Jerusalem, do not stir up or awaken love until it is ready!

THE MAN

Who is that coming up from the wilderness, leaning upon her beloved? Under the apple tree I awakened you. There your mother was in labor with you; there she who bore you was in labor.

THE WOMAN

Set me as a seal upon your heart, as a seal upon your arm; for love is strong as death, passion fierce as the grave. Its flashes are flashes of fire, a raging flame. Many waters cannot quench love, neither can floods drown it. If one offered for love all the wealth of one's house, it would be utterly scorned. We have a little sister, and she has no breasts. What shall we do for our sister, on the day when she is spoken for? If she is a wall, we will build upon her a battlement of silver; but if she is a door, we will enclose her with boards of cedar. I was a wall, and my breasts were like towers; then I was in his eyes as one who brings peace. Solomon had a vineyard at Baal-hamon; he entrusted the vineyard to keepers; each one was to bring for its fruit a thousand pieces of silver. My vineyard, my very own, is for myself; you, O Solomon, may have the thousand, and the keepers of the fruit two hundred! O you who dwell in the gardens, my companions are listening for your voice; let me hear it. Make haste, my beloved, and be like a gazelle or a young stag upon the mountains of spices!

A passage in the book Ecclesiastes is also noteworthy for its celebration of love and the enjoyment of love's pleasures. It reads, "Go, eat your bread with enjoyment, and drink your wine with a merry heart; for God has long ago approved what you do. Let your garments always be white; do not let oil be lacking on your head. Enjoy life with the wife whom you love, all the days of your vain life that are given you under the sun, because that is your portion in life and in your toil at which you toil under the sun" (Eccles. 9:7–9).

There are a few other stories of romantic love in the Old Testament. Two are found in Genesis. The second creation story tells us something about this sort of love. After the creation of his partner the man cries out, "This at last is bone of my bones and flesh of my flesh; this one shall be called Woman, for out of Man this one was taken" (2:23). The narrator of the story follows this with, "Therefore a man leaves his father and his mother and clings to his wife, and they become one flesh" (2:24). These two verses express a passionate desire for human intimacy. Sex and the desire for intimacy are part of the divine ordering of creation. In Genesis we also read of Isaac's love for Rebekah (24:67). The first love story in the Bible, however, appears later in Genesis with the story of Jacob and his love for Rachel.

Genesis 29: 1–30
Then Jacob went on his journey, and came to the land of the people of the east. As he looked, he saw a well in the field and three flocks of sheep lying there beside it; for out of that well the flocks were watered. The stone

on the well's mouth was large, and when all the flocks were gathered there, the shepherds would roll the stone from the mouth of the well, and water the sheep, and put the stone back in its place on the mouth of the well.

Jacob said to them, "My brothers, where do you come from?" They said, "We are from Haran." He said to them, "Do you know Laban son of Nahor?" They said, "We do." He said to them, "Is it well with him?" "Yes," they replied, "and here is his daughter Rachel, coming with the sheep." He said, "Look, it is still broad daylight; it is not time for the animals to be gathered together. Water the sheep, and go, pasture them." But they said, "We cannot until all the flocks are gathered together, and the stone is rolled from the mouth of the well; then we water the sheep."

While he was still speaking with them, Rachel came with her father's sheep; for she kept them. Now when Jacob saw Rachel, the daughter of his mother's brother Laban, and the sheep of his mother's brother Laban, Jacob went up and rolled the stone from the well's mouth, and watered the flock of his mother's brother Laban. Then Jacob kissed Rachel, and wept aloud. And Jacob told Rachel that he was her father's kinsman, and that he was Rebekah's son; and she ran and told her father.

When Laban heard the news about his sister's son Jacob, he ran to meet him; he embraced him and kissed him, and brought him to his house. Jacob told Laban all these things, and Laban said to him, "Surely you are my bone and my flesh!" And he stayed with him a month.

Then Laban said to Jacob, "Because you are my kinsman, should you therefore serve me for nothing? Tell me, what shall your wages be?" Now Laban had two daughters; the name of the elder was Leah, and the name of the younger was Rachel. Leah's eyes were lovely, and Rachel was graceful and beautiful. Jacob loved Rachel; so he said, "I will serve you seven years for your younger daughter Rachel." Laban said, "It is better that I give her to you than that I should give her to any other man; stay with me." So Jacob served seven years for Rachel, and they seemed to him but a few days because of the love he had for her.

Then Jacob said to Laban, "Give me my wife that I may go in to her, for my time is completed." So Laban gathered together all the people of the place, and made a feast. But in the evening he took his daughter Leah and brought her to Jacob; and he went in to her. (Laban gave his maid Zilpah to his daughter Leah to be her maid.) When morning came, it was Leah! And Jacob said to Laban, "What is this you have done to me? Did I not serve with you for Rachel? Why then have you deceived me?" Laban said, "This is not done in our country—giving the younger before the firstborn.

Complete the week of this one, and we will give you the other also in return for serving me another seven years." Jacob did so, and completed her week; then Laban gave him his daughter Rachel as a wife. (Laban gave his maid Bilhah to his daughter Rachel to be her maid.) So Jacob went in to Rachel also, and he loved Rachel more than Leah. He served Laban for another seven years.

The book of Tobit contains another memorable love story. Commentators describe this book as a folk tale and a romance. The love story fits within the larger message of the book, namely God's justice, mercy, and freedom.[28] This folk tale presents an interesting theology of love. The angel Raphael tells Tobias that Sarah was "set apart for you before the world was made" (6:18) and "it has been decreed from heaven that she be given to you. . . . from today and forever (7:11). That is to say, the bond between them was "fashioned by God from all eternity."[29] In common, everyday language, the author is saying that the couple was "meant" to be together and they will always be together. The Jewish tradition has several sayings that express this same view. One is, "God's occupation is sitting and arranging marriages." Another is, "Forty days before a child is created, it is proclaimed in heaven, 'This man's daughter shall marry that man's son.'"[30]

The excerpt below picks up with Tobias on a journey accompanied by the angel Raphael. Raphael takes him to the home of Raguel, father of the ill-fated Sarah with whom Tobias falls in love. The story contains a few enjoyable ironies. Note, for example, when Raguel refers to Tobias's father, Tobit, who has recently become blind. Earlier in the text we read that poor Tobit was blinded when bird droppings hit him in his eyes (2:10)!

Tobit 6–8

Chapter 6: The young man went out and the angel went with him; and the dog came out with him and went along with them. So they both journeyed along, and when the first night overtook them they camped by the Tigris river. Then the young man went down to wash his feet in the Tigris river. Suddenly a large fish leaped up from the water and tried to swallow the young man's foot, and he cried out. But the angel said to the young man, "Catch hold of the fish and hang on to it!" So the young man grasped the fish and drew it up on the land. Then the angel said to him, "Cut open the fish and take out its gall, heart, and liver. Keep them with you, but throw away the intestines. For its gall, heart, and liver are useful as medicine." So after cutting open the fish the young man gathered together the gall, heart, and liver; then he roasted and ate some of the fish, and kept some to be salted.

The two continued on their way together until they were near Media. Then the young man questioned the angel and said to him, "Brother Azariah, what medicinal value is there in the fish's heart and liver, and in the gall? He replied, "As for the fish's heart and liver, you must burn them to make a smoke in the presence of a man or woman afflicted by a demon or evil spirit, and every affliction will flee away and never remain with that person any longer. And as for the gall, anoint a person's eyes where white films have appeared on them; blow upon them, upon the white films, and the eyes will be healed."

When he entered Media and already was approaching Ecbatana, Raphael said to the young man, "Brother Tobias." "Here I am," he answered. Then Raphael said to him, "We must stay this night in the home of Raguel. He is your relative, and he has a daughter named Sarah. He has no male heir and no daughter except Sarah only, and you, as next of kin to her, have before all other men a hereditary claim on her. Also it is right for you to inherit her father's possessions. Moreover, the girl is sensible, brave, and very beautiful, and her father is a good man." He continued, "You have every right to take her in marriage. So listen to me, brother; tonight I will speak to her father about the girl, so that we may take her to be your bride. When we return from Rages we will celebrate her marriage. For I know that Raguel can by no means keep her from you or promise her to another man without incurring the penalty of death according to the decree of the book of Moses. Indeed he knows that you, rather than any other man, are entitled to marry his daughter. So now listen to me, brother, and tonight we shall speak concerning the girl and arrange her engagement to you. And when we return from Rages we will take her and bring her back with us to your house."

Then Tobias said in answer to Raphael, "Brother Azariah, I have heard that she already has been married to seven husbands and that they died in the bridal chamber. On the night when they went in to her, they would die. I have heard people saying that it was a demon that killed them. It does not harm her, but it kills anyone who desires to approach her. So now, since I am the only son my father has, I am afraid that I may die and bring my father's and mother's life down to their grave, grieving for me—and they have no other son to bury them."

But Raphael said to him, "Do you not remember your father's orders when he commanded you to take a wife from your father's house? Now listen to me, brother, and say no more about this demon. Take her. I know that this very night she will be given to you in marriage. When you enter the bridal chamber, take some of the fish's liver and heart, and put them on the embers of the incense. An odor will be given off; the demon will smell it and flee, and will never be seen near her any more. Now when you are about to go to bed with her, both of you must first stand up and pray, imploring the Lord of heaven that mercy and safety may be granted to you. Do not be afraid, for she was set apart for you before the world was made. You will save her, and she will go with you. I presume that you will have children by her, and they will be as brothers to you. Now say no more!" When Tobias heard the words of Raphael and learned that she was his kinswoman, related through his father's lineage, he loved her very much, and his heart was drawn to her.

Chapter 7: Now when they entered Ecbatana, Tobias said to him, "Brother Azariah, take me straight to our brother Raguel." So he took him to Raguel's house, where they found him sitting beside the courtyard door. They greeted him first, and he replied, "Joyous greetings, brothers; welcome and good health!" Then he brought them into his house. He said to his wife Edna, "How much the young man resembles my kinsman Tobit!" Then Edna questioned them, saying, "Where are you from, brothers?" They answered, "We belong to the descendants of Naphtali who are exiles in Nineveh." She said to them, "Do you know our kinsman Tobit?" And they replied, "Yes, we know him." Then she asked them, "Is he in good health?" They replied, "He is alive and in good health." And Tobias added, "He is my father!" At that Raguel jumped up and kissed him and wept. He also spoke to him as follows, "Blessings on you, my child, son of a good and noble father! O most miserable of calamities that such an upright and beneficent man has become blind!" He then embraced his kinsman Tobias and wept. His wife Edna also wept for him, and their daughter Sarah likewise wept. Then Raguel slaughtered a ram from the flock and received them very warmly.

When they had bathed and washed themselves and had reclined to dine, Tobias said to Raphael, "Brother Azariah, ask Raguel to give me my kinswoman, Sarah." But Raguel overheard it and said to the lad, "Eat and drink, and be merry tonight. For no one except you, brother, has the right to marry my daughter Sarah. Likewise I am not at liberty to give her to any other man than yourself, because you are my nearest relative. But let me explain to you the true situation more fully, my child. I have given her to seven men of our kinsmen, and all died on the night when they went in to her. But now, my child, eat and drink, and the Lord will act on behalf of you both." But Tobias said, "I will neither eat nor drink anything until you settle the things that pertain to me." So Raguel said, "I will do so. She is given to you in accordance with the decree in the book of Moses, and it has been decreed from heaven that she be given to you. Take your kinswoman; from now on you are her brother and she is your sister. She is given to you from today and forever. May the Lord of heaven, my child, guide and prosper you both this night and grant you mercy and peace." Then Raguel summoned his daughter Sarah. When she came to him he took her by the hand and gave her to Tobias, saying, "Take her to be your wife in accordance with the law and decree written in the book of Moses. Take her and bring her safely to your father. And may the God of heaven prosper your journey with his peace." Then he called her mother and told her to bring writing material; and he wrote out a copy of a marriage contract, to the effect that he gave her to him as wife according to the decree of the law of Moses. Then they began to eat and drink.

Raguel called his wife Edna and said to her, "Sister, get the other room ready, and take her there." So she went and made the bed in the room as he had told her, and brought Sarah there. She wept for her daughter. Then, wiping away the tears, she said to her, "Take courage, my daughter; the Lord of heaven grant you joy in place of your sorrow. Take courage, my daughter." Then she went out.

Chapter 8: When they had finished eating and drinking they wanted to re-tire; so they took the young man and brought him into the bedroom. Then Tobias remembered the words of Raphael, and he took the fish's liver and heart out of the bag where he had them and put them on the embers of the incense. The odor of the fish so repelled the demon that he fled to the re-motest parts of Egypt. But Raphael followed him, and at once bound him there hand and foot.

When the parents had gone out and shut the door of the room, To-bias got out of bed and said to Sarah, "Sister, get up, and let us pray and implore our Lord that he grant us mercy and safety." So she got up, and they began to pray and implore that they might be kept safe. Tobias began by saying, "Blessed are you, O God of our ancestors, and blessed is your name in all generations forever. Let the heavens and the whole creation bless you forever. You made Adam, and for him you made his wife Eve as a helper and support. From the two of them the human race has sprung. You said, 'It is not good that the man should be alone; let us make a helper for him like himself.' I now am taking this kinswoman of mine, not because of lust, but with sincerity. Grant that she and I may find mercy and that we may grow old together." And they both said, "Amen, Amen." Then they went to sleep for the night.

But Raguel arose and called his servants to him, and they went and dug a grave, for he said, "It is possible that he will die and we will become an object of ridicule and derision." When they had finished digging the grave, Raguel went into his house and called his wife, saying, "Send one of the maids and have her go in to see if he is alive. But if he is dead, let us bury him without anyone knowing it." So they sent the maid, lit a lamp, and opened the door; and she went in and found them sound asleep together. Then the maid came out and informed them that he was alive and that nothing was wrong. So they blessed the God of heaven, and Raguel said, "Blessed are you, O God, with every pure blessing; let all your chosen ones bless you. Let them bless you forever. Blessed are you because you have made me glad. It has not turned out as I expected, but you have dealt with us according to your great mercy. Blessed are you because you had compassion on two only children. Be merciful to them, O Master, and keep them safe; bring their lives to fulfillment in happiness and mercy." Then he ordered his servants to fill in the grave before daybreak.

After this he asked his wife to bake many loaves of bread; and he went out to the herd and brought two steers and four rams and ordered them to be slaughtered. So they began to make preparations. Then he called for Tobias and swore on oath to him in these words: "You shall not leave here for fourteen days, but shall stay here eating and drinking with me; and you shall cheer up my daughter, who has been depressed. Take at once half of what I own and return in safety to your father; the other half will be yours when my wife and I die. Take courage, my child. I am your father and Edna is your mother, and we belong to you as well as to your wife now and forever. Take courage, my child."

The Old Testament, while at times delighting in romantic love, also limits sexuality and sexual relations within specific relations. Given the moral significance of sex, many references are of a more restrictive note. Leviticus 18, for example, gives a detailed listing of inappropriate sexual relations. The Scriptures also contain stories of misuse of sex and passion. The message is that love demands responsible behavior. Its primary consideration is the other and not self-gratification. Tobias, for example, prays, "I am now taking this kinswoman of mine, not because of lust, but with sincerity. Grant that she and I may find mercy and that we may grow old together" (Tobit 8:7). The Old Testament illustrates the probability of tragedy and abuse when self-gratification, power, lust, and sex are mistakenly thought of as love. The rape of Tamar (2 Samuel 13) and the rape of Dinah (Genesis 34), as well as David's adulterous relationship with Bathsheba (2 Samuel 11) and Samson's troubled love life (Judges 14–16), all illustrate this well.

The book of Proverbs also points to this idea. It records the words of a teacher warning young men about the dangers of straying from their wives (note who is the victim and who the aggressor in these verses!).

Proverbs 5; 6:20–35; 7

Chapter 5: My child, be attentive to my wisdom; incline your ear to my understanding, so that you may hold on to prudence, and your lips may guard knowledge. For the lips of a loose woman drip honey, and her speech is smoother than oil; but in the end she is bitter as wormwood, sharp as a two-edged sword. Her feet go down to death; her steps follow the path to Sheol. She does not keep straight to the path of life; her ways wander, and she does not know it.

And now, my child, listen to me, and do not depart from the words of my mouth. Keep your way far from her, and do not go near the door of her house; or you will give your honor to others, and your years to the merciless, and strangers will take their fill of your wealth, and your labors will go to the house of an alien; and at the end of your life you will groan, when your flesh and body are consumed, and you say, "Oh, how I hated discipline, and my heart despised reproof! I did not listen to the voice of my teachers or incline my ear to my instructors. Now I am at the point of utter ruin in the public assembly." Drink water from your own cistern, flowing water from your own well.

Should your springs be scattered abroad, streams of water in the streets? Let them be for yourself alone, and not for sharing with strangers. Let your fountain be blessed, and rejoice in the wife of your youth, a lovely deer, a graceful doe. May her breasts satisfy you at all times; may you be intoxicated always by her love. Why should you be intoxicated, my son, by another woman and embrace the bosom of an adulteress? For human ways are under the eyes of the Lord, and he examines all their paths. The iniquities of the wicked ensnare them, and they are caught in the toils of their sin. They die for lack of discipline, and because of their great folly they are lost.

Chapter 6:20–35: My child, keep your father's commandment, and do not forsake your mother's teaching. Bind them upon your heart always; tie them around your neck. When you walk, they will lead you; when you lie down, they will watch over you; and when you awake, they will talk with you. For the commandment is a lamp and the teaching a light, and the reproofs of discipline are the way of life, to preserve you from the wife of another, from the smooth tongue of the adulteress. Do not desire her beauty in your heart, and do not let her capture you with her eyelashes; for a prostitute's fee is only a loaf of bread, but the wife of another stalks a man's very life. Can fire be carried in the bosom without burning one's clothes? Or can one walk on hot coals without scorching the feet? So is he who sleeps with his neighbor's wife; no one who touches her will go unpunished. Thieves are not despised who steal only to satisfy their appetite when they are hungry. Yet if they are caught, they will pay sevenfold; they will forfeit all the goods of their house. But he who commits adultery has no sense; he who does it destroys himself. He will get wounds and dishonor, and his disgrace will not be wiped away. For jealousy arouses a husband's fury, and he shows no restraint when he takes revenge. He will accept no compensation, and refuses a bribe no matter how great.

Chapter 7: My child, keep my words and store up my commandments with you; keep my commandments and live, keep my teachings as the apple of your eye; bind them on your fingers, write them on the tablet of your heart. Say to wisdom, "You are my sister," and call insight your intimate friend, that they may keep you from the loose woman, from the adulteress with her smooth words.

For at the window of my house I looked out through my lattice, and I saw among the simple ones, I observed among the youths, a young man without sense, passing along the street near her corner, taking the road to her house in the twilight, in the evening, at the time of night and darkness. Then a woman comes toward him, decked out like a prostitute, wily of heart. She is loud and wayward; her feet do not stay at home; now in the street, now in the squares, and at every corner she lies in wait. She seizes him and kisses him, and with impudent face she says to him: "I had to offer sacrifices, and today I have paid my vows; so now I have come out to meet you, to seek you eagerly, and I have found you! I have decked my couch with coverings, colored spreads of Egyptian linen; I have perfumed my bed with myrrh, aloes, and cinnamon. Come, let us take our fill of love until morning; let us delight ourselves with love. For my husband is not at home; he has gone on a long journey. He took a bag of money with him; he will not come home until full moon.

With much seductive speech she persuades him; with her smooth talk she compels him. Right away he follows her, and goes like an ox to the slaughter or bounds like a stag toward the trap until an arrow pierces its entrails. He is like a bird rushing into a snare, not knowing that it will cost him his life.

And now, my children, listen to me, and be attentive to the words of my mouth. Do not let your hearts turn aside to her ways; do not stray into her paths. For many are those she has laid low, and numerous are her victims. Her house is the way to Sheol, going down to the chambers of death.

Conflicting Loves

Two nations are in your womb, and two peoples born of you shall be divided, the one shall be stronger than the other, the elder shall serve the younger.

—Genesis

The story of Ruth is one of family ties, kinship, and rightly ordered love prevailing. Not all familial loves in the Old Testament, however, work out on such a happy note as Ruth's does. The book of Deuteronomy, for example, addresses the problem of a man loving one of his wives more than another and the ramifications of this for the rights of the first-born son (Deut. 21:15–17). The book of Genesis narrates the destructive possibilities of conflicting loves through three stories covering three generations of family life. The first story narrates the dramatic conflict in Abraham's life between his love for his son, Isaac, and the word of God. The second concerns the love of two parents, Isaac and Rebekah, for their sons, Esau and Jacob. The final narrative tells of problems that arise with Jacob's preferential love for his youngest son Joseph.

Genesis 22:1–19
After these things God tested Abraham. He said to him, "Abraham!" And he said, "Here I am." He said, "Take your son, your only son Isaac, whom you love, and go to the land of Moriah, and offer him there as a burnt offering on one of the mountains that I shall show you." So Abraham rose early in the morning, saddled his donkey, and took two of his young men with him, and his son Isaac; he cut the wood for the burnt offering, and set out and went to the place in the distance that God had shown him. On the third day Abraham looked up and saw the place far away. Then Abraham

said to his young men, "Stay here with the donkey; the boy and I will go over there; we will worship, and then we will come back to you." Abraham took the wood of the burnt offering and laid it on his son Isaac, and he himself carried the fire and the knife. So the two of them walked on together. Isaac said to his father Abraham, "Father!" And he said, "Here I am, my son." He said, "The fire and the wood are here, but where is the lamb for a burnt offering?" Abraham said, "God himself will provide the lamb for a burnt offering, my son." So the two of them walked on together.

When they came to the place that God had shown him, Abraham built an altar there and laid the wood in order. He bound his son Isaac, and laid him on the altar, on top of the wood. Then Abraham reached out his hand and took the knife to kill his son. But the angel of the Lord called to him from heaven, and said, "Abraham, Abraham!" And he said, "Here I am." He said, "Do not lay your hand on the boy or do anything to him; for now I know that you fear God, since you have not withheld your son, your only son, from me." And Abraham looked up and saw a ram, caught in a thicket by its horns. Abraham went and took the ram and offered it up as a burnt offering instead of his son. So Abraham called that place "The Lord will provide"; as it is said to this day, "On the mount of the Lord it shall be provided."

The angel of the Lord called to Abraham a second time from heaven, and said, "By myself I have sworn, says the Lord: Because you have done this, and have not withheld your son, your only son, I will indeed bless you, and I will make your offspring as numerous as the stars of heaven and as the sand that is on the seashore. And your offspring shall possess the gate of their enemies, and by your offspring shall all the nations of the earth gain blessing for themselves, because you have obeyed my voice." So Abraham returned to his young men, and they arose and went together to Beer-sheba; and Abraham lived at Beer-sheba.

Isaac survives God's demand to Abraham and later marries Rebekah. The couple has great difficulty having children. They wait twenty years for Rebekah to conceive. Finally Rebekah is pregnant with twins. The happiness they must feel is mixed with a concern about the future of the children. As the narrator writes, the "children struggled together within her" (25:22). The twin boys are named Esau and Jacob. The parents' preferential love for them becomes the source of tension and indeed deception in the family.

Genesis 25:19–34

These are the descendants of Isaac, Abraham's son: Abraham was the father of Isaac, and Isaac was forty years old when he married Rebekah, daughter of Bethuel the Aramean of Paddan-aram, sister of Laban the Aramean. Isaac prayed to the Lord for his wife, because she was barren; and the Lord granted his prayer, and his wife Rebekah conceived. The children struggled together within her; and she said, "If it is to be this way, why do I live?" So she went to inquire of the Lord. And the Lord said to her, "Two nations are in your womb, and two peoples born of you shall be divided; the one shall be stronger than the other, the elder shall serve the younger." When her time to give birth was at hand, there were twins in her womb. The first came out red, all his body like a hairy mantle; so they named him Esau. Afterward his brother came out, with his hand gripping Esau's heel; so he was named Jacob. Isaac was sixty years old when she bore them.

When the boys grew up, Esau was a skillful hunter, a man of the field, while Jacob was a quiet man, living in tents. Isaac loved Esau, because he was fond of game; but Rebekah loved Jacob.

Once when Jacob was cooking a stew, Esau came in from the field, and he was famished. Esau said to Jacob, "Let me eat some of that red stuff, for I am famished!" (Therefore he was called Edom.) Jacob said, "First sell me your birthright." Esau said, "I am about to die; of what use is a birthright to me?" Jacob said, "Swear to me first." So he swore to him, and sold his birthright to Jacob. Then Jacob gave Esau bread and lentil stew, and he ate and drank, and rose and went his way. Thus Esau despised his birthright.

Isaac is now on his deathbed and ready to give his blessing to his oldest son Esau, but Rebekah has different plans. She and Jacob conspire to cheat Esau out of his rightful blessing.

Genesis 27

When Isaac was old and his eyes were dim so that he could not see, he called his elder son Esau and said to him, "My son"; and he answered, "Here I am." He said, "See, I am old; I do not know the day of my death. Now then, take your weapons, your quiver and your bow, and go out to the field, and hunt game for me. Then prepare for me savory food, such as I like, and bring it to me to eat, so that I may bless you before I die."

Now Rebekah was listening when Isaac spoke to his son Esau. So when Esau went to the field to hunt for game and bring it, Rebekah said to her son Jacob, "I heard your father say to your brother Esau, 'Bring me game,

and prepare for me savory food to eat, that I may bless you before the Lord
before I die.' Now therefore, my son, obey my word as I command you.
Go to the flock, and get me two choice kids, so that I may prepare from
them savory food for your father, such as he likes; and you shall take it to
your father to eat, so that he may bless you before he dies." But Jacob said
to his mother Rebekah, "Look, my brother Esau is a hairy man, and I am
a man of smooth skin. Perhaps my father will feel me, and I shall seem to
be mocking him, and bring a curse on myself and not a blessing." His
mother said to him, "Let your curse be on me, my son; only obey my word,
and go, get them for me." So he went and got them and brought them to
his mother; and his mother prepared savory food, such as his father loved.
Then Rebekah took the best garments of her elder son Esau, which were
with her in the house, and put them on her younger son Jacob; and she put
the skins of the kids on his hands and on the smooth part of his neck. Then
she handed the savory food, and the bread that she had prepared, to her
son Jacob.

So he went in to his father, and said, "My father"; and he said, "Here
I am; who are you, my son?" Jacob said to his father, "I am Esau your firstborn. I have done as you told me; now sit up and eat of my game, so that
you may bless me." But Isaac said to his son, "How is it that you have found
it so quickly, my son?" He answered, "Because the Lord your God granted
me success." Then Isaac said to Jacob, "Come near, that I may feel you, my
son, to know whether you are really my son Esau or not." So Jacob went
up to his father Isaac, who felt him and said, "The voice is Jacob's voice,
but the hands are the hands of Esau." He did not recognize him, because
his hands were hairy like his brother Esau's hands; so he blessed him. He
said, "Are you really my son Esau?" He answered, "I am." Then he said,
"Bring it to me, that I may eat of my son's game and bless you." So he
brought it to him, and he ate; and he brought him wine, and he drank.
Then his father Isaac said to him, "Come near and kiss me, my son." So he
came near and kissed him; and he smelled the smell of his garments, and
blessed him, and said, "Ah, the smell of my son is like the smell of a field
that the Lord has blessed. May God give you of the dew of heaven, and of
the fatness of the earth, and plenty of grain and wine. Let peoples serve
you, and nations bow down to you. Be lord over your brothers, and may
your mother's sons bow down to you. Cursed be everyone who curses you,
and blessed be everyone who blesses you!"

As soon as Isaac had finished blessing Jacob, when Jacob had scarcely
gone out from the presence of his father Isaac, his brother Esau came in

from his hunting. He also prepared savory food, and brought it to his father. And he said to his father, "Let my father sit up and eat of his son's game, so that you may bless me." His father Isaac said to him, "Who are you?" He answered, "I am your firstborn son, Esau." Then Isaac trembled violently, and said, "Who was it then that hunted game and brought it to me, and I ate it all before you came, and I have blessed him?—yes, and blessed he shall be!" When Esau heard his father's words, he cried out with an exceedingly great and bitter cry, and said to his father, "Bless me, me also, father!" But he said, "Your brother came deceitfully, and he has taken away your blessing." Esau said, "Is he not rightly named Jacob? For he has supplanted me these two times. He took away my birthright; and look, now he has taken away my blessing." Then he said, "Have you not reserved a blessing for me?" Isaac answered Esau, "I have already made him your lord, and I have given him all his brothers as servants, and with grain and wine I have sustained him. What then can I do for you, my son?" Esau said to his father, "Have you only one blessing, father? Bless me, me also, father!" And Esau lifted up his voice and wept.

Then his father Isaac answered him: "See, away from the fatness of the earth shall your home be, and away from the dew of heaven on high. By your sword you shall live, and you shall serve your brother; but when you break loose, you shall break his yoke from your neck."

Now Esau hated Jacob because of the blessing with which his father had blessed him, and Esau said to himself, "The days of mourning for my father are approaching; then I will kill my brother Jacob." But the words of her elder son Esau were told to Rebekah; so she sent and called her younger son Jacob and said to him, "Your brother Esau is consoling himself by planning to kill you. Now therefore, my son, obey my voice; flee at once to my brother Laban in Haran, and stay with him a while, until your brother's fury turns away—until your brother's anger against you turns away, and he forgets what you have done to him; then I will send, and bring you back from there. Why should I lose both of you in one day?"

Then Rebekah said to Isaac, "I am weary of my life because of the Hittite women. If Jacob marries one of the Hittite women such as these, one of the woman of the land, what good will my life be to me?"

Esau is furious and plans to kill his brother. Jewish lore has it that the reason Jacob was tricked in his attempt at marriage with Rachel was divine retribution for taking the blessing from his brother! The Jacob and Esau story, however, does not end with this tension. Years later, the brothers meet. Jacob bows down to Esau and seems hesitant to greet his brother. Esau is overcome with joy at the sight of his brother and accepts him warmly and lovingly.

Genesis 33

Now Jacob looked up and saw Esau coming, and four hundred men with him. So he divided the children among Leah and Rachel and the two maids. He put the maids with their children in front, then Leah with her children, and Rachel and Joseph last of all. He himself went on ahead of them, bowing himself to the ground seven times, until he came near his brother.

But Esau ran to meet him, and embraced him, and fell on his neck and kissed him, and they wept. When Esau looked up and saw the women and children, he said, "Who are these with you?" Jacob said, "The children whom God has graciously given your servant." Then the maids drew near, they and their children, and bowed down; Leah likewise and her children drew near and bowed down; and finally Joseph and Rachel drew near, and they bowed down. Esau said, "What do you mean by all this company that I met?" Jacob answered, "To find favor with my lord." But Esau said, "I have enough, my brother; keep what you have for yourself." Jacob said, "No, please; if I find favor with you, then accept my present from my hand; for truly to see your face is like seeing the face of God—since you have received me with such favor. Please accept my gift that is brought to you, because God has dealt graciously with me, and because I have everything I want." So he urged him, and he took it.

Then Esau said, "Let us journey on our way, and I will go alongside you." But Jacob said to him, "My lord knows that the children are frail and that the flocks and herds, which are nursing, are a care to me; and if they are overdriven for one day, all the flocks will die. Let my lord pass on ahead of his servant, and I will lead on slowly, according to the pace of the cattle that are before me and according to the pace of the children, until I come to my lord in Seir."

So Esau said, "Let me leave with you some of the people who are with me." But he said, "Why should my lord be so kind to me?" So Esau returned that day on his way to Seir. But Jacob journeyed to Succoth, and built himself a house, and made booths for his cattle; therefore the place is called Succoth.

Jacob came safely to the city of Shechem, which is in the land of Canaan, on his way from Paddan-aram; and he camped before the city.

And from the sons of Hamor, Shechem's father, he bought for one hundred pieces of money the plot of land on which he had pitched his tent. There he erected an altar and called it EI-Elohe-Israel.

The love for a child causes yet another family problem in the next generation. Jacob, now an old man and called Israel, shows particular preference for his youngest son Joseph. This causes a great hatred and jealousy among his other sons.

Genesis 37

Jacob settled in the land where his father had lived as an alien, the land of Canaan. This is the story of the family of Jacob.

Joseph, being seventeen years old, was shepherding the flock with his brothers; he was a helper to the sons of Bilhah and Zilpah, his father's wives; and Joseph brought a bad report of them to their father. Now Israel loved Joseph more than any other of his children, because he was the son of his old age; and he had made him a long robe with sleeves. But when his brothers saw that their father loved him more than all his brothers, they hated him, and could not speak peaceably to him.

Once Joseph had a dream, and when he told it to his brothers, they hated him even more. He said to them, "Listen to this dream that I dreamed. There we were, binding sheaves in the field. Suddenly my sheaf rose and stood upright; then your sheaves gathered around it, and bowed down to my sheaf." His brothers said to him, "Are you indeed to reign over us? Are you indeed to have dominion over us?" So they hated him even more because of his dreams and his words.

He had another dream, and told it to his brothers, saying, "Look, I have had another dream: the sun, the moon, and eleven stars were bowing down to me." But when he told it to his father and to his brothers, his father rebuked him, and said to him, "What kind of dream is this that you have had? Shall we indeed come, I and your mother and your brothers, and bow to the ground before you?" So his brothers were jealous of him, but his father kept the matter in mind.

Now his brothers went to pasture their father's flock near Shechem. And Israel said to Joseph, "Are not your brothers pasturing the flock at Shechem? Come, I will send you to them." He answered, "Here I am." So he said to him, "Go now, see if it is well with your brothers and with the flock; and bring word back to me." So he sent him from the valley of Hebron.

He came to Shechem, and a man found him wandering in the fields; the man asked him, "What are you seeking?" "I am seeking my brothers," he said; "tell me, please, where they are pasturing the flock." The man said, "They have gone away, for I heard them say, 'Let us go to Dothan.'" So Joseph went after his brothers, and found them at Dothan. They saw him from a distance, and before he came near to them, they conspired to kill him. They said to one another, "Here comes this dreamer. Come now, let us kill him and throw him into one of the pits; then we shall say that a wild animal has devoured him, and we shall see what will become of his dreams." But when Reuben heard it, he delivered him out of their hands, saying, "Let us not take his life." Reuben said to them, "Shed no blood; throw him into this pit here in the wilderness, but lay no hand on him"— that he might rescue him out of their hand and restore him to his father. So when Joseph came to his brothers, they stripped him of his robe, the long robe with sleeves that he wore; and they took him and threw him into a pit. The pit was empty; there was no water in it.

Then they sat down to eat; and looking up they saw a caravan of Ishmaelites coming from Gilead, with their camels carrying gum, balm, and resin, on their way to carry it down to Egypt. Then Judah said to his brothers, "What profit is it if we kill our brother and conceal his blood? Come, let us sell him to the Ishmaelites, and not lay our hands on him, for he is our brother, our own flesh." And his brothers agreed. When some Midianite traders passed by, they drew Joseph up, lifting him out of the pit, and sold him to the Ishmaelites for twenty pieces of silver. And they took Joseph to Egypt.

When Reuben returned to the pit and saw that Joseph was not in the pit, he tore his clothes. He returned to his brothers, and said, "The boy is gone; and I, where can I turn?" Then they took Joseph's robe, slaughtered a goat, and dipped the robe in the blood. They had the long robe with sleeves taken to their father, and they said, "This we have found; see now whether it is your son's robe or not." He recognized it, and said, "It is my son's robe! A wild animal has devoured him; Joseph is without doubt torn to pieces." Then Jacob tore his garments, and put sackcloth on his loins, and mourned for his son many days. All his sons and all his daughters sought to comfort him; but he refused to be comforted, and said, "No, I shall go down to Sheol to my son, mourning." Thus his father bewailed him. Meanwhile the Midianites had sold him in Egypt to Potiphar, one of Pharaoh's officials, the captain of the guard.

CHAPTER TWO

Love in the New Testament: The Great Commandment

Agape

Teacher, which commandment in the law is the greatest?

—Matthew

This chapter continues the examination of love in the Bible through an exploration of the use and meaning of love in the New Testament. Every Christian knows that love plays a significant role in the New Testament. It is fundamental to Christian teaching that God is love and Christians ought to love God and love their neighbors. It would not be accurate, however, to say that the central teaching of Jesus was love or that the unifying theme of the New Testament is love.[1] Jesus preached and lived the Kingdom of God. His teachings and actions were a witness and a proclamation of the Kingdom present in his life. The authors of the New Testament understood the imperative to love within the context of the Kingdom, which they understood as God's present and active rule in the world.[2] The New Testament stories, themes, and teachings on love developed within the cultural setting of a community formed by the Old Testament, but in relation to the broader Greek culture and in reflection on the life, teachings, and death of Jesus.

The dominant and almost exclusive word for love in the New Testament is the Greek word *agape*. This is interesting, given that Jesus did not speak Greek. He never used the word *agape*. The entire New Testament, however, was originally written in Greek, specifically *Koine* Greek. The reason for this is that Christianity rapidly spread from Palestine and the world of Jesus to the Hellenistic world and to Rome. Norman Perrin writes, "Though earliest Christianity was an apocalyptic sect within Palestinian Judaism and though Jesus himself was a Palestinian Jew, Palestinian Judaism is not really the world of the New Testament.

Hellenism, the civilization created by the conquests of Alexander the Great . . . is the world of the New Testament."[3] Greek was the common language, indeed the common culture, within the areas where Christianity developed and during the time period in which the New Testament was written. The books that came to be accepted as the "New Testament" were written, then, in the common language of the people.

The fact that the New Testament was written in Greek adds an interesting twist to our examination of the meaning of love. Because the Greek language had several words referring to love, the authors of the New Testament had to make a decision which word to use. To resolve this issue, the authors of the New Testament had a precedent. The Old Testament had been translated into Greek (the translation is called the Septuagint) about 250 years before the birth of Jesus. The translators of the Old Testament chose the word *agape* to interpret the Hebrew words for love. Before we consider the meaning of *agape* in classical Greek, let's examine the two dominant Greek words for love that the translators of the Old Testament could have chosen, but did not—namely, *philia* and *eros*.

In classical Greek, *philia* "designates the relationship between a person and any other person(s) or being(s) which that person regards as peculiarly his own and to which he has a particular attachment. This included the bond holding the members of any association together, regardless of whether the association is the family, the state, a club, a business partnership, or even the business relation between buyer and seller."[4] Philia suggests a level of mutuality and sharing between persons "and would not ordinarily imply sexual desire."[5] It is most often translated into English as friendship.

Eros is the love characterized by desiring or longing for someone or something. In classical Greek *eros* had sexual connotations. A lover, for example, longs to be with the beloved and desires the beloved's physical presence. This meaning carries over into today in our use of the term erotic, although erotic has more limited connotations than did *eros*. *Eros* in classical Greek included desires beyond merely sexual desires.

Plato's book *The Symposium* is cited as the authoritative ancient text on *eros*. The book narrates a dialogue in which the characters discuss the meaning of the term. Plato's teacher, Socrates, offers the definitive account. For Socrates, *eros* is "the means of actualizing the highest potentialities of human being through achieving an understanding of the ultimate principle of beauty, which is the ultimate object of eros."[6] *Eros* is not beauty or good itself; it is a thirst or "a desire for beauty, for the good, for wisdom, for happiness, for immortality, for the Absolute."[7] Giovanni Reale describes this as true love. He writes, "The *true lover* is one who knows how to pursue the beloved in all things until he reaches the supreme vision, until he achieves a vision of that which is absolutely beautiful."[8] There is a hierarchy, or gradation, of things to be loved. There are those who love the physical bodies of others, there are "lovers of souls, lovers of arts, lovers of justice and laws, lovers of pure knowledge . . . and finally, at the summit of the scale of love there is . . . Absolute Beauty."[9] In *The Symposium* Socrates, quoting Diotima, describes "arriving" at the "notion of absolute beauty" and "knowing the essence of beauty." The "life above all others which man should live," he says, is "the contemplation of beauty absolute." Socrates offers a question that is at once an aspiration and an inspiration. "But what if man had eyes to see the true beauty—the divine beauty, I mean, pure and clear and unalloyed, not clogged with the pollutions of mortality and all the colors and vanities of human life— thither looking, and hold converse with the true beauty simple and divine?"[10]

Neither *philia* nor *eros* were chosen to translate the words for love in the Old Testament or the New Testament even though there might have been an occasion to use them. *Eros*, for example, might have been used to describe the type of love between the couple in the Song of Solomon. *Philia* would seem descriptive of the relationship between David and Jonathan. The word used for love in the Septuagint and the New Testament is *agape*. William Klassen writes, "Words from the agape family occur 341 times and are found in every book of the New Testament."[11] *Eros* is not mentioned in the New Testament and *philia* appears just a handful of times.

In classical Greek the meaning for *agape* was broad; it was used to suggest a variety of loves, such as affection, fondness, and contentedness.[12] The translators probably chose this term because its use was less common and its meaning more unspecified than either *philia* or *eros*. The irony here is that a classic Greek word with a relatively unspecified meaning becomes the most well-known Greek word in the Christian vocabulary. Whatever the reason for the choice of the word, the implication is clear. An interpretation of *agape* "must be found in the text's substantive claims, rather than in the linguistic meaning of the word."[13] The meaning of *agape* is to be found in the pages of the Bible not in the writings of philosophers. Scripture scholar G. Johnston puts it simply, "Jesus revealed the meaning of love by his life."[14] Reflection on the life Jesus lived, on the words he preached, and on the act of his death provides, for the Christian, the meaning of *agape*.

The Great Commandment

You shall love the Lord your God with all your heart, and with all your soul, and with all your mind. This is the greatest and first commandment. And the second is like it: You shall love your neighbor as yourself.

—Matthew

The most appropriate place to start a review of love in the New Testament is with the Great Commandment. The New Testament follows the Old Testament in that love is commanded. For Jesus, it is the primary commandment. Paul repeats this point in the Letter to the Galatians, when he writes, "For the whole law is summed up in a single commandment, 'You shall love your neighbor as yourself'"(Gal. 5:14). Likewise the author of the First Letter of John writes, "And this is his commandment, that we should believe in the name of his Son Jesus Christ and love one another just as he has commanded us" (1 John 3:23). The Great Commandment passages are found in three Gospels, Matthew, Mark, and Luke. Here is Mark's version of the Great Commandment:

> One of the scribes came near and heard them disputing with one another, and seeing that he answered them well, he asked him, "Which commandment is the first of all?" Jesus answered, "The first is, 'Hear, O Israel: the Lord our God, the Lord is one; you shall love the Lord your God with all your heart, and with all your soul, and with all your mind, and with all your strength.' The second is this, 'You shall love your neighbor as yourself.' There is no other commandment greater than these." Then the scribe said to him, "You are right, Teacher; you have truly said that 'he is one, and beside him there is no other'; and to love him with all the heart, and with all the understanding, and with all the strength, and 'to love one's neighbor as oneself,' this is much more important than all whole burnt offerings and sacrifices." When Jesus saw that he answered wisely, he said to him, "You are not far from the kingdom of God." (Mk 12:28–34)

Here is Matthew's version of the Greatest Commandment:

> When the Pharisees heard that he had silenced the Sadducees, they gathered together, and one of them, a lawyer, asked him a question to test him. "Teacher, which commandment in the law is the greatest?" He said to him, "'You shall love the Lord your God with all your heart, and with all your soul, and with all your mind. This is the greatest and first commandment. And the second is like it: 'You shall love your neighbor as yourself.' On these two commandments hang all the law and the prophets." (Matt. 22:34–40)

Here is Luke's version of the Greatest Commandment:

> Just then a lawyer stood up to test Jesus. "Teacher," he said, "what must I do to inherit eternal life?" He said to him, "What is written in the law? What do you read there?" He answered, "You shall love the Lord your God

with all your heart, and with all your soul, and with all your strength, and
with all your mind; and your neighbor as yourself." And he said to him,
"You have given the right answer; do this, and you will live." (Luke 10:25–28)

Luke then follows the story with the lawyer asking Jesus, "And who is my neighbor?" to which Jesus responds with the story of the Good Samaritan. Although
the Great Commandment includes love of God, self, and other, in terms of number and prominence of texts, the priority is much more on neighbor love than
on love for God. Beyond the texts above, there is nothing said on love for self.

God's Love

Beloved, since God loves us so much, we also ought to love one another.

—1 John

The New Testament presents several texts describing God's love. In John's Gospel
we read, "For God so loved the world that he gave his only Son, so that everyone who believes in him may not perish but may have eternal life" (John 3:16).
Paul writes in his Letter to the Romans, "For while we were still weak, at the
right time Christ died for the ungodly. Indeed, rarely will anyone die for a righteous person—though perhaps for a good person someone might actually dare
to die. But God proves his love for us in that while we still were sinners Christ
died for us" (Rom. 5:6–8). The First Letter of John, as it often does in discourse
on love, dramatically summarizes this theme.

> Beloved, let us love one another, because love is from God; everyone
> who loves is born of God and knows God. Whoever does not love does
> not know God, for God is love. God's love was revealed among us in
> this way: God sent his only Son into the world so that we might live
> through him. In this is love, not that we loved God but that he loved
> us and sent his Son to be the atoning sacrifice for our sins. Beloved,
> since God loves us so much, we also ought to love one another. No one
> has ever seen God; if we love one another, God lives in us, and his love
> is perfected in us. (1 John 4:7–12)

Jesus often describes God's love through parables. In chapter 15 of the Gospel
of Luke, we hear Jesus tell three stories about God's love. The first is about a man
who loses one of his one hundred sheep and goes out to find it. The second is
about a woman who loses one of her ten silver pieces and diligently searches to

find it. The desire of this man and this woman to seek out the lost even when they have so much seems foolish. Their intensity seems a bit overboard by customary standards, but for Luke, the efforts and attitudes of this man and this woman depict the expansiveness and boundlessness of God's love.[15] The final parable in chapter 15 is about a family who "loses" a member and is most dramatic in its statement of the nature of God's love. Much can be said about this rich story. We can reflect for example on the troubled brothers, the younger one and his choices, or the older one and his reaction to his returning brother. Think about the "loves" of the younger brother and his struggles to find love in life. We might also consider the older brother and his narrow view of love, a view that seems unable to get beyond his feelings of resentment. In the middle of the story, however, we hear about a love, strong and clear, that is reminiscent of Hosea's description of God's love. It is the enduring love of a parent. Recall Hosea: "When Israel was a child I loved him. . . . It was I who taught Ephraim to walk. . . . I led them with cords of human kindness, with bands of love. I was to them like those who lift infants to their cheeks. I bent down to them and fed them" (Hos. 11:1, 3–4). As Raymond Brown suggests, "the portrayal of the father running to the younger son and kissing him before he can give the prepared speech of repentance"[16] is a moving description of God's love.

> Then Jesus said, "There was a man who had two sons. The younger of them said to his father, 'Father, give me the share of the property that will belong to me.' So he divided his property between them. A few days later the younger son gathered all he had and traveled to a distant country, and there he squandered his property in dissolute living. When he had spent everything, a severe famine took place throughout that country, and he began to be in need. So he went and hired himself out to one of the citizens of that country, who sent him to his fields to feed the pigs. He would gladly have filled himself with the pods that the pigs were eating; and no one gave him anything. But when he came to himself he said, 'How many of my father's hired hands have bread enough and to spare, but here I am dying of hunger! I will get up and go to my father, and I will say to him, "Father, I have sinned against heaven and before you; I am no longer worthy to be called your son; treat me like one of your hired hands."' So he set off and went to his father. But while he was still far off, his father saw him and was filled with compassion; he ran and put his arms around him and kissed him. Then the son said to him, 'Father, I have sinned against heaven and before you; I am no longer worthy to be called your son.' But the father said to his slaves, 'Quickly, bring out a robe—the best one—and

put it on him; put a ring on his finger and sandals on his feet. And get the fatted calf and kill it, and let us eat and celebrate; for this son of mine was dead and is alive again; he was lost and is found!' And they began to celebrate.

"Now his elder son was in the field; and when he came and approached the house, he heard music and dancing. He called one of the slaves and asked what was going on. He replied, 'Your brother has come, and your father has killed the fatted calf, because he has got him back safe and sound.' Then he became angry and refused to go in. His father came out and began to plead with him. But he answered his father, 'Listen! For all these years I have been working like a slave for you, and I have never disobeyed your command; yet you have never given me even a young goat so that I might celebrate with my friends. But when this son of yours came back, who has devoured your property with prostitutes, you killed the fatted calf for him!' Then the father said to him, 'Son, you are always with me, and all that is mine is yours. But we had to celebrate and rejoice, because this brother of yours was dead and has come back to life; he was lost and has been found.'" (Luke 15:11–31)

As Ruth loves Naomi, Hosea loves Gomer, and the father loves his lost son, so God loves us. Indeed, the parables of the lost coin, the lost sheep, and the lost son describe the very nature of God. For not only does God love, but according to the author of the First Letter of John, "God is love" (1 John 4:8, 4:16). "God is love": these few words are "the closest the New Testament comes to telling us about the 'being' of God."[17] Paul has the most passionate expression of God's love in the New Testament. In his Letter to the Romans he writes:

What then are we to say about these things? If God is for us, who is against us? He who did not withhold his own Son, but gave him up for all of us, will he not with him also give us everything else? Who will separate us from the love of Christ? Will hardship or distress, or persecution, or famine, or nakedness, or peril, or sword? As it is written, "For your sake we are being killed all day long; we are accounted as sheep to be slaughtered." No, in all these things we are more than conquerors through him who loved us. For I am convinced that neither death, nor life, nor angels, nor rulers, nor things present, nor things to come, nor powers, nor height, nor depth, nor anything else in all creation, will be able to separate us from the love of God in Christ Jesus our Lord. (Rom. 8:31–32, 35–39)

Love of Neighbor

A man was going down from Jerusalem to Jericho, and fell into the hands
of robbers, who stripped him, beat him, and went away, leaving him half
dead.

—Luke

Eight times the New Testament commands us to love our neighbors as we love
ourselves (Matt. 19:19, 22:39; Mark 12:31 33; Luke 10:27; Rom. 13:9; Gal. 5:14; James
2:8). We will begin the discussion of neighbor love in an obvious place, the parable of the Good Samaritan. The people in Luke's audience might have defined
"the neighbor" as one's friend or a member of the community.[18] Jesus, however,
by making the moral hero a person outside the community, explodes the general
preconception of the neighbor. This parable, writes Pheme Perkins, "ignores social
boundaries and all the reasonable sorts of calculations people make."[19] As William
Klassen writes, in the gospels "the neighbor is described concretely: tax collec-
tor, prostitute, victim of a robbery, debtor, woman threatened with divorce. Likewise the deed of love is concretely viewed and described: table fellowship, emer-
gency aid, release from debt, healing."[20] The neighbor is not limited to the person
who lives next door, or to an acquaintance, or even to a fellow community member. The neighbor is, as Victor Furnish notes, the next person you meet.[21]

> Jesus replied, "A man was going down from Jerusalem to Jericho, and fell
> into the hands of robbers, who stripped him, beat him, and went away,
> leaving him half dead. Now by chance a priest was going down that road;
> and when he saw him, he passed by on the other side. So likewise a Levite,
> when he came to the place and saw him, passed by on the other side. But
> a Samaritan while traveling came near him; and when he saw him, he was
> moved with pity. He went to him and bandaged his wounds, having poured
> oil and wine on them. Then he put him on his own animal, brought him
> to an inn, and took care of him. The next day he took out two denarii, gave
> them to the innkeeper, and said, 'Take care of him; and when I come back,
> I will repay you whatever more you spend.' Which one of these three, do
> you think, was a neighbor to the man who fell into the hands of the rob-
> bers?" He said, "The one who showed him mercy." Jesus said to him, "Go
> and do likewise." (Luke 10: 30–37)

There is a story in Luke's gospel about Jesus and the sinner that, like the
parable of the Good Samaritan, captures an essential element of neighbor love.

Luke precedes this famous story with an extended narrative relating John the
Baptist and his work to Jesus and his work. At one point, Luke has Jesus clari-
fying his relationship to John. Among the points Jesus mentions is that John and
he share a common experience; both are rejected by the people. In a strongly
worded remark, Jesus reprimands those who reject John because they think he
is possessed by a demon, due to his leading a very austere life "eating no bread
and drinking no wine" (7:33). Jesus, on the other hand, is rejected for the opposite reason. He is called a "glutton and a drunkard" because he eats and drinks.
He is, moreover, condemned for being "a friend of tax collectors and sinners"
(7:34). Luke then tells a story that confirms both the charges people make against
Jesus. In the story Jesus eats and drinks and he befriends a sinner. It is as if Luke
is saying, "Yes, this is who Jesus is and this is part of his message."

    The story has three characters: a woman described as a sinner (although she
is not accused of any specific sin), Jesus, and a Pharisee named Simon. Simon
invites Jesus for a meal at his house and while they are sitting at the table, an un-
invited person, the woman, enters. She barges in on the event and performs a
most dramatic act. Jesus responds to her actions saying her sins were forgiven
and that "she has shown great love." Raymond Brown writes that there is some
debate as to whether she "was forgiven because she loved much or whether she
loved much because she had already been forgiven."[22] Regardless of which came
first, the story shows this woman heaping love on Jesus and Jesus responding. In
the dusty and dry land where they lived, the woman cares for Jesus and meets
his needs. In response Jesus meets her pressing need, to be relieved of her sin, her
burden. Jesus' parable is an analogy to make a point to Simon. The woman ful-
fills the duty (or debt) of the host to a guest, and does so, moreover, without hesitation. In Jesus' time washing feet "might be performed by the master's slaves
when welcoming a dignitary to the house."[23] The woman is "like the great debtor
who had the greatest debt forgiven him: thus she loves all the more."[24] The host
is then like the man forgiven the smaller debt. His love is less. Her actions and
Simon's reactions encourage Jesus to fashion a parable. We have then a story
within a story. Luke concludes the narrative with Jesus associating the characters
in the parable with Simon and the woman.

> One of the Pharisees asked Jesus to eat with him, and he went into the
> Pharisee's house and took his place at the table. And a woman in the city,
> who was a sinner, having learned that he was eating in the Pharisee's house,
> brought an alabaster jar of ointment. She stood behind him at his feet,
> weeping, and began to bathe his feet with her tears and to dry them with

her hair. Then she continued kissing his feet and anointing them with the ointment. Now when the Pharisee who had invited him saw it, he said to himself, "If this man were a prophet, he would have known who and what kind of woman this is who is touching him—that she is a sinner." Jesus spoke up and said to him, "Simon, I have something to say to you." "Teacher," he replied, "Speak." "A certain creditor had two debtors; one owed five hundred denarii, and the other fifty. When they could not pay, he canceled the debts for both of them. Now which of them will love him more?" Simon answered, "I suppose the one for whom he canceled the greater debt." And Jesus said to him, "You have judged rightly." Then turning toward the woman, he said to Simon, "Do you see this woman? I entered your house; you gave me no water for my feet, but she has bathed my feet with her tears and dried them with her hair. You gave me no kiss, but from the time I came in she has not stopped kissing my feet. You did not anoint my head with oil, but she has anointed my feet with ointment. Therefore, I tell you, her sins, which were many, have been forgiven; hence she has shown great love. But the one to whom little is forgiven, loves little." Then he said to her, "Your sins are forgiven." But those who were at the table with him began to say among themselves, "Who is this who even forgives sins?" And he said to the woman, "Your faith has saved you; go in peace." (Luke 7:36–50)

Luke's narrative is striking in that it dramatically points out that Jesus has different standards of love, acceptance, forgiveness, and "who counts" than does Simon.[25] Jesus forgives her and sends her on her way in peace. The irony of this story is that the woman is being like Jesus to Jesus. Indeed in a story very reminiscent of the sinful woman, Jesus illustrates his love for his disciples as he washes their feet. Here John clearly links the love that Jesus had for his disciples with direct, basic human service to them. Service, whether washing feet, "feeding my sheep," feeding the hungry, nourishing the thirsty, helping the stranger, clothing the naked, caring for the sick, or visiting those in prison, is the substance of love. Following and loving Jesus are then "identical with care of the needy."[26] As Hallett writes, "It is not merely that acts of love are the surest signs of love; in the final analysis, love is defined in relation to behavior."[27] John records the following during the Last Supper.

Now before the festival of the Passover, Jesus knew that his hour had come to depart from this world and go to the Father. Having loved his own who were in the world, he loved them to the end. The devil had already put it into the heart of Judas son of Simon Iscariot to betray him. And during supper Jesus, knowing that the Father had given all things into his hands, and that he had come from God and was going to God, got up from the table, took off his outer robe, and tied a towel around himself. Then he poured water into a basin and began to wash the disciples' feet and to wipe them with the towel that was tied around him. He came to Simon Peter, who said to him, "Lord, are you going to wash my feet?" Jesus answered, "You do not know now what I am doing, but later you will understand," Peter said to him, "You will never wash my feet." Jesus answered, "Unless I wash you, you have no share with me." Simon Peter said to him, "Lord, not my feet only but also my hands and my head!" Jesus said to him, "One who has bathed does not need to wash, except for the feet, but is entirely clean. And you are clean, though not all of you." For he knew who was to betray him; for this reason he said, "Not all of you are clean." After he had washed their feet, had put on his robe, and had returned to the table, he said to them, "Do you know what I have done to you? You call me Teacher and Lord—and you are right, for that is what I am. So if I, your Lord and Teacher, have washed your feet, you also ought to wash one another's feet. For I have set you an example, that you also should do as I have done to you." (John 13:1–15)

Paul writes that Jesus took the "form of a slave" (Phil. 2:7) and that he, Paul, "made himself a slave to all" (1 Cor. 9:19). He thus implores Christians to do the same as he encourages the Galatians to "become slaves to one another" through love (Gal. 5:13). On six occasions in Matthew, Mark, and Luke, we hear the authors equate service with greatness (see Matt. 20: 24–38, 32:11; Mark 9:35, 10:42–45; and Luke 22:26–27). In Luke's account of the Last Supper, for example, immediately after Jesus shares the bread and wine and identifies them with his body and his blood, his disciples get into an argument about who is the greatest. Jesus' answer is clear. Luke writes, "A dispute also arose among them as to which one of them was to be regarded as the greatest. But he said to them, 'The kings of the Gentiles lord it over them; and those in authority over them are called benefactors. But not so with you; rather the greatest among you must become like the youngest, and the leader like one who serves. For who is greater, the one who is at the table or the one who serves? Is it not the one at the table? But I am among you as one who serves" (Luke 22:26–27). "The most significant fact about the role of Jesus," writes Johnston, "is that his mission was thought of in terms derived from the image of the Servant of the Lord."[28]

Neighbor Love: Enemies

But I say to you, love your enemies and pray for those who persecute you.
—Matthew

Jesus demands a very broad view of who counts as a neighbor; he holds that one's neighbor may indeed be one's enemy. The neighbor may be one who wishes for your downfall or even seeks your destruction. The neighbor may be quite unlovable or even repulsive. The people who first heard Jesus and Paul speak of loving enemies had enemies. The early Christian communities who came to write down these words of Jesus had enemies. Enemies are real and, like neighbors, were concretely understood. There are four possible groups that the authors of the New Testament might have had in mind when they referred to enemies: national-political enemies, local people who persecuted people in Jesus' audience, Jews who removed the early Jewish-Christians from the community, and perhaps even members within local Christian communities. Regarding the first interpretation, Piper writes, "In Jesus' own environment . . . where nationalistic feelings ran high, the command 'love your enemies!' struck home with discomforting concreteness."[29] Jesus and his people, after all, were held as a conquered colony of the Roman empire. There were members of his community, known as the Zealots, who were strongly anti-Roman and worked for the overthrow of the Romans. The enemies in this sense were very real and very present.

Other biblical commentators argue that love of enemy refers more to the "squabbles of local life" than to political enemies.[30] When Jesus lived there were social tensions between the few who were rich (the landowners and employers) and the many who were poor. There were also tensions between the Jews and other groups. The parable of the Good Samaritan is not only a story about loving the neighbor. Samaritans were enemies of the Jews, not in the sense of being a military threat but of a religious and cultural threat. As the Good Samaritan cared for the person in need, he loved his enemy.

A third interpretation of the notion of the enemy is based on the place of the first Christians in their world. These earliest Christians had to deal with the conflicts associated with being a sectarian movement within a dominant and exclusive religion. They were expelled from the local religious centers, often misunderstood and negatively stereotyped by their neighbors. The concerns of these first Christians were, "How shall we act toward the unbeliever, the hostile townspeople, the ridiculing old friends?" Indeed enemies to members of the early Church "were specifically described: revilers (1 Pet. 3:9; 1 Cor. 4:12), persecutors (Rom. 12:14), those who do evil to you (1 Thess. 5:15; Rom. 12:17; 1 Pet. 3:9)."[31]

The final interpretation is intra-Christian rather than between Christians and the world. Evidently not all the early groups of Christians gelled together in loving communities. There was, for example, bickering and disagreement about issues of leadership as well as faith and morals. Paul, for example, is concerned that in Corinth some Christians were excluding other members (1 Cor. 11:17). He had an overriding concern for the health of these communities and preached love as the corrective for these internal tensions.

The famous "love your enemy" text appears in two Gospels—Matthew and Luke—as well as in Paul's Letter to the Romans. All three texts follow. In the first two passages Jesus is speaking, in the third it is Paul who is speaking. Love of enemy in Matthew:

> "You have heard that it was said, 'you shall love your neighbor and hate your enemy.' But I say to you, Love your enemies and pray for those who persecute you, so that you may be children of your Father in heaven; for he makes his sun rise on the evil and on the good, and sends rain on the righteous and on the unrighteous. For if you love those who love you, what reward do you have? Do not even the tax collectors do the same? And if you greet only your brothers and sisters, what more are you doing than others? Do not even the Gentiles do the same? Be perfect, therefore, as your heavenly Father is perfect." (Matt. 5:43–48)

Love of enemy in Luke:

> "But I say to you that listen, Love your enemies, do good to those who hate you, bless those who curse you, pray for those who abuse you. If anyone strikes you on the cheek, offer the other also; and from anyone who takes away your coat do not withhold even your shirt. Give to everyone who begs from you; and if anyone takes away your goods, do not ask for them again. Do to others as you would have them do to you. If you love those who love you, what credit is that to you? For even sinners love those who love them. If you do good to those who do good to you, what credit is that to you? For even sinners do the same. If you lend to those from whom you hope to receive, what credit is that to you? Even sinners lend to sinners, to receive as much again. But love your enemies, do good, and lend, expecting nothing in return. Your reward will be great, and you will be children of the Most High; for he is kind to the ungrateful and the wicked. Be merciful, just as your Father is merciful. Do not judge, and you will not be judged; do not condemn, and you will not be condemned. Forgive, and you will be forgiven; give, and it will be given to you." (Luke 6:27–38)

Paul's version of love of enemy in the Letter to the Romans:

> Bless those who persecute you; bless and do not curse them. Rejoice with
> those who rejoice, weep with those who weep. Live in harmony with one
> another; do not be haughty, but associate with the lowly; do not claim to
> be wiser than you are. Do not repay anyone evil for evil, but take thought
> for what is noble in the sight of all. If it is possible, so far as it depends on
> you, live peaceably with all. Beloved, never avenge yourselves, but leave
> room for the wrath of God; for it is written, "Vengeance is mine, I will
> repay, says the Lord." No, "if your enemies are hungry, feed them; if they
> are thirsty, give them something to drink; for by doing this you will heap
> burning coals on their heads." Do not be overcome by evil, but overcome
> evil with good. (Rom. 12:14–21)

This radical love Jesus demands may have dramatic consequences. The writers of the New Testament, for example, equate giving up one's life, as Jesus did,
with *agape*. In John's gospel, Jesus says, "This is my commandment, that you
love one another as I have loved you. No one has greater love than this, to lay
down one's life for one's friend." (John 15:12–13)

Neighbor Love: Friendship and Personal Relationships

See how he loved him.

—John

It is well known that the four gospels highlight different aspects of Jesus' life.
Catherine Cory writes, "The authors of the gospels selected and arranged these
stories and sayings [of Jesus], with special attention to the particular situation of
the communities for which they were writing."[32] The Gospel of John is distinctive in several ways, one of which is it describes Jesus having personal friendships.
John "allows for and even encourages special relationships of love and friendship
in a way that no other Gospel writer does."[33] The Gospel shows us a Jesus who
had strong feelings for particular people. Three stories stand out, namely, his love
for Lazarus, his relationship with the "beloved" disciple, and his reference to followers as his friends.

In chapter 11 we hear about the death of Jesus' friend Lazarus. Lazarus becomes sick and his sister thinks Jesus ought to know, so she sends a messenger
to give Jesus the message, "Lord, he whom you love is ill" (John 11:3). Jesus, interestingly enough, is in no hurry to see him. He takes his time getting to
Lazarus's house. By the time he arrives, Lazarus has been dead for four days. John

writes, "When Mary came where Jesus was and saw him, she knelt at his feet and said to him, 'Lord, if you had been here, my brother would not have died.' When Jesus saw her weeping, and the Jews who came with her also weeping, he was greatly disturbed in spirit and deeply moved. He said, 'Where have you laid him?' They said to him, 'Lord, come and see.' Jesus began to weep. So the Jews said, 'See how he loved him!'" (John 11:32–36). Jesus then goes to the cave where Lazarus is buried and prays. After his prayer, "he cried out in a loud voice, 'Lazarus, come out!' The dead man came out, his hands and feet bound with strips of cloth, and his face wrapped in a cloth" (John 11:43–44).

John also tells us about Jesus' special and unnamed friend known as the "Beloved Disciple." In his narrative of the Last Supper we read, "One of his disciples, the one whom Jesus loved, was reclining next to him" (John 13:23). Furthermore, John describes an incident as Jesus hung on the cross very near death. "When Jesus saw his mother and the disciple whom he loved standing beside her, he said to his mother, 'Woman, here is your son.' Then he said to the disciple, 'Here is your mother.' And from that hour the disciple took her into his own home" (John 19: 26–27). Finally, in the last chapter of his gospel, John again mentions this disciple. John writes that there was a rumor in the community that this disciple would not die. Jesus responds, "if it is my will that he remain until I come, what is that to you?" (John 21: 20–23). Jesus, like you and me, had a small group of people, namely, Lazarus, Mary, Martha, and the Beloved Disciple, whom he called friends.

On several occasions John also speaks of Jesus' love for his followers. Indeed Jesus' love for his followers is a dominant theme in John's telling of the Last Supper. In this moving narrative we hear the words of a man who realizes his death is near. Jesus openly expresses his love for his friends and encourages them to love each other as he loved each of them. "Now before the festival of the Passover, Jesus knew that his hour had come to depart from this world and go to the Father. Having loved his own who were in the world, he loved them to the end" (John 13:1). After the meal Jesus tells his many disciples gathered, "I give you a new commandment, that you love one another. Just as I have loved you, you also should love one another. By this everyone will know that you are my disciples, if you have love for one another" (John 13:34–35). He continues, "I will not leave you orphaned; I am coming to you. In a little while the world will no longer see me, but you will see me; because I live, you also will live. On that day you will know that I am in my Father, and you in me, and I in you. They who have my commandments and keep them are those who love me; and those who love me will be loved by my Father, and I will love them and reveal myself to them" (14:18–21). Repeatedly speaking of love (see 14: 23–24 and 14: 28–31), Jesus goes on to say, "As the Father has loved me, so I have loved you; abide in my love. If you keep my commandments, you will abide in my love, just as I have kept my Father's commandment and abide in his love. I have said these things to you so that my joy may be in you and that your joy may be complete. This is my commandment, that you love one another as I have loved you" (John 15: 9–12); and, "I am giving you these commands so that you may love one another" (John 15:17).

John ends his Last Supper account with Jesus offering a long prayer that includes this concern for all his followers:[34]

> The glory that you have given me I have given them, so that they may be one, as we are one, I in them and you in me, that they may become completely one, so that the world may know that you have sent me and have loved them even as you have loved me. Father, I desire that those also, whom you have given me, may be with me where I am, to see my glory, which you have given me because you loved me before the foundation of the world. Righteous Father, the world does not know you, but I know you; and these know that you have sent me. I made your name known to them, and I will make it known, so that the love with which you have loved me may be in them, and I in them. (John 17: 22–26)

As we read through the New Testament we detect a shift in the presentation of *agape*. In the Gospels of Matthew, Mark, and Luke we see a Jesus reaching out and expecting his followers to love their neighbors, with the latter being broadly enough construed to include their enemies. In John's Gospel and the First Letter of John as well as many of the Pauline letters, we hear not "love your enemy" but love your "brothers and sisters." That is, love your fellow Christians. The reason for this is that after the death of Jesus the community of his followers experienced some dramatic challenges. The very first Christians were Jews who in their new beliefs and practices developed into a sect within established Judaism. This was cause for great tension both between Christians themselves (Did, for example, new members who were not Jewish have to follow Jewish religious laws to be truly Christian?) and between the Christian Jews and the Jews. Not long after the fall of the temple in 70 C.E., Christians were excluded from Jewish life. This expulsion, as one can imagine, "caused painful wounds and left scars on the community's tradition."[35] (Thus some commentators, as was suggested earlier, think the command "love your enemy" may have meant love for those responsible for excluding Christians from the Jewish community.) As Christians were banned from Jewish life they also "lost the protection that had been granted to Judaism as a tolerated religion in the Roman Empire. With the loss of this legal protection Christianity became vulnerable to persecution."[36] Christianity at that time was under considerable pressure. Individual communities were forced to foster unity and integrity of faith in face of an increasingly hostile world. Indeed as the author of the First Letter of John writes, the world is an evil, threatening place. "Do not be astonished, brothers and sisters, that the world hates you" (1 John 3:13). Richard Hays comments, "Love for the brothers and sisters within the community of faith, under these siege conditions, becomes not only an act of communal self-preservation but also of prophetic resistance: in a world governed by hate, pride in riches, and the power of the Evil One, the love of the believing community for one another stands as a sign of the light that shines in the darkness and has not been extinguished."[37]

Paul, writing before John, was not as concerned with the tension between Christianity and the world. He was, however, concerned with the health of particular Christian communities. Paul, for example, often comments on the love he sees witnessed in these communities. He greets the Thessalonians as follows: "Timothy has just now come to us from you, and has brought us the good news of your faith and love" (1 Thess. 3:6, see also Col. 1:3–4). Paul is never satisfied. Thus he continually encourages Christians to love more (see 1 Thess. 3:12). "And this is my prayer, that your love may overflow" (Phil. 1:9). Thus, in striking language, he says Christians ought to "put on the breastplate of faith and love" (1 Thess. 5:8). After listing various virtues needed for community life, he says, "Above all, clothe yourselves with love, which binds everything together in perfect harmony" (Col. 3:14). Other Pauline letters continue this concern. The author of the Letter to the Ephesians, for example, tells his audience to "speak the truth in love" (Eph. 4:16). The Letter to the Hebrews states, "And let us consider how to provoke one another to love and good deeds" (Heb. 10:24).

The life of the Christian community depended on the character of the relationships between its members. The New Testament indicates, however, that there were tensions in some communities (see, for example, 1 Cor. 1:10–17). In his Letter to the Romans Paul describes a community as a body with different members. He then exhorts the Roman community, "Let love be genuine; hate what is evil, hold fast to what is good; love one another with mutual affection; outdo one another in showing honor" (Rom. 12:9–10). "Walking in love" includes, for Paul, not causing scandal to those weaker in faith (Rom. 14:13–16).

In the Corinthian community there seems to have been particular tension and division among members. In his most famous statement on love, Paul both defends a diversity of members and chastises certain members of the community. "Love is patient; love is kind; love is never envious or boastful or arrogant or rude. It does not insist on its own way; it is not irritable or resentful; it does not rejoice in wrongdoing, but rejoices in the truth. It bears all things, believes all things, hopes all things, endures all things" (1 Cor. 13:4–7). Note that this description of love is really a personification of love. Love takes on characteristics of people. "The 15 verbs all involve another person and were chosen in order to highlight virtues neglected by the Corinthians. The strong were not 'patient and kind.' The sexual ascetics tended to 'insist on their own way.' The community 'rejoiced at wrong.'"[38]

Biblical scholar Raymond Brown describes love as the driving force in Paul's life and work. In Christ, "Paul, who already knew the love shown by the God of his Israelite ancestors, discovered a love that went beyond his previous imagination."[39] Paul writes, "For the love of Christ urges us on, because we are convinced that one has died for all; therefore all have died. And he died for all so that those who live might live no longer for themselves, but for him who died and was raised for them" (2 Cor. 5:14–15). Paul calls Christians to imitate God's love, *agape*, in service and even in suffering. "God in Christ has forgiven you. Therefore be imitators of God, as beloved children, and live in love, as Christ loved us and gave himself up for us, a fragrant offering and sacrifice to God" (Eph. 5:1–3). Thus for Paul, "If the love of God was manifested in the self-giving of Christ, how could the love of Christ be shown to others except in the same way?"[40] Joseph Fitzmeyer describes Paul's understanding of *agape* as "an openness, an outgoing concern and respect of one person for another/others in concrete acts that result in the diminution of the lover's 'self.'"[41] Brendan Byrne writes that Paul believes that love "flows from a free disposition to unseat the concern for self as the driving force of life and replace it with a practical concern for others."[42]

Paul's most famous thoughts on love are found in his First Letter to the Corinthians:

> If I speak in the tongues of mortals and of angels, but do not have love, I am a noisy gong or a clanging cymbal. And if I have prophetic powers, and understand all mysteries and all knowledge, and if I have all faith, so as to remove mountains, but do not have love, I am nothing. If I give away all my possessions, and if I hand over my body so that I may boast, but do not have love, I gain nothing. Love is patient; love is kind; love is not envious or boastful or arrogant or rude. It does not insist on its own way; it is not irritable or resentful; it does not rejoice in wrongdoing, but rejoices in the truth. It bears all things, believes all things, hopes all things, endures all things. Love never ends. But as for prophecies, they will come to an end; as for tongues, they will cease; as for knowledge, it will come to an end. . . . And now faith, hope, and love abide, these three; and the greatest of these is love. (1 Cor. 13:1–8, 13)

In several of his letters to local churches, Paul extends the notion of love from life in community into the daily life of the Christian families. He borrows and then transforms the general cultural expectations of his Greco-Roman world about the roles of men and women. The culture in which Paul lived, as does any culture, had expectations about the ordering of authority in family life. This was a male-dominated society where women were not citizens and fathers were to rule their families. Paul repeated these standards, that have come to be known as the "Household Codes," but not without some transformation. Paul's presentation of the Household Codes was progressive for his time. That was, however, almost 2,000 years ago. By our contemporary standards Paul's words are harder to classify. At times they defend the equality of men and women and advocate mutual subordination in marriage, and at other times they promote only the subordination of women.

A discussion of the Household Codes begins with Paul's concern to establish a foundational equality between the members of the Christian communities. In his Letter to the Galatians, for example, he writes, "As many of you as were baptized into Christ have clothed yourselves with Christ. There is no longer Jew or Greek, there is no longer slave or free, there is no longer male and female; for all of you are one in Christ Jesus" (Gal. 3:27–27). Paul repeats the theme of unity in Christ in Colossians (Col. 3:11). In his Letter to the Philippians he counsels love, unity, and mutual service in the community. "Do nothing from selfish ambition or conceit, but in humility regard others as better than yourselves. Let each of you look not to your own interests, but to the interests of others. Let the same mind be in you that was in Christ Jesus, who, though he was in the form of God, did not regard equality with God as something to be exploited, but emptied himself, taking the form of a slave, being born in human likeness. And being found in human form, he humbled himself and became obedient to the point of death—even death on a cross" (Phil. 2:3–8). In First Corinthians Paul likewise reminds community members that although they have different gifts, they are all one (1 Cor. 12).

As Paul considers household relationships, he continues his concern for equality and mutual subordination. Thus in a discussion of marriage in First Corinthians, he writes, "The husband should give to his wife her conjugal rights, and likewise the wife to her husband. For the wife does not have authority over her body, but the husband does; likewise the husband does not have authority over his own body, but the wife does" (1 Cor. 7:3–4). The demand for mutuality between Christian partners in marriage as preached by Paul stood in contrast to the rule of male authority that was part of his culture.[43] The authors of a recent study on marriage in the Christian tradition are correct when they write,

"When placed within its full historical context, early Christianity appears as a progressive influence on the family: in contrast to the surrounding Greco-Roman world, it inspired heightened degrees of female equality, a chastened patriarchy, higher levels of male responsibility and servanthood, less of a double standard in sexual ethics and deeper respect for children. But all of this progress was accomplished with ambivalence, hesitation, compromise and some defensiveness."[44]

In his most detailed commentary on the household, Paul (or one of Paul's disciples writing in his name[45]) affirms mutual subordination, but at the same time accepts some of his culture's dominant social expectations.

> Be subject to one another out of reverence for Christ. Wives, be subject to your husbands as you are to the Lord. For the husband is the head of the wife just as Christ is the head of the church, the body of which he is the Savior. Just as the church is subject to Christ, so also wives ought to be, in everything, to their husbands. Husbands, love your wives, just as Christ loved the church and gave himself up for her, in order to make her holy by cleansing her with the washing of water by the word, so as to present the church to himself in splendor, without a spot or wrinkle or anything of the kind—yes, so that she may be holy and without blemish. In the same way, husbands should love their wives as they do their own bodies. He who loves his wife loves himself. For no one ever hates his own body, but he nourishes and tenderly cares for it, just as Christ does for the church, because we are members of his body. "For this reason a man will leave his father and mother and be joined to his wife, and the two will become one flesh." This is a great mystery, and I am applying it to Christ and the church. Each of you, however, should love his wife as himself and a wife should respect her husband." (Eph. 5:21–33)

In less nuanced words in the Letter of the Colossians, Paul repeats the husband's obligation to love his wife, "Wives, be subject to your husbands, as is fitting in the Lord. Husbands, love your wives and never treat them harshly" (Col. 3:18).

Love for God

> For those who do not love a brother or a sister whom they have seen, cannot love God who they have not seen.
>
> —1 John

There are several occasions in the New Testament where we read direct references to loving God or loving Jesus. Paul speaks of loving God five times.[46] In Second Thessalonians, for example, he writes "May the Lord direct your hearts to the love of God and to the steadfastness of Christ" (3:5). In First Corinthians he states, "anyone who loves God is known by him" (8:3); and "What no eye has seen, nor ear heard, nor the human heart conceived, what God has prepared for those who love him" (2:9). Paul ends this letter with, "Let anyone be accursed who has not love for the Lord. Our Lord, come! The grace of the Lord Jesus be with you. My love be with all of you in Christ Jesus" (16:22–24). Finally in his Letter to the Romans Paul writes, "We know that all things work together for good, for those who love God, who are called according to his purpose" (8:28). There is a direct link between loving Jesus and/or God and loving one's neighbor in the New Testament. As Victor Furnish writes, "Not only in the Great Commandment, but wherever New Testament writers stress the centrality of the love command, one's love for the neighbor is vitally related to his relationship to God."[47] Johnston repeats this theme, "All through the New Testament it will be seen that the love of God may virtually be equated with love for the neighbor."[48] In the New Testament itself, this is best stated in the First Letter of John, where on three occasions the author links loving God and loving neighbor: "How does God's love abide in anyone who has the world's goods and sees a brother or sister in need and yet refuses help?" (1 John 3:17); "No one has ever seen God; if we love one another, God lives in us, and his love is perfected in us" (1 John 4:12); "Those who say, 'I love God,' and hate their brothers and sisters are liars; for those who do not love a brother or a sister whom they have seen, cannot love God whom they have not seen" (1 John 4:20). The New Testament identifies loving God with loving, through direct service, the neighbor. As the author of First John writes, "Little children, let us love, not in word or speech, but in truth and action" (1 John 3:18).

An important New Testament story about loving Jesus is found in the last chapter of John's Gospel. The risen Jesus appears to his disciples by the Sea of Tiberias and equates loving him with direct service to others.

> When they had finished breakfast, Jesus said to Simon Peter, "Simon son of John, do you love me more than these?" He said to him, "Yes Lord; you know that I love you." Jesus said to him, "Feed my lambs." A second time he said to him, "Simon son of John, do you love me?" He said to him, "Yes, Lord; you know that I love you." Jesus said to him, "Tend my sheep." He said to him the third time, "Simon son of John, do you love me?" Peter felt hurt because he said to him the third time, "Do you love me?" And he said to him, "Lord, you know everything; you know that I love you." Jesus said to him, "Feed my sheep." (John 21:15–17)

A second story from the Gospel of Matthew is relevant here. At the very end of Jesus' pubic ministry we hear him speak of the end of time.

"When the Son of Man comes in his glory, and all the angels with him, then he will sit on the throne of his glory. All the nations will be gathered before him, and he will separate people one from another as a shepherd separates the sheep from the goats, and he will put the sheep at his right hand and the goats at the left. Then the king will say to those at his right hand, 'Come, you that are blessed by the Father, inherit the kingdom prepared for you from the foundation of the world; for I was hungry and you gave me food, I was thirsty and you gave me something to drink, I was a stranger and you welcomed me, I was naked and you gave me clothing, I was sick and you took care of me, I was in prison and you visited me.' Then the righteous will answer him, 'Lord, when was it that we saw you hungry and gave you food, or thirsty and gave you something to drink? And when was it that we saw you a stranger and welcomed you, or naked and gave you clothing? And when was it that we saw you sick or in prison and visited you?' And the king will answer them, 'Truly I tell you, just as you did it to one of the least of these who are members of my family, you did it to me.' Then he will say to those at his left hand, 'You that are accursed, depart from me into the eternal fire prepared for the devil and his angels; for I was hungry and you gave me no food, I was thirsty and you gave me nothing to drink, I was a stranger and you did not welcome me, naked and you did not give me clothing, sick and in prison and you did not visit me.' Then they also will answer, 'Lord, when was it that we saw you hungry or thirsty or a stranger or naked or sick or in prison, and did not take care of you?' Then he will answer them, 'Truly I tell you, just as you did not do it to one of the least of these, you did not do it to me.' And these will go away into eternal punishment, but the righteous into eternal life." (Matt. 25:31–46)

The Summation of *Agape*?

Whoever does not love does not know God, for God is love.

—1 John

The presentation of love in The First Letter of John has been cited as the summary of love in the New Testament, the summation of *agape*. Although missing the direct imperative to love enemies, the text does seem to include all the aspects of love discussed in this chapter. The text includes the primary affirmation that God is love. It includes loving God and loving neighbor. It suggests, moreover, that we experience and know God's love in daily life. John gives us reasons, of both the heart and the head, to support the notion that we experience God's love. The text includes the language of moral imperative. Christians must love. The imperative is a command yet it is also presented as the only appropriate response to love already given. For John, this love is of the heart and expressed in action. Indeed, as Gustafson suggests, there is a behavioral test here.[49] If you say you love God but you hate a brother or a sister, you are a liar! Here are some of the most important examples:

From 1 John
Whoever says, "I have come to know him," but does not obey his commandments, is a liar, and in such a person the truth does not exist; but whoever obeys his word, truly in this person the love of God has reached perfection. By this we may be sure that we are in him: whoever says, "I abide in him," ought to walk just as he walked.

Beloved, I am writing you no new commandment, but an old commandment that you have had from the beginning; the old commandment is the word that you have heard. Yet I am writing you a new commandment that is true in him and in you, because the darkness is passing away and the true light is already shining. Whoever says, "I am in the light," while hating a brother or sister, is still in the darkness. Whoever loves a brother or sister lives in the light, and in such a person there is no cause for stumbling. But whoever hates another believer is in the darkness, walks in the darkness, and does not know the way to go, because the darkness has brought on blindness. . . .

Do not love the world or the things in the world. The love of the Father is not in those who love the world; for all that is in the world—the desire of the flesh, the desire of the eyes, the pride in riches—comes not from the Father but from the world. . . .

See what love the Father has given us, that we should be called children of God; and that is what we are. The reason the world does not know us is that it did not know him. Beloved, we are God's children now; what we will be has not yet been revealed. What we do know is this: when he is revealed, we will be like him, for we will see him as he is. And all who have this hope in him purify themselves, just as he is pure. . . .

The children of God and the children of the devil are revealed in this way: all who do not do what is right are not from God, nor are those who do not love their brothers and sisters.

For this is the message you have heard from the beginning, that we should love one another. We must not be like Cain who was from the evil one and murdered his brother. And why did he murder him? Because his own deeds were evil and his brother's righteous. Do not be astonished, brothers and sisters, that the world hates you. We know that we have passed from death to life because we love one another. Whoever does not love abides in death. All who hate a brother or sister are murderers, and you know that murderers do not have eternal life abiding in them. We know love by this, that he laid down his life for us—and we ought to lay down our lives for one another. How does God's love abide in anyone who has the world's goods and sees a brother or sister in need and yet refuses help?

Little children, let us love, not in word or speech, but in truth and action. And by this we will know that we are from the truth and will reassure our hearts before him whenever our hearts condemn us; for God is greater than our hearts, and he knows everything. Beloved, if our hearts do not condemn us we have boldness before God; and we receive from him whatever we ask, because we obey his commandments and do what pleases him.

And this is his commandment, that we should believe in the name of his Son Jesus Christ and love one another, just as he has commanded us. All who obey his commandments abide in him, and he abides in them. And by this we know that he abides in us, by the Spirit that he has given us. . . .

Beloved, let us love one another, because love is from God; everyone who loves is born of God and knows God. Whoever does not love does not know God, for God is love. God's love was revealed among us in this way: God sent his only Son into the world so that we might live through him. In this is love, not that we loved God but that he loved us and sent his Son to be the atoning sacrifice for our sins. Beloved, since God loved us so much, we also ought to love one another. No one has ever seen God; if we love one another, God lives in us, and his love is perfected in us.

By this we know that we abide in him and he in us, because he has given us of his Spirit. And we have seen and do testify that the Father has sent his Son as the Savior of the world. God abides in those who confess that Jesus is the Son of God, and they abide in God. So we have known and believe the love that God has for us.

God is love, and those who abide in love abide in God, and God abides in them. Love has been perfected among us in this: that we may have boldness on the day of judgment, because as he is, so are we in this world. There is no fear in love, but perfect love casts out fear; for fear has to do with punishment, and whoever fears has not reached perfection in love. We love because he first loved us. Those who say, "I love God," and hate their brothers or sisters, are liars; for those who do not love a brother or sister whom they have seen, cannot love God whom they have not seen. The commandment we have from him is this: those who love God must love their brothers and sisters also.

Everyone who believes that Jesus is the Christ has been born of God, and everyone who loves the parent loves the child. By this we know that we love the children of God, when we love God and obey his commandments. For the love of God is this, that we obey his commandments. (2:4–11, 15–16; 3:1–3, 10–24; 4:7–5:3)

Augustine: Love God and Love All Things in God

Conversions

For when we ask how good a man is, we do not ask what he believes or
what he hopes for, but what he loves.

—Augustine, *Enchiridian*

St. Augustine, a bishop in the late fourth century and early fifth century, was the dominant voice for Christianity during his lifetime. He lived at a time in which Christianity experienced both tremendous growth and dramatic challenges. Augustine's influence, however, goes far beyond his times. Theologian John Mahoney notes that Augustine's thinking on such issues as suicide, lying, abortion, sexual morality, just war, the virtues, and sin remain even today highly influential.[1] Indeed, as John Noonan comments, "You cannot go anywhere in theology without finding that he was there first."[2] Augustine's written legacy illustrates his influence. He is the author of over 100 books, over 200 published letters, and over 500 published sermons.

Augustine plays a particularly important role in this study. It is not an exaggeration to say that his "insistence on the supreme importance of love of God in the Christian life"[3] has been very influential on the Christian tradition. As Daniel Day Williams remarks, "St. Augustine formulated the conception of love at a critical time in the development of early Christianity, and his vision in some way informs all subsequent Christian thought in the West."[4]

Love is a dominant, perhaps the dominant, feature in Augustine's understanding of the moral life. However, it is not all that easy to discuss his thinking. Augustine scholar John Rettig writes, "Love is a prominent and frequent topic, an essential element in his understanding of the Christian life, but nowhere dealt with by itself and separately from other elements and aspects of his theology."[5]

Augustine was a brilliant and creative thinker. He also was involved deeply in the dramatic religious issues of his day. Some of his writings are systematic, some are not. Peter Brown writes that Augustine's writings are "littered with lines of thought that are not worked through to their conclusion."[6] At times, his thoughts on love appear this way. Indeed, this chapter includes some of Augustine's short pithy statements on love. All of this is to say that commentary on Augustine's thought is faced with the challenge of trying to describe an idea that is scattered throughout many sources. At the outset it can be said that Augustine's understanding of love is simple: we are to love God and all things in God.

Augustine's life was as complex as it is interesting. He was born in North Africa in 354 in what is now Algeria. Augustine's mother was a devoted Christian while his father remained aloof from religion until late in life. As a young adult Augustine had a keen interest in religion and philosophy, as well as, he tells us, the sensual pleasures of the world. When he was around twenty years old, he became a member of a religious group known as the Manichees. The basic tenet of Manicheism was its dualistic view of reality. Manicheism held that "from the beginning of time there have existed two fundamental realities: a principal power of good (the kingdom of Light) and a power of evil (the kingdom of Darkness). The kingdom of Light consisted of spirit, and the kingdom of Darkness consisted of matter and the dark elements, such as smoke. These two powers, according to the Manichees, were coeternal and coequal."[7] The physical, material world was associated with evil while spiritual things were good.

After some nine years, Augustine found this religion intellectually unsatisfying. Upon rejecting the dualism of Manicheism, he toyed with astrology and finally, before converting to Christianity, found that the philosophy of Plato, as taught by Plotinus and Porphyry, offered him a more compelling view of reality. This school of philosophy later became known as "neoplatonism." One commentator explains that neoplatonism was the "intellectual bridge" that allowed Augustine to move from pagan life to Christian life.[8] Peter Brown writes that neoplatonism was "grafted almost imperceptibly into his writings as the ever present basis of his thought."[9] David Hunter suggests that Augustine found neoplatonism to be "profoundly compatible" with Christianity.[10] For the purposes of this study we need not press the issue of Augustine's use of neoplatonic philosophy on the whole of his thought. Certainly there were elements he rejected.[11] He was, in the end, a Christian not a neoplatonist. Suffice it to say that Augustine used this philosophy in the service of Christianity but that some Christian beliefs were irreconcilable with neoplatonism. The neoplatonists of this time saw themselves as orthodox followers of Plato but, interestingly enough, anti-Christian.[12]

A striking example of the influence of Plato on Augustine, and indeed on later Christian understanding of love, is Augustine's critical appropriation of the ancient concept of eros. Plato's *Symposium* is perhaps the most influential text on the philosophy of love in European literature.[13] An important component of this philosophy can be seen in the "famous poetic image of the ladder of love, with its powerful suggestion that all early loves are, rightly understood, continuous with and, finally, but a vehicle for the love of Being itself and of its highest principles."[14] This notion that in reality there is a hierarchy, or ladder, of being and good serves as the backbone for Augustine's theology of love. As Henry Chadwick notes, "Throughout his writing Augustine holds to a doctrine of gradations of goodness. The good of the body is inferior to that of the soul; the will, in itself midway, may turn to higher or lower things, and may err by preferring inferior good to superior."[15]

The excerpt below includes the ladder of love passage, but begins by picking up Plato's narrative of Socrates' discussion of the nature of *eros*. After addressing several friends on the issue, Socrates explains what he learned about *eros* from Diotima. There are a few things to note in this brief selection. First, *eros* not only concerns thinking about the good and the beautiful, but also "requires the active pursuit of it so as to possess it."[16] Second, *eros* recognizes a scale of beauty and of good. We read about the movement from bodies, to forms, to thoughts, to institutions and law, to science, and to absolute or ideal beauty. "The philosopher's movement up the ladder of love is an ascent toward the things that are always, as opposed to those that come into being and pass away."[17] Stated in other words, *eros* moves us from physical things, that is, things that change, to permanent things. Diotima teaches, or in Plato's words, seeks to initiate Socrates in the mysteries of *eros*. She narrates the stages of development on the scale of things beautiful:

> He who is to move correctly in this matter must begin while young to go to beautiful bodies. And first of all . . . he must love one body. . . . Then he must realize that the beauty that is in any body whatsoever is related to that in another body. . . . And with this realization he must be the lover of all beautiful bodies and in contempt slacken this [erotic] intensity for only one body. . . . After this he must believe that the beauty in souls is more honorable than that in the body . . . so that he may come to believe that the beauty of the body is something trivial. After these pursuits he must lead [the beloved] on to the science, so that he [himself, the lover] may see the beauty of science and in looking at the beautiful, which is now so vast, no

longer be content with the beauty of one . . . human being, or of one practice . . . but, with a permanent turn to the vast open sea of the beautiful,
there strengthened and increased, he may discern a certain single philosophical science, which has as its object the following sort of beauty.[18]

As Diotima describes this beauty, note the characteristics she ascribes to it; it is
everlasting and absolute.

For whose sake alone all the prior labors were undertaken—something
that is, first of all, always being and neither coming to be nor perishing,
nor increasing nor passing away; and secondly, not beautiful in one respect
and ugly in another, nor at one time so, and at another time not . . .
but as it is alone by itself and with itself, always being of a single form.[19]

She continues:

Beginning from these beautiful things here, always to proceed on up
for the sake of that beauty, using these beautiful things here as steps:
from one to two, and from two to all beautiful bodies; and from beautiful bodies to beautiful pursuits; and from pursuits to beautiful lessons,
and from lessons to end at that lesson, which is the lesson of nothing
else than the beautiful itself; and at last to know what is beauty itself.[20]

In the experience of this true beauty one sees true virtue and becomes "dear to
god."[21] Socrates concludes his speech as follows: "And in this state of conviction,
I try to persuade others that for this possession one could not easily get a better
co-worker with human nature than Eros. Accordingly, I assert that every real
man must honor Eros, as I myself honor erotics and train myself."[22]

Neoplatonism provides then a framework that helps Augustine understand
the God of the Bible. God is the greatest good, that Being on which the good
of all other things rest. Only God is immutable and thus worthy of our true love.
For Augustine, "we will only be made perfectly happy when we achieve permanent possession of God, the infinite being, the being that encompasses all good
in every possible world."[23] We can see evidence of Augustine's indebtedness to
neoplatonism in the following selection from his book *The Confessions*. He writes:

Because, I think, in your Gift we find rest, and there we enjoy you, our true
place is where we find rest. We are borne toward it by love, and it is your
good Spirit who lifts up our sunken nature from the gates of death. In

goodness of will is our peace. A body gravitates to its proper place by its own weight. This weight does not necessarily drag it downward, but pulls it to the place proper to it: thus fire tends upward, a stone downward. Drawn by their weight, things seek their rightful places. If oil is poured into water, it will rise to the surface, but if water is poured onto oil it will sink below the oil: drawn by their weight, things seek their rightful places. They are not at rest as long as they are disordered, but once brought to order they find their rest.[24]

As we read Augustine, we come to see how important the theme of movement and rest of the soul is for him. Notice the quotations from the book of Psalms in the excerpts above and below. Augustine uses the Psalms to express and explain his ideas. Indeed he finds links with the ideas of the Psalms and neoplatonic theology.[25] He continues describing his love.

Now, my weight is my love, and wherever I am carried, it is this weight that carries me. Your Gift sets us afire and we are borne upward; we catch his flame and up we go. In out hearts we climb those upward paths, singing the songs of ascent. By your fire, your beneficent fire, are we enflamed, because we are making out way up to the peace of Jerusalem. For I rejoiced when I was told, "We are going to the Lord's house." There shall a good will find us a place, that we may have no other desire but to abide there for ever.[26]

In 386 Augustine converted to Christianity, and with it, to a celibate lifestyle. Five years later he was ordained and within five more years he became a bishop, one of 700 in Africa at the time. For the next thirty years of his life, until his death in 428, Augustine was deeply involved in many religious controversies and debates.[27]

When Augustine looked to the Bible, as he so often did for his theological reflections, he did not come across the words *hesed* or *agape*. Augustine did not read the Hebrew version of the Old Testament nor did he read the Greek New Testament. The Bible he used was a second century Old Latin translation. It was translated from the Greek New Testament and from the Greek translation of the Old Testament (the Septuagint).[28] Again, in our review of love in the Christian tradition, we have been encountering new words. The history of translation repeats itself here. As did the translators of the Septuagint, the Latin translators of the Greek Bible had several possible words for love to choose from. Like the earlier Greek choice of *agape*, the Latin *caritas* was chosen more for what it did not stand for than for what it did. The word was chosen to "avoid the unwanted connotations" of particular attachments to others."[29]

This is a very significant development in the Christian understanding of love. With the Latin translation of the Bible, *caritas* becomes the word for Christian love from the Patristic Ages on through the Middle Ages and into the Reformation. As one commentator notes, "Early Christian writers tended to avoid *amor* and *amare*, because of their association with passionate and physical love."[30] The translation problems do not end here, for the usual English translation of *caritas* is "charity." Certainly there are liturgical prayers and hymns that still use the term charity as a type of love. It is not unusual even today, for example, to hear "Faith, Hope and Charity." The meaning of charity in popular language today, however, is much different than its meaning in Patristic and Medieval use. When we hear charity we usually think of giving to those in need, which is not what the early Christian writers meant by *caritas*. To make matters a bit more interesting, Augustine does not strictly follow the preference of the early, and indeed later, Christian writers. He uses the Latin words *amor* and *dilectio*, as well as *caritas* when he speaks of love. Some English translations of Augustine translate *caritas* as "charity," while others, wary of the limited understanding of "charity" in contemporary conversation, prefer simply to use the word love for *caritas*.[31] Augustine's terminology, as Etienne Gilson notes, is "flexible" on this point.[32]

Augustine acknowledges this himself in *The City of God*. In the following excerpt, note his reliance on the Latin translation of the Bible as authoritative.

> Anyone who resolves to love God and to love his neighbor as himself, not in a purely human way but according to the will of God, may certainly, because of this love, be called a man of good will. Holy Scripture usually expresses this attitude by the word "caritas," but it also uses the word "amor."
>
> The reason why it seems to me that this point should be mentioned is that there are some who think that dilectio or caritas is one thing and amor another. They maintain that dilectio is understood in a good sense and amor in a bad sense. . . . What is certain is that their writings make clear that they use the word amor to express esteem for the love of good things and even of God Himself. My point has been to prove that the Scriptures of our religion, whose authority I prefer to all other writings, make no distinction between, amor, dilectio, and caritas.[33]

For purposes of interpretation, it must be noted that the work of most philosophers and theologians can be read and understood apart from their personal lives.

This is not true with Augustine. His theology is very closely linked to his life and to the decisions he made in his life.

Misdirected Love

> Human friendship is also a nest of love and gentleness because of the unity it brings about between many souls. . . . Friendship can be a dangerous enemy, a seduction of the mind lying beyond the reach of investigation.
> —Augustine, *The Confessions*

Throughout his writings, Augustine portrays himself as a lover. As he does this he is not simply making an autobiographical point. Augustine is making an anthropological claim. That is, while *The Confessions* is about his life, it is also, for Augustine, about humankind. He is saying that we all are lovers. Loving is an essential part of our nature as persons. Note his broad use of the term love. That is, he uses the term to refer not only to human relationships, but also to human desires. When Augustine says we are lovers, he is saying that we are naturally attracted to things and to people. John Burnaby describes Augustine's notion of desiring as the dominant element in his understanding of love. For Augustine, all of us have this desiring, this "unsatisfied longing of the homesick heart."[34] The lesson Augustine is trying to teach his readers, through reflection on his own experience, is that we must think about what we love and how we love the things we love. In his view, it is better to love some things than others. Augustine suggests that our desires, our loves, can only be satisfied in God. The often quoted passage from the first paragraph of *The Confessions* illustrates his thinking. Speaking to God, he prays, "You stir man to take pleasure in praising you, because you have made us for yourself, and our heart is restless until it rests in you."[35]

We are lovers. We have loves. We can have good loves and bad loves. The judgment of which depends on the evaluation of whom or what the person loves and how the person loves the other or the thing. Loving, moreover, is at the seat of other emotions. That is to say, from loving comes other emotions such as joy, fear, and grief. The following short excerpt suggests the complexities of Augustine's thinking on love. In his *The City of God* he writes: "A righteous will, then, is a good love; and a perverted will is an evil love. Therefore, love striving to possess what it loves is joy; love fleeing what it is adverse to is fear; and love undergoing such adversity when it occurs is grief. Accordingly, these feelings are bad if the love is bad, and good if it is good."[36] Love is essentially a motion of the soul or the heart.

There is, in fact, an important passage in *Eighty-Three Different Questions* that addresses this very question. But first, Augustine's reasons for writing this book are interesting enough in their own right to warrant some attention here. After his conversion to Christianity and before he became bishop, Augustine formed two small communities. The first one was in Cassiciacum, Italy, at the foothills of the Alps. Here he was the master with a handful of young students, including his son. The community was dedicated to study and philosophy. Several years later, after the death of his son and after his return to Africa, Augustine formed a community of a different sort. This community resembled a monastery. Augustine became the spiritual father to this group of men. Both situations suggest that Augustine valued interpersonal relationships. During the years he spent in these communities, students often asked him questions about various aspects of the faith. Augustine writes, "When I became bishop, I ordered that the questions be gathered together and made up into a single book, and that numbers be added so that anyone could easily find what he wanted to read."[37] Thus we have *Eighty-Three Different Questions*, a collection of Augustine's answers to his students' questions.

The following excerpts are from Question 35, "What Ought to Be Loved?" Here Augustine wonders if love itself ought to be loved. He answers, "But if love is loved for the sake of the other things which ought to be loved, it is a mistake to say that it ought to be loved. For to love is nothing other than to desire something for its own sake. Accordingly love ought not be sought for itself, should it, when unmistakable misery follows on the loss of what is loved?"[38] He then describes what we might call the psychology of love. "Then again, since love is a kind of motion, and since there is no motion except it be toward something, when we seek what ought to be loved we are looking for something to which this motion ought to direct us."[39] We then do love love, yet we ought not make that judgment until the object of the love, that toward which the love is moving, is described. "For this reason, if love ought to be loved, surely not every kind of love ought to be. For there is a base love by means of which the soul chases after things inferior to itself, and this love is more properly called *covetousness*, that is to say 'the root of all evils.'"[40]

Love then is a desire, a motion of the soul. True love is the desire for something for its own sake. Augustine speaks of possessing and enjoying such love, and the greatest of these is loving that which is eternal. In his discussion of love as desire, Augustine brings a philosophical or psychological nuance to the Christian tradition on love. A stirring of our heart is a love, but as we shall see more developed in later sections of this chapter, true love is not just desire. True love includes an act of the will, a choice, to love goods in their appropriate manner.

The following selections are from *The Confessions*. Written while he was a bishop, Augustine recounts his conversion to Christianity. The text is written in a style unusual for us, but not for his time. It is part memoir and part prayer. Readers hear him talking to them while at the same time he is talking to God. In the excerpt that follows, Augustine describes some of his youthful adventures. He is writing as an adult about things he did and attitudes he had while a teenager. Augustine was something of an irresponsible youth. Notice the many ways he uses the term "love" here.

> Now I want to call to mind the foul deeds I committed, those sins of the flesh that corrupted my soul, not in order to love them, but to love you, my God. Out of love for loving you I do this, recalling my most wicked ways and thinking over the past with bitterness so that you may grow ever sweeter to me; for you are a sweetness that deceives not, a sweetness bliss-ful and serene. I will try now to give a coherent account of my disintegrated self, for when I turned away from you, the one God, and pursued a mul-titude of things, I went to pieces. There was a time in adolescence when I was afire to take my fill of hell. I boldly thrust out rank, luxuriant growth in various furtive love affairs; my beauty wasted away and I rotted in your sight, intent on pleasing myself and winning favor in the eyes of men.[41]

Augustine says that he was driven by lust confused as love.

> What was it that delighted me? Only loving and being loved. But there was no proper restraint, as in the union of mind with mind, where a bright boundary regulates friendship. From the mud of my fleshly desires and my erupting puberty belched out murky clouds that obscured and darkened my heart until I could not distinguish the calm light of love from the fog of lust. The two swirled about together and dragged me, young and weak as I was, over the cliffs of my desires, and engulfed me in a whirlpool of sins.[42]

In a very descriptive paragraph he tells of his father's "intoxication" and "perverse will directed to inferior things."

> Owing to the state of family finances in this sixteenth year of my life there was an interval of leisure for me, during which, being free from all schooling, I began to spend time in my parents' company. The thorn-bushes of my lust shot up higher than my head, and no hand was there to root them out. Least of all my father's; for when at the baths

one day he saw me with unquiet adolescence my only covering, and
noted my ripening sexuality, he began at once to look forward eagerly
to grandchildren, and gleefully announced his discovery to my mother.
His glee sprang from that intoxication which has blotted you, our creator, out of this world's memory and led it to love the creature instead,
as it drinks the unseen wine of its perverse inclination and is dragged
down to the depths. In my mother's soul, however, you had already
begun to build your temple and prepare for your holy indwelling.[43]

Augustine writes of his mother's concern and warning, which he ignored, and
his friends' challenges, which he listened to.

Whose, then, were the words spoken to me by my mother, your faithful
follower? Were they not your words, the song you were constantly singing
into my ears? None of it sank down to my heart, though, to induce me to
act on it. She urged me to keep clear of fornication, and especially not to
commit adultery with any man's wife. I remember in my inmost heart the
intense earnestness with which she cautioned me against this; but these
warnings seemed to me mere woman's talk, which I would have blushed to
heed. In truth they came from you, but I failed to realize that, and assumed
that you were silent and she alone was talking. By using her you were not
silent to me at all; and when I scorned her I was scorning you—I, her son,
the son of your handmaid, I your servant. But I was quite reckless; I rushed
on headlong in such blindness that when I heard other youths of my own
age bragging about their immoralities I was ashamed to be less depraved
than they.[44]

I was under no compulsion of need, unless a lack of moral sense can
count as need, and a loathing for justice, and a greedy, full-fed love of sin.
Yet I wanted to steal, and steal I did. I already had plenty of what I stole,
and of much better quality too, and I had no desire to enjoy it when I resolved to steal it. I simply wanted to enjoy the theft for its own sake, and
the sin. Close to our vineyard there was a pear tree laden with fruit. This
fruit was not enticing, either in appearance or in flavor. We nasty lads went
there to shake down the fruit and carry it off at dead of night, after pro-
longing our games out of doors until that late hour according to our abom-
inable custom. We took enormous quantities, not to feast on ourselves but
perhaps to throw to the pigs; we did eat a few, but that was not our motive: we derived pleasure from the deed simply because it was forbidden.[45]

By most anyone's standards, there are bigger sins than stealing pears from a tree. But it is not the act so much as the fact that he loved sinning and his own moral ruin.

> The beautiful form of material things attracts our eyes, so we are drawn to gold, silver and the like. We are powerfully influenced by the feel of things agreeable to the touch; and each of our other senses finds some quality that appeals to it individually in the variety of material objects. There is the same appeal in worldly rank, and the possibility it offers of commanding and dominating other people: this too holds its attraction, and often provides an opportunity for settling old scores. We may seek all these things, O Lord, but in seeking them we must not deviate from your law. The life we live here is open to temptation by reason of a certain measure and harmony between its own splendor and all these beautiful things of low degree. Again, the friendship which draws human beings together in a tender bond is sweet to us because out of many minds it forges a unity. Sin gains entrance through these and similar good things when we turn to them with immoderate desire, since they are the lowest kind of goods and we thereby turn away from the better and higher: from you yourself, O Lord our God, and your truth and your law. These lowest goods hold delights for us indeed, but no such delights as does my God, who made all things; for in him the just man finds delight, and for upright souls he himself is joy.[46]

Friends are a great source of joy for Augustine but he admits that without his friends he would not have stolen the fruit.

> What fruit did I ever reap from those things which I now blush to remember, and especially from that theft in which I found nothing to love save the theft itself, wretch that I was? It was nothing, and by the very act of committing it I became more wretched still. And yet, as I recall my state of mind at the time, I would not have done it alone; I most certainly would not have done it alone. It follows, then, that I also loved the camaraderie with my fellow-thieves. So it is not true to say that I loved nothing other than the theft? Ah, but it is true, because that gang-mentality too was a nothing. What was it in fact? Who can teach me, except the One who illumines my heart and distinguishes between its shadows? Why has this question come into my mind now, to be examined and discussed and considered? If the object of my love had been the pears I stole, and I simply wanted to enjoy them, I could have done it alone; similarly, if the act of

committing the sin had sufficed by itself to yield me the pleasure I sought, I would not have further inflamed my itching desire by the stimulation of conspiracy. But since my pleasure did not lie in the pears, it must have been in the crime as committed in the company of others who shared in the sin.

What kind of attitude was that? An extremely dishonorable one, certainly; alas for me, that I entertained it! Yet what exactly was it? Who understands his faults? The theft gave us a thrill, and we laughed to think we were outwitting people who had no idea what we were doing, and would angrily stop us if they knew. Why could I not have derived the same pleasure from doing it alone? Perhaps because it is not easy to enjoy a joke by oneself? Not easy, to be sure, but it does sometimes happen that people who are entirely alone, with no one else present, are overcome by laughter, if something very funny presents itself to their senses or their thoughts. Possibly . . . but I would not have done that deed alone; in no way would I have done it alone. In your presence I declare it, my God, this is my soul's vivid remembrance. On my own I would not have perpetrated that theft in which I felt no desire for what I stole, but only for the act of stealing; to do it alone would have aroused no desire whatever in me, nor would I have done it.[47]

Augustine writes that he "rushed headlong into love" but it was an empty, unsatisfying love.

So I arrived at Carthage, where the din of scandalous love-affairs raged cauldron-like around me. I was not yet in love, but I was enamored with the idea of love, and so deep within me was my need that I hated myself for the sluggishness of my desires. In love with loving, I was casting about for something to love; the security of a way of life free from pitfalls seemed abhorrent to me, because I was inwardly starved of that food which is yourself, O my God. Yet this inner famine created no pangs of hunger in me. I had no desire for the food that does not perish, not because I had my fill of it, but because the more empty I was, the more I turned from it in revulsion. My soul's health was consequently poor. It was covered with sores and flung itself out of doors, longing to soothe its misery by rubbing against sensible things; yet these were soulless, and so could not be truly loved. Loving and being loved were sweet to me, the more so if I could also enjoy a lover's body; so I polluted the stream of friendship with my filthy desires and clouded its purity with hellish lusts; yet all the while, befouled and disgraced though I was, my boundless vanity made me long to appear elegant and sophisticated. I blundered headlong into the love which I hoped would hold me captive, but in your goodness, O my God, my mercy, you sprinkled bitter gall over my sweet pursuits. I was loved, and I secretly entered into an enjoyable liaison, but I was also trammeling myself with fetters of distress.[48]

Friendship

There is no greater consolation than the unfeigned loyalty and mutual love of good men who are true friends.

—Augustine, *The City of God*

There is little doubt that Augustine valued friendship. Friendship was an important and very powerful element of his life. Peter Brown writes, "Augustine . . . will hardly ever spend a moment of his life without some friend, even some blood-relative, close by him. No thinker in the Early Church was so preoccupied with the nature of human relationships."[49] Augustine wrote, "In this world two things are essential: a healthy life and friendship."[50] The following quotation, taken from a letter to a friend, demonstrates his emotional ties. "My great and only joy is that I am unable to avoid delight when you are with me and I am unable to avoid sorrow when you are far away. My only consolation now comes from bravely accepting my sadness."[51] Brown comments further, "Augustine needed the constant response and reassurance of a circle of friends: both to know that he was loved, and to know that there was someone worth loving, encouraged him greatly to love in return."[52] Friendship is a consistent part of Augustine's life. "Seldom do we find him thinking alone." [53] He is always in dialogue with friends. Recall, however, the ambivalence of Augustine in *The Confessions*. Friendship, he writes, is "a nest of love and gentleness because of the unity it brings about between many souls." It can also be "a seduction of the mind" and "a dangerous enemy." How are we to make sense of this? In the following section, also from *The Confessions*, Augustine describes the appropriate love in friendship. The context is that he has to face the death of a good friend.

At this same period, when I first began to teach in the town where I was born, I had a friend who shared my interests and was exceedingly dear to me. He was the same age as myself and, like me, now in the flower of young manhood. As a boy he had grown up with me; we had gone to school together and played together. He was not then such a friend to me as he was to become later, though even at the later time of which I speak our union fell short of true friendship, because friendship is genuine only when you bind fast together people who cleave to you through the charity poured abroad in our hearts by the Holy Spirit who is given to us. I did love him very tenderly, though, and similarity of outlook lent warmth to our relationship; for I had lured him from the true faith, which he had held in a thoroughly immature way and without conviction, to the superstitious and baneful fables which my mother deplored in me. Already this man was intellectually astray along with me, and my soul could not bear to be without him. Ah, but you were pursuing close behind us, O God of vengeance who are the fount of all mercy and turn us back to yourself in wondrous ways. You took him from this life after barely a year's friendship, a friendship sweeter to me than any sweetness I had known in all my life.[54]

His friend, who was his "other self" and with whom he shared his soul was dead. Augustine's life was shattered.

But why am I talking thus? This is no time for asking questions, but for confessing to you. I was miserable, and miserable too is everyone whose mind is chained by friendship with mortal things, and is torn apart by their loss, and then becomes aware of the misery that it was in even before it lost them. This was my condition at the time; I wept very bitterly and found repose in the bitterness. Miserable as I was, I held even this miserable life dearer than my friend; for although I might wish to change it, I would have been even less willing to lose it than I was to lose him. I do not even know if I would have been willing to lose it for him, after the manner of Orestes and Pylades, who wanted to die for one another or, failing that, to die together, because for either to live without the other would have been worse than death—or so the story goes, though it may not be true. Some kind of emotion opposed to this had sprung up in me, so that although my weariness with living was intense, so too was my fear of dying. I believe that the more I loved him, the more I hated death, which had taken him from me; I hated it as a hideous enemy, and feared it, and pictured it as ready to devour all human beings, since it had been able to make away with him. Yes, this was my state of mind: I remember it.

Look upon my heart, O my God, look deep within it. See, O my hope, who cleanse me from the uncleanness of such affections, who draw my eyes to yourself and pull my feet free from the snare, see that this is indeed what I remember. I was amazed that other mortals went on living when he was dead whom I had loved as though he would never die, and still more amazed that I could go on living myself when he was dead—I, who had been like another self to him. It was well said that a friend is half one's own soul. I felt that my soul and his had been but one soul in two bodies, and I shrank from life with loathing because I could not bear to be only half alive; and perhaps I was so afraid of death because I did not want the whole of him to die, whom I had loved so dearly.

Woe to the madness which thinks to cherish human beings as though more than human! How foolish the human heart that anguishes without restraint over human ills, as I did then! Feverishly I thrashed about, sighed, wept and was troubled, and there was no repose for me, nor any counsel. Within me I was carrying a tattered, bleeding soul that did not want me to carry it, yet I could find no place to lay it down. Not in pleasant country-side did it find rest, nor in shows and songs, nor in sweet-scented gardens, nor in elaborate feasts, nor in the pleasures of couch or bed, nor even in books and incantations. All things loured at me, even daylight itself, and everything that was not what he was seemed to me offensive and hateful, except for mourning and tears, in which alone I found some slight relief. Whenever my soul was drawn away from this, it burdened me with a great load of misery. I should have lifted it up to you, Lord.[55]

After some time, Augustine's grief subsided and he began to put his loves in perspective. He notes that his mistake was that he loved his friend too much. Or better stated, he loved his friend with a love that should be reserved for God.

Time does not stand still, nor are the tolling seasons useless to us, for they work wonders in our minds. They came and went from day to day, and by their coming and going implanted in me other hopes and other memories. Little by little they set me up again and turned me toward things that had earlier delighted me, and before these my sorrow began to give ground. Yet its place was taken, not indeed by fresh sorrows, but by the seeds of fresh sorrows; for how had that sorrow been able so easily to pierce my inmost being, if not because I had poured out my soul into the sand by loving a man doomed to death as though he were never to die? What restored and re-created me above all was the consolation of other friends, in whose company I loved what I was loving as a substitute for you. This was a gross fable and a long-sustained lie, and as our minds itched to listen they were corrupted by its adulterous excitation, but the fable did not die for me when any of my friends died.[56]

This is not to say that we ought not have friends, but rather that we love friends in the appropriate and limited fashion.

> There were other joys to be found in their company which still more powerfully captivated my mind—the charms of talking and laughing together and kindly giving way to each other's wishes, reading elegantly written books together, sharing jokes and delighting to honor one another, disagreeing occasionally but without rancor, as a person might disagree with himself, and lending piquancy by that rare disagreement to our much more frequent accord. We would teach and learn from each other, sadly missing any who were absent and blithely welcoming them when they returned. Such signs of friendship sprang from the hearts of friends who loved and knew their love returned, signs to be read in smiles, words, glances and a thousand gracious gestures. So were sparks kindled and our minds were fused inseparably, out of many becoming one.
>
> This is what we esteem in our friends, and so highly do we esteem it that our conscience feels guilt if we fail to love someone who responds to us with love, or do not return the love of one who offers love to us, and this without seeking any bodily gratification from the other save signs of his goodwill. From this springs our grief if someone dies, from this come the darkness of sorrow and the heart drenched with tears because sweetness has turned to bitterness, so that as the dying lose their life, life becomes no better than death for those who live on. Blessed is he who loves you, and loves his friend in you and his enemy for your sake. He alone loses no one dear to him, to whom all are dear in the One who is never lost. And who is this but our God, the God who made heaven and earth and fills them, because it was by filling them that he made them? No one loses you unless he tries to get rid of you, and if he does try to do that, where can he go, whither does he flee, but from you in your tranquility to you in your anger? Does he not encounter your law everywhere, in his own punishment? Your law is truth, as you yourself are truth.[57]

Physical, created things are transient. They come and go and are thus no place to find rest.

> Turn us toward yourself, O God of Hosts, show us your face and we shall be saved; for wheresoever a human soul turns, it can but cling to what brings sorrow unless it turns to you, cling though it may to beautiful things outside you and outside itself. Yet were these beautiful things

not from you, none of them would be at all. They arise and sink; in their rising they begin to exist and grow toward their perfection, but once perfect they grow old and perish; or, if not all reach old age, yet certainly all perish. So then, even as they arise and stretch out toward existence, the more quickly they grow and strive to be, the more swiftly they are hastening toward extinction. This is the law of their nature. You have endowed them so richly because they belong to a society of things that do not all exist at once, but in their passing away and succession together form a whole, of which the several creatures are parts. So is it with our speaking as it proceeds by audible signs: it will not be a whole utterance unless one word dies away after making its syllables heard, and gives place to another.

Let my soul use these things to praise you,
    O God, creator of them all,
but let it not be glued fast to them by sensual love,
    for they are going whither they were always destined to go,
        toward extinction;
and they rend my soul with death-dealing desires,
    for it too longs to be, and loves to rest in what it loves.
But in them it finds no place to rest,
    because they do not stand firm;
they are transient,
    and who can follow them with the senses of the body?
Or who can seize them, even near at hand?
Tardy is carnal perception, because it is carnal;
    such is the law of its nature.
Sufficient it is for another purpose, for which it was made,
    but insufficient to catch the fleeting things
    that rush past from their appointed beginning to their
        appointed end.
In your Word, through whom they are created,
    they hear your command,
From here begin, and thus far you shall go.[58]

In *The City of God* Augustine offers another reflection on friendship. Because we are so emotionally involved with friends, he writes, we are vulnerable to being hurt when they are hurt or when they turn on us. The death of a friend is a particularly hard time for true friends. A quick note on the book *The City of God* before we read the excerpt: This thousand-plus-page manuscript was written over some thirteen years and finished twenty-six years after *The Confessions*. In the book Augustine addresses the challenges of pagan critics who argued that the dramatic growth of Christianity and the subsequent rejection of traditional religious practices caused the destruction of the Roman empire. Augustine argued that the "pagan religion was both morally and spiritually bankrupt. As for the fall of the empire, Augustine noted that it had largely been built on the lust of domination and that Christians had to look elsewhere for the 'city of God.'"[59] Note Augustine's powerful description of the joys and anxieties that are inherent in deep friendships.

> Another of the not uncommon miseries of our human life is to mistake, by a misunderstanding close to madness, enemies for friends and friends for enemies. This apart, even granted the ordinary miseries and mistakes, of which all human relationship is full, there is no greater consolation than the unfeigned loyalty and mutual love of good men who are true friends. Yet, the more friends we have, and the more scattered they are locally, the more widely stretched are our heartfelt fears, lest any of the mountainous miseries of life befall them. We become apprehensive not only about possible afflictions of famine, war, sickness, imprisonment, or such unimaginable sufferings as may be their lot in slavery. What is far harder to swallow is our fear that they may fail us in faithfulness, turn to hate us and work us harm. If and when our fear becomes a fact, and we find it out (and the more friends we have, the more source of such heartbreak), the fire of pain is whipped to such a blazing in our heart as none can guess who has not felt the smart. Indeed, we should rather hear that our friends are dead.[60]

Augustine describes the great pain one feels upon the death of a friend.

> Yet here is another source of sadness, for the death of those who can never leave us free from grief whose friendship during life was a solace and delight. There are some who say men should not grieve. Then, let them try, if they can, to ban all loving interchange of thought, cut off and outlaw all friendly feelings, callously break the bonds of all human fellowship, or claim that such human relationships must be emptied of all tenderness. And if this is utterly impossible, it is no less impossible for us not to taste as bitter the death of those whose life for us was such a source of sweetness. It is, in fact, because such grief, in a broken heart, is like a wound or open sore that men feel it a duty to offer us the balm of their condolences. And

if the heart is more easily and quickly healed the more virtuous a man is, that does not mean that there was no wound to heal.[61]

Yet, not every death of every friend strikes us so powerfully. When a friend dies a holy death, the Christian feels a certain joy amid the grief.

> There is no escape, then, from that misery of human life which is caused, in varying degrees, by the deaths of very close friends, especially if they have played some important role in public life. Yet it is easier to watch any of our loved ones die, in this sense, than to learn that they have lost heir faith, or have fallen into grievous sin, and thus are spiritually dead. It is because of the immensity of this misery filling the earth that the Scripture asks: "Is not the life of man upon earth a trial?" No wonder the Lord said: "Woe to the world because of scandals," and again: "Because iniquity hath abounded, the charity of many shall grow cold." . . . That is why we Christians can feel a real joy when our friends die a holy death. Their death, of course, afflicts our heart, but faith gives us the surer consolation, that they are now freed from those evils of this present life which threaten the best of men with either failure or defilement—and sometimes with both.[62]

Augustine never married, at least in the technical sense, and he had very little to say about love in marriage. Indeed in his book *The Good of Marriage* he has only a few words on the topic. He describes companionship as a good of marriage and writes that, "in a good marriage, although one of many years, even if the ardor of youth has cooled between man and woman, the order of charity still flourishes between husband and wife."[63] Before his conversion, however, he was matched with a girl for marriage. His prospective bride was only ten years old. Roman law said that he had to wait until she was twelve; that would make Augustine about thirty-two years old at the time. Before he was matched with the girl, he was involved in a relationship with another woman. He met her when he was about eighteen. In *The Confessions* he writes:

> At this time too I lived with a girl not bound to me in lawful wedlock but sought out by the roving eye of reckless desire; all the same she was the only girl I had, and I was sexually faithful to her. This experience taught me at first hand what a difference there is between a marriage contracted for the purpose of founding a family, and a relationship of love charged with carnal desire in which children may be born even against the parents' wishes—though once they are born one cannot help loving them.[64]

Augustine lived with the woman for some thirteen years. It is with her that he had his son. This kind of relationship was not unusual in Augustine's time. Surprisingly, the Catholic Church recognized such relationships "so long as the couple remained faithful to one another."[65] A concubine would be of a lower class than the man and would function also as a housekeeper. In 385 Augustine rejected this woman, whom he never names, in order to climb the social ladder through marriage with the young girl. He writes:

> Meanwhile my sins were multiplying, for the woman with whom I had been cohabiting was ripped from my side, being regarded as an obstacle to my marriage. So deeply was she engrafted into my heart that it was left torn and wounded and trailing blood. She had returned to Africa, vowing to you that she would never give herself to another man, and the son I had fathered by her was left with me. But I was too unhappy to follow a woman's example: I faced two years of waiting before I could marry the girl to whom I was betrothed, and I chafed at the delay, for I was no lover of marriage but the slave of lust. So I got myself another woman, in no sense a wife, that my soul's malady might be sustained in its pristine vigor or even aggravated, as it was conducted under the escort of inveterate custom into the realm of matrimony.
>
> The wound inflicted on me by the earlier separation did not heal either. After the fever and the immediate acute pain had dulled, it putrefied, and the pain became a cold despair.[66]

At this stage of his life, it is hard to take Augustine as a moral authority. He has much to confess in *The Confessions*! Yet as he reflects on his choices much later in life he describes some important patterns and thoughts. Like Augustine, we all make bad decisions. We all, at times, love the wrong things in life. Hopefully we have friends or family members who can carry us through our bad times. In a section that follows from the above excerpt, Augustine writes:

> Nor did I in my wretchedness consider what stream it was whence flowed to me the power to discuss even these distasteful things with my friends and still find sweetness in our talk, or whence came my inability to be happy, even in the sense in which I then understood happiness, without my friends, however lavishly supplied I might be with carnal luxuries. I loved these friends for their own sake, and felt myself loved by them for mine.[67]

Friends are essential, Augustine says. But how are we to choose and make friends? The next selection is taken from Question 71 of *Eighty-Three Different Questions*. Augustine writes on "On the Scripture: 'Bear One Another's Burdens, and in This Way Will You Fulfill the Law of Christ.'" Here he reflects on meeting new people, and things one ought to think about as one meets others.

> Next, one must reflect on this: there is no man who could not have some good quality, albeit hidden, which you do not yet have [and] by which he could doubtlessly be superior to you. This consideration is of importance in crushing and subduing pride, lest you think, because certain of your own good qualities stand out and are conspicuous, that no one else therefore has any good qualities, even hidden and perhaps of greater significance, by which he excels you without your knowing it. For the Apostle enjoins us not to deceive, or rather, not to empty flattery, when he says: "not by strife nor by empty conceit, but in lowliness of mind, the one valuing the other as superior to himself." We ought not to value the other in such a way that we do not value him but instead pretend to value him. Rather, let us genuinely consider the possibility of there being something hidden in the other by which he may be superior to us, even though our moral fitness, by which we seem to be superior to the other, is not hidden. These reflections, which crush pride and kindle charity, result in brothers carrying one another's burden, not only with equanimity, but also with the greatest willingness. Moreover, in the case of some man whom one does not know, one must not pass any judgment at all; and no one is known except through friendship. And for this reason do we bear more steadfastly the bad points of our friends, because their good points delight and captivate us.[68]

Augustine considers several roadblocks to new friendships. What if the person is of a different social status than you? What if a potential friend has some obvious negative characteristics?

> Accordingly one must not reject the friendship of anyone who offers himself for the association of friendship. [It is] not that he should be received immediately, but he should be desired as one worthy of being received, and he should be so treated that he can be received. For we can say that a person has been received into friendship to whom we dare pour out all our plans. And if there is someone who lacks the courage to offer himself [to us] in the making of friendship, because restrained by some temporal honor

or rank of ours, we must come down to him and must offer to him with a
certain gentleness and humility of soul what he himself does not of himself dare ask. Although somewhat rarely, of course, nonetheless it does happen from time to time in regard to someone whom we want to receive into
friendship that we learn of his bad qualities before we learn of his good,
and offended and, as it were, driven back by them, we give up on him and
do not pursue an investigation of his good qualities, which are perhaps
somewhat hidden. For this reason the Lord Jesus Christ, who desires that
we become followers of his example, admonishes us to bear that person's
weaknesses so that through the steadfast endurance of love we may be led
to certain wholesome qualities which bring us joy—a joy which satisfies.[69]

Friendship has a spiritual purpose and theological meaning for Augustine. By
being friends with sinners we have opportunities to bring them to love God.

> For he says: "The whole have no need of a physician—only the ill." There-
> fore, we ought not, for the sake of Christ's love, to reject from our lives a
> person who is ill in possibly every respect, since he can be made whole by
> the Word of God. [If this is so,] how much less [ought we to reject] him
> who can appear to us to be totally ill for the reason that we could not en-
> dure certain ills of his in the very beginnings of friendship, and, what is
> more serious, for the reason that we dared, in our displeasure, to pass a rash
> and prejudiced judgment on this whole man, nor fearing the words: "Judge
> not, that you be not judged," and: "the measure with which you measure,
> the same will be used in turn to measure you."[70]

Perhaps the problem that occurs most often is that one makes friends with a nice
person only to find out that this person has some negative characteristics. Augustine cautions people not to be naive about new friends. No one is perfect.

> Often, however, the good qualities appear first. In regard to these you must
> also beware of rash judgment which springs from goodwill, lest, when you
> think the person completely good, his bad qualities afterwards come to
> light and find you free of doubt and unprepared, and they shock you all
> the more, so that the one whom you had thoughtlessly loved you will hate
> more intensely, which is absolutely wrong. For even if none of his good
> qualities precede, and [even if] the first qualities to stand out were the ones
> [mentioned above] which afterwards appeared bad, still they ought to have
> been endured until you had done everything with him which ordinarily

brings healing to such ills. [This being so], how much more [is it necessary] when those good qualities preceded which ought, like pledges, to constrain us to put up with what comes afterwards![71]

Loving another one must love God, and through this love for Christ we can love others, even those with negative characteristics.

> Therefore it is the very law of Christ that we bear one another's burdens. Moreover, by loving Christ we easily bear the weakness of another, even him whom we do not yet love for the sake of his own good qualities, for we realize that the one whom we love is someone for whom the Lord has died. This is the love which the apostle Paul pressed upon us when he said: "And the weak one will perish because of your knowledge, the brother for whom Christ has died." Paul's intent was that if, because of the moral failing whereby he is weak, we love that weak person less, we should then consider the person in relation to him who died on his behalf. For this reason, with great care and the mercy of God having been implored, we must purpose not to neglect Christ because of the weak person, since we ought to love him because of Christ.[72]

The Order of Love

Some things are to be enjoyed, others to be used.
—Augustine, *On Christian Doctrine*

Biographer Peter Brown calls *On Christian Doctrine* Augustine's most original work.[73] Augustine started the book soon after he became bishop, but it took him nearly twenty-six years to finish. The underlying premise of *On Christian Doctrine* is that the Bible is the basis of Christian culture, yet the meanings of biblical texts are often not clear. Augustine is addressing an issue that concerns us even today. The Bible was and is often very hard for people, even educated people, to understand. Biblical interpretation was and still is an age-old problem. Augustine addresses this question in *On Christian Doctrine*. He writes, "But many and varied obscurities and ambiguities deceive those who read casually, understanding one thing instead of another; indeed, in certain places they do not find anything to interpret erroneously, so obscurely are certain sayings covered with a most dense mist."[74] *On Christian Doctrine* then can be read as "an introduction to the interpretation and explanation of the Bible."[75] Augustine's first principle of interpretation, the one that underlies his more specific interpretive principles, is *caritas*.[76] He writes, "Whoever, therefore, thinks that he understands the divine Scriptures or any part of them so that it does not build the double love of God and of our neighbor does not understand it at all."[77]

According to Augustine, some parts of the Bible are to be read literally and others figuratively. Love helps us understand the meaning of biblical texts. He writes:

> To this warning that we must beware not to take figurative or transferred expressions as though they were literal, a further warning must be added lest we wish to take literal expressions as though they were figurative. Therefore a method of determining whether a locution is literal or figurative must be established. And generally this method consists of this: that whatever appears in the divine Word that does not literally pertain to virtuous behavior or to the truth of faith you must take to be figurative. Virtuous behavior pertains to the love of God and of one's neighbor; truth of faith pertains to the knowledge of God and one's neighbor. For the hope of everyone lies in his own conscience in so far as he knows himself to be becoming more proficient in the love of God and of his neighbor.[78]

The Great Commandment is then the key to understanding Scripture. This statement invites a deeper question. What does it mean to love God and to love our neighbor? Augustine addresses this question in *On Christian Doctrine*. The following excerpt contains his famous distinction between love as use and love as enjoyment.

> Some things are to be enjoyed, others to be used, and there are others which are to be enjoyed and used. Those things which are to be enjoyed make us blessed. Those things which are to be used help and, as it were, sustain us as we move toward blessedness in order that we may gain and cling to those things which make us blessed. If we who enjoy and use things, being placed in the midst of things of both kinds, wish to enjoy those things which should be used, our course will be impeded and sometimes deflected, so that we are rewarded in obtaining those things which are to be enjoyed, or even prevented altogether, shackled by an inferior love.
>
> To enjoy something is to cling to it with love for its own sake. To use something, however, is to employ it in obtaining that which you love, provided that it is worthy of love. For an illicit use should be called rather a waste or an abuse. Suppose we were wanderers who could not live in blessedness except at home, miserable in our wandering and desiring to end

it and to return to our native country. We would need vehicles for land and sea which could be used to help us to reach our homeland, which is to be enjoyed. But if the amenities of the journey and the motion of the vehicles itself delight us, and we were led to enjoy those things which we should use, we should not wish to end our journey quickly, and entangled in a perverse sweetness, we should be alienated from our country, whose sweetness would make us blessed. Thus in this mortal life, wandering from God, if we wish to return to our native country where we can be blessed we should use this world and not enjoy it, so the "invisible things" of God "being understood by the things that are made" may be seen, that is, so that by means of corporal and temporal things we may comprehend the eternal and spiritual.[79]

In *Eighty-Three Different Questions* he writes: "Consequently every human perversion (also called vice) consists in the desire to use what ought to be enjoyed and to enjoy what ought to be used. In turn, good order (also called virtue) consists in the desire to enjoy what ought to be enjoyed and to use what ought to be used."[80] In his short book, *Enchiridian, or Faith, Hope, and Charity* (written late in his life, after a request was made for a short book on Christian doctrine, the book is "a commentary on the Apostles' Creed and the Lord's Prayer"[81]), Augustine summarizes this point in one of his characteristically powerful sentences. He writes, "For when we ask how good a man is, we do not ask what he believes or what he hopes for, but what he loves."[82]

In *On Christian Doctrine* Augustine continues:

> The things which are to be enjoyed are the Father, the Son, and the Holy Spirit, a single Trinity, as certain supreme thing common to all who enjoy it, if, indeed, it is a thing and not rather the cause of all things, or both a thing and a cause. . . . All three have the same eternity, the same immutability, the same majesty, and the same power. In the Father is unity, in the Son equality, and in the Holy Spirit a concord of unity and equality; and these three qualities are all one because of the Father, all equal because of the Son, and all united because of the Holy Spirit.[83]

We have seen this theme presented before. Recall Augustine's reflections on the death of his friend in *The Confessions*. He realizes that it was "madness" to love his friend as deeply as he did. People grow old and die. There is no permanence, "no point of rest" in people. The only focus of true love, of enjoyment, is that which is eternal and unchangeable, namely, God. Does this mean we are then to love others as a means to God? Augustine writes:

Therefore, among all these things only those are to be enjoyed which we
have described as being eternal and immutable; others are to be used so
that we may be able to enjoy those. In the same way we who enjoy and
use other things are things ourselves. A great thing is man, made in the
image and likeness of God, not in that he is encased in a mortal body, but
in that he excels the beast in the dignity of a rational soul. Thus there is a
profound question as to whether men should enjoy themselves, use themselves, or to do both. For it is commanded to us that we should love one
another, but it is to be asked whether man is to be loved by man for his
own sake or for the sake of something else. If for his own sake, we enjoy
him; if for the sake of something else we use him. But I think that man is
to be loved for the sake of something else. In that which is to be loved for
its own sake the blessed life resides; and if we do not have it for the present, the hope for it now consoles us. But "cursed be the man that trusteth
in man."[84]

In the above passage Augustine begins to describe the proper ordering of our
loves. We are to love others, not in themselves, but for the sake of God. This was
the mistake Augustine confesses in *The Confessions*. He loved his friends for their
own sake. Again, the point is that it is good to love friends, but you have to love
them in the right way, that is, for the sake of God. Elsewhere in *The Confessions*
Augustine, again addressing God, is concerned with why some people desire to
be loved by others. He writes, "The temptation is to wish to be feared or loved
by people for no reason other than the joy derived from such power, which is
not joy at all. It is a wretched life, and vanity is repulsive. This is the main cause
why I fail to love and fear you in purity. . . . Let it be for your sake that we are
loved, and let it be your word in us which is feared."[85]

Augustine continues his theology of love in *On Christian Doctrine* by considering love of self.

But no one ought to enjoy himself either, if you observe the matter closely,
because he should not love himself on account of himself but on account
of Him who is to be enjoyed. For he is the best man who turns his whole
life toward the immutable life and adheres to it with all his affection. But
if he loves himself on his own account he does not turn himself toward
God, but, being turned toward himself, he does not care for anything immutable. . . . If, therefore, you should love yourself not on your own account but on account of Him who is most justly the object of your love,
no other man should feel angry with you if you love him also on account

of God. . . . Thus all your thoughts and all your life and all your understanding should be turned toward Him from whom you receive these powers. . . . But whatever else appeals to the mind as being lovable should be directed into that channel into which the whole current of love flows. Whoever, therefore, justly loves his neighbor should so act toward him that he also loves God with his whole heart, with his whole soul, and with his whole mind. Thus, loving his neighbor as himself, he refers the love of both to that love of God which suffers no stream to be led away from it by which it might be diminished.[86]

It is clear that for Augustine the term love is not limited to feelings or desire. Love, properly understood, includes action. If a person loves God, the person acts in certain ways. This idea directs Augustine's view of neighbor love. To love the neighbor does not simply mean to have warm feelings for or kind thoughts about one's neighbors. In his *On the Morals of the Catholic Church*, Augustine writes:

For it is impossible for one who loves God not to love himself. For he alone has a proper love for himself who aims diligently at the attainment of the chief and true good; and this is nothing else but God. . . . Yea, verily; so that we can think of no surer step toward the love of God than the love of man to man. . . . Now you love yourself suitably when you love God better than yourself. What, then, you aim at in yourself you must aim at in your neighbor, namely, that he may love God with a perfect affection. For you do not love him as yourself, unless you try to draw him to that good which you are yourself pursuing. For this is the one good which has room for all to pursue it along with thee. From this precept proceed the duties of human society, in which it is hard to keep from error. But the first thing to aim at is, that we should be benevolent, that is, that we cherish no malice and no evil design against another. For man is the nearest neighbor of man.[87]

There is a direct relationship between loving the neighbor and loving God. Augustine continues, "But as a man may sin against another in two ways, either by injuring him or by not helping him when it is in his power, and as it is for these things which no loving man would do. . . . and if we cannot attain to good unless we first desist from working evil, our love of our neighbor is a sort of cradle of our love to God."[88]

Augustine compares these two loves in human experience. Which, for example, comes first? How are we to love our neighbor? He continues,

But there is a sense in which these either rise together to fullness and perfection, or, while the love of God is first in beginning, the love of our neighbor is first in coming to perfection. For perhaps divine love takes hold on
us more rapidly at the outset, but we reach perfection more easily in lower
things. However that may be, the main point is this, that no one should
think that while he despises his neighbor he will come to happiness and
to the God whom he loves. And would that it were as easy to seek the good
of our neighbor, or to avoid hurting him, as it is for the well trained and
kindhearted to love his neighbor! These things require more than mere
good-will, and can be done only by a high degree of thoughtfulness and
prudence, which belongs only to those to whom it is given by God, the
source of all good.[89]

For Augustine, there are two ways to love the neighbor. We must care for
those in need and, more importantly, we must draw them to God. Augustine
continues, "Man, then, as viewed by his fellowman, is a rational soul with a mortal and earthly body in its service. Therefore he who loves his neighbor does good
partly to the man's body, and partly to his soul. What benefits the body is called
medicine, what benefits the soul, discipline."[90] Under care for the body, along
with medicine Augustine includes all that enables good health,—food, shelter,
and clothing. As he says, "For hunger and thirst, and cold and heat, and all violence from without, produce loss of that health."[91] Compassion, he says, "requires us to ward off these distresses from others. The law to do no harm to others "forbids the infliction" of these distresses.[92]

Augustine argues that bodily medicine is not sufficient. Without the medicine of the mind, what Augustine calls discipline, there is no salvation. Discipline includes both fear of God and love of God. Augustine concludes, "He, then
who loves his neighbor endeavors all he can to procure his safety in body and
in soul, making the health of the mind the standard in his treatment of the body.
And as regards the mind, his endeavors are in this order, that he should first fear
and then love God. This is true excellence of conduct, and thus the knowledge
of truth is acquired which we are ever in the pursuit of."[93]

John Burnaby argues that Augustine sees the New Testament command to
love to be a higher level of love compared to the natural relationships of friends
and family. Commenting on Augustine's theology, Burnaby writes that

The love of the new commandment "makes new men," the New People
of God, the brothers of His beloved Son. It is to be, like Christ's love for

His own, a creative love, loving men not for what they are but in order that they may become, leading them to the goal where God is all in all. In that sense Augustine can say that God is the real object of Christ's love for us, and that all holy love of our neighbor seeks God in him. . . . God is the end as He is the beginning of all true love of neighbor.[94]

He continues, "Augustine never says we love our neighbor because he has a capacity for God; he says we love him 'in order that God may be in him.'"[95] Love for others demands that we help them love God. Charity is contagious. It spreads. "The 'love of men which is the will for them to live righteously' is realised in the love of neighbor 'in God and for God.'"[96] As he says in *On Christian Doctrine*, "Whoever, therefore, justly loves his neighbor should so act toward him that he also love God with his whole heart, and his whole soul, and with his whole mind."[97] For, as he says in a sermon, "If we love them for another reason, we hate them more than love them."[98]

Love binds the lover and the beloved together. It is formed both by the desires of the lover and by that which is loved in the beloved. A discussion in *The Trinity* captures this tension and gives a direct answer to the question of what we are to love in the other.

But what is love or charity, which the divine Scripture praises and proclaims so highly, if not the love of the good? Now love is of someone who loves, and something is loved with love. So then there are three: the lover, the beloved, and the love. What else is love, therefore, except a kind of life which binds or seeks to bind some two together, namely the lover and the beloved? And this is so even in external and carnal love. But that we may draw from a purer and clearer source, let us tread the flesh under foot and mount up to the soul. What does the soul love in a friend except the soul? And, therefore, even here there are three: the lover, the beloved, and the love.[99]

If we are to love the soul in the other we cannot stand by idly when another sins. Love compels us to correct and indeed to discipline the sinner, yet our intention must be love. Augustine gives two examples to illustrate the priority of the appropriate intention over the act. In the first example, a father beats his son. Judging only the physical action, the act seems like a terrible act. In the second example, a person is nice to, indeed flatters another person, yet the person knows that the other is a sinner. Augustine comments, "In the case of different acts we find a man made raging by love and one made fawning by iniquity. . . . If you should propose two things, blows and fawns, who would not choose fawning and flee from blows? If you should look to the persons, love lashes out, iniquity fawns." The father beats his son out of love. He does so for his son's own good. For Augustine, the intention to love makes the act moral and appropriate. (Note that some commentators argue that Augustine, in advocating coercion for another's good, contradicts other elements of his theology.[100]) In the other example, the person ignores the sin, indeed seems to support the sin, as he is nice to the sinner. Augustine continues,

> See what we are pointing out, that the acts of men are distinguished only from the root of love. For many things can happen that have a good appearance on the exterior and do not proceed from the root of love. Even thorn bushes have flowers. But some things seem harsh, seem savage, but they are done for discipline under the direction of love. Once for all, therefore, a short precept is presented to you: Love and do what you will. If you should be silent, be silent out of love; if you should cry out, cry out of love. If you should correct, correct out of love; if you should spare, spare out of love. Let the root of love be within; from this root only good can emerge.[101]

In another place Augustine addresses the same theme.

> We should never undertake the task of chiding another's sin unless, cross-examining our own conscience, we can assure ourselves, before God, that we are acting from love. If reproaches or threats or injuries, voiced by the one you are calling to account, have wounded your spirit, then, for that person to be healed by you, you must not speak till you are healed yourself, lest you act from worldly motives, to hurt, and to make your tongue a sinful weapon against evil, returning wrong for wrong, curse for curse. Whatever you speak out of a wounded spirit is the wrath of an avenger, not the love of an instructor. Act as you desire, so long as you are acting with love. Then there will be no meanness in what may sound mean, while you are acutely aware that you are striving with the sword of God's word to free another from the grip of sin. And if, as often happens, you begin some course of action from love, and are proceeding with it in love, but a different feeling insinuates itself because you are resisted, deflecting you from reproach of a man's sin and make you attack the man himself—it were best, while watering the dust with your tears, to remember that we have no right to crow over another's sin, since we sin in the very reproach of sin, if anger at sin is better at making us sinners than mercy is at making us kind.[102]

On Christian Doctrine presents an ordered love. That is, there is a hierarchy of being or goodness and this hierarchy ought to be reflected in our loves. We must love the right things in the right way, "respecting the 'more' or 'less' which we discern in the order of things." The structure of Augustine's order is thus: We are to love and enjoy God. We are to love and use our selves, our neighbors, and our bodies. We are to use but not love material things.[103] Donald Burt comments, "My place as a human being is thus in the middle of reality. Some parts are above me and some are below me. Augustine concludes from this that happiness can come only from the possession of a good that is greater than human beings and, indeed, is that good than which there is no greater."[104] It must be noted that Augustine's hierarchy of good is also an argument against the Manichees. Recall the theology of the Manichees; they held that material and physical things were evil and only spiritual things were truly good. In contrast to this, Augustine writes in *The City of God* that "the things of earth are not merely good; they are undoubtedly gifts from God."[105]

It is not the material world that is evil, evil results in how we love the things of the world. Augustine continues, "if men so love the goods of earth as to believe that these are the only goods or if they love them more than the goods they know to be better, then the consequence is inevitable: misery and more misery."[106]

Indeed Augustine himself attests to this misery. Returning to *The Confessions*, we hear him, again in prayer, lamenting his early choices in life. He loved physical and earthly goods over the ultimate beauty of God. This is a striking paragraph and thus is often quoted. Note the emotional and sensual language Augustine uses to describe both his early love for creating things and his current love for the creator.

> Late have I loved you, Beauty so ancient and so new,
> late have I loved you!
> Lo, you were within,
> but I outside, seeking there for you,
> and upon the shapely things you have made I rushed headlong,
> I, misshapen.
> You were with me, but I was not with you.
> They held me back far from you,
> those things which would have no being
> were they not in you.
> You called, shouted, broke through my deafness;
> you flared, blazed, banished my blindness;
> you lavished your fragrance, I gasped, and now I pant for you;

I tasted you, and I hunger and thirst;
you touched me, and I burned for your peace.[107]

We make choices in our loves. The choices have consequences. In *Eighty-Three Different Questions* Augustine addresses how our choices create the conditions for *caritas* to flourish or alternatively how our choices can poison *caritas*.

> Charity denotes that whereby one loves those things whose worth, in comparison to the lover itself, must not be thought to be of lesser value, those things being the eternal and what can love the eternal. Therefore in its consummate and purest sense charity is used only of the love of God and of the soul by which he is loved (and this is also appropriately called *dilectio*).
>
> However, when God is loved more than the soul so that a man prefers to belong to him rather than to himself, then is it that we are genuinely mindful in the highest degree of the soul and consequently also of the body. . . . However, the poison of charity is the hope of getting and holding onto temporal things. The nourishment of charity is the lessening of covetousness. . . . Accordingly whoever wants to nourish charity in himself, let him pursue the lessening of covetous desires (covetousness being the love of getting and holding onto temporal things).[108]

In contrast to the teaching of the Manichees, evil does not rest in physical things but rather in our choices to love such goods inappropriately. Yet at times Augustine is quite suspicious of physical pleasure or what he calls bodily delights. He warns, "God alone is to be loved; and all this world, that is all sensible things, are to be despised, while, however, they are to be used as this life requires."[109]

He says of the New Testament that it requires "us not to love anything in this world, especially in that passage where it is said, 'Be not conformed to this world,' for the point is to show that a man is conformed to whatever he loves."[110] He concludes:

> For when you consider things beneath yourself to be admirable and desirable, what is this but to be cheated and misled by unreal goods? The man, then, who is temperate in such mortal and transient things has his rule of life confirmed by both Testaments, that he should love none of these things, nor think them desirable for their own sakes, but should use them as far as is required for the purposes and duties of life, with the moderation of an employer instead of the ardor of a lover.[111]

Returning to *On Christian Doctrine* we read more about the hierarchy of things to love.

> Not everything which is to be used is to be loved, but only those things which either by a certain association pertain to God, like man or an angel, or pertain to use and require the favor of God through us, like the body. For undoubtedly the martyrs did not love the evil of those who persecuted them, even though they used it to merit God. Although there are four kinds of things which may be loved—first, the kind which is above us; second, the kind which constitutes ourselves; third, the kind which is equal to us; and fourth, the kind which is below us—no precepts need to be given concerning the second and the fourth. However much a man departs from the truth, there remains in him the love of himself and of his body. For the spirit, having fled from the immutable light which reigns overall, acts so that it may rule itself and its own body, and thus cannot do otherwise than love itself and its own body.[112]

Augustine distinguished true self-love from false self-love, describing the former as hate. He singles out those who usurp God's claim on people and demand that others serve them as an example of false self-love. People, by nature, do not hate themselves but they can hate themselves by choice. In *The Trinity*, Augustine comments, "Hence, he who knows how to love himself loves God; on the other hand, he who does not love God, even though he loves himself which is naturally implanted in him, is not unfittingly said to hate himself, since he does that which is opposed to himself, and pursues himself as though he were his own enemy."[113]

As if continuing down the ladder to Diotima's first rung, Augustine considers love of one's body.

> Thus no one hates himself. And, indeed this principle was never questioned by any sect. Neither does anyone hate his body, and what the Apostle says concerning this is true, "No man ever hated his own flesh. " And that which some say, that they would rather be without a body, arises from a complete delusion: they hate not their bodies but the corruption and solidity of their bodies. They do not wish to have no bodies at all but rather incorruptible and most agile bodies.[114]

Augustine cites St. Paul's words in his Letter to Galatians that the flesh lusts against the spirit and the spirit against flesh. Would not that suggest that we ought to hate our bodies? Augustine rejects this. Again, it is not the flesh itself but the habits of the flesh. He writes, "Since after the resurrection the body will thrive in complete peace immortally in subjection to the spirit, in the present life we should seek that the habit of the flesh should be changed for the better lest it resist the spirit with inordinate demands."[115] He explains:

> Thus the spirit acts in dominating the flesh that it may destroy the evils of habit as if they constituted a perverse covenant, and it creates the peace of good custom. However, not even those who, depraved by a false opinion, detest their bodies, would be prepared to lose one eye even without pain, not even if the one left could see as well as both together, unless something else which might be valued more demanded it.[116]

For Augustine, we share a basic sense of self-love, which includes love for our bodies, with animals. This, he says, is natural, so we need no laws directing us. We do need laws concerning loving things equal to us and things that are greater than us: thus the great commandments given by Jesus. He writes, "Therefore, since there was no need for a precept that anyone love himself and his own body, because we love that which we are and that which is below us . . . there remained a necessity only that we receive precepts concerning that which is equal to us and that which is above us."[117] After stating the Great Commandment, he continues,

> Thus if you think of yourself as a whole embracing both a soul and a body and your neighbor also as a whole embracing both a soul and a body— for the soul and the body constitute a man—nothing which is to be loved is to be omitted from these two precepts. For when love of God is placed first and the character of that love is seen to be described so that all other loves must flow into it, it may seem that nothing has been said about love of yourself. But when it is said, "Thou shalt love thy neighbor as thy self" as the same time, it is clear that love yourself is not omitted.[118]

Not only are we commanded to love, but Augustine holds for any commandment of God to be followed properly persons must be "directed to the love of God and of one's neighbor for God's sake." All commandments from God are directed toward charity.[119]

Augustine summarizes his theology of love and indeed the whole of Christian life as being in two stages. He first describes loving abstractly. Augustine writes, "He lives in justice and sanctity who is an unprejudiced assessor of the intrinsic value of things. He is a man who has an ordinate love: he neither loves what should not be loved nor fails to love what should be loved; he neither loves more what should be loved less, loves equally what should be loved less or more, nor loves less or more what should be loved equally."[120] Augustine then fills in the abstract categories with concrete examples.

No sinner should be loved in that he is a sinner, and every man should be loved for his own sake. And if God is to be loved more than any man, everyone should love God more than himself. Again, another man is to be loved more than our own bodies; for all of these things are to be loved for the sake of God, and another man can enjoy God with us while our bodies cannot do this, for the body has life only through the soul by means of which we enjoy God.[121]

Augustine offers criteria by which we can decide how to love others.

All other men are to be loved equally; but since you cannot be of assistance to everyone, those especially are to be cared for who are most closely bound to you by place, time, or opportunity, as if by chance. Thus suppose you had an abundance of something which it would be well to give to someone else who lacked it, but you could not give it to two. If two came to you of whom neither took precedence either in need or in any special connection with you, you could do nothing more just than to decide by lot which one should be given that which you could not give to both. Thus in the same way among men, not all of whom you can care for, you must consider as if selected by lot each one as he is able to be more closely associated with you in time.[122]

He also briefly mentions love of enemies.

And He wishes to be loved, not for selfish ends, but so that He may confer an eternal reward on those who love Him, which is the very object of their love. Thus it is that we also love our enemies. For we do not fear them, since they cannot take away that which we love. Rather are we sorry for them, for the more they hate us, the further removed are they from that which we love. If they were to turn to Him and love Him as the source of blessedness, they would necessarily love us also as companions in the great good.[123]

Earlier in this chapter, it was noted that there are two types of love for Augustine, love that lifts one upward like fire to God and the other that is like the stone that falls down taking us away from God, *caritas* and *cupiditas*. In *On Christian Doctrine* he affirms this distinction. "I call 'charity' the motion of the soul toward the enjoyment of God for His own sake, and the enjoyment of one's self and of one's neighbor for the sake of God; but 'cupidity' is a motion of the soul toward the enjoyment of one's self, one's neighbor, or any other corporal thing for the sake of something other than God."[124] It is in considering the different directions of the soul's movement, then, that we can speak of moral goodness and sinfulness.

> That which uncontrolled cupidity does to corrupt the soul and its body is called "vice"; what it does in such a way that someone else is harmed is called a "crime." And these are the two classes of all sins, but vices occur first. When vices have emptied the soul and led it to a kind of extreme hunger, it leaps into crimes by means of which impediments to the vices may be removed or the vices themselves sustained. On the other hand, what charity does to the charitable person is called "utility"; what it does to benefit one's neighbor is called "beneficence." And here utility occurs first, for no one may benefit another with that which he does not have himself. The more the reign of cupidity is destroyed, the more charity is increased.[125]

In a sermon given late in his life, Augustine preached:

> In this life there are two loves wrestling with each other in every trial and temptation: love of the world and love of God. And whichever of these two wins, that's where it pulls the lover as by the force of gravity. It isn't, you see, on wings or on foot that we come to God, but on the power of our desires. And again, it isn't with knots and chains that we find ourselves stuck to the earth, but with contrary desires. Christ came to change our love, and to make lovers of the heavenly life out of earthly lovers.[126]

Reflecting on his youth he writes, "At that time I did not know this. I loved beautiful things of a lower order, and I was going down to the depths."[127]

Ordered Love and Family Relationships
Love your father, but not above your Lord.
—Augustine, *Sermon 344*

The category of that "which is equal to us" is huge. It includes all persons. Augustine gives us, however, some help in discerning how to love all these people. He says, we are particularly to love those "who are most closely bound" to us "by place, time, or opportunity." He picks up this theme in *The City of God* and develops the idea of responsibilities within particular relationships. Note his driving concern that we ought to help others love God.

> Meanwhile, God teaches him two chief commandments, the love of God and the love of neighbor. In these precepts man finds three beings to love, namely, God, himself, and his fellow man, and know that he is not wrong in loving himself so long as he loves God. As a result, he must help his neighbor (whom he is obliged to love as himself) to love God. Thus, he must help his wife, children, servants, and all other whom he can influence. He must wish, moreover, to be similarly helped by his fellow man, in case he himself needs such assistance. Out of all this love he will arrive at peace, as much as in him lies, with every man—at that human peace which is regulated fellowship. Right order here means, first that he harm no one, and, second, that he help whomever he can. His fundamental duty is to look out for his own home, for both by natural and human law he has easier and readier access to their requirements.[128]

An element of Augustine's writing that we have not spent much time on in this chapter is his sermons. In comparison to the more scholarly and theoretical books we have been citing, Augustine also preached his theology of love to people in churches. Sermons are of a different genre than philosophical or theological treatises. Augustine's sermons, for example, seem spontaneous and extemporaneous. He probably did not write them out before he delivered them. His students or followers probably recorded the texts. Augustine, like other preachers, tended to use rhetorical tools that might not occur in more abstract writing. He repeated simple phrases and he moved easily from the topic at hand to address a specific current event. His tone appears more conversational than formal and certainly he intends to motivate or to uplift his audience.[129] A striking feature of Augustine's sermons, in comparison to his other works, is their practicality. For example, in the following sermon Augustine preaches about loving one's family members. Note how rightly ordered love makes specific demands on how we ought to understand particular relationships. Augustine deeply valued friends and he affirms the natural loves in the family. We ought to love our parents. We ought to love our wives. We ought to love our children. We are to love all these people, indeed all people, in a limited and relative way. That is, to truly love a friend or a parent or a spouse or a child, one must love them "in reference to God." We must "in them love nothing but Christ." He is speaking about Jesus here.

He didn't abolish love of parent, wife, children, but put them in their right order. He didn't say "Whoever loves," but "Whoever loves above me." That's what the Church is saying in the Song of Songs: He put charity in order for me (Sg. 2:4). Love your father, but not above your Lord; love the one who begot you, but not above the one who created you. Your father begot you, but didn't himself fashion you; because who or what would be born to him, when he sowed the seed, he himself did not know. Your father reared you, but when you were hungry he didn't provide bread for you from his own body. Finally, whatever your father is keeping for you on earth, he has to pass away for you to succeed to it; he will leave space for your life by his death. But what God your Father is keeping for you, he is keeping with himself, so that you may possess the inheritance with your Father, and not, as his successor, be waiting for his demise, but rather may cleave to him who is always going to abide, and may always abide yourself in him. So love your father, but not above your God.[130]

After spending a good deal of time on loving one's father, he addresses loving one's mother, wife, and children, albeit in a much shorter space.

Love your mother, but not above the Church, who bore you to eternal life. Finally, from the love you have for your parents weigh up how much you ought to love God and the Church. After all, if those who bore you, only to die in due course, are to be loved as much, with how much charity are those to be loved who have borne you in order to enter eternity, in order to remain in eternity? Love your wife, love your children after God, in such a way that you take care they too worship God with you; when you're joined to him, you will fear no separation. The reason you ought not to love them more than God is that you love them in a totally bad way if you neglect to bring them to God together with you.[131]

In the following sermon, he breaks legitimate love into two categories, human and divine, but he says that the human legitimate love is not sufficient. The selection is longer than most in this chapter. We read the words of an impassioned preacher attempting to move and motivate everyday Christians. He begins his discussion of the three loves (note that previously we heard him refer to only two loves), by comparing how a man would love his wife to how he would love a prostitute.

So, to give a quick instance, the human charity by which one's wife is loved is lawful; by which a prostitute, or someone else's wife is loved, unlawful.

Even in the streets and market place, the lawful kind of charity is preferred to the prostitute variety; which in the house of God, in the temple of God, in the city of Christ, in the body of Christ, the love of a prostitute leads the lover straight to hell. So have the lawful kind of charity; it's human, but as I said, it's lawful. It's not only lawful, though, in the sense that it's permitted; but also lawful in the sense that if it's lacking, you are very much at fault. It's absolutely right for you to love your wives, to love your children, to love your friends, to love your fellow citizens with human charity. All these names, you see, imply a bond of relationship, and the glue, so to say, of charity.[132]

We see human charity evidenced throughout the world. It is natural for humans to love in this manner; indeed, argues Augustine, even animals love their young.

But you will observe that this sort of charity can be found also among the godless, that is, among pagans, Jews, heretics. Which of them, after all, does not naturally love wife, children, brothers, neighbors, relations, friends, etc.? So this kind of charity is human. So if anyone is affected by such hardness of heart that he loses even the human feeling of love, and doesn't love his children, doesn't love his wife, he isn't fit even to be counted among human beings. A man who loves his children is not thereby particularly praiseworthy; but one who does not love his children is certainly blameworthy, I mean, he should observe with whom he ought to have this kind of love in common; even wild beasts love their children; adders love their children; tigers love their children; lions love their children. There is no wild creature, surely, that doesn't gently coo or purr over its young. I mean, while it may terrify human beings, it cherishes its young. The lion roars in the forest, so that nobody dare walk through it; it goes into its den, where it has its young, it lays aside all its rabid ferocity. . . . So a man who doesn't love his children is worse than a lion. These are human sentiments, but they are lawful.[133]

Augustine warns against unlawful loves and he graphically illustrates the difference between unlawful and lawful human loves. "Now just as one flesh is effected in the lawful congress of man and wife; so too one flesh is effected in the unlawful congress of harlot and lover. So since one flesh is effected, you should be shaken to the core."[134] He continues:

Let us question divine charity, and let us set before her the two human kinds of charity, and let us say to her, "Here is lawful human charity, with which wives are loved, and daughters, and other secular relations. Here on

the other side is the unlawful sort, by which harlots are loved, by which
one's maidservants are loved, by which another man's daughter is loved,
when she has been neither asked for nor promised in marriage, by which
another man's wife is loved. In front of you are two sorts of charity; with
which of the two do you wish to stay?"

The man who chooses to stay with that lawful human love doesn't stay
with the unlawful variety. You should none of you say to yourselves, "I
have them both." If you have them both by admitting into yourself the
love of a harlot, you are doing wrong to divine charity, who is living there
as the lady of the house. I rather think, you see, that if you are a married
man, and are in love with a harlot, you don't bring the harlot into your
house, to live with your lady wife. You aren't quite as advanced as all that.
You look for the cover of darkness, you look for out-of-the-way corners,
you don't parade your shameful behavior. But even those who don't have
wives, and are the lovers of harlots slightly less unlawfully, as it were (the
reason I said "as it were," is that they too stand condemned, if they are already believers); I rather imagine that even a young man who hasn't yet got
a wife will not, if he loves a harlot, bring her to live with his sister, will not
bring her to live with his mother, for fear of insulting ordinary human decency, for fear of offending against the honor of his blood. So if you don't
bring along the harlot you are in love with to live with your mother, with
your sister, for fear, as I said, of offending against the honor of your blood;
are you going to bring the love of a harlot along to live in your heart together with the love of God, and offend against the honor of the blood of
Christ?[135]

Human action itself illustrates the difference between these loves. After affirming natural human love, Augustine pushes forward. Such love pales in comparison to divine charity.

Love God; you can't find anything better to love. You love silver, because
it's better than iron or brass; you love gold more, because it's better than
silver; you love precious stones more, because they exceed even the value
of gold; finally you love this light of day, which everyone who is afraid of
death dreads leaving behind. . . . Love Christ; long for the light which
Christ is. If that man longed for the light of the body, how much more
ought you all to long for the light of the heart? Let us cry out to him, not
with our voices, but with our behavior. Let us lead good lives, let us scorn
the world; for us, let everything that passes away be nothing.[136]

Divine charity is concerned with the immutable, that which does not change. This is the only place where one's heart can truly rest. Divine charity is love for God. This love gives direction to lawful human loves.

> Love your children, love your wives, even if it's only in worldly matters and a worldly way. Because of course you ought to love them with reference to Christ, and take thought for them with reference to God, and in them love nothing but Christ, and hate it in your nearest and dearest if they don't want to have anything to do with Christ. Such, you see, is that divine sort of charity. What good, after all, would be done them by your fleeting and mortal charity? Still, when you do love them in a human way, love Christ more. I'm not saying you shouldn't love your wife; but love Christ more. I'm not saying you shouldn't love your father, not saying you shouldn't love your children; but love Christ more. Listen to him saying it himself, in case you should suppose these are just my words: "Whoever loves father or mother more than me, is not worthy of me" (MT 10:37).[137]

Love for God

What then do I love when I love my God? Who is he who is higher than the highest element in my soul? Through my soul I will ascend to him. I will rise above the force by which I am bonded to the body and fill its frame with vitality."

—Augustine, *The Confessions*

For Augustine, love of God, love of self, and love of neighbor are hierarchically arranged yet intertwined. One cannot truly love oneself unless one loves God; one cannot truly love the neighbor unless one loves God; and one cannot truly love God without neighbor and self love. In *The Trinity*, Augustine writes, "We, therefore, love God and our neighbor from one and the same love, but we love God on account of God, and ourselves and our neighbor on account of God."[138] In commenting on loving God and loving neighbor in the same book, he notes that at times the Bible only mentions loving God and at other times the Bible only mentions loving neighbor. In response to the former he writes, "For he who loves God must logically do what God has commanded, and love Him just as much as he does so; therefore, he must also love his neighbor since God has commanded this."[139] Regarding the latter he states, "And we find many other passages in the Sacred Scriptures where love of our neighbor alone seems to be commanded for perfection, and the love of God is passed over in silence. . . . But this also follows logically, for he who loves his neighbor must also love love itself above everything else. But 'God is love, and he who abides in love abides in God.' Therefore, he must needs love God above everything else."[140]

How does one love God? For Augustine, loving God is ultimately linked to one's mind. He writes in *The Trinity*:

> For something can be known and not loved; but what I am asking is, whether something can be loved that is not known? If that is impossible, then no one loves God before he knows Him. And what does it mean to love God, except to see Him and to perceive him steadfastly with our mind? For He is not a body to be sought for with bodily eyes.
>
> But even before we are capable of seeing and perceiving God, as He can be perceived, which is granted to the clear of heart, for "blessed are the clean of heart, for they shall see God," he must be loved by faith; other wise, the heart cannot be cleansed so as to be fit and ready to see Him. For where are those three, faith, hope, and charity, for the building up of which in the soul, all the divine books have been composed and work together, except in the soul that believes what it does not yet see, and hopes for and loves what it believes? Therefore, even He who is not known, but in whom one believes, is already loved.[141]

The mind is where believing takes place. The mind is where one comprehends God. In *Eighty-Three Questions*, Question 35, Augustine states:

> For of all things, the most excellent is what is eternal, and therefore we cannot possess it except by that part of ourselves in which lies our excellence, i.e., by our mind. But whatever is possessed by the mind is had by knowing, and no good is completely known which is not completely loved. Nor is it the case, since the mind alone can know, that thus it alone can love. For love is a kind of desire. . . . If this desire is in accord with the mind and reason, it will be possible for the mind to contemplate what is eternal in great peace and tranquillity.[142]

In the following selection, from *The Confessions*, Augustine considers the deeper question of what it means to love God. He first thinks of the wonderful pleasures of life as things he ought to love to love God.

> But what am I loving when I love you? Not beauty of body, not transient grace, not this fair light which is now so friendly to my eyes, not melodi-

ous song in all its lovely harmonies, not the sweet fragrance of flowers or ointments or spices, not manna or honey, not limbs that draw me to carnal embrace: none of these do I love when I love my God. And yet I do love a kind of light, a kind of voice, a certain fragrance, a food and an embrace, when I love my God: a light, voice, fragrance, food and embrace for my inmost self, where something limited to no place shines into my mind, where something not snatched away by passing time sings for me, where something no breath blows away yields to me its scent, where there is savor undiminished by famished eating, and where I am clasped in a union from which no satiety can tear me away. This is what I love, when I love my God.[143]

Augustine looks to creation and the beauty in creation to find God. He discovers that creation is not God but that it points to God. He starts with the lowest part of creation, the sea, and works up to the stars.

And what is this?
I put my question to the earth, and it replied, "I am not he";
I questioned everything it held, and they confessed the same.
I questioned the sea and the great deep,
and the teeming live creatures that crawl, and they replied,
"We are not God; seek higher."
I questioned the gusty winds,
and every breeze with all its flying creatures told me,
"Anaximenes was wrong: I am not God."
To the sky I put my question, to sun, moon, stars,
but they denied me: "We are not the God you seek."
And to all things which stood around the portals of my flesh I said,
"Tell me of my God.
You are not he, but tell me something of him."
Then they lifted up their mighty voices and cried,
"He made us."
My questioning was my attentive spirit,
and their reply, their beauty.[144]

Augustine exhausts the external world in his search for God. He examines sensual pleasure and the beauty of creation and finds only traces of God. Where can he turn to next? All that is left is the internal. Gilson describes Augustine's method as "a path leading from the exterior to the interior and from the interior to the superior."[145] Commenting on the same, Charles Taylor concludes, "By going inward, I am drawn upward."[146] The significance of the internal, the mind, is that only through it can the external be known.

> Then toward myself I turned, and asked myself, "Who are you?" And I answered my own question: "A man." See, here are the body and soul that make up myself, the one outward and the other within. Through which of these should I seek my God? With my body's senses I had already sought him from earth to heaven, to the farthest place whither I could send the darting rays of my eyes; but what lay within me was better, and to this all those bodily messengers reported back, for it controlled and judged the replies of sky and earth, and of all the creatures dwelling in them, all those who had proclaimed, "We are not God," and "He made us." My inner self recognized them all through the service of the outer. I, who was that inmost self, I, who was mind, knew them through the senses of my body; and so I questioned the vast frame of the world concerning my God, and it answered, "I am not he, but he made me."[147]

The path, the principal way to God is inward.[148] That is not to equate the soul with God or to confuse the road with the destination. Turning inward is the route to God, not God. Augustine continues:

> What is it, then, that I love when I love my God? Who is he who towers above my soul? By this same soul I will mount to him. I will leave behind that faculty whereby I am united to a body and animate its frame. Not by that faculty do I find my God, for horse and mule would find him equally, since the same faculty gives life to their bodies too, yet they are beasts who lack intelligence. There is another power by which I do more than give life to my flesh: with this I endow with senses the flesh that God has fashioned for me, commanding the eye not to hear and the ear not to see, giving to my organ of seeing and my organ of hearing and to all my other senses what is proper to them in their respective places and for their particular work.[149]

Not long after his conversion and baptism, Augustine wrote *On the Morals of the Catholic Church* and a companion volume *On the Morals of the Manicheans*. The purpose of the books was to refute Manichean heresy. *On the Morals of the Catholic Church* contains an extended argument on loving God. We see in the following text these same themes of inwardness and loving God.

Following after God is the desire of happiness; to reach God is happiness itself. We follow after God by loving Him; we reach Him, not by becoming entirely what He is, but in nearness to Him, and in wonderful and immaterial contact with Him, and in being inwardly illuminated and occupied by His truth and holiness. . . . For those who love the Lord all things issue in good. . . . If, then, to those who love God all things issue in good, and if, as no one doubts, the chief or perfect good is not only to be loved, but to be loved so that nothing shall be loved better, as is expressed in the words, "With all thy soul, with all thy heart, and with all thy mind," who, I ask, will not at once conclude, when these things are all settled and most surely believed, that our chief good which we must hasten to arrive at in preference to all other things is nothing else than God?[150]

Where is it where we come near to God? Where are we illuminated? For Augustine it is through our mind and our understanding, that is, our intellect.

Now, as God also can be known by the worthy, only intellectually, exalted though He is above the intelligent mind as being its Creator and Author. . . . For the mind becomes like God, to the extent vouchsafed by its subjection of itself to Him for information and enlightenment. . . . The farther, then, the mind departs from God, not in space, but in affection and lust after things below Him, the more it is filled with folly and wretchedness. So by love it returns to God, a love which places it not along with God, but under Him . . . But then again, it must take care that it be not separated by the love of the other creature, that is, of this visible world, from the love of God Himself, which sanctifies it in order to lasting happiness.[151]

Things of this world can be distractions from the internal life and its pursuit of the love for God. The distractions can be quite serious because there is a clear link between the object of our desires and who we are as people. In short, we become like what we love. We become what our love is.[152] Thus Augustine speaks of being conformed to God and not the world. Note his consideration of living well and things internal in the following selection.

If, then, we ask what it is to live well . . . it must assuredly be to love virtue, to love wisdom, to love truth with all the heart, with all the soul, and with all the mind; virtue which is inviolable and immutable, wisdom which never gives place to folly, truth which knows no change or variation from its uniform character. Through this the Father Himself is seen, for it is said, "No man cometh unto the Father but by me." To this we cleave by sanctification. For when sanctified we burn with full and perfect love, which is the only security for our not turning away from God, and for our being conformed to Him rather than to this world. . . . It is through love, then, that we become conformed to God; and by this conformation, and configuration, and circumcision from this world we are not confounded with the things which are properly subject to us.[153]

The following excerpt is Augustine's famous reflection on temperance, fortitude, justice, and prudence, the classical virtues articulated by Plato in Book Four of his *Republic*. Virtues, writes Augustine, are possessed in the mind and control the body.[154] The object of the virtues, however, is not simply the self nor is it the public order. The object of the virtues according to Augustine is the love for God. Indeed if virtues "aim at any other purpose or possession than God," they "are in point of fact vices rather than virtues."[155] A commentator on the following text writes, "It would be difficult to find in Christian literature a more beautiful and satisfactory exposition of love of God. The Neo-Platonic influence is manifest, but it is Neo-Platonism thoroughly Christianized."[156]

> As to the virtue leading us to a happy life, I hold virtue to be nothing else than perfect love of God. For the fourfold division of virtue I regard as taken from four forms of love. For these four virtues (would that all felt their influence in their minds as they have their names in their mouths!), I should have no hesitation in defining them: that temperance is love giving itself entirely to that which is loved; fortitude is love readily bearing all things for the sake of the loved object; justice is love serving only the loved object, and therefore ruling rightly; prudence is love distinguishing with sagacity between what hinders it and what helps it. The object of this love is not anything, but only God, the chief good, the highest wisdom, the perfect harmony. So we may express the definition thus: that temperance is love keeping itself entire and incorrupt for God; fortitude is love bearing everything readily for the sake of God; justice is love serving God only, and therefore ruling well all else, as subject to man; prudence is loving making a right distinction between what helps it towards God and what might hinder it.[157]

He discusses each virtue in turn.

First, then, let us consider temperance, which promises us a kind of integrity and incorruption in the love by which we are united to God. The office of temperance is in restraining and quieting the passions which make us pant for those things which turn us away from the laws of God and from the enjoyment of His goodness, that is, in a word, from a happy life. . . . The whole duty of temperance, then, is to put off the old man, and to be renewed in God, that is, to scorn all bodily delights, and the popular applause, and to turn the whole love to things divine and unseen.[158]

If temperance is "not seeking earthy things," fortitude is "bearing the loss of them."[159] The most significant earthy thing for each of us is our own body. Augustine writes that the soul is shaken by the fear of toil, pain, and death, but he notes that the soul loves the body from the force of habit. Love for God transforms the natural love of the body and indeed transforms one's interpretation of suffering. It enables us to bear and even look forward to toil, pain, and death. Note again the role of the mind in love for God.

But when the soul turns to God wholly in this love, it knows these things, and so will not only disregard death, but will even desire it.

Then there is the great struggle with pain. But there is nothing, though of iron hardness, which the fire of love cannot subdue. And when the mind is carried up to God in this love, it will soar above all torture free and glorious, with wings beauteous and unhurt, on which chaste love rises to the embrace of God. Otherwise God must allow the lovers of gold, the lovers of praise, and the lovers of women, to have more fortitude than the lovers of Himself, though love in those cases is rather to be called passion or lust. And yet even here we may see with what force the mind presses on with unflagging energy, in spite of all alarms, towards what it loves; and we learn that we should bear all things rather than forsake God, since those men bear so much in order to forsake Him.[160]

On justice and prudence Augustine writes:

The lover, then, whom we are describing, will get from justice this rule of life, that he must with perfect readiness serve the God whom he loves, the highest good, the highest wisdom, the highest peace; and as regards all other things, must either rule them as subject to himself, or treat them with a view to their subjection. This rule of life, is, as we have shown, confirmed by the authority of both Testaments. . . . With equal brevity we must treat prudence, to which it belongs to discern between what is to be desired and what is to be shunned. . . . It is the part of prudence to keep watch with most anxious vigilance, lest any evil influence should stealthily creep in upon us.[161]

He concludes,

I need say no more about right conduct. For if in God is man's chief good, which you cannot deny, it clearly follows, since to seek the chief good is to live well, that to live well is nothing else but to love God with all the heart, with all the soul, with all the mind; and, as arising from this, that this love must be preserved entire and incorrupt, which is the part of temperance; that it give way before no troubles, which is the part of fortitude; that it serve no other, which is the part of justice; that it be watchful in its inspection of things lest craft or fraud steal in, which is the part of prudence. This is the one perfection of man, by which alone he can succeed in attaining to the purity of truth.[162]

CHAPTER FOUR

Mystical Love: Union with God

The sources for this chapter are medieval mystics. The medieval times, or the Middle Ages, are generally understood to be from 500 to 1500. This chapter includes a review of the theology of love from Bernard of Clairvaux, who lived from 1090 to 1153, Hadewijch, who wrote around 1220, and Julian of Norwich who lived from 1342 to 1416. These three writers are recognized as Christian mystics and as such they represent an important strand in the history of Christian reflection on love. We can follow the lead of Richard McBrien, who defines mysticism as "the graced transformation of the consciousness that follows upon a direct or immediate experience of the presence of God leading to deeper union with God."[1] Mystics experience God in a profound manner. In such experiences the mystic is said to have a deep and unique sense of union with or nearness to God. Mystical experiences include an enhanced state of knowledge as well as an enhanced sense of joy and fulfillment. The life of a mystic is changed and indeed charged by these experiences. Others would note the mystic's humility, devotion, service, and perhaps submissive suffering as enduring character traits.[2] The mystics addressed in this chapter speak movingly of God's love and thus offer a unique contribution to the Christian theology of love.

Bernard of Clairvaux

For when God loves, he wants nothing but to be loved; he loves for no other purpose than to be loved, knowing that those who love him are blessed by their very love."

—Bernard of Clairvaux, *On Loving God*

From the vantage point of the twenty-first century, Bernard of Clairvaux is a fascinating historical figure and a man of interesting contradictions. He was born into a family of the minor nobility in 1090 in the French town of Fontaines-les-

Dijon and died sixty-three years later on August 20, 1153, in the place with which he is forever identified, Clairvaux. The story of Bernard's life takes shape in the year IIII when he, along with thirty friends and relations who followed him, entered the "poor and obscure house of Citeaux" to join the Cistercian religious order.[3]

Jean Leclercq, the foremost authority on Bernard, writes of Bernard's ardor about joining the religious life. "His great enthusiasm made him unwilling to keep his ideal to himself and he managed to bring his uncle, his brothers, and a group of young noblemen to the same vocation. He even persuaded his sister, Humbeline, to leave her husband and become a nun."[4] Bernard was a bold, intelligent, and deeply religious man, and his leadership ability was soon recognized by the Cistercians. Just three years after he entered the monastery, he was sent out to found a new monastery at Clairvaux. By the time of his death some 164 monasteries across Europe were under his authority.

Bernard was not merely concerned with the growth and development of the Cistercian order. He was a spirited defender of the Christian faith. Indeed, Bernard wrote letters challenging both the King of France and the Pope. Bruno James comments, "From the first he was fearless in his condemnations of the folly and vice of those in high places. No one, no matter how exalted, was exempt from the sometimes very scathing rebukes of the young Abbott of Clairvaux."[5] As his reputation spread, Bernard soon found himself being consulted by bishops. The event that catapulted Bernard onto the wider public scene was in 1130. The Church was faced with a schism as the cardinals in Rome elected two popes on the same day, Innocent II and Anacletus.[6] James narrates, "for a time the fate of the two popes swung in the balance, but it was Bernard who turned the scales in favor of Innocent. He stormed through Europe persuading, encouraging, and threatening." Bernard tried to convince Emperor Lothair to support Innocent but the Emperor would only do so on the condition that he receive some benefit in return. James comments that Bernard "fearlessly rebuked" him "before all the assembled bishops, whereupon the Emperor quailed, and gave way."[7] Bernard worked for eight long years struggling to bring resolution to the schism, which ended with the death of Anacletus in 1138.

In 1139 Bernard was asked to challenge the theology of Peter Abelard publicly. Abelard (whom we will hear more about later in a quite different context) was a brilliant and creative theologian whose work pushed generally accepted theological notions. Bernard's theology, on the other hand, was conventional and conservative.[8] From Bernard's theological position, Gillian Evans writes, "it is more important not to rock the boat than to push the boat a little farther out to sea."[9] Bernard, and others, saw Abelard's innovations as a threat to the faith.

So under the direction of some religious authorities, Bernard attacked Abelard and Abelard's theology. Leclercq describes the exchange as an "intellectual tournament" that "brought together the two greatest minds of the time."[10] Yet the "tournament" did not remain solely on an intellectual level. It was a nasty exchange with both men condemning the other and both seeking backing by the Church. Leclercq comments that in the writing of both, "the violence of the tone is extreme."[11] In the end Bernard's aggressiveness and his "propaganda campaign"[12] of insults and accusations[13] eventually won, and the pope condemned Abelard's teaching. That Bernard was a man of passion is illustrated in the fervor and tactics he used in his debate with Abelard. We will see the same temperament in his writings on love.

In 1146, Pope Eugenius III, a Cistercian like Bernard, ordered Bernard to preach a Crusade. The Crusade was called to protect Christian places in the Holy Land from control by non-Christians. Bernard's job was to drum up support. He had to defend and encourage participation in an event that people would not necessarily be interested in. He called for a religious war, and that meant calling for recruits as well as monetary support. Bernard's preaching here was innovative. The previous crusade (proclaimed by Pope Urban II in 1095) was promoted by the Church with "the promise of indulgence, privileges, and other advantages" for participants and supporters. Bernard's theological motivation was different. He "described the Crusade as a spiritual undertaking, an opportunity to renounce sin and turn to God and to increase one's love for Jesus Christ."[14] The Crusade ended in disaster and Bernard, its main spokesperson, was blamed. It was the first time in his life Bernard was associated with a losing project.[15] James comments, "And so like many other great and holy men Bernard died under a cloud of disappointment and failure."[16]

Reading this brief narrative, one would think that Bernard's primary vocation was political activist. This is not the case. Bernard was a monk, who by vocation withdrew from the world. As a leader in the religious order, his work was to encourage others to develop their interior life. He was a contemplative as well as an activist. He was a man of contradictions, who spoke enthusiastically of loving God while advocating participation in war. Brian McGuire captures the ambiguity of Bernard's life in the title of his biography of Bernard, *The Difficult Saint.*[17]

Bernard's primary audience, for the texts we are considering, was the monks of his monasteries. He wanted to motivate the monks and encourage their spiritual experience. Leclercq describes the distinct genre within which Bernard works.

> The aim of ancient and medieval spiritual authors was not to provide food
> for reflection; rather, they sought to encourage an experience through rec-

ollections of a poetical nature. They gave free rein to their imagination in a way that to us, seems more like fantasy than thought. They wrote playfully of symbols and were given to variations on biblical themes that appear more rhapsodic than strictly theological.[18]

Leclercq continues, "The art of writing is the art of astonishing. Bernard knew this. He submitted himself to the demands of the profession. He sought effect."[19] Gillian Evans describes Bernard as an "affective and impulsive" writer. Leclercq writes, "We are dealing here with a poet, rather than a professor, who freely casts his ideas in every direction."[20]

Bernard's writings give us a strong example of the mystical love for God tradition. His theology had an enormous effect on the monastic tradition and Catholic mysticism. He also had some influence on the Protestant reformers, Martin Luther and John Calvin. One commentator refers to Bernard as Martin Luther's "theological mentor"; Bernard has over five hundred citations in Luther's works.[21] Another commentator observes that Calvin quotes Bernard often and favorably.[22] Bernard invites readers, medieval and modern, to think not only about abstract ideas of God but about our experiences of God. Gillian Evans writes, "Bernard's God is huge and present and compelling, and he ought to be the focus of the most gigantic of human passions; that is what he demands and what he rewards. At the same time he is gentle and tender and woos a love from his 'bride', the soul, which is freely given and infinitely pleasurable."[23]

The excerpts in this chapter are taken from two sources, Bernard's *Sermons on the Song of Songs*, started in 1135 and left unfinished at his death eighteen years later, and his Treatise *On Loving God*, written sometime between 1125 and 1141.[24] In the first chapter of this book, "Love in the Old Testament," we read the Song of Solomon or the Song of Songs and discussed it as a love poem, or series of love poems, between a man and a woman. During Bernard's time, the book was read much differently. For Bernard and his contemporaries, the appropriate interpretation of the Song of Songs was not literal but spiritual and allegorical. Thus in the following excerpts we hear Bernard giving spiritual meaning to language that we normally reserve for romantic or sexual love. In Bernard's interpretation of the Song of Songs, for example, the Bridegroom stands for Jesus and the Bride signifies the Church and the soul of the individual. Bernard likewise interprets other words found in the Song in a spiritual sense, words like kisses and intoxication.[25] Contemporary commentators on the Song of Songs do not recommend an allegorical interpretation. Unlike the traditional interpretation that Bernard so clearly represents, contemporary biblical scholars suggest that the book "refers to love between humans" and readers ought not give a transferred meaning to details in the poem.[26]

The excerpts from Bernard begin with his description of love from Sermon 83 of the *Sermons on the Song of Songs*.

> It is its own merit and its own reward. Love needs no cause, no fruit besides itself; its enjoyment is its use (Augustine, *De Doctrine Christiana* 1.1). I love because I love; I love that I may love. Love is a great thing; as long as it returns to its beginning, goes back to its origin, turns again to its source, it will always draw afresh from it and flow freely. In love alone, of all the movements of the soul and the senses and affections, can the creature respond to its Creator, if not with an equal, at least with a like return of gift for gift. For example, if God is angry with me, can I return his anger? Not at all; I shall be afraid and tremble and beg for his pardon. If he accuses me, I shall not return his accusation, but concede that he is right. If he judges me, I shall not judge him but adore him; and in saving me he does not seek to be saved by me in return, nor does he need to be set free by anyone in return when he frees all. If he commands it is for me to obey; if he gives me orders it is for me to do what he says and not ask service or obedience from the Lord in return. Now you see how different it is with love. For when God loves, he wants nothing but to be loved; he loves for no other purpose than to be loved, knowing that those who love him are blessed by their very love.[27]

Bernard notes that love is to be understood in relation to God. Yet God is not seen in all loves; this is because there are different levels or degrees of love. He continues here describing pure love.

> Love is a great thing, but there are degrees of love. The Bride stands at the high point. For children love, but they are thinking of their inheritance, and as long as they fear they may lose it in some way they honor more than love him from whom they hope to have it. I am suspicious of love which seems to be prompted by hope of gain. It is weak if when hope is gone it either vanishes or diminishes. It is impure when it desires something else, other than the beloved. Pure love does not hope for gain. Pure love does not draw its strength from hope; nor is it weakened by mistrust. Love is the very being of the Bride. She is full of it, and the Bridegroom is satisfied with it. He asks nothing else. That is why he is the Bridegroom and she the Bride. This love belongs only to them; no one else can share it, not even a child.[28]

The second verse of the first chapter of the Song of Songs reads "Let him kiss me with the kisses of his mouth." For Bernard the kiss is the Holy Spirit. Leclercq writes, "Christ gives the kiss to his spouse, the bride, whom he fills with the Spirit."[29] The bride is the Church and the individual's soul. The following excerpts are from Sermon 2 and Sermon 3.

> But he, the one whom they proclaim, let him speak to me, 'let him kiss me with the kiss of his mouth.' I have no desire that he should approach me in their person, or address me with their words, for they are 'a watery darkness, a dense cloud'; rather in his own person 'let him kiss me with the kiss of his mouth'; let him whose presence is full of love, from whom exquisite doctrines flow in streams, let him become 'a spring inside me, welling up to eternal life.' Shall I not receive a richer infusion of grace from him whom the Father has anointed with the oil of gladness above all his rivals, provided that he will bestow on me the kiss of his mouth? For his living, active word is to me a kiss, not indeed an adhering of the lips that can sometimes belie a union of hearts, but an unreserved infusion of joys, a revealing of mysteries, a marvelous and indistinguishable mingling of the divine light with the enlightened mind, which, joined in truth to God, is one spirit with him. . . . I must ask you to try to give your whole attention here. The mouth that kisses signifies the Word who assumes human nature; the nature assumed receives the kiss; the kiss however, that takes its being both from the giver and the receiver, is a person that is formed by both, none other than "the one mediator between God and mankind, himself a man, Christ Jesus."[30]

> A fertile kiss therefore, a marvel of stupendous self-abasement that is not a mere pressing of mouth upon mouth; it is the uniting of God with man. Normally the touch of lip on lip is the sign of the loving embrace of hearts, but this conjoining of natures brings together the human and divine, shows God reconciling "to himself all things, whether on earth or in heaven." "For he is the peace between us, and has made the two into one." This was the kiss for which just men yearned under the old dispensation, foreseeing as they did that in him they would "find happiness and a crown of rejoicing," because in him were hidden "all the jewels of wisdom and knowledge."[31]

> Today the text we are to study is the book of our own experience. You must therefore turn your attention inwards, each one must take note of his own particular awareness of the things I am about to discuss. I am attempting to discover if any of you has been privileged to say from his heart: "Let him kiss me with the kiss of his mouth." Those to whom it is given to utter these

words sincerely are comparatively few, but any one who has received this mystical kiss from the mouth of Christ at least once, seeks again that intimate experience, and eagerly looks for its frequent renewal. I think that nobody can grasp what it is except the one who receives it. For it is "a hidden manna," and only he who eats it still hungers for more. It is "a sealed fountain" to which no stranger has access; only he who drinks still thirsts for more.[32]

There are stages of kissing, stages in courtship. One kiss leads to another; a quick kiss leads to a more passionate kiss. Kissing often brings on more passion instead of settling passion. Yet there are appropriate levels of intimacy. Intimacy develops slowly over time. Evans comments, "The kissing of the foot is repentance. By the kissing of the hand, Christ raises man to newness of life. The kiss of the mouth is mystical union with Christ."[33]

> Though you have made a beginning by kissing the feet, you may not presume to rise at once by impulse to the kiss of the mouth; there is a step to be surmounted in between, an intervening kiss on the hand for which I offer the following explanation. If Jesus says to me: "Your sins are forgiven," what will it profit me if I do not cease from sinning? . . . For these various reasons I must confess that I am not entirely satisfied with the first grace by which I am enabled to repent of my sins; I must have the second as well, and so bear fruits that befit repentance, that I may not return like the dog to its vomit.
>
> I am now able to see what I must seek for and receive before I may hope to attain to a higher and holier State. I do not wish to be suddenly on the heights, my desire is to advance by degrees. The impudence of the sinner displeases God as much as the modesty of the penitent gives him pleasure. You will please him more readily if you live within the limits proper to you, and do not set your sights at things beyond you. It is a long and formidable leap from the foot to the mouth, a manner of approach that is not commendable. . . . First of all you must glorify him because he has forgiven your sins, secondly because he has adorned you with virtues.[34]

You have seen the way that we must follow, the order of procedure: first, we cast ourselves at his feet, we weep before the Lord who made us, deploring the evil we have done. Then we reach out for the hand that will lift us up, that will steady our trembling knees. And finally, when we shall have obtained these favors through many prayers and tears, we humbly dare to

raise our eyes to his mouth, so divinely beautiful, not merely to gaze upon
it, but—I say it with fear and trembling—to receive its kiss. "Christ the
Lord is a Spirit before our face," and he who is joined to him in a holy kiss
becomes through his good pleasure, one spirit with him.[35]

The soul experiences different emotions as its love for God matures. In the
early stages, it is fearful. Bernard compares the relationship between the soul and
God to that of a slave to a master. Fear moves to hope as love grows. Bernard
suggests that the soul then moves into a relationship with God much like that
of an employee to an employer. As love continues, the soul becomes like a disciple to a master and the predominant feeling is obedience. Later, the dominant
emotion is respect and the allegorical relationship is child to parent. Finally, the
deepest emotion is the true love found between spouses.[36]
    In simple but rich language, Bernard describes this level and the third kiss.

I should think that by now I have said enough about these two kisses, so
we shall pass on to the third. "Let him kiss me with the kiss of his mouth,"
she said. Now who is this "she"? The bride. But why bride? Because she is
the soul thirsting for God. In order to clarify for you the characteristics of
the bride, I shall deal briefly with the diverse affective relationships between
persons. Fear motivates a slave's attitude to his master, gain that of wage-
earner to his employer, the learner is attentive to his teacher, the son is re-
spectful to his father. But the one who asks for a kiss, she is a lover. Among
all the natural endowments of man love holds first place, especially when
it is directed to God, who is the source whence it comes. No sweeter names
can be found to embody that sweet interflow of affections between the
Word and the soul, than bridegroom and bride. Between these all things
are equally shared, there are no selfish reservations, nothing that causes division. They share the same inheritance, the same table, the same home,
the same marriage-bed, they are flesh of each other's flesh. "This is why a
man leaves his father and mother and joins himself to his wife, and they
become one body." The bride for her part is bidden to "forget her nation
and her ancestral home," so that the bridegroom may fall in love with her
beauty. Therefore if a love relationship is the special and outstanding characteristic of the bride and groom, it is not unfitting to call the soul that
loves God a bride. Now one who asks for a kiss is in love. It is not for liberty that she asks, nor for an award, not for an inheritance nor even knowledge, but for a kiss. It is obviously the request of a bride who is chaste, who
breathes forth a love that is holy, a love whose ardor she cannot entirely dis-

guise. For note how abruptly she bursts into speech. About to ask a great favor from a great personage, she does not resort, as others do, to the arts of seduction, she makes no devious or fawning solicitations for the prize that she covets. There is no preamble, no attempt to conciliate favor. No, but with a spontaneous outburst from the abundance of her heart, direct even to the point of boldness, she says: "Let him kiss me with the kiss of his mouth."

Does not this seem to you to indicate that she wished to say: "Whom have I in heaven but you? And there is nothing upon earth that I desire besides you."[37]

Love, desire, and indeed drunkenness are addressed in this final excerpt.

Her love is surely chaste when it seeks the person whom she loves, and not some other thing of his. It is a holy love, the impulse of an upright spirit rather than of carnal desire. And it is an ardent love, blinded by its own excess to the majesty of the beloved. For what are the facts? He is the one at whose glance the earth trembles, and does she demand that he give her a kiss? Can she be possibly drunk? Absolutely drunk! And the reason? It seems most probable that when she uttered those passionate words she had just come out from the cellar of wine; afterwards she boasts of having been there. David in his turn cried out to God concerning people such as the bride: "They shall be inebriated with the plenty of your house; and you will make them drink of the torrent of your pleasure." How great this power of love: what great confidence and freedom of spirit! What is more manifest than that fear is driven out by perfect love!

There is a certain modesty in the fact that she directs that utterance of hers not to the Bridegroom himself but to others, as if he were absent: "Let him kiss me," she exclaimed, "with the kiss of his mouth."[38]

When romantic relationships deepen in commitment the couples often think of marriage. In Sermon 85 Bernard writes:

The soul which has attained this degree now ventures to think of marriage. Why should she not, when she sees that she is like him and therefore ready for marriage? His loftiness has no terrors for her, because her likeness to him associates her with him, and her declaration of love is a betrothal. This is the form of that declaration: 'I have sworn and I purpose to keep your righteous judgements' (Ps. 118:106). The apostles followed this when they

said, 'See, we have left everything to follow you' (Matt. 19:27). There is a
similar saying which pointing to the spiritual marriage between Christ and
the Church, refers to physical marriage: 'For this shall a man leave his father and mother and be joined to his wife, and they two shall be one flesh'
(Eph. 5:31); and the prophet says of the Bride's glory: 'It is good to me to
cling to good, and to put my hope in the Lord.' (Ps. 72:28). When you see
a soul leaving everything (Luke 5:11) and clinging to the Word with all her
will and desire, living for the Word, ruling her life by the Word, conceiv-
ing by the Word what it will bring forth by him, so that she can say, 'For
me to live is Christ, and to die is gain', (Phil. 1:21) you know that the soul
is the spouse and bride of the Word. The heart of the Bride groom has faith
(Prov. 31:11) in her, knowing her to be faithful, for she has rejected all things
as dross to gain him (Phil. 3:8). He knows her to be like him of whom it
was said, 'He is a chosen vessel for me' (Acts 9:15). Paul's soul indeed was
like a tender mother and a faithful wife when he said, 'My little children,
with whom I travail in birth again, until Christ shall be formed in you'
(Gal. 4:11).[39]

Marriage usually leads to children and thus Bernard continues his allegory speaking of the offspring from spiritual marriage. Note how he distinguishes the love
for a spouse, and the intensity of the love between spouses, from the love of the
parent for the child.

But notice that in spiritual marriage there are two kinds of birth, and thus
two kinds of offspring, though not opposite. For spiritual persons, like holy
mothers, may bring souls to birth by preaching, or may give birth to spiritual insights by meditation. In this latter kind of birth the soul leaves even
its bodily senses and is separated from them, so that in her awareness of the
Word she is not aware of herself. This happens when the mind is enrap-
tured by the unutterable sweetness of the Word, so that it withdraws, or
rather is transported, and escapes from itself to enjoy the Word. The soul
is affected in one way when it is made fruitful by the Word, in another
when it enjoys the Word: in the one it is considering the needs of its neighbor; in the other it is allured by the sweetness of the Word. A mother is
happy in her child; a bride is even happier in her bridegroom's embrace.
The children are dear, they are pledge of his love, but his kisses give her
greater pleasure. It is good to save many souls but there is far more pleasure in going aside to be with the Word (2 Cor. 5:13). But when does this
happen, and for how long? It is sweet intercourse, but lasts a short time and

is experienced rarely! This is what I spoke of before, when I said that the final reason for the soul to seek the Word was to enjoy him in bliss.

There may be someone who will go on to ask me, "What does it mean to enjoy the Word?" I would answer that he must find someone who has experience of it, and ask him. Do you suppose, if I were granted that experience, that I could describe to you what is beyond description?[40]

It is Bernard's experience that one comes to truly love God slowly, in distinct stages and through much prayer. In his treatise, *On Loving God*, he describes four such stages.[41] Note that Bernard's stages of love, though focusing on the love of God, illustrate degrees of love or stages in love evident in interpersonal relationships. These stages are not different types of love; they express the developmental continuum of love. John Sommerfeldt comments, "Where does love begin? Bernard's answers seem equivocal. Love begins with empathy, love for others. Yet one cannot have empathy until one knows and loves oneself. But one cannot truly love oneself except in God. . . . For Bernard, all loves are part of one love which is the proper ordering of the will toward the good."[42]
The first degree of love, writes Bernard, is when a person loves oneself for one's own sake. He writes, "Since we are carnal and born of concupiscence of the flesh, our cupidity or love must begin with the flesh, and when this is set in order, our love advances by fixed degrees, led on by grace, until it is consummated in the spirit, for 'Not what is spiritual comes first, but what is animal then what is spiritual.'"[43] Bernard continues, "It is necessary that we bear first the likeness of an earthly being, then that of a heavenly being. Thus man first loves himself for himself because he is carnal and sensitive to nothing but himself."[44]

> Since nature has become more fragile and weak, necessity obliges man to serve it first. This is carnal love by which a man loves himself above all for his own sake. He is only aware of himself; as St Paul says: "What was animal came first, then what was spiritual." Love is not imposed by a precept; it is planted in nature. Who is there who hates his own flesh? . . . Yet should love, as it happens, grow immoderate, and, like a savage current, burst the banks of necessity, flooding the fields of delight, the overflow is immediately stopped by the commandment which says: "You shall love your neighbor as yourself." It is just indeed that he who shares the same nature should not be deprived of the same benefits, especially that benefit which is grafted in that nature. Should a man feel overburdened at satisfying not only his brethren's just needs but also their pleasures, let him restrain his own if he does not want to be a transgressor. He can be as indulgent as he likes for

himself providing he remembers his neighbor has the same rights. . . . Then your love will be sober and just if you do not refuse your brother that which he needs of what you have denied yourself in pleasure. Thus carnal love becomes social when it is extended to others. . . . Nevertheless, in order to love one's neighbor with perfect justice, "one must have regard to God. In other words, how can one love one's neighbor with purity, if one does not love him in God? But it is impossible to love in God unless one loves God. It is necessary, therefore, to love God first; then one can love one's neighbor in God." Thus God makes himself lovable and creates whatever else is good.[45]

From experience one learns that loving oneself for one's own sake is insufficient.

In this way, man who is animal and carnal, knows how to love only himself, yet starts loving God for his own benefit, because he learns from frequent experience that he can do everything that is good for him in God and that without God he can do nothing good.[46]

Elsewhere Bernard writes, "Then when he sees he cannot subsist by himself, he begins to seek for God by faith and to love him as necessary to himself."[47] Thus the second degree of love is when one loves God for one's own good.

Man, therefore, loves God, but for his own advantage and not yet for God's sake. Nevertheless, it is a matter of prudence to know what you can do by yourself and what you can do with God's help to keep from offending him who keeps you free from sin. If man's tribulations, however, grow in frequency and as a result he frequently turns to God and is frequently freed by God, must he not end, even though he had a heart of stone in a breast of iron, by realizing that it is God's grace which frees him and come to love God not for his own advantage but for the sake of God?[48]

The third degree of love is when one comes to love God for God's sake.

Thus man first loves himself for himself because he is carnal and sensitive to nothing but himself. Then when he sees he cannot subsist by himself, he begins to seek for God by faith and to love him as necessary to himself. So in the second degree of love, man loves God for man's sake and not for God's sake.

When forced by his own needs he begins to honor God and care for him by thinking of him, reading about him, praying to him, and obeying him, God reveals himself gradually in this kind of familiarity and consequently becomes lovable. When man tastes how sweet God is, he passes to the third degree of love in which man loves God not now because of himself but because of God. No doubt man remains a long time in this degree, and I doubt if he ever attains the fourth degree during this life, that is, if he ever loves only for God's sake.[49]

In another place Bernard writes:

Man's frequent needs oblige him to invoke God more often and approach him more frequently. This intimacy moves man to taste and discover how sweet the Lord is. Tasting God's sweetness entices us more to pure love than does the urgency of our own needs. Hence the example of the Samaritans who said to the woman who had told them the Lord was present: "We believe now not on account of what you said; for we have heard him and we know he is truly the Savior of the world." We walk in their footsteps when we say to our flesh, "Now we love God, not because of your needs; for we have tasted and know how sweet the Lord is." The needs of the flesh are a kind of speech, proclaiming in transports of joy the good things experienced. A man who feels this way will not have trouble in fulfilling the commandment to love his neighbor. He loves God truthfully and so loves what is God's. He loves purely and he does not find it hard to obey a pure commandment, purifying his heart, as it is written, in the obedience of love. He loves with justice and freely embraces the just commandment. This love is pleasing because it is free. It is chaste because it does not consist of spoken words but of deed and truth. It is just because it renders what is received. Whoever loves this way, loves the way he is loved, seeking in turn not what is his . . . but what belongs to Christ, the same way Christ sought not what was his, but what was ours, or rather, ourselves. He so loves who says: "Confess to the Lord for he is good." Who confesses to the Lord, not because he is good to him but because the Lord is good, truly loves God for God's sake and not for his own benefit. He does not love this way of whom it is said: "He will praise you when you do him favors." This is the third degree of love: in it God is already loved for his own sake.[50]

Bernard argues that the fourth and final degree of love is when one loves himself for the sake of God. Although he is suspicious about whether this level can be experienced in life, "No doubt man remains a long time in this degree [the third degree], and I doubt if he ever attains the fourth degree during this life, that is, if he ever loves only for God's sake."[51] Bernard is very descriptive of its characteristics but is at the same time suspects that one cannot reach this stage in this life. Perhaps some people have. The reader gets conflicting messages about Bernard's own experience here.[52]

> Happy the man who has attained the fourth degree of love, he no longer even loves himself except for God. . . . When will this sort of affection be felt that, inebriated with divine love, the mind may forget itself and become in its own eyes like a broken dish, hastening towards God and clinging to him, becoming one with him in spirit, saying: "My flesh and my heart have wasted away; O God of my heart, O God, my share for eternity." I would say that man is blessed and holy to whom it is given to experience something of this sort, so rare in life, even if it be but once and for the space of a moment. To lose yourself, as if you no longer existed, to cease completely to experience yourself, to reduce yourself to nothing is not a human sentiment but a divine experience.[53]

This love is, in a sense, natural, given the intention of God the creator.

> All the same, since Scripture says God made everything for his own purpose, the day must come when the work will conform to and agree with its Maker. It is therefore necessary for our souls to reach a similar state in which, just as God willed everything to exist for himself, so we wish that neither ourselves nor other beings to have been nor to be except for his will alone; not for our pleasure. The satisfaction of our wants, chance happiness, delights us less than to see his will done in us and for us, which we implore every day in prayer saying: " . . . your will be done on earth as it is in heaven . . . ." O pure and sacred love! O sweet and pleasant affection! O pure and sinless intention of the will, all the more sinless and pure since it frees us from the taint of selfish vanity, all the more sweet and pleasant, for all that is found in it is divine. It is deifying to go through such an experience.[54]

At this stage we love like God. Bernard suggests that the self disappears or dissolves in the will of God.

> As a drop of water seems to disappear completely in a big quantity of wine, even assuming the wine's taste and color; . . . just as red, molten iron becomes so much like fire it seems to lose its primary state; just as the air on

a sunny day seems transformed into sunshine instead of being lit up; so it is necessary for the saints that all human feelings melt in a mysterious way and flow into the will of God. Otherwise, how will God be all in all if something human survives in man? No doubt, the substance remains though under another form, another glory, another power.[55]

Those experiencing the fourth degree of love are free from their body in the sense that the torments of the flesh do not seem to affect the mind. The mind and the soul perceive the body in a new way. Although Bernard did not have a negative view of the body, part of moving up to the highest degree of love is mastering the impulses of the body.[56]

At the fourth level bodily impulses are fully mastered. Indeed the stage seems almost angelic. Evans comments, "Human virtue is marked by a freedom from enslavement to bodily desires and an ability to think without bodily assistance. The creature goes out of itself and transcends itself. Then the eyes of the mind 'see' internally, not prompted by outward things."[57]

I do not think that can take place for sure until the word is fulfilled: "You will love the Lord your God with all your heart, all your soul, and all your strength," until the heart does not have to think of the body and the soul no longer has to give it life and feeling as in this life. Freed from this bother, its strength is established in the power of God. For it is impossible to assemble all these and turn them toward God's face as long as the care of this weak and wretched body keeps one busy to the point of distraction. Hence it is in a spiritual and immortal body, calm and pleasant, subject to the spirit in everything, that the soul hopes to attain the fourth degree of love, or rather to be possessed by it; for it is in God's hands to give it to whom he wishes, it is not obtained by human efforts. I mean he will easily reach the highest degree of love when he will no longer be held back by any desire of the flesh or upset by troubles as he hastens with the greatest speed and desire toward the joy of the Lord. All the same, do we not think the holy martyrs received this grace, at least partially, while they were still in their victorious bodies? The strength of this love seized their souls so entirely that, despising the pain, they were able to expose their bodies to exterior torments. No doubt, the feeling of intense pain could only upset their calm; it could not overcome them. But what about those souls which are already separated from their bodies? We believe they are completely engulfed in that immense ocean of eternal light and everlasting brightness.[58]

Citing biblical passages from both Testaments, Bernard describes loving as a banquet with much food and much drink. Note how he uses the idea of drinking and being drunk found in the Song of Songs.

> This is what is meant by the Bridegroom in the Canticle saying: "Eat, my friends, and drink; dearest ones, be inebriated." Eat before death, drink after death, be inebriated after the resurrection. It is right to call them dearest who are drunk with love; they are rightly inebriated who deserve to be admitted to the nuptials of the Lamb, eating and drinking at his table in his kingdom when he takes his Church to him in her glory without a blemish, wrinkle, or any defect of the sort. By all means he will then intoxicate his dearest ones with the torrent of his delight, or in the Bridegroom and bride's most passionate yet most chaste embrace, the force of the river's current gives joy to the city of God. I think this is nothing other than the Son of God who in passing waits on us as he in a way promised: "The just are feasting and rejoicing in the sight of God, delighting in their gladness." Here is fullness without disgust; here is insatiable curiosity without restlessness; here is that eternal, inexplicable desire knowing no want. At last, here is that sober intoxication of truth, not from overdrinking, not reeking with wine, but burning for God. From this then that fourth degree of love is possessed forever, when God alone is loved in the highest way, for now we do not love ourselves except for his sake, that he may be the reward of those who love him, the eternal recompense of those who love him forever.[59]

Hadewijch

I wish to devote all my time to noble thoughts about great Love.
—Hadewijch, *Poems in Stanzas*

Very few details are known about the life of Hadewijch. She lived in The Netherlands probably in the first part of the thirteenth century. "Her main literary activity took place between 1220 and 1240, if not earlier."[60] Hadewijch was a beguine, a member of a woman's religious community. Beguines were often educated and from higher socioeconomic families. They were, however, not nuns. Like nuns, beguines lived lives of poverty and contemplation; however they did not take vows as did nuns. Columba Hart comments, "Apparently they rejected not only the narrow life of the lady in the castle, but the strict obliga-

tions of the nun in the cloister."[61] Apparently Hadewijch was a leader of a beguine community and some of her writings appear to be directed to the younger
members of the group. A fairly substantial body of her writing remains, including letters, poems (she wrote in stanzas and in couplets), as well as narratives of
her visions.

Hadewijch was consumed by love. Indeed, the "theme of love appears on
practically every page" of her writing.[62] Harvey Egan writes, "The main theme
throughout Hadewijch's writings is the tumultuous longing for the infinite joy
of possessing a God who is love. . . . She experienced that she became the brave
knight of divine Love who knows what love teaches with love and how love hon-
ors the loyal lover with love."[63] Her work fuses the love for God tradition we saw
in Bernard and Augustine with the elements of courtly love. She seems well
versed in each. Hart notes that just as Bernard "used the Song of Songs to express his own intimate and personal experience of God, Hadewijch used the poetry of courtly love to express the emotional tensions of the longing for God."[64]
In Hadewijch secular images are given spiritual meaning. In place of courtly
love's service to the lady, Hadewijch placed service of the soul to God. At times
Hadewijch saw herself as a knight "courting dangers and adventures" in God's
honor "riding down the roads of the land of love."[65] The distance between the
beloved and the lover, that is, the unattainability of the lover in courtly love, images perfectly the distance between the soul and God. Hadewijch does not, however, simply repeat what others said before her. She formed a new genre of mystical love or love mysticism.[66] "Love mysticism contends that God allows himself
to be experienced as Love by a person who ardently desires to love and to be
united with God in this life."[67] Indeed an authority on her work suggests she is
"one of the loftiest figures in the Western mystical tradition."[68] Like Bernard, she
gives personal experience a privileged position in her writings.

The word Hadewijch uses for love (she wrote in Flemish) was *minne. Minne,*
a feminine word, means the dynamic love of a person for God.[69] The word suggests "the union with God on earth as a love relationship."[70] It is "the way the
soul experiences its relation to God."[71] This love does not come easily. It takes
time and experience. Hadewijch marks the time in twelve stages, or hours. These
hours fall into three categories. During the first four hours the mind seeks to
know love. Love is something one continually strives for, but something that
continually brings suffering. Indeed she describes these hours as "unspeakable."
Why does she use this term, a term one would associate with something negative when she talks about love? Her reason for this is that "our longing for God
is an agony of desire in which we sense our own finite limitations, our inability

to be fully united with the beloved." In her communications with the younger beguines, "she counsels patience in spiritual growth and likens the growth of the love of God who is Love Itself as carrying a pregnancy to term."[72] There is a necessary link between love and suffering. Hadewijch recalls that Jesus freely accepted suffering and "we likewise must accept human misery and sufferings because he did so."[73] She believes that suffering and perseverance help us attain deep love for God.[74] Love, for Hadewijch, this dynamic love for God, is a paradox. A consequence of love is pain and suffering as well as a strong desire to have more love and deeper love. The beloved is present but distant and the lover can do nothing but live for this love.[75]

> The nature from which true love springs has twelve hours which drive love out of herself and bring her back in herself. And when love comes back in herself she brings with her all that makes the unspeakable hours drive her out of herself: a mind that seeks to know, a heart full of desire, and a soul full of love. And when love brings these back she throws them into the abyss of the mighty nature in which she was born and nurtured. Then the unspeakable hours enter nature unknown. Then love has come to herself and rejoices in her nature, below, above, and around. And all those who stay below this knowledge shudder at those who have fallen into the abyss and work there and live and die. For such is love's command and her nature.[76]
>
> In the first unspeakable hour of the twelve that draw the soul into love's nature, love reveals herself and touches the soul unexpected and uninvited when her nobility leads us to least suspect it. No matter how strong-natured, the soul fails to understand, for this is truly an unspeakable hour.
>
> In the second unspeakable hour love makes the heart taste a violent death, and the heart goes through death, but it does not die. And yet the soul has not known love for long, and has barely moved from the first to the second hour.
>
> In the third unspeakable hour love shows how one may die and live in her, and how one cannot love without great suffering.
>
> In the fourth unspeakable hour love makes the soul taste her hidden designs, which are deep and darker than the abyss. Then love reveals how miserable the soul is without love. But the soul does not yet partake of love's nature. This hour is truly unspeakable, for the beloved is made to accept love's designs before he possesses love.[77]

In the next stage, the fifth through eight hours, we move from the mind seeking to understand to the desire of the heart.

In the fifth unspeakable hour love seduces the heart and the soul, and the soul is driven out of herself and out of love's nature and back into love's nature. The soul has then ceased to wonder about the power and darkness of love's designs, and has forgotten the pains of love. Then the soul knows love only through love herself, which may seem lower but is not. For where knowledge is most intimate the beloved knows least.

In the sixth unspeakable hour love despises reason and all that lies within reason and above it and below. Whatever belongs to reason stands against the blessed state of love. For reason cannot take away anything from love or bring anything to love, for love's true reason is a flood that rises forever and knows no peace.

In the seventh unspeakable hour nothing can dwell in love or touch her except desire. And touch is love's most secret name, and touch springs from love herself. For love is always touch and desire and feasts on herself forever. Yet love is perfect in herself.

Love cannot dwell in all things. Love can dwell in charity, but charity cannot dwell in love. Mercy and humility cannot dwell in love, nor can reason or fear, hardship or moderation, or any other thing. But love dwells in them all and gives them all sustenance, though she receives no other food than the wholeness of herself.

The eighth unspeakable hour brings bewilderment when the beloved learns that he cannot know love's nature from her face. Yet the face is held to reveal the inmost nature, and that is most hidden in love. For that she is herself in herself. Love's other limbs and her works are easier to know and understand.[78]

The final level describes the loving soul. The language is not clear, perhaps indicating the gap between the lover and the beloved, between the soul and God.

The ninth unspeakable hour brings love's fiercest storm, harshest touch, and deepest desires. The face is sweetest there, at peace, and most winsome. And the deeper love wounds the one she assails, the sweeter she drowns him in herself with the soft splendor of her face. And there she shows herself in her loveliness.

The tenth unspeakable hour is that when no one judges love, but when love judges all things. From God she takes the power to judge all she loves. Love does not yield to saints or men, or angels, heaven or earth, and she enfolds the divine in her nature. To love she calls the hearts who love, in a voice that is loud and untiring. The voice has great power and it tells of things more terrible than thunder. This word is the rope love uses to bind her prisoners, this is the sword she turns on those whom she touches, it is the rod she uses to chastise her children, this is the craft she teaches her companions.

In the eleventh unspeakable hour love possesses the beloved by force. For not a moment can he stray from her, or his heart desire or his soul love. And love makes the memory shrink and the beloved cannot think of saints or men, or angels, heaven or earth, God or himself, but of love alone who has possessed him in a present ever new.

In the twelfth unspeakable hour love is the likeness of her uppermost nature. Only now she breaks out of herself and she works with herself and sinks deep in herself, utterly satisfied with her nature. She fully rejoices in herself, and even if no one loved her the name of love would give her enough loveliness in the nature of her splendid self. Her name which is her nature inside her, her name which is her works outside her, her name which is her crown above her, her name which is the soil under her.

These are the twelve unspeakable hours of love. For in none of the twelve can love be understood, except by those I mentioned, those who have been thrown into the abyss of love's mighty nature and those who belong there, and they believe in love more than they understand her.[79]

Love is a dramatic and dominant theme in her poetry. The selections below are representative of her work and her ideas.

31.1. I wish to devote all my time
To noble thoughts about great Love.
For she, with her infinite strength,
So enlarges my heart
That I have given myself over to her completely,
To obtain within me the birth of her high being.
But if I wish to take free delights,
She casts me into her prison!

31.2. I fancied I would suffer without harm,
Being thus fettered in love,
If she willed to make me understand
All the narrowest paths of her requirements.
But if I think of reposing in her grace,
She storms at me with new commands.

She deals her blows in a wonderful way:
The greater her love, the more crushing her burden![80]

32.1. In Love, I place my salvation,
And my power in her hands;
I demand no other consolation from her
Than to remain wholly in her chains.[81]

32.4. Love is master of contraries;
She is ready to give bitter and sweet;
Since I first experienced the taste of her,
I lie at her feet continually;
I pray her it may be her pleasure
That I endure, for her honor's sake,
Suffering, to the death, without recovery,
And I will not complain of it to aliens.[82]

32.8. People are afraid of any pains in love
Certainly cannot understand
What can be won by souls
Who are always submissive to Love,
Who receive from her hand heavy blows
Of which they remain wholly unhealed.
And who mount on high and are knocked down again
Before they please Love.[83]

33.3. But they who spare any pain for Love,
Thus betraying his baseness,
And expect profit from joys unrelated to love,
Inevitably find the service burdensome.[84]

34.2. Bitter and dark and desolate
Are Love's ways in the beginning of love;
Before anyone is perfect in Love's service,
He often becomes desperate:
Yet where we imagine losing, it is all gain.
How can one experience this?
By sparing neither much nor little,
But giving oneself totally in love.[85]

34.4. In love no action is lost
That was ever performed for Love's sake;
Love always repays, late or soon;
Love is always the reward of love.
Love knows with love the courtly manners of Love;
Her receiving is always giving;
Not least she gives by her adroitness
Many a death in life.[86]

37.11. Love wills that the loving soul lovingly demand total love.
She has set up her highest banner.
From this we learn what kind of works she requires,
With clear truth and without doubt.

37.13 Love wills all love from noble spirits,
And that they bring their works into conformity with it,
And that they rejoice with memory
And delight in Love with joy.
Praise and honor be to Love,
To her great power, to her rich teaching;
And by her consolation may she heal the pain
Of all who gladly brave Love's vicissitudes.[87]

Julian of Norwich

It is true that sin is the cause of all this suffering, but all shall be well, and
all shall be well, and all manner of things shall be well."
—Julian, *Revelations of Divine Love*

This section contains the writings of a person who wished to remain anonymous.
We do not know her name and we know nothing of her background. She is called
Julian of Norwich because she spent the last twenty years of her life in a small
house attached to the church of St. Julian in Norwich, England. Julian was a mystic; her life was one of meditation, prayer, and advising others in the spiritual life.
A singular event catapulted her life into history. On May 8, 1373, she received a
series of visions, which she referred to as "showings." "The showings were so compelling and so rich in meaning that Julian understood them to come directly from
God and to be messages not just to herself but to all Christians."[88] Julian recorded
the visions in the book *Showings* (also known as *Revelations of Divine Love*) and

in doing so became the first woman English writer. Twenty years later, after much prayer and reflection on the meanings of the showings, she finished a longer version. A. C. Spearing comments, "Julian is manifestly a woman of exceptional intelligence, and she shows not just an understanding of theology, the province of learned male clerics, but a capacity for powerful new theological thought; moreover, her prose, while owing much to speech, is distinctive and distinguished."[89]

Julian was born in 1342, five years after the start of the Hundred Years War and six years before the outbreak of the Black Death, which is said to have killed a third of the population of Europe. As a young woman she prayed to receive three graces from God. She desired "to have an understanding of Christ's passion; to experience bodily suffering when she turned thirty (the same age as Christ when he began his public life); and to have the three 'wounds' of contrition, compassion and earnest longing for God."[90] In May 1373, when she was just over thirty years old, she became very ill. A priest visited her on what seemed to be her deathbed. As he held a crucifix up for her to gaze upon, her pain ceased and she experienced the fifteen showings. Julian saw Jesus in excruciating agony expressing his love for all. In the concluding chapter of *Showings*, after fully describing her visions, Julian writes.

> And from the time that it was revealed, I desired many times to know in what was our Lord's meaning. And fifteen years after and more, I was answered in spiritual understanding, and it was said: What, do you wish to know our Lord's meaning in this thing? Know it well, love was his meaning. Who reveals it to you? Love. What did he reveal to you? Love. Why does he reveal it to you? For love. Remain in this, and you will know more of the same. But you will never know differently, without end.[91]

The striking message one gets from reading Julian is the incredible and gentle, everlasting and comforting love of God. Julian speaks of her experience of this great love in a "homey" or, in her words, "homely" way. God's love is fully affirming, accepting, and familiar. Thus Julian describes the "hideous" vision of the bleeding Jesus as sweet, lovely, comforting and courteous.[92] Indeed Jesus loves us so much that he would happily go through the passion and crucifixion every day for us.[93]

The following excerpts are from the longer version of *Showings*:

> And at this, suddenly I saw the red blood running down from under the crown, hot and flowing freely and copiously, living stream, just as it was at the time when the crown of thorns was pressed on his blessed head.[94]

The great drops of blood fell from beneath the crown like pellets. Looking as if they came from the veins. And as they issued they were a brown-
ish red. For the blood was very thick, and as they spread they turned bright
red. And as they reached the brows they vanished; and even so the bleeding continued until I had seen and understood many things.[95]

I saw that he is to us everything which is good and comforting for our help.
He is our clothing, who wraps and enfolds us for love, embraces us and
shelters us, surrounds us for his love, which is so tender that he may never
desert us. And so in this sight I saw that he is everything which is good, as
I understand.

And in this he showed me something small, no bigger than a hazel-
nut, lying in the palm of my hand, as it seemed to me, and it was as
round as a ball. I looked at it with the eye of my understanding and
thought: What can this be? I was amazed that it could last. For I thought
that because of its littleness it would suddenly have fallen into nothing.
And I was answered to my understanding: It lasts and always will, because God loves it; and thus everything has being through the love of
God.

In this little thing I saw three properties. The first is that God made
it, the second is that God loves it, the third is that God preserves it.[96]

The message of this love is a clear and solid affirmation even in our sin. Indeed there was never a time that God "began" to love us. God has loved us since
before time began.[97]

And because of the tender love which our good Lord has for all who will
be saved, he comforts readily and sweetly, meaning this: It is true that sin
is the cause of all this pain, but all will be well, and every kind of thing will
be well.[98]

So it would be most unkind of me to blame God or marvel at him on account of my sins, since he does not blame me for sin.[99]

Though our Lord revealed to me that I should sin, by me is understood
everyone. And in this I conceive a gentle fear, and in answer to this our
Lord said: I protect you very safely. This word was said with more love and
assurance of protection for my soul than I can or may tell.[100]

And our Lord revealed this to me in the completeness of his love, that we are standing in his sight, yes, that he loves us now whilst we are here as well as he will when we are there, before his blessed face; but all our travail is because love is lacking on our side.[101]

Peace and love are always in us, living and working, but we are not always in peace and in love; but he wants us to take heed that he is the foundation of our whole life in love, and furthermore that he is our everlasting protector, and mightily defends us against our enemies, who are very cruel and very fierce towards us.[102]

Reflection on God's love gives Julian insight into the nature of God.

For this was revealed, that our life is all founded and rooted in love, and without love we cannot live. And therefore to the soul which by God's special grace sees so much of his great and wonderful goodness as that we are endlessly united to him in love, it is the most impossible thing which could be that God might be angry, for anger and friendship are two contraries; for he dispels and destroys our wrath and makes us meek and mild—we must necessarily believe that he is always one in love, meek and mild, which is contrary to wrath.[103]

And for the great endless love that God has for all mankind, he makes no distinction in love between the blessed soul of Christ and the least soul that will be saved . . . where the blessed soul of Christ is, there is the substance of all the souls which will be saved by Christ.[104]

As to the first, I saw and understood that the high might of the Trinity is our Father, and the deep wisdom of the Trinity is our Mother, and the great love of the Trinity is our Lord; and all these we have in nature and in our substantial creation. And furthermore I saw that the second person, who is our Mother, substantially the same beloved person, has now become our mother sensually.[105]

So Jesus Christ, who opposes good to evil, is our true Mother. We have our being from him, where the foundation of motherhood begins, with all the sweet protection of love which endlessly follows. As truly as God is our Father, so truly God is our Mother.[106]

The mother's service is nearest, readiest and surest: nearest because it is most natural, readiest because it is most loving, and surest because it is truest.[107]

The mother can give her child to suck of her milk, but our precious Mother Jesus can feed us with himself, and does, most courteously and most tenderly, with the blessed sacrament, which is the precious food of true life.[108]

The mother can lay her child tenderly to her breast, but our tender Mother Jesus can lead us easily into his blessed breast through his sweet open side, and show us there a part of the godhead and of the joys of heaven.[109]

To the property of motherhood belong nature, love, wisdom and knowledge, and this is God.[110]

The kind, loving mother who knows and sees the need of her child guards it very tenderly, as the nature and condition of motherhood will have. And always as the child grows in age and in stature, she acts differently, but she does not change her love. And when it is even older, she allows it to be chastised to destroy its faults, so as to make the child receive virtues and grace. This work, with everything which is lovely and good, our Lord performs in those by whom it is done. So he is our Mother.[111]

CHAPTER FIVE

Troubadours and Troubled Romance

R eading the mystics one might get the idea that the talk of love among Christians in the Middle Ages focused on God's intense love for people and the attempt of Christians to seek union with God. This chapter suggests otherwise. The first section describes the phenomenon of courtly love. Courtly love developed during the twelfth century, around the time of Bernard. It had an immense impact during the Middle Ages, as its songs and stories entertained people for centuries. Indeed, St. Ignatius Loyola, writing in 1530s, lamented the amount of time he spent as a youth reading such romances. A biographer of Ignatius wrote, however, that the ideals of courtly love, "courage, generosity, fidelity, courtesy, honor and truthfulness," influenced Ignatius "all the days of his life."[1] The phenomenon of courtly love was contemporaneous with the love for God tradition, yet contrasts with it in many ways. The second section of the chapter narrates the famous love story of Heloise and Abelard. Their relationship, which embodied features of courtly love, was an illicit affair marked by scandal and suffering. It is here that we read for the first time in this book the writings of a woman on romantic love. As Heloise exchanges letters with Abelard, one cannot help but wonder if women and men think differently about the meaning of love.

Courtly Love

A true lover is constantly and without intermission possessed by the thought of his beloved.
—Andreas Capellanus, *The Art of Courtly Love*

As Bernard developed his upward-looking transcendent love in the monastery, there was a strong movement among lay people in the courts and castles toward developing an outward-looking romantic love. The phenomenon has come to be called "courtly love."[2] The story of the development of courtly love, beginning in southern France during the twelfth century and spreading throughout Europe during the next 200 years, is quite interesting. The sources are obscure, although commentators often cite two influences, the work of the first century B.C.E. Roman poet Ovid, and the eleventh century Moslem author Ibn Hazam.[3] Indeed some have speculated that Bernard's mysticism may have contributed to this movement.[4] Whatever the origins, the phenomenon of courtly love stands in both radical contrast to, as well as partial continuity with, accepted Christian practices of the day. Some commentators have suggested that indeed it might be more of a satire than an expression of a movement because courtly love is quite ironic. On the one hand, it claims moral high ground as it celebrates virtue expressed in such terms as service, humbleness, and faithfulness between lovers. On the other hand, this virtue is said to form within illicit, often adulterous, love affairs.

In an age when women were subservient to men, courtly love raised the beloved, the lady, onto a pedestal. The man was expected to serve his love without question and to meet any challenge or obstacle to win her love. Service and chivalry were foundational virtues of courtly love. C. S. Lewis writes, "The lover is always abject. Obedience to his lady's lightest wish, however whimsical, and silent acquiescence in her rebukes, however unjust, are the only virtues he dares to claim."[5] Courtly love praised the glories of impossible and secret loves, a knight for a queen, for an example. In doing so it advocated adultery. Note that people of this time did not generally marry for love. Most marriages came about as a result of negotiations between the man and the woman's father and were thus based on an agreement or contract rather than love.[6] Courtly love celebrated sensuality in an age that considered sensuality a hindrance to union with God.[7] This sensuality was more reserved, however, than our contemporary notions of sex. Romance in courtly love was marked by dedication and secrecy. Instead of instant gratification we hear about suffering love and a longing heart. Irving Singer describes courtly love as a "humanization of Christian and Platonic love."[8] He writes, "What the transcendental idealizations had tried to achieve by getting beyond nature, courtly love duplicated on the level of human relations in nature. Not God or the Good but other men and women became objects of devotion."[9] Even though there are these rather large differences between courtly love and mystical love, this is not to say that there were not parallels. In place of the theologian, courtly love has the troubadour. Instead of God (or in some instances Mary), courtly love posits the lady. In place of the monastery, monks, and contemplation, courtly love speaks of the courts, knights, and battle.

The troubadours are credited with spreading courtly love through Europe. They were traveling entertainers. "A clever singer, full of soap-operalike stories and bloodcurdling adventures, was a welcome guest"[10] among the aristocracies of Europe. Diane Ackerman writes, "Thanks to the troubadours, affairs of the heart became a favorite theme of poetic sagas, and so the love story first entered European literature."[11] Lewis describes the effects of the troubadour love poetry as a revolution in literature. He writes:

> It seems—or it seemed to us till lately—a natural thing that love (under certain conditions) should be regarded as a noble and ennobling passion; it is only if we imagine ourselves trying to explain this doctrine to Aristotle, Virgil, St. Paul, or the author of *Beowulf*, that we become aware how far from natural it is. Even our code of etiquette, with its rule that women always have precedence, is a legacy from courtly love, and is felt to be far from natural in modern Japan or India. . . . French poets, in the eleventh century, discovered or invented, or were the first to express, that romantic species of passion. . . .They effected a change which has left no corner of our ethics, our imagination, or our daily life untouched.[12]

The defining ideals of courtly love are associated with Queen Eleanor of Aquitaine and her daughter Countess Marie. The most famous manuscript on courtly love was written around 1186 at the request of Countess Marie by Andreas Capellanus, a chaplain in her court. Capellanus' book is a detailed analysis of love. He gives rules of love, characteristics of love, case studies of love, precise directions on who may love and how to keep love. He begins his treatise defining his subject matter. Note the role of suffering, of anguish of the heart, so present in his view of love. Also note how this love differs from platonic love. Recall Plato's ladder of love. At an early stage, one is to love the beauty of a particular other person, but this is just a step to loving absolute beauty. Courtly love extols and exalts the beauty of the particular other.

> Love is a certain inborn suffering derived from the sight of and excessive meditation upon the beauty of the opposite sex, which causes each one to wish above all things the embraces of the other and by common desire to carry out all of love's precepts in the other's embrace.
>
> That love is suffering is easy to see, for before the love becomes equally balanced on both sides there is no torment greater, since the lover is always in fear that his love may not gain its desire and that he is wasting his efforts. He fears, too, that rumors of it may get abroad, and he fears everything that might harm it in any way, for before things are perfected a slight disturbance often spoils them. If he is a poor man, he also fears that the woman

may scorn his poverty; if he is ugly, he fears that she may despise his lack of beauty or may give her love to a more handsome man; if he is rich, he fears that his parsimony in the past may stand in his way. To tell the truth, no one can number the fears of one single lover. This kind of love, then, is a suffering which is felt by only one of the persons and may be called "single love." But even after both are in love the fears that arise are just as great, for each of the lovers fears that what he has acquired with so much effort may be lost through the effort of someone else, which is certainly much worse for a man than if, having no hope, he sees that his efforts are accomplishing nothing, for it is worse to lose the things you are seeking than to be deprived of a gain you merely hope for. The lover fears, too, that he may offend his loved one in some way; indeed he fears so many things that it would be difficult to tell them.

That this suffering is inborn I shall show you clearly, because if you will look at the truth and distinguish carefully you will see that it does not arise out of any action; only from the reflection of the mind upon what it sees does this suffering come. For when a man sees some woman fit for love and shaped according to his taste, he begins at once to lust after her in his heart; then the more he thinks about her the more he burns with love, until he comes to a fuller meditation. Presently he begins to think about the fashioning of the woman and to differentiate her limbs, to think about what she does, and to pry into the secrets of her body, and he desires to put each part of it to the fullest use. Then after he has come to this complete meditation, love cannot hold the reins, but he proceeds at once to action; straightway he strives to get a helper and to find an intermediary. He begins to plan how he may find favor with her, and he begins to seek a place and a time opportune for talking; he looks upon a brief hour as a very long year, because he cannot do anything fast enough to suit his eager mind. It is well known that many things happen to him in this manner. This inborn suffering comes, therefore, from seeing and meditating. Not every kind of meditation can be the cause of love, an excessive one is required for a restrained thought does not, as a rule, return to the mind, and so love cannot arise from it.[13]

Capellanus looks to the root meaning of love to explore the term.

Love gets its name (amor) from the word for hook (amus), which means "to capture" or "to be captured," for he who is in love is captured in the chains of desire and wishes to capture someone else with his hook. Just as a skillful fisherman tries to attract fishes by his bait and to capture them on his crooked hook, so the man who is a captive of love tries to attract another person by his allurements and exerts all his efforts to unite two different hearts with an intangible bond, or if they are already united he tries to keep them so forever.[14]

Love has dramatic effects upon a person; it transforms the lover. It turns him into a new man. Love strengthens one's moral character and makes one a person of high moral standards.

Now it is the effect of love that a true lover cannot be degraded with any avarice. Love causes a rough and uncouth man to be distinguished for his handsomeness; it can endow a man even of the humblest birth with nobility of character; it blesses the proud with humility; and the man in love becomes accustomed to performing many services gracefully for everyone. O what a wonderful thing is love, which makes a man shine with so many virtues and teaches everyone, no matter who he is, so many good traits of character! There is another thing about love, that we should not praise in few words: it adorns a man, so to speak, with the virtue of chastity, because he who shines with the light of one love can hardly think of embracing another woman, even a beautiful one. For when he thinks deeply of his beloved the sight of any other woman seems to his mind rough and rude.[15]

People are attracted to one another five ways, writes Capellanus, through beauty, character, cleverness, wealth, and the "readiness with which one grants that which is sought."[16] He rejects the latter two out of hand and then shows why loving because of beauty or cleverness does not last. Both men and women ought to seek lovers for their character. Women ought to beware of a man "who anoints himself all over" and "makes a rite of the care of the body."[17] Men ought to be weary of a woman who wears much makeup because a "woman who puts all her reliance on her rouge usually doesn't have any particular gifts of character."[18] Capellanus concludes, "Character alone, then, is worthy of the crown of love."[19]

Twice in *The Art of Courtly Love*, Capellanus lists the rules of love. The first list cites twelve and the second cites thirty-one. Both are said to be from the King of Love. Here is the first list:

I. Thou shalt avoid avarice like the deadly pestilence and shalt embrace its opposite.

II. Thou shalt keep thyself chaste for the sake of her whom thou lovest.

III. Thou shalt not knowingly strive to break up a correct love affair that someone else is engaged in.

IV. Thou shalt not choose for thy love anyone whom a natural sense of shame forbids thee to marry.

V. Be mindful completely to avoid falsehood.

VI. Thou shalt not have many who know of thy love affair.

VII. Being obedient in all things to the commands of ladies, thou shalt ever strive to ally thyself to the service of Love.

VIII. In giving and receiving love's solaces let modesty be ever present.

IX. Thou shalt speak no evil.

X. Thou shalt not be a revealer of love affairs.

XI. Thou shalt be in all things polite and courteous.

XII. In practicing the solaces of love thou shalt not exceed the desires of thy lover.[20]

Here is the second list.

I. Marriage is no real excuse for not loving.

II. He who is not jealous cannot love.

III. No one can be bound by a double love.

IV. It is well known that love is always increasing or decreasing.

V. That which a lover takes against the will of his beloved has no relish.

VI. Boys do not love until they arrive at the age of maturity.

VII. When one lover dies, a widowhood of two years is required of the survivor.

VIII. No one should be deprived of love without the very best of reasons.

IX. No one can love unless he is impelled by the persuasion of love.

X. Love is always a stranger in the home of avarice.

XI. It is not proper to love any woman whom one would be ashamed to seek to marry.

XII. A true lover does not desire to embrace in love anyone except his beloved.

XIII. When made public love rarely endures.

XIV. The easy attainment of love makes it of little value; difficulty of attainment makes it prized.

XV. Every lover regularly turns pale in the presence of his beloved.

XVI. When a lover suddenly catches sight of his beloved his heart palpitates.

XVII. A new love puts to flight an old one.

XVIII. Good character alone makes any man worthy of love.

XIX. If love diminishes, it quickly falls and rarely revives.

XX. A man in love is always apprehensive.

XXI. Real jealousy always increases the feeling of love.

XXII. Jealousy, and therefore love, are increased when one suspects his beloved.

XXIII. He whom the thought of love vexes eats and sleeps very little.

XXIV. Every act of a lover ends in the thought of his beloved.

XXV. A true lover considers nothing good except what he thinks will please his beloved.

XXVI. Love can deny nothing to love.

XXVII. A lover can never have enough of the solaces of his beloved.

XXVIII. A slight presumption causes a lover to suspect his beloved.

XXIX. A man who is vexed by too much passion usually does not love.

XXX. A true lover is constantly and without intermission possessed by the thought of his beloved.

XXXI. Nothing forbids one woman being loved by two men or one man by two women.[21]

Abelard and Heloise

Our desires left no stage of lovemaking untried.
—Abelard, *Historica calamitatum*

God is my witness to the depth of my love. Even if Augustus, ruler of the entire world, thought me worthy of the honor of marriage and gave me the whole world for my possession, I would consider it more valuable and more of an honor to be called your whore than to be called his empress.
—Heloise, "The First Letter of Heloise to Abelard"

There was in Paris at the time a young girl named Heloise, the niece of Fulbert, one of the canons, and so much loved by him that he had done everything in his power to advance her education in letters. In looks she did not rank lowest, while in the extent of her learning she stood supreme. A gift for letters is so rare in women that it added greatly to her charm and had won her renown throughout the realm. I considered all the usual attractions for a lover and decided she was the one to bring to my bed, confident that I should have an easy success; for at that time I had youth and exceptional good looks as well as my great reputation to recommend me, and feared no rebuff from any woman I might choose to honor with my love.[22]

So Peter Abelard describes the beginnings of his infamous relationship with Heloise. Abelard, born in Brittany in 1079, was a man who "had it all." Thought of by many as a brilliant intellectual, he opened his own school, complete with tuition-paying students, at age twenty-two. By his mid-thirties he was head of the prestigious Cloister School of Notre Dame in Paris. Abelard was as eloquent as he was bright. Betty Radice comments, "All accounts agree that he was a wonderful teacher, with a rare gift for kindling enthusiasm in his pupils and inspiring devotion."[23] He was moreover a talented poet and songwriter. Ackerman describes him as "the pluperfect professor, superstar, hunk."[24]

It so happened that Heloise, at age seventeen, had finished the highest level of education available for a woman at the time. Her uncle, who was her guardian (she may have been an orphan) wanted her to continue studies. He thus looked for a tutor. Abelard, who was perhaps bored upon reaching the pinnacle of his career at age forty, was more than willing to get to know Heloise. Fulbert hired him as her tutor and Abelard moved in. Abelard was a cleric, who by custom was celibate.[25] Soon Abelard was upon Heloise. He wrote later that his "nights were sleepless with lovemaking" and "our desires left no stage of lovemaking untried, and if love could devise something new, we welcomed it."[26] At some time amid the passion and secrecy, caution gave way. Abelard composed love songs to Heloise that became public. People were said to be singing them in the streets. He gave up teaching and indeed became a bit reckless. All of this happened under Fulbert's naïve nose, until one day he found them in a compromising position. He excused Abelard but that did not end the relationship. Heloise became pregnant and Abelard removed her from the house. They had a boy while living at Abelard's sister's house.

Abelard wanted to make things right, so he contacted Fulbert and offered to marry Heloise, so long as the marriage was kept a secret. Heloise would not agree to such an arrangement. She believed that marriage would most certainly jeopardize Abelard's career and, moreover, a secret marriage would not ultimately satisfy Fulbert's public embarrassment. Abelard got his way once again and they married in secret. Heloise was correct in her estimation of her Uncle Fulbert; he did not keep the marriage secret. Things got nasty and Abelard again took Heloise away. This time he dressed her as a nun and put her into a convent. The nun's clothing and the religious environment did nothing to inhibit their passion as they made love in various places within the convent. Fulbert thought Abelard hid Heloise away so he could keep his place in society and have her as his secret mistress. This angered him and he plotted revenge. Abelard writes, "One night as I lay sleeping in my chamber, one of my servants, corrupted by gold, delivered me to their vengeance, which the world would learn of to its stupefaction: they cut off those parts of my body with which I committed the offense they deplored."[27] Humiliated, he withdrew from society and he demanded that Heloise, now nineteen, become a nun. Abelard went to the Abbey of St. Denis to become a monk. After she took her vows, which included celibacy, he took his. They did not communicate for ten years.

Over the years, each moved into leadership positions in their religious orders. Abelard's career, however, continued to be rocky. He was expelled from one community, threatened in another. The event that caused their meeting was that her religious community was having difficulties and his religious community was in a situation to help. When they met after all those years, he addressed her as his "sister in Christ rather than my wife."[28] Abelard was able to help found a new community for the women. Communication between them ceased.

In the following years Abelard wrote his autobiography, which he titled *Story of His Misfortunes*. The book, written as a letter to an unnamed friend, was somehow forwarded to Heloise. She read it and felt that she had to respond to him. Her response initiated a series of letters between the two. In very engaging writing, Heloise at once challenges and commits herself to Abelard.

She reviews his life story saying that is was "full of so much suffering" as it retold "the tragic story of our lives, our conversion, and the crosses which you alone continue to carry."[29] With a bit of stinging sarcasm she notes the persecutions and injury he suffered. His enemies, she notes, even attacked his "glorious theological work."[30] After reviewing his list of misfortune and pain, she concludes, "I do not think anyone could read or hear what you say and have dry eyes."[31] She, however, does not dwell on his self-pity. In fact, she takes him to task for his lack of responsibility, first for wasting his time writing this book when he should be writing to the community of women he helped organize. They need his encouragement. She writes, "I implore you to heal us whom you have hurt . . . do you not owe us as much out of friendship?"[32] Her indictment does not end there. "Although I omit the rest, think of how obligated you are to me. The debt that you owe to these women as a community you owe more abundantly to one who is yours alone."[33] Radice comments, "For twelve years or more she has brooded over his apparent indifference in never giving her a word of recognition for the sacrifice she made in entering monastic life. He knows very well that she did it only for love of him, but his neglect has forced her to the conclusion that what he had felt for her was no more than lust and, when physical desire had gone, any warmth of affection had gone with it."[34] In the excerpt that follows, taken from her first letter to Abelard, Heloise speaks passionately about her loss and her suffering.

As you know, I am the one to whom you were bound by the great obligation of love, an obligation that became even greater when it was reinforced
by the lasting bonds of the sacrament of marriage. You know that you have
been made subject to me by the great love with which I have always sur-
rounded you, a love which has been publicly exposed as excessive. My
beloved, you and everyone else knows that I lost much in losing you.

Truly, the greater the cause of any sorrow, the greater must be the
means to remedy or console it. Since you alone are the cause of my sorrow,
the consolation must come only from you. Only you can bestow the grace
of consolation. Insofar as you alone are the one who brings me sadness, you
alone can bring me joy. You alone owe me the most, for I have done everything you ordered. I did this so completely that I found strength in your
command to enter this abbey, since I was unable to oppose you in anything
you desired. It was at your command that I instantly changed my dress
along with my mind to prove to you that my heart, my body, and soul were
your possession.

God knows that I asked nothing of you except yourself. My love for
you was not motivated by any desire for your possessions. I did not expect
you to marry me, nor did I expect you to give me any marriage portion. I
can truly say that I never tried to satisfy my own pleasure and wishes, but
only yours. You yourself surely know this. Even if the name of wife sounds
holier and truer to others, the word mistress will always remain sweeter to
me. If you do not get angry at this, even the name of concubine or prostitute is sweet to me. I choose these so as to win fuller gratitude from you as
well as to do less damage to the glory of your reputation.

You have not forgotten all this if the letter sent to console your friend
can be used as an example. In that letter you explained that I did not wish
us to enter into a public marriage. However, you did not give the main reasons for my claim that I preferred love over marriage, or liberty over chains.
God is my witness to the depth of my love. Even if Augustus, ruler of the
entire world, thought me worthy of the honor of marriage and gave me the
whole world for my possession, I would consider it more valuable and more
of an honor to be called your whore than to be called his empress.[35]

Heloise addresses the question of guilt for their former lives. How can she
be judged a sinner? She believes that because she acted out of love her actions
were justified. She writes, "Although I am considered most guilty, you know that
I am most innocent. It is not only the thing done, but, more importantly, the
intention of the doer that makes the crime. Therefore justice ought to weigh not

on the actions alone but on what was in the heart. You alone can judge what I have had in my heart toward you, for you have put it to the test."[36]

But was she a fool? She admits to desire and lust, but it was in the name of love, a love she experienced as a bond unlike any other. But she wonders, was it really mutual? It appears to her that Abelard's love for her was cut the moment he was castrated. Did he ever really love her or was he simply following lustful desires?

> My desire joined me to you more powerfully than friendship, and the fires of my lust united me to you more powerfully than ever. Therefore, when what you desired ceased to be possible, your display of affection vanished with it. Beloved, this is not my conjecture alone. Everyone believes this. My opinion is not one opinion among many but expresses the universal view. This view is not only held in private but is expressed in public. If this were my personal opinion only, and others could find excuses for your love, that would lessen my sorrow. If I could fabricate excuses for you that would cover up your cheap behavior toward me, I would.[37]

Her love is true and strong. It has not diminished over the years.

> I beg you to pay attention to what I am about to ask, for it is a small and easy thing for you to do. Since I am deprived of your physical presence, at least send me a letter, a sweet image of yourself in words. You have enough of those. If I have to put up with your stinginess in words, I surely wait in vain for generous deeds. Yet I still believe that you will do much for me because I have done everything for you. I am obedient to you even now. It was your command, not religious devotion, that forced me to embrace the monastic way of life while I was still a young woman. You can judge my situation for yourself. If you do nothing for me, are not my efforts in vain?
>
> I cannot expect God to reward me for anything I have done up to now. Love for God has not been my motivation. I only followed you when you were hastening after God. I took the religious habit before you did. As if moved by the memory of Lot's wife who turned back, you gave only God the title to me by monastic investiture and profession. This was before you yourself made that commitment. I suffered violently because of this. I was ashamed that you had so little confidence in my love in this situation. God knows that I would not have hesitated either to precede you or to follow you if you commanded it.
>
> My soul belonged to you more than to me. In fact, it is more yours now, for if it is not with you, it does not exist. Without you, there is no

purpose for my existence. I beg you to treat my soul well so that it may remain with you. If it experiences your kindness, if you repay gracious acts with my gracious act, a small grace in return for my great deed, mere words in return for my love, my soul will flourish in your possession. I beg you to remember what I have done and consider how much you owe me. When I enjoyed carnal pleasure with you, many were uncertain whether I acted through love or lust. The end of the affair now shows its origin. I have given up all pleasure in order to serve you. Weigh your injustice with care. I beg you to send your presence to me the only way you can. Write some comforting message to me, or at least agree to do so. Then my obedience will be revived and I will again be at peace for God.

Farewell, my only love.[38]

Heloise addressed her letter to Abelard as follows, "To her master, or rather her father, husband, or rather brother; his handmaid, or rather his daughter, wife, or rather sister; to Abelard, Heloise."[39] When Abelard responds, he addresses his letter, "To Heloise, his dearly beloved sister in Christ, Abelard her brother in Christ."[40] As much as she writes with passion, he writes with restraint. In the letter he refers to her as "my sister once dear in the world and now dearest in Christ."[41] Radice notes, "He writes as abbot to abbess."[42]

Heloise does not back down. In her return letter she writes with even more passion for the man she loves. "It is most difficult," she says "to tear the longing for supreme pleasures from the heart."[43]

Love, passion, and commitment to Abelard all emerge within Heloise in contrast to Abelard's abstract and detached love for her "in Christ."

Indeed, the delights that we enjoyed together as lovers were so sweet that I can neither hate them nor forget them except with the greatest difficulty. There are present to me and so is my longing for them wherever I turn. I am not even spared their illusions when I sleep. Their unclean visions take such complete possession of my unhappy soul even during the solemn moments of the Mass when prayer should be the most fervent. Yet even then, my thoughts are fixed on vileness rather than on prayer. When I ought to be deeply sorrowful for what I have done, I am lamenting for what I have lost. It is not only what we actually did that afflicts me. I live the past over and over again in my mind, the very places and moments we shared together. I have no relief from this even when I sleep. An unguarded word or a movement of my body betrays my thoughts. I am a most unhappy woman. I can truly utter the complaint of the afflicted Paul. "O wretched that I am! Who shall deliver me from the body of this death?" I wish I could add with truth what follows: "I thank God through Jesus Christ our Lord." You, my beloved, have that grace that came to you though you did not seek it. A single wound to your body has healed you from these torments and also healed any wounds in your soul. God has proved to be kind to you, in spite of the apparent cruelty. The Lord is a good physician who causes pain to heal. For me it is not that easy. I am young and passionate. Because I have known the most intense pleasures of love, the attacks directed against me are most fierce, for my nature is frail.[44]

Abelard responds by recalling events in their past. The romance is gone and he prefers to speak of their sins and their shame instead of their bond. He sees his castration now as divine grace that cleansed him, instead of an act that deprived him.[45] Abelard calls upon Heloise to love God. "It was he who truly loved you, not I. My love, which brought us both to sin, should be called lust, not love. I took my fill of my wretched pleasures in you, and this was the sum total of my love."[46] He concludes with a prayer that includes the line, "Lord . . . those whom thou hast parted for a time on earth, unite forever to thyself in heaven."[47]

Heloise writes another letter to Abelard. She admits she must show some restraint, as hard as that may be. "For nothing is less under our control than the heart," she writes, "having no power to command it we are forced to obey."[48] Yet written words are different from spoken words. "I will therefore hold my hand from writing words which I cannot restrain my tongue from speaking; would that a grieving heart would be as ready to obey as a writer's hand!"[49] Here she seems to let go of the past and push on into the future. The remainder of this letter and Abelard's two later letters to her are about issues in running a monastery.

Abelard died in 1142 at the age of sixty-three amid theological controversy. Heloise performed a final act of devotion and asked the abbot of Cluny for absolution for Abelard's sins. The request was granted and Abelard was laid to rest in good standing with the Church. Heloise died some twenty years later. Radice comments, "The romantically minded have liked to think that she died, like Abelard, at the age of sixty-three."[50] Indeed, the romantically minded have a more fantastic tale. Story has it that her body was placed in his tomb. Ackerman writes, "Rumor at the time said that, as her body was placed there, his arms fell open to embrace her."[51]

CHAPTER SIX

Thomas Aquinas: Friendship with God

The *Summa Theologica*

Charity is the friendship of man for God.
—Thomas Aquinas, *Summa Theologica*

There is much to be said by way of introduction to Thomas Aquinas, most of it regarding his writing. Unlike Augustine or even Bernard, a detailed knowledge of Thomas's life is not necessary to understand his work. He was born in 1224 or 1225 in the Italian town of Roccasecca and died in 1274. Thomas was a Dominican priest, teacher, and scholar who is remembered as the most important Christian systematic theologian in history.

"Systematic" theology refers to a comprehensive and coherent study of basic Christian beliefs and the relationship between such beliefs. His most famous book is the *Summa Theologica*, or "Summary of Theology." The book is a comprehensive and systematic approach to theology. Some editions of it are 4,000 pages long![1] Thomas was heir to the great biblical tradition of love passed on primarily by Augustine. But by no means is Augustine his exclusive source. Thomas also draws directly from the Bible as well as from prominent theologians from the tradition including Bernard. Unlike Bernard, however, Thomas "pushed the theological boat out to sea." One of his greatest accomplishments is that he integrated the writings of the ancient Greek philosopher Aristotle into Christian theology.[2] Although Thomas lived some 850 years ago his theology and theological method still influence the Catholic Church and Catholic theologians today.

Although written for "beginners" in theology, the *Summa* is a complicated book. An outstanding feature most students notice when reading it is that Thomas constantly makes distinctions. The first thing he does when he approaches a question is to pick it apart and analyze its components. He is a most careful thinker. As such, he does not let simple ideas or generalizations get by without scrutiny. To the novice reader (and indeed even to those who have read him many times), his distinctions can seem to make the issue more complicated. His point, however, is to speak with precise words on clearly defined issues.

Our use of Thomas here is quite limited and as a result we will only briefly review the general outline of the *Summa*. This will put the discussion on love into a broader context. The organizing principle of the book is that all things are from God and all things return to God. The three divisions of the *Summa* follow this principle. The first part argues that we come from God and that we are made in the image of God. The second part of the *Summa* is the largest part and is divided into two sections. The second part considers our end or our destination. By nature we are directed to God. This part also narrates the path to God, namely, the practice of virtues and the avoidance of vices. The third part considers how Jesus Christ, through the sacraments, enables us to practice virtue and avoid vice, so we are able to return to God.[3]

Our discussion of Thomas addresses two main issues, his understandings of love as *amor* and as *caritas* (normally translated as "charity"). The first is found in the First Part of the Second Part of the *Summa Theologica* where Thomas describes the nature of human actions, indeed the nature of being human. Among characteristics of human nature, he describes the human passions (emotions), and first among the passions is love. The major discussion of *caritas* is found in the Second Part of the Second Part under the section on theological virtues. Thomas lists faith and hope as such virtues along with *caritas*.

Amor and Friendship

The name love is given to the principle of movement toward the end loved.
—Thomas Aquinas, *Summa Theologica*

By way of introduction we can note five distinctive ways in which Thomas uses the word love. We will call them the structure of love, basic love, unreciprocated love, friendship love, and *caritas* love. The "structure of love" refers to the overall experience of loving as described by Augustine, that is, the subjective element of love, the lover, the object of love, the beloved, and the love or unity between the lover and the beloved.

Turning our attention to the lover, we can speak of the second way Thomas uses love, namely, as basic love or *amor*. Love, for Thomas, in its most fundamental sense, is a passion. Relying on Augustine, he notes that love is a movement of an internal aspect of a person toward a particular object. For Thomas human action results from some apprehension of the good and a subsequent attraction to that good. What we think is good, on whatever level, moves us to act. Love in its most basic sense is then this attraction toward something we perceive as good. Thomas holds that there are several levels in our nature and thus we have several levels of love. We have an aspect we share with all of creation, which he calls the natural; an aspect we share to some extent with animals, which he calls the sensitive; and a unique aspect he refers to as the rational. The rational directs the other two aspects of human nature. Thus, while love is a passion, something that arises in the person, it is also an act. That is, people can make choices and direct their loves.

If love is a movement, it must be going somewhere and it must be moved by something. For Thomas, that which is loved, the beloved, is something like a magnet for the lover. The object causes the attraction because the lover finds the object good. The range of goods we experience is vast. We love some things because they give us pleasure—wine, for instance. We all have, at one time or another, said we loved a certain food. We love other things on different levels. We love other people in that we wish them well and we act kindly toward them. Aquinas uses the word "benevolence" here to describe our feelings toward things in this second group. He continues with a further distinction concerning benevolent love. In some loves, benevolence is mutual or reciprocal, in other loves it is not. My wife and I love each other. Our love is mutual. On the other hand, as a teacher, I try to love all my students. Some days, however, I do not get the sense that they all love me in return. We can call this unreciprocated love. Thomas does not spend much time describing this sort of love. He does, however, spend a great deal of time talking about relationships characterized by mutual benevolence, that is, friendships.

Friendships are a crucial part of our lives. We all have friends and we all have different levels of friendships. Friendship is a basic element of human existence. One of the things that makes Thomas's approach to love so interesting is that while he tends to be very analytical, the data of his research is common human experience. I think most of us would agree with Thomas when he says that in true friendship a person loves the friend not merely for the pleasure the other gives or for how useful the other might be. In true friendship we share essential values. We have some strong common ground.

In true friendship we love the other for who the other is. Recall the distinction above about our natural, sensitive, and rational natures. In true friendship the love emanates from our highest level and is directed to the other on the same level. This is not to belittle the sensitive and physical nature of the beloved, but it is to say that we do not ultimately love them because of these features. Thus, writes Thomas, the friend is "not satisfied with a superficial apprehension of the beloved, but strives to gain an intimate knowledge of everything pertaining to the beloved."[4] Certainly the friend takes pleasure in the other's company, but in true friendship, the friend feels the friend's feelings. If something good happens to my friend, I too feel good. If my friend suffers, I too suffer.

Love unites. Thomas knows this from experience and thus he offers some strong and interesting words on friendship. He believes the bonds of true friendship are so strong that the friend becomes like another self. He writes: "When a man loves another with the love of friendship, he wills good to him, just as he wills good to himself: wherefore he apprehends him as his other self, in so far, to wit as he wills good to him as to himself. Hence a friend is called a man's other self."[5] True friendship is union. It pushes one out of oneself without the person negating one's true self. Thomas continues, "He who loves, goes out from himself, in so far as he wills the good of his friend and works for it. Yet he does not will the good of his friend more than his own good; and so it does not follow that he loves another more than himself."[6] True friendship is union in that it makes both partners better people because it requires that each do good and be good for the other. In Thomas's view, you cannot sin for the good of the friend; that is, you cannot harm your own essential good for the beloved. Thomas, quoting Aristotle, writes that there are five things proper to friendship. For in the first place, every friend wishes his friend to be and to live; second, he desires good things for him; third, he does good things to him; fourth, he takes pleasure in his company; fifth, he is of one mind with him, rejoicing and sorrowing in almost the same things.[7]

Thomas believes that not all friendships are the same. Consider your own relationships for a moment. You probably have a couple or perhaps several people whom you would call "good" friends. But you would not limit your friends to this group. There is also a wider group of people whom you might simply refer to as friends. Always the one to analyze experience, Thomas describes different ways to think of your different levels of friends. Some relationships are dictated by the terms of character of the relationship. Is your relationship based on pleasure, usefulness, or some deeper connection? Some relationships, he argues, are founded on the specific commonality shared between the friends. Is this person your friend simply because you are in the same class or because you belong to the same group?

All of this has interesting implications. If you are involved in a friendship that is one-sided, it is not a true friendship. If you continually feel belittled in a relationship or are constantly being put down, it is not a true friendship. If the relationship is based solely on pleasure or you feel you are being used, the relationship is not true friendship. Thomas writes, "Love of suitable good perfects and betters the lover; but love which is unsuitable to the lover, wounds and worsens him. Wherefore man is perfected and bettered chiefly by the love of God; but is wounded and worsened by the love of sin."[8] This is not to say that a lover does not have negative feelings in loving. From love springs all other passions and feelings. Love is not a simple affection. Thomas notes that there are four such effects of love. There is first a "melting" feeling, a "softening of the heart" where one opens up to the beloved. If the beloved is present, the lover experiences pleasure and enjoys the company of the other. In the beloved's absence, the lover experiences two feelings. The lover is at once sad and also has an intense desire to be with the beloved.[9] Thomas goes further when he suggests that even hate is caused by love. Hate occurs when something gets in the way of that which we love.

Friendship and *Caritas*

Man's third pursuit is to aim chiefly at union with and enjoyment of God.
—Thomas Aquinas, *Summa Theologica*

As the outline of the *Summa* suggested, Thomas's primary concern is not simply with having good friends. Thomas ultimately is concerned with our return to God, that is, our salvation and eternal happiness with God. The most significant relationship for Thomas is the relationship one has with God. In a very interesting move, he describes this relationship as friendship. He defines love for God, which he calls *caritas*, as friendship with God. To understand *caritas* we must first understand friendship. Here are several statements about friendship as it relates to *caritas*.

1. Friendship is a natural activity for persons. It is as if we are programmed to have friends. Can you imagine life without friends? There is a dynamic link between our experience of friends and friendship and our relationship to God. Thomas describes *caritas* as a virtue and thus something natural to us. Virtue is a perfection of our nature. *Caritas* is founded on the goodness of God and the natural inclination of persons toward God. *Caritas* is then the nexus around which the moral life moves. According to Thomas, it should be the central love in one's life. *Caritas* is the "foundation or root" of the moral life "as all other virtues draw their sustenance and nourishment" from it.[10]

2. Friendship involves mutual choice. Thomas holds together two seemingly opposite views. In one place he describes love as "a spontaneous movement of the lover towards the beloved,"[11] and in another he writes, "the passion of love

is not aroused suddenly, but it is born of an earnest consideration of the object loved."[12] How are these contradictory statements held together? Consider your experience. You come into contact with many people every day, yet only a select few are your friends. I use the term "select" on purpose here. Not everyone you meet is your friend. You choose your friends. Maybe your friends are not chosen through "earnest consideration" but you did make choices. On the other hand, if one is your friend for some time, if you love someone, you do not have to choose your feelings. Your feelings arise spontaneously toward the one you love. Repeated over time, your love for the other becomes like a habit. It just flows. Thus love is both a passion and a choice.

All friendship is love, but not all love is friendship. Some loves are not reciprocated. As friendship is mutual love so is *caritas*. Here again the language of virtue helps. That is to say, *caritas* is a result of God's grace. *Caritas* is given to us. Consider how this relates to friendship. Friendship essentially is a choice, one chooses one's friends, but it is not an individual choice. How do I become a friend with another person? Can I do things to make another person like me? The answer to this is yes and no. By doing certain things I can get another's attention and perhaps he or she will like the things that I do, but that is not the same as getting the person to like me as a person. Friendship ultimately is a gift. We do not go out and get a friend. The potential friend has to see some common ground between us and give me the gift of his or her friendship. The same is true with *caritas*. We cannot do things to win God's love. On the other hand, doing good things makes us more able to see God's love in the world and to receive God's love. In Thomas's words, acts "dispose" one "to receive the infusion of" *caritas*.[13] Friendship is mutual and depends on the mutual assent of each person. It rests on my choice but it is ultimately beyond my choice.

3. Friendships change. Friendships go through stages, which we can designate beginning, middle, and mature (or perfect). These stages are based on many factors including the intensity of the relationship and the quality of interaction between the friends. As friendships grow, so does *caritas*. Thomas writes, "In like manner charity does not actually increase through every act of charity, but each act of charity disposes to an increase of charity, in so far as one act of charity makes man more ready to act again according to charity, and this readiness increasing, man breaks out into an act of more fervent love, and strives to advance in charity, and then his charity increases actually."[14] There is no limit to the increase in *caritas* as the "heart is enlarged" and "there is a corresponding increased ability to receive a further increase" in it.[15] Thomas notes that there are three distinct stages of *caritas*. They are distinguished

according to the different pursuits to which man is brought by the increase of charity. For at first it is incumbent on man to occupy himself chiefly with avoiding sin and resisting his concupiscences [desires from sensitive nature], which move him in opposition to charity: this concerns beginners, in whom charity has to be fed or fostered lest it be destroyed: in the second place man's chief pursuit is to aim at progress in good, and this is the pursuit of the proficient, whose chief aim is to strengthen their charity by adding to it: while man's third pursuit is to aim chiefly at union with and enjoyment of God: this belongs to the perfect who "desire to be dissolved and to be with Christ."[16]

Events along the way can have a negative effect on a friendship. You know yourself that friendships can be vulnerable. A word here or an action there can harm a friendship. In human friendships either party can break or end the relationship. One can tire of the other or grow out of the relationship or simply not feel the need to continue the relationship. *Caritas* is different, because the other party, God, is stable and always loving. We can, however, act in certain ways that challenge or even lessen our *caritas*. Again, it is our choice. In *caritas* a person loves God and follows God. By disobeying God we choose sin over God. Although a single sin can break the relationship, the good person, Thomas notes, does not suddenly fall from *caritas*. He writes, "For God does not turn away from man, more than man turns away from Him."[17]

If *caritas* is the perfect form of love, can we ever have it perfectly? Thomas answers,

> The perfection of charity may be understood in two ways: first with regard to the object loved, secondly with regard to the person who loves. With regard to the object loved, charity is perfect, if the object be loved as much as it is lovable. Now God is as lovable as He is good, and His goodness is infinite, wherefore He is infinitely lovable. But no creature can love Him infinitely since all created power is finite. Consequently no creature's charity can be perfect in this way; the charity of God alone can, whereby He loves Himself. On the part of the person who loves, charity is perfect, when he loves as much as he can.[18]

We cannot overstate the importance of friendship in our lives. True friendships and good friends make us better people. Such relationships are the best and fullest way of understanding our relationship to God.

Love for God and Love for Neighbor

Love can begin at once where knowledge ends, namely in the thing itself
which is known through another thing.

—Thomas Aquinas, *Summa Theologica*

As *caritas* is friendship with God, it is similar to other relationships one might
have. As it is friendship with God, it is also very different from such relationships. *Caritas* directs all other loves. Though the aim and end of *caritas* is God,
Thomas holds that this love is not exclusive. He uses several metaphors to describe *caritas* and how through loving God one necessarily loves others. *Caritas*
is like a furnace, he says. A fire, by its very nature, makes things around it hot.
The stronger the fire in the furnace, the more heat it radiates through a house.
The stronger the *caritas*, the more one is able to love others. The very same fire
that unites us with God unites us with others. Thomas also compares *caritas* to
seeing a color. As we see a color we also see the light that enables us to see the
color. One does not see colors in a dark closet. We cannot distinguish the two
acts. Likewise, Thomas suggests the same act of loving God is the act of loving
the neighbor.

In our reading of Augustine, Bernard, and Hadewijch, we encountered
strong and determined language for loving God. If there is a criticism of this view
in the Christian tradition it is that at times people, in their desire to love God,
focus on God so exclusively that they forget, ignore, or even reject their neighbor. Thomas is keenly aware of this danger. Thus he speaks of two types of love
for God, a false and a true. In the first type, one loves God alone. In the second
one loves one's neighbors for God's sake. "In this way love of our neighbor includes love of God, while love of God does not include love of our neighbor."
The latter is "perfect love for God" while the former, says Thomas, is "inadequate and imperfect love for God."[19] According to Thomas if one is a friend with
God, if one has *caritas*, one necessarily loves the neighbor. Note, however, how
we are to love our neighbor. For Thomas neighbor love is not based on a particular quality the person has. Nor is it based on some inherent dignity all possess. We love the neighbor in that the neighbor "may be in God."[20]

Thomas is very careful in his thinking. He is quite balanced and sees truth
and insight from different positions. His theology of love is difficult to catego-
rize. He does not hold that we ought to love God first and neighbors second or
that we ought to love our neighbors first and love God through loving neighbors. He recognizes the problems when either approach is carried to an extreme,

the dangers of over "spiritualizing" love or mistaking creation for the Creator. For Thomas there is a "circular movement" of *caritas*.[21] Love flows from God to creation. So we know God's love through other things. Thus we are drawn to God. There is then a unity between loving God and loving the neighbor for Thomas. But, to ask a famous question, "Who is my neighbor?" Thomas speaks of the neighbor in a generic sense. Anybody and everybody is my neighbor. But he cannot remain on this general level. Thomas knows that distinctions make a difference. His experience tells him that we tend to love different people differently. At the same time, however, *caritas* does not simply affirm our experience of the natural order of the world. As a part of God's grace, it transforms and perfects the natural order. In order to consider how *caritas* directs human love, let us return to the model of love discussed above.

The intensity of any love, the emotion, rests in the lover. When we look to the beloved, that is, to the person who is loved, we get the type or form of the love. Thomas calls this the "species" of love. As we all know, the love for a parent is different from the love for an enemy, love for a child, love for a spouse, love for a stranger, and so on. Thomas notes that there are two characteristics that determine the species of a love. Both refer to a quality in the beloved. First, all people are deserving of our love simply because they are persons. Humans are, says Thomas, like God.[22] All people, by their very nature, have a capacity to share the goodness of God and thus are deserving of our love. But Thomas does not remain on this level of general love of humanity. Along with a basic humanness, all people have unique determining features. As we consider loving others in *caritas*, two such features are important for Thomas. They are the relationship the person has to the lover and the relationship the person has with God. Thomas expects that we love those who are close to us, family members, for example, more than we love those who are not close to us. He also holds that people who are closer to God are more deserving of our love than those who are distant from God.

The third element in the model of love, after the lover and the beloved, is that which is shared by the lovers. We might say that that which is shared by the lovers is what the relationship is based on. In life it is, of course, impossible to separate these three aspects, but on paper it can be a helpful tool with which to reflect on a relationship. The most fundamental feature between persons, that is, the basic good individuals have in common, is God. All persons share the prospect for eternal happiness. *Caritas*-based love for neighbor, that is, true love for others, according to Thomas, begins and ends with this fact. The final element of the model of love is the level of unity or intimacy. It is a result of the mixture of the other three elements and thus cannot be described in the abstract. You may feel more closely united to a friend than you do to your brother or sister. On the other hand, you may feel closer to a brother or sister than you do to a person you are dating.

Two of the more interesting sections of Thomas's writing on *caritas* describe particular relationships. In one section he considers the hard questions of such love, that is, the place of self-love, love of enemies, love of sinners, and love of animals. Returning to our model of love, we can see why these are hard questions. The issues are, what are we to love in these objects (how can I love a sinner?) and what do we share with these objects (I do not seem to share anything with my enemy)? In the second section he addresses the variety of loves that make up day-to-day lives.

As Thomas addresses the "objects" of love and the "order" of love, we can note two characteristics of his thinking. The first is that while *caritas* requires certain loves, it never limits love. The fire in the furnace of love can be infinitely stoked and the love can radiate out a long distance from the lover. On the other hand, when we read Thomas on love, we see that he is realistic. *Caritas* is demanding but the demands seem to be within the lover's concrete ability. There is no love "heroism" in Thomas. The next two sections will address Thomas's particular decisions on whom we are to love and how we are to love them.

Animals, Enemies, Sinners, and Angels

> For since man loves his neighbor, out of charity, for God's sake, the more he loves God, the more does he put enmities aside and shows love towards his neighbor.
>
> —Thomas Aquinas, *Summa Theologica*

Caritas is love for God. The very same love we have for God radiates out to others. Before Thomas looks to the neighbor, however, he considers the question of self-love. We have already seen in his discussion of friendship that one loves the self before the other and that one cannot harm one's essential self for the other. That is to say, one cannot sin for the good of the other. For Thomas, if one has *caritas*, one has appropriate love of self. For we love God neither with our basic nature nor with our sensitive nature, we love God with our intellectual nature. This is where our spiritual self resides. So if we love God we are acting from our intellectual nature and thus by default we love ourselves. This sort of self-love is very different from the self-love of sinners, according to Thomas. Sinners love their sensitive nature at the expense of their rational nature. They love their physical self, thinking it is their essential nature. Their love is misdirected love. Thomas does not reject loving one's physical nature. We ought to love our bodies as they are part of God's creation. That is to say, we have to love it in the right way. The body, unlike our intellect, does not reach happiness directly. It reaches happiness "by a kind of overflow."[23] The body, with its desires and limitations, "weighs down the soul, so as to hinder it from seeing God."[24]

Does *caritas* require the love of animals? Not necessarily, says Thomas. His conclusion hinges on his view of the bonds of *caritas*. It is through our rational nature that we are united to others in a fellowship of happiness. We experience the common good which is God. Animals do not have a rational nature and are thus incapable of experiencing this good. In the strict sense, an animal is not our neighbor (although an angel is). Thomas says that true friendship with an animal is impossible. That, however, is not his final answer. He says we can speak of being friends with animals metaphorically. "Nevertheless we can love irrational creatures out of charity, if we regard them as the good thing that we desire for others, in so far, to wit, as we wish for their preservation, to God's honor and man's use; thus too does God love them out of charity."[25]

Does *caritas* require that we love sinners? Thomas's answer is again nuanced. We are to love sinners, but in a certain way. We are to love them in their nature but we are to hate them in their guilt. Love the sinner; hate the sin. Indeed, as Thomas says, "hatred of a person's evil is equivalent to love of his good."[26] As sinners have the capacity for eternal happiness, they must be loved. But what if one's friend is a sinner? Thomas reckons that it is the duty of one to help a friend in sin to recover virtue. In some instances, however, the friend may be beyond help. Thomas's comments here include a startling conclusion.

> When, however, they fall into very great wickedness, and become incurable, we ought no longer to show them friendliness. It is for this reason that both Divine and human laws command such like sinners to be put to death, because there is greater likelihood of their harming others than of their mending their ways. Nevertheless the judge puts this into effect, not out of hatred for the sinners, but out of the love of charity, by reason of which he prefers the public good to the life of the individual. Moreover the death inflicted by the judge profits the sinner, if he be converted, unto the expiation of his crime; and, if he be not converted, it profits so as to put an end to the sin, because the sinner is thus deprived of the power to sin any more.[27]

In such instances, though perhaps rare, *caritas* demands that we kill. This follows from Thomas's thinking. Recall what we love in neighbors. We love the capacity for happiness in them. We share this fellowship with them. This idea is similar to but not simply transferable to our contemporary notion of human dignity. For Thomas, we (meaning society through appropriate legal measures) ought to kill the incurable sinner for two reasons. The first is to protect the community from further harm. We thus kill the sinner for the love of the community. The second is to protect the sinner from the probability of sinning more. We thus kill the sinner out of love for him or her. Killing out of love, particularly out of *caritas*, makes little sense to us today. There are important theological and social differences between Thomas's time and ours. Theologically, the development of human dignity and human rights language is significant. The most obvious pragmatic difference is that we have many other means of restraint available to us. We do not have to kill to protect people from "incurable sinners."

Does *caritas* require that we love our enemies? By now we expect Thomas to address this question on a number of levels. He does not disappoint us. He divides his answer into three parts. The first two are not new to us. In the third, however, he makes some interesting qualifications.

> Love of one's enemies may be understood in three ways. First, as though we were to love our enemies as such: this is perverse, and contrary to charity, since it implies love of that which is evil in another. Secondly, love of one's enemies may mean that we love them as to their nature, but in general: and in this sense charity requires that we should love our enemies, namely, that in loving God and our neighbor, we should not exclude our enemies from the love given to our neighbor in general. Thirdly, love of one's enemies may be considered as specially directed to them, namely, that we should have a special movement of love towards our enemies. Charity does not require this absolutely, because it does not require that we should have a special movement of love to every individual man, since this would be impossible. Nevertheless charity does require this, in respect of our being prepared in mind, namely, that we should be ready to love our enemies individually, if the necessity were to occur. That man should actually do so, and love his enemy for God's sake, without it being necessary for him to do so, belongs to the perfection of charity. For since man loves his neighbor, out of charity, for God's sake, the more he loves God, the more does he put enmities aside and show love towards his neighbor.[28]

Caritas never limits love; it does, however, require love. In the case of loving the enemy, it demands a readiness and willingness to love. Being open to and receiving God's grace is not a "once and forever" event. We grow in *caritas*. Thomas can thus make the distinction between perfect *caritas* and the *caritas* that most of us experience, namely imperfect and developing *caritas*. The greater the love for God, the more able we are to love enemies.

Loving Some More than Others

A thing is loved more in two ways: first because it has the character of a
more excellent good, secondly by reason of a closer connection.

—Thomas Aquinas, *Summa Theologica*

It has already been established that in *caritas* one loves oneself and one loves one's
neighbor. But how does self-love compare to neighbor love? Thomas relies on his
distinction between the levels of the person to answer this question. According
to one's intellectual and spiritual level, in *caritas*, a person loves oneself "more
than he loves any other person."[29] While it is clear then that self-love is a priority
for Thomas, it is a qualified love. When he applies the spiritual/physical distinction to love of neighbor, he says that we are to love the neighbor's spiritual
good over our own physical good. In this way, we love the neighbor more than
we love our self. What Thomas has introduced here is the language of preferential love. We are to love some people more than others. Indeed he argues that it
is unreasonable to think that we ought to love all people equally. He writes,

> Love can be unequal in two ways: first on the part of the good we wish
> our friend. On this respect we love all men equally out of charity: because
> we wish them all one same generic good, namely everlasting happiness. Sec-
> ondly love is said to be greater through its action being more intense: and
> in this way we ought not to love all equally.[30]

But, as usual, his first answer is not his final answer. He makes the distinction
between love as beneficence, the active doing good for another, and benevolence,
the intention or desire for the good of the other. He continues, "Or we may reply
that we have unequal love for certain persons in two ways: first, through our loving some and not loving others. As regards beneficence we are bound to observe
this inequality, because we cannot do good to all: but as regards benevolence,
love ought not to be thus unequal."[31]

The major tension in Thomas's presentation on the order of love is between
loving those who are close to God and loving those who are close to us. If God
is the object of *caritas*, should not we love those who are closer to God? Thomas
answers,

> Every act should be proportionate both to its object and to the agent. But
> from its object it takes its species, while, from the power of the agent it
> takes the mode of its intensity: thus movement has its species from the term
> to which it tends, while the intensity of its speed arises from the disposi-

tion of the thing moved and the power of the mover. Accordingly love takes its species from its object, but its intensity is due to the lover. Now the object of charity's love is God, and man is the lover. Therefore the specific diversity of the love which is in accordance with charity, as regards the love of our neighbor, depends on his relation to God, so that, out of charity, we should wish a greater good to one who is nearer to God.[32]

This however is not his conclusion. He continues,

On the other hand, the intensity of love is measured with regard to the man who loves, and accordingly man loves those who are more closely united to him, with more intense affection as to the good he wishes for them, than he loves those who are better as to the greater good he wishes for them. Again a further difference must be observed here: for some neighbors are connected with us by their natural origin, a connection which cannot be severed, since that origin makes them to be what they are. But the goodness of virtue, wherein some are close to God, can come and go, increase and decrease, as was shown above (Q. 24, Arts. 4, 10, 11). Hence it is possible for one, out of charity, to wish this man who is more closely united to one, to be better than another, and so reach a higher degree of happiness.

Moreover there is yet another reason for which, out of charity, we love more those who are more nearly connected with us, since we love them in more ways. For, towards those who are not connected with us we have no other friendship than charity, whereas for those who are connected with us, we have certain other friendships, according to the way in which they are connected. . . . Consequently this very act of loving someone because he is akin or connected with us, or because he is a fellow-countryman or for any like reason that is referable to the end of charity, can be commanded by charity, so that, out of charity both eliciting and commanding, we love in more ways those who are more nearly connected with us.[33]

A person who is more closely united to us is to be loved more.

Loving good people or loving a friend generally comes easily. Love of enemies, however, is difficult. Thomas notes that the only reason we would have to love an enemy is God. We love friends in any number of ways. Thus, he says, "Hence our love for God is proved to be so much the stronger, as the more difficult are the things we accomplish for its sake."[34] Does this mean that it is better to love an enemy than it is to love a friend? Thomas responds, "Yet just as the same fire acts with greater force on what is near than on what is distant, so too, charity loves with greater fervor those who are united to us than those who are far removed; and in this respect the love of friends, considered in itself, is more ardent and better than the love of one's enemy."[35]

These are hard questions. Thomas, however, asks more difficult ones. Do you think a person ought to love his or her parents more than his or her children? Do you think you ought to love your father more than your mother? How about your spouse compared to your parents? Thomas's answers to these questions illustrate his concern for the proper ordering of *caritas* as well as his thirteenth century context.

Delving into particular loves and the comparison between such loves Thomas asks, "Whether a man ought, out of charity, to love his children more than his father?"

> I answer that, As stated above, the degrees of love may be measured from two standpoints. First, from that of the object. In this respect the better a thing is, and the more like to God, the more is it to be loved: and in this way a man ought to love his father more than his children, because, to wit, he loves his father as his principle, in which respect he is a more exalted good and more like God.
>
> Secondly, the degrees of love may be measured from the standpoint of the lover, and in this respect a man loves more that which is more closely connected with him, in which way a man's children are more lovable to him than his father, as the Philosopher states (Ethic. viii). First, because parents love their children as being part of themselves, whereas the father is not part of his son, so that the love of a father for his children, is more like a man's love for himself. Secondly, because parents know better that so and so is their child than vice versa. Thirdly, because children are nearer to their parents, as being part of them, than their parents are to them to whom they stand in the relation of a principle. Fourthly, because parents have loved longer, for the father begins to love his child at once, whereas the child begins to love his father after a lapse of time; and the longer love lasts, the stronger it is.[36]

A child's love for parents "consists chiefly in honor" writes Thomas. The love of parents for children, on the other hand, is "one of care."[37] On loving parents, Thomas asks, "Whether a man ought to love his mother more than his father?"

> I answer that, In making such comparisons as this, we must take the answer in the strict sense, so that the present question is whether the father

as father, ought to be loved more than the mother as mother. The reason is that virtue and vice may make such a difference in such like matters, that friendship may be diminished or destroyed, as the Philosopher remarks (Ethic. viii, 7). Hence Ambrose [Origen, Hom. ii in Cant.] says: "Good servants should be preferred to wicked children."

Strictly speaking, however, the father should be loved more than the mother. For father and mother are loved as principles of our natural origin. Now the father is principle in a more excellent way than the mother, because he is the active principle, while the mother is a passive and material principle. Consequently, strictly speaking, the father is to be loved more.[38]

Thomas's answer is based on "scientific" knowledge. In this case, the biology of his day, known from empirical evidence, indicated that in the act of sexual intercourse, the man implants a seed in a woman. The biology of the day was that in the act of sex the man was like a farmer, planting a seed in the "passive" woman. Passive in the sense that she, like the soil, necessarily contributed in a secondary way to the beginning of life. This biology, "true" in his day but false in ours, informs his moral theory. This implies that his conclusions on sexual issues, based as they are on faulty descriptions of reality, are themselves false. Given that he consulted knowledge from all fields in his work, one would think that his conclusions on this aspect of love and indeed all other questions of sex and sexuality would be strikingly different today. There is some irony, however, in Thomas's hierarchy of love. Later, in a discussion on whether it is better to love or be loved, he argues that it is better to love. He gives two examples, the love of a friend and the love of a mother. He writes, "a mother, whose love is the greatest, seeks rather to love than to be loved."[39] So a mother loves a child more than a father, but the child is to love the father more than the mother!

A final question we will review is "Whether a man ought to love his wife more than his father and mother?" Thomas's answer is based on the distinction he has been working with throughout this section. "The degrees of love," he notes, "may be taken from the good (which is loved), or from the union between those who love." Regarding the good, we ought to love our parents more. Regarding the union and that a wife is "united with her husband, as one flesh," one ought to love his wife more. Thomas concludes, "Consequently a man loves his wife more intensely, but his parents with greater reverence."[40]

CHAPTER SEVEN

Martin Luther:
The Christian Is Servant to All

Justification by Grace through Faith

*If I were to paint a picture of God, I would so draw him that there
would be nothing else in the depth of his divine nature than that fire and
passion which is called love for people.*

—Martin Luther, *Werke*

If love has a history," writes Daniel Day Williams, "then here is the point at
which that history is shaped by a new understanding."[1] The new understanding of which he speaks is Martin Luther's rejection of Medieval theology with its dependence on ancient Greek philosophy and his insistence on reform in the church and a return to the Bible. It was Luther who sparked the Protestant Reformation of the sixteenth century and who is the reason we have the Lutheran Church today.

Martin Luther was born on November 10, 1483, in a town now located in Germany. At the age of twenty-one and after completing a master's degree, he decided, against his family's wishes, to become a monk. Luther joined an order named for Augustine, called the Observant Augustinians. Within a year, he was ordained a priest and sent off by his order for further study to be a teacher. By any standard, Luther was a very serious monk. He prayed often and went to daily confession. Even though he lived the monastic life with a great deal of vigor he did not feel right with God. Biographer Roland Bainton writes, "Luther probed every resource of contemporary Catholicism for assuaging the anguish of a spirit alienated from God. He tried the way of good works and discovered that he could never do enough to save himself."[2] All the religious prescriptions, the prayers, the sacraments, the masses, fasting, vigils, and so on, did nothing for him. His restlessness was not easily resolved. The resolution to Luther's spiritual anguish came slowly and over time through his study of the Bible. Luther had an insight into God that changed his thinking, changed his life, and in the end changed the course of the Christian tradition. He came to believe that religious actions, such as worship and fasting, do nothing to make one right with God. Being right with God, what he calls "justification," comes only through faith. The phrase that summarizes his belief is "justification by grace through faith."

Luther's theology directly challenged the love for God tradition. The focus of that tradition is the self as lover and the moral directive is to love the right things in the right way. The highest human activity is contemplation of and union with God. The love for God tradition is based on an optimistic view of persons. We are naturally lovers and we are naturally inclined toward the good. Luther, on the other hand, was deeply impressed by human sinfulness. He held that as a result of the Fall of Adam and Eve, the image of God in people was seriously distorted. Luther's narrative of the movement of love is then the opposite of the love for God tradition. As sinners we cannot possibly reach up and love God. The drama of life is not humans moving up the scale of love, but God's love moving down to humans. Commenting on Luther's theology, Paul Althaus writes, "God 'showers us with his own being.' He gives us what he is. For Luther, God's sharing of himself is the highest expression of the fact that God is God."[3] God's love for us is, in a sense, irrational because we do not deserve it. We deserve God's punishment. Shirley Jordon comments, "As sinners, humans do not deserve it and they can do absolutely nothing to earn it. . . . They need to depend completely and entirely on Christ, not on what they do."[4] At the heart of Luther's theology is grace. We are saved by what God has done for us in Christ. In the words of Brian Gerrish, it is simply not "possible for man to prepare himself for grace . . . there can be no preparation for grace on man's side."[5] Indeed faith itself, "the willingness to risk anything and everything for Christ,"[6] is a gift from God. Instead of highlighting our love for God, Luther speaks of God's love of us.

The immediate effect of God's love of us is that we are to love others. We are to love like God loves. Luther describes God's love flowing like a stream out from us to others. We are like tubes that carry God's love to others. In place of contemplation in the monastery, Luther calls us to direct service of others in the world. In a way, Luther identifies love of God as love of neighbor. Althaus comments, "Since God has become man, our love for God should show itself as love for men. God is very close to us, that is, in men."[7] In Luther's words, "You will find Christ in every street and just outside your door. Do not stand around staring at heaven and say, 'Oh, if I could just only see our Lord God, how I would do everything possible for him.'"[8]

In 1525, four years after he was excommunicated, Luther married Katharina von Bora, a former nun. Jordon comments, "Although Luther had taught for several years that celibacy and monastic asceticism were contrary to the Bible and that priests, monks and nuns should be free to marry, he had not indicated any desire to do so himself."[9] Indeed it was Katharina who suggested that they marry and he agreed! Although they did not marry for love, "genuine affection and love developed between" them.[10] Luther's marriage and his reference to his marriage in his preaching added an important new element for reflection on Christian life. A legacy of this element of Luther's theology and the Reformation in general is what Charles Taylor refers to as the "affirmation of ordinary life." Luther and other reformers rejected the notion of a priestly caste of people in favor of the belief in the priesthood of all believers. "They also rejected the special vocation to the monastic life and affirmed the spiritual value of lay life."[11] Taylor comments, "The denial of a special status to the monk was also an affirmation of ordinary life as more than profane, as itself hallowed and in no way second class. . . . The repudiation of monasticism was a reaffirmation of lay life as a central locus for the fulfillment of God's purpose."[12]

Taylor notes that a particular feature of contemporary life is that we place such high significance on love in marriage. That is to say, love comes "to be seen as a crucial part of what makes life worthy and significant."[13] The fact that we make so much of love, he argues, can be traced to Luther. Lawrence Stone reviewing the history of "passionate attachments" writes, "What is certain is that every advice book, every medical treatise, every sermon and religious homily of the sixteenth and seventeenth centuries firmly rejected both romantic passion and lust as suitable basis for marriage. In the sixteenth century marriage was thought to be best arranged by parents who could be relied upon to choose socially and economically suitable partners."[14] Luther's life and theology planted the seeds for the development of a Christian theology of married, romantic love. Luther "affirmed that the fullness of Christian existence was to be found within activities of this life, in one's calling and in marriage and the family."[15] He preached that "no station in life is morally superior to marriage,"[16] and described marriage as a "school of character."[17] Speaking from experience, he noted the many struggles couples face, and suggested that through them spouses "learn the difficult art of patiently subjecting themselves to God's will."[18] Indeed, he wrote, "Marriage presents innumerable opportunities for demonstrating love and patience that are not available to the celibate."[19] For Luther the highest calling in life was not contemplation of God in a monastery but loving and serving one's neighbor at home and on the street.

Pure Love and "Crummy" Love

This love says: I love you, not because you are good or bad; for I draw my love, not from your goodness, as from another's fountain, but from my own little spring, from the Word, which is grafted in my heart and which bids me to love my neighbor.

—Martin Luther, "Sermon on the Sum of the Christian Life"

In the following two excerpts, taken from his "1535 Lectures on Galatians," Luther discusses the primacy of faith and the necessity of love.

Love can sometimes be neglected without danger, but the Word and faith cannot. It belongs to love to bear everything and to yield to everyone. On the other hand, it belongs to faith to bear nothing whatever and to yield to no one. Love yields freely, believes, condones, and tolerates everything. Therefore it is often deceived. Yet when it is deceived, it does not suffer any hardship that can really be called a hardship; that is, it does not lose Christ, and therefore it is not offended but keeps its constancy in doing good even toward those who are unthankful and unworthy.[20]

Both faith and love have confidence, but their objects are different. Faith has confidence in God; therefore it cannot be deceived. Love has confidence in men; therefore it is often deceived. The confidence that love has is so necessary for this present life that without it life on earth could not go on. If one man did not believe and trust another, what would our life on earth be?[21]

The paradox of love for Luther is that we are commanded to love, yet true love is not something we can do on our own. He writes, "He who refuses to obey this commandment is hereby informed that he is not a Christian, even though he may be called a Christian."[22]

It is the law and commandment of Christ that one must love him with the whole soul, the whole mind, and all powers, and the neighbor as one's self; and he who has this has everything and God dwells in him; this is certain. But you may say: Oh, it is utterly impossible for a person to keep these two commandments. Yes, it is impossible for you to keep or perform them. You cannot do it; God must do it in you, for him it is possible.[23]

Luther does not have much time or patience with those who preach love and act otherwise. The following excerpts are from his "Sermon on the Sum of the Christian Life."

> What, then, is the sum total of what should be preached? St Paul's answer is: "The aim of our charge is love that issues from a pure heart and a good conscience and sincere faith."
>
> There it is; there you have everything in a nutshell, expressed in the finest and fullest way and yet briefly and quickly said and easily retained. . . . What must be there is what the law really requires, and that is love, and the kind of love that flows like a rivulet, a stream, or a spring from a heart which is pure and a good conscience and sincere, unfeigned faith. If that's the way it goes, it's right; if not, then the meaning and sense of the whole law is missed.
>
> Now these other teachers also use this word. They preach and puff a lot about love. But they do so only from their own angle and turn it to their own advantage, just as the heretics, the godless, and the rascals also have love, but only among themselves and for those who are like them, but meanwhile they hate and persecute all good Christians and would gladly murder them if they could. But it is still a long way from being love when I select a person or two who please me and do what I wish and treat them kindly and favorably and nobody else. This is a crummy love [*parteken liebe*] which does not issue from a pure heart but is nothing but a filthy mess.
>
> True love flows from a pure heart. God has commanded me to let my love go out to my neighbor and be kindly disposed to all, whether they be my friends or enemies, just as our heavenly Father himself does. He allows his sun to rise and shine on the good and evil and is most kind to those who are constantly dishonoring him and misusing his goods through disobedience, blasphemy, sin, and shame. He sends rain on the grateful and the selfish [Matt. 5:45; Luke 6:35] and gives even to the worst rascals on earth many good things from the earth, and money and possessions besides. Why does he do this? Out of sheer, pure love, of which his heart is full to overflowing, and which he pours out freely over every one without exception, be he good or bad, worthy or unworthy. This is a real, divine, total, and perfect love, which does not single out one person nor cut and divide itself, but goes out freely to all. The other kind of love—when I am a good friend to one who can serve and help me and who esteems me, and hate the one who disregards me and is not on my side—is false love. For

it does not issue from a heart which is basically good and pure, the same toward all alike, but which rather seeks only its own and is stuffed full with love for itself and not for others; for he loves nobody except for his own advantage, regards only what will serve him, and seeks in everyone his own profit, not the neighbor's. If you praise and honor that kind of a person, he smiles; but if you make a sour face at him or say something he doesn't like to hear, he flares up, begins to scold and curse, and the friendship is over.

On the contrary, he who has a pure heart should be so in accord with God's Word and his example that he will wish everyone well and do good to all, as God wishes him well and gives his divine love to him. If God can bestow all good upon Judas the traitor or Caiaphas, as well as upon his good children, why should I not also do the same? For what can we give to him which he has not more richly given to us?

Yes, you say, but he is my enemy and he does nothing but evil to me. Yes, my dear man, he is God's enemy too and he does far more evil to him than he can do to you or to me. But my love should not grow dim or cease because he is evil and unworthy of it. If he is evil, he will find it out; but his wickedness must not overcome me. On the contrary, if through love, I can rebuke and admonish him or pray for him, that he may amend his ways and escape punishment, this I should do and do gladly. But to want to fly out at him and become his enemy and do evil to him besides, this will not do; for what good will it do me? It will not make me any better and it only makes him worse.

But what is it that makes the heart pure? The answer is that there is no better way of making it pure than through the highest purity, which is God's Word. Get that into your heart and order your life by it, and your heart will become pure. For example, take this saying: "You shall love your neighbor as yourself" [Matt. 19:19], and order your life by that, and you will see very well whether it will not wash it clean and scour out the selfishness and self-love which is there. For when he commands you to love your neighbor he excludes nobody, be he friend or enemy, good or evil. For even though he be a bad man and one who does evil to you, he does not on that account lose the name of neighbor but remains your flesh and blood and is included in the words: Love your neighbor. Therefore I say to you, if you look at him in the way the Word teaches and directs you, your heart will become pure and your love true, so that you will make no false distinction between persons nor will you look upon him as anything but another person who is good and does good to you.[24]

Pure love is like a stream flowing from one's heart, Luther says. Its quality is not derived from the person loved but from the Word, Jesus Christ.

> It is true, of course, that the good man is more likeable and everybody naturally is glad to associate with him, whereas one shies away from rough, evil people. But this is still flesh and blood and not yet the true Christian love, for a Christian must not derive his love from the person, as the world does, as a young man is attracted by a good looking wench, a skinflint by money and property, or a lord or prince by honor and power. All this is a derived or borrowed love, which cleaves outwardly to the good it sees in a person and lasts no longer than this good lasts and can be enjoyed. This love, however, should be a flowing love, which flows from the inside of the heart like a fresh stream that goes on flowing and cannot be stopped or dried up. This love says: I love you, not because you are good or bad; for I draw my love, not from your goodness, as from another's fountain, but from my own little spring, from the Word, which is grafted in my heart and which bids me to love my neighbor. Then it flows out abundantly and is there for all who need it, touching both the good and the bad, friend and foe. Indeed, it is ready most of all for enemies, because they are the ones who have more need that I should help them out of their misery and sins and especially for the greatest good I can do them, namely, to pray for them and do whatever I can that they too may become good and be delivered from sins and the devil. Look this is a love that flows out of the heart, not into it; for it finds nothing in it from which it can draw this love, but because he is a Christian and lays hold of the Word which in itself is altogether pure, it also makes his heart so pure and full of genuine love that he lets his love flow out to every man and does not stop at anybody, no matter who the person is.[25]

Luther has no time for lukewarm Christianity, no time for hypocrites, and no time for those who have a soft view of Christian love. The following excerpts are from his 1535 "Lectures on Galatians." The "sophists" he refers to are some of his contemporary theologians.

> The notion that the sophists have about the word "love" is completely cold and vain. They say that "to love" means nothing else than to wish someone well, or that love is a quality inhering in the mind by which a person elicits the motivation in his heart or the action which they call "wishing well." This is a completely bare, meager, and mathematical love, which does not

become incarnate, so to speak, and does not go to work. By contrast, Paul says that love should be a servant, and that unless it is in the position of a servant, it is not love.[26]

Therefore let no one think that he knows this commandment, "You shall love your neighbor," perfectly. It is very short, and so far as its words are concerned, it is very easy. But show me the preachers and hearers who truly practice and produce it in their teaching and living. I see both groups taking it easy! Thus the words "Through love be servants of one another" and "You shall love your neighbor as yourself" are eternal words, which no one can adequately ponder, teach, and practice. It is amazing that godly people have this trial: their conscience is immediately wounded if they omit some trifling thing that they should have done, but not if, as happens every day, they neglect Christian love and do not act toward their neighbor with a sincere and brotherly heart. They do not put as high an estimate on the commandment of love as they do on their own superstitions, from which they are never completely free in this life.

Therefore Paul is chiding the Galatians with the words "The whole Law is fulfilled in one word." It is as though he were saying: "You are fine people! You are immersed in your superstitions and ceremonies about special places, seasons, and foods, which are of no benefit either to you or to anyone else; meanwhile you neglect love, which is the only thing that has to be observed. How insane you are!" Thus Jerome also says: "We punish our bodies with vigils, fasts, and labors; but we neglect love, which is the lord and master of all works." This is especially evident in the monks. They rigidly observe their traditions about ceremonies, food, and clothing; if someone neglects anything here, be it ever so small, he commits a mortal sin. But they are not the least bit frightened by the fact that they not only neglect love but even hate one another bitterly. [27]

The following excerpts illustrate Luther's affirmation of ordinary life as well as the link between service and love.

So also serving another person through love seems to reason to mean performing unimportant works such as the following: teaching the erring; comforting the afflicted; encouraging the weak; helping the neighbor in whatever way one can; bearing with his rude manners and impoliteness; putting up with annoyances, labors, and the ingratitude and contempt of men in both church and state; obeying the magistrates; treating one's par-

ents with respect; being patient in the home with a cranky wife and an un-
manageable family, and the like. But believe me, these works are so outstanding and brilliant that the whole world cannot comprehend their usefulness and worth; indeed, it cannot estimate the value of even one tiny
truly good work, because it does not measure works or anything else on the
basis of the Word of God but on the basis of a reason that is wicked, blind,
and foolish.[28]

It is a brief statement, expressed beautifully and forcefully: "You shall love
your neighbor as yourself." No one can find a better, surer, or more available pattern than himself; nor can there be a nobler or more profound attitude of the mind than love; nor is there a more excellent object than one's
neighbor. Therefore the pattern, the attitude and the object are all superb.
Thus if you want to know how the neighbor is to be loved and want to
have an outstanding pattern of this, consider carefully how you love yourself. In need or in danger you would certainly want desperately to be loved
and assisted with all the counsels, resources, and powers not only of all men
but all of creation. And so you do not need any book to instruct and admonish you how you should love your neighbor, for you have the loveliest and best of books about all laws right in your own heart. You do not
need any professor to tell you about this matter; merely consult your own
heart, and it will give you abundant instruction that you should love your
neighbor as you love yourself. What is more, love is the highest virtue. It
is ready to be of service not only with its tongue, its hands, its money, and
its abilities but with its body and its very life. It is neither called forth by
anything that someone deserves nor deterred by what is undeserving and
ungrateful. A mother cherishes and cares for her child simply because she
loves him.[29]

Now our neighbor is any human being, especially one who needs our help,
as Christ interprets it in Luke 10:30–37. Even one who has done me some
sort of injury or harm has not shed his humanity on that account or
stopped being flesh and blood, a creature of God very much like me; in
other words, he does not stop being my neighbor. Therefore as long as
human nature remains in him, so long the commandment of love remains
in force, requiring of me that I not despise my own flesh and not return
evil for evil but overcome evil with good (Rom. 12:21). Otherwise love will
never "bear, endure," etc. (1 Cor. 13:7). It does not amputate a diseased limb
but cherishes it and takes care of it. "And those parts of the body which

we think less honorable," Paul says (1 Cor. 12:23), "we invest with the greater honor." But many people are so unmindful of this commandment that even when they know someone who is endowed with many outstanding qualities and virtues, but can find even one little flaw or blemish in him, they will look only at this and will forget all his good qualities and assets. You will find many mockers so inhuman and spiteful that they do not refer to the objects of their malice by their proper names but describe them with some contemptuous nickname like "Cockeyed" or "Hooknose" or "Bigmouth." In short, the world is the kingdom of the devil, which, in its supreme smugness, despises faith and love and all the words and deeds of God.

This is why Paul commends love to the Galatians and to all Christians, and exhorts them through love to be servants of one another.[30]

Self-Love

Thus you do wrong if you love yourself, an evil from which you will not be free unless you love your neighbor in the same way, that is, by ceasing to love yourself.

—Martin Luther, *Lectures on Romans*

If Luther is wary of the idea that we can love God, he is deeply suspicious of the idea that we ought to love ourselves. Because of sin we are inclined toward excessive self-love; we are, he says, "curved in" on ourselves. Luther discusses true love of self as love of neighbor.

Let each of us please his neighbor. "In this way," as blessed Gregory says, "love reaches out to another person, so that it can be love. For no one is said to have charity for himself." And in the gloss I pointed out that charity is love not for oneself but for another. Likewise as soon as the apostle rejected self-complacency, he immediately went on to teach that we should please our neighbor. Therefore to please our neighbor means not to please oneself. But this statement of Gregory's and our own statement appear to be contradicted by the famous definition of the different ways of loving and their order. For in accord with blessed Augustine, the Master of the Sentences affirms: "First we must love God, then our own soul, then the soul of our neighbor, and finally our own body." Ordered love therefore begins with itself. The answer to this is that this is one of the things by which we are led away from love as long as we do not fully understand it. For as long as we first use each good for ourselves, we are not concerned about our neighbor. But true love for yourself is hatred of yourself. As our Lord said: "For whoever would love his life, will lose it, and he who hates his life will find it" (cf. Mark 8:35). And the apostle in Phil. 2:4 says: "Let each of you look not only to his own interests, but also to the interests of others." And 1 Cor. 13:5: "Love does not insist on its own way." Therefore he who hates himself and loves his neighbor, this person truly loves himself. For he loves himself outside of himself, thus he loves himself purely as long as he loves himself in his neighbor.

Hence with all respect for the judgment of others and with reverence for the fathers, I want to say what is on my mind, even if I speak like a fool: This does not seem to be a correct understanding of the law of love toward our neighbor when it is interpreted in such a way that we say that in this commandment the person who loves is the model (forma) by which one loves his neighbor, obviously because the commandment says "as yourself." Thus people conclude: It is necessary that you first love yourself and thus in keeping with this example (exemplar) of your love you then love your neighbor.

I believe that with this commandment "as yourself" man is not commanded to love himself but rather is shown the sinful love with which he does in fact love himself, as if to say: "You are completely curved in upon yourself and pointed toward love of yourself, a condition from which you will not be delivered unless you altogether cease loving yourself and, forgetting yourself, love your neighbor. For it is a perversity that we want to be loved by all and want to seek our interests in all people; but it is uprightness that if you do to everyone else what in your perverseness you want done to yourself, you will do good with the same zeal as you used to do evil. . . . So it also says here: "Love your neighbor as yourself", but not in the sense that you should love yourself; otherwise that would have been commanded. But now it is not commanded in this way, that the commandment is founded on this principle. Thus you do wrong if you love yourself, an evil from which you will not be free unless you love your neighbor in the same way, that is, by ceasing to love yourself.[31]

Married Love

In Scripture, therefore, He also commanded man and woman to love each other, and He shows that the sexual union of husband and wife is also most pleasing to Him. Hence this desire and love must not be absent, for it is a good fortune and a great pleasure, if only it continues as long as possible.
—Martin Luther, *Sermons on the Sermon on the Mount*

In the following excerpts we hear Luther describe married love as the greatest of human loves.

> God makes distinctions between the different kinds of love, and shows that the love of a man and woman is (or should be) the greatest and purest of all loves. For he says, "A man shall leave his father and mother and cleave to his wife" [Gen. 2:24], and the wife does the same, as we see happening around us every day. Now there are three kinds of love: false love, natural love, and married love. False love is that which seeks its own, as a man loves money, possessions, honor, and women taken outside of marriage and against God's command. Natural love is that between father and child, brother and sister, friend and relative, and similar relationships. But over and above all these is married love, that is, a bride's love, which glows like a fire and desires nothing but the husband. She says, "It is you I want, not what is yours: I want neither your silver nor your gold; I want neither. I want only you. I want you in your entirety, or not at all." All other kinds of love seek something other than the loved one: this kind wants only to have the beloved's own self completely. If Adam had not fallen, the love of bride and groom would have been the loveliest thing. Now this love is not pure either, for admittedly a married partner desires to have the other, yet each seeks to satisfy his desire with the other, and it is this desire which corrupts this kind of love. Therefore, the married state is now no longer pure and free from sin. The temptation of the flesh has become so strong and consuming that marriage may be likened to a hospital for incurables which prevents inmates from falling into graver sin. Before Adam fell it was a simple matter to remain virgin and chaste, but now it is hardly possible, and without special grace from God, quite impossible.[32]

As we are sinners, we need God's grace in all areas of our lives. Marriage is no exception.

> When a man does not look at his wife, on the basis of the Word of God, as the one whom God gives him and whom He blesses, and when instead he turns his gaze to another woman, this is the principal cause of adultery, which then is almost inevitable. Soon the heart follows the eyes, bringing on the desire and appetite that I ought to reserve for my wife alone. Flesh and blood is curious enough anyway. It soon has its fill and loses its taste for what it has, and it gapes at something else. With the devil's promptings, a person sees only his wife's faults, losing sight of her good and laudable

qualities. As a consequence, every other woman seems more beautiful and better to my eyes than my own wife. Indeed, many a man with a truly beautiful and pious wife lets himself be hoodwinked into hating her and taking up with some vile and ugly bag.

As I have pointed out more fully in my other discussions of marriage and married life, it would be a real art and a very strong safeguard against all this if everyone learned to look at his spouse correctly, according to God's Word, which is the dearest treasure and the loveliest ornament you can find in a man or a woman. If he mirrored himself in this, then he would hold his wife in love and honor as a divine gift and treasure. And if he saw another woman, even one more beautiful than his own wife, he would say: "Is she beautiful? As far as I am concerned, she is not very beautiful. And even if she were the most beautiful woman on earth, in my wife at home I have a lovelier adornment, one that God has given me and has adorned with His Word beyond the others, even though she may not have a beautiful body or may have other failings. Though I may look over all the women in the world, I cannot find any about whom I can boast with a joyful conscience as I can about mine: 'This is the one whom God has granted to me and put into my arms.' I know that He and all the angels are heartily pleased if I cling to her lovingly and faithfully. Then why should I despise this precious gift of God and take up with someone else, where I can find no such treasure or adornment?"

This argument and inquiry has come from some: "Is it sinful for a man and a woman to desire each other for the purpose of marriage?" This is ridiculous, a question that contradicts both Scripture and nature. Why would people get married if they did not have desire and love for each other? Indeed, that is just why God has given this eager desire to bride and bridegroom, for otherwise everybody would flee from marriage and avoid it. In Scripture, therefore, He also commanded man and woman to love each other, and He shows that the sexual union of husband and wife is also most pleasing to Him. Hence this desire and love must not be absent, for it is a good fortune and a great pleasure, if only it continues as long as possible. Without it there is trouble: from the flesh, because a person soon gets tired of marriage and refuses to bear the daily discomfort that comes with it; and from the devil, who cannot stand the sight of a married couple treating each other with genuine love and who will not rest until he has given them an occasion for impatience, conflict, hate, and bitterness. Therefore it is an art both necessary and difficult, and one peculiarly Christian, this art of loving one's husband or wife properly, of bearing the other's faults and all the accidents and troubles. At first everything goes all right, so that, as the saying goes, they are ready to eat each other up for love. But when their curiosity has been satisfied, then the devil comes along to create boredom in you, to rob you of your desire in this direction, and to excite it unduly in another direction.[33]

The whole basis and essence of marriage is that each gives himself or herself to the other, and they promise to remain faithful to each other and not give themselves to any other. By binding themselves to each other, and surrendering themselves to each other, the way is barred to the body of anyone else, and they content themselves in the marriage bed with their one companion. In this way God sees to it that the flesh is subdued so as not to rage wherever and however it pleases, and, within this plighted troth, permits even more occasion than is necessary for the begetting of children. But, of course, a man has to control himself and not make a filthy sow's sty of his marriage.[34]

CHAPTER EIGHT

Christian Love Is Sacrificial Love

The sources of this chapter are three influential Protestant theologians of the nineteenth and twentieth centuries, Soren Kierkegaard (1813–1855), Anders Nygren (1890–1977), and Reinhold Niebuhr (1892–1971). The three describe Christian love in a bold and exclusive manner. In contrast to love in the mystical tradition, love for these theologians is to be concretely expressed. We are to love our neighbors. In contrast to interpretations of Christian love that include a positive place for self-regard, these theologians highlight self-sacrifice. This chapter can be read as a continuation and development of Martin Luther's theology.

Soren Kierkegaard: On Genuine Love

When you open the door which you shut in order to pray to God, the first person you meet as you go out is your neighbor whom you *shall* love.
—Soren Kierkegaard, *Works of Love*

Soren Kierkegaard was one of those rare creative persons whose contemporaries find strange and fanatical, but later generations find interesting, if not compelling.[1] He was born in Copenhagen in 1813, and he lived there most of his life until his death in 1855. Georg Lukacs writes that in Copenhagen Kierkegaard lived "as a noted eccentric; his peculiar ways made him a constant target for the humorous papers, and although his writings, published under a variety of pen-names, found some admirers because they were so full of wit, they were hated by the majority" of readers. "His later works made still more open enemies for him—namely, all the leaders of the ruling Protestant Church."[2]

Kierkegaard was born into a strict religious household, yet he found that his Danish Lutheran upbringing could not answer his most pressing questions. After rejecting religion and living a life of pleasure, he returned to the church and studied to become a pastor. An event often cited as pivotal is Kierkegaard's short-term engagement to Regine Olsen in 1840. Although he broke off the engagement after a year, thinking he could not marry, Regine remained in his thoughts and writings. Regine eventually married, while Kierkegaard remained single throughout his life. After ending the engagement Kierkegaard decided not to pursue the ministry and lived a solitary life as an author.[3] "He believed himself to be an exception to the rule of marriage and, on the other hand, quite clearly destined for a life of religiously oriented authorship."[4] Lukacs, in critical voice, describes Kierkegaard as both a troubadour and a Platonist. "In the woman-glorifying poetry of the Provencal troubadours, great faithlessness was the basis for great faithfulness; a woman had to belong to another in order to become the ideal, in order to be loved with real love. But Kierkegaard's faithfulness was even greater than the troubadour's, and for that reason even more faithless: even the deeply beloved woman was only a means, only a way towards the great, the only absolute love, the love for God."[5]

Kierkegaard was a prolific writer. One commentator suggests that on review of his many works "he could justly qualify as a novelist, essayist, satirist, philosopher, humorist, theologian, psychologist, journalist, sociologist, poet."[6] He was a writer with a dramatic message. "To be a Christian, he said, is not simply to be born in a Christian country and grow up with the Christian virtues of decency, tolerance, and graciousness. To be a Christian is to become contemporary with the Christ who suffered and was persecuted, who castigated the Pharisees and was crucified."[7] Although there were plenty of good people around, true Christianity, he argued, no longer existed. For Kierkegaard philosophy was not about the development of abstract systems; philosophy was about the "expression of individual existence." The school of thought he is associated with is existentialism. The existentialist quality of Kierkegaard's writing is perhaps best captured by quoting the epitaph he composed for himself: "That individual."[8]

This section considers Kierkegaard's 1847 book *Works of Love*. The subtitle of the book, "Some Christian Reflections in the Form of Discourses," indicates that Kierkegaard's aim was to teach something new to the reader. He begins with the assumption that the reader knows nothing about true love.[9] The purpose of the book is to enable the reader to reflect objectively on his or her own life and "to consider anew God's command to him. *Works of Love* is an appeal for self-examination; it is to be read as though it speaks solely to *me* about *my* life."[10] Kierkegaard argues that Christian love, what he calls "genuine" love, is radically different from our usual views of love. Indeed, he says, "If anyone thinks that by falling in love or finding a friend he has learned Christian love, he is in profound error."[11] Kierkegaard argues there are several differences between genuine love and romantic love, or what he calls erotic love or friendship. The object of Christian love is the neighbor rather than the self. Christian love is stable and enduring; it is not subject to the ups and downs of emotions. Christian love is commanded not chosen.

> The object of both erotic love and friendship has therefore also the favourite's name, the beloved, the friend, who is loved in distinction from the rest of the world. On the other hand, the Christian teaching is to love one's neighbor, to love all mankind, all men, even enemies, and not to make exceptions, neither in favouritism nor in aversion.[12]

> Erotic love is based on disposition which, explained as inclination, has its highest, its unconditional, artistically unconditional, unique expression in that there is only one beloved in the whole world. . . . Christian love teaches love of all men, unconditionally all. Just as decidedly as erotic love strains in the direction of the one and only beloved, just as decidedly and powerfully does Christian love press in the opposite direction.[13]

> Erotic love is determined by its object; friendship is determined by the object; only love to one's neighbor is determined by love.[14]

> Erotic love and friendship are preferential and the passion of preference. Christian love is self-renunciation's love. . . . But the most passionate boundlessness of preference in excluding others is to love only the one and only; self-renunciation's boundlessness in giving itself is not to exclude a single one.[15]

> Christian love also has a one and only object, one's neighbor, but one's neighbor is as far as possible from being only one person, one and only, infinitely removed from this, for one's neighbour is all men.[16]

> Christianity has misgivings about erotic love and friendship because preference in passion or passionate preference is really another form of self-love.[17]

> Self-love and passionate preferences are essentially the same; but love of one's neighbor—that is genuine love.[18]

> Just as self-love in the strictest sense has been characterised as self-deification, so love and friendship . . . are essentially idolatry.[19]

To love oneself in the right way and to love one's neighbor correspond perfectly to one another; fundamentally they are one and the same thing.[20]

Christianity, however, teaches a man immediately the shortest way to find the highest good: shut your door and pray to God—for God is still the highest . . . when you open the door which you shut in order to pray to God, the first person you meet as you go out is your neighbor whom you *shall* love.[21]

Therefore he who in truth loves his neighbor loves also his enemy. . . . Men think that it is impossible for a human being to love his enemies, for enemies are hardly able to endure the sight of one another. Well, then, shut your eyes—and your enemy looks just like your neighbor.[22]

Your neighbor is every man, for on the basis of distinctions he is not your neighbor, nor on the basis of likeness to you as being different from other men. He is your neighbor on the basis of equality with you before God; but this equality absolutely every man has, and has it absolutely.[23]

Christian love is commanded and permanent. Other loves, says Kierkegaard, are spontaneous and thus depend on the circumstances.

Spontaneous love can be changed within itself; it can be changed to its opposite, to hate. . . . True love . . . is never changed, it has integrity; it loves—and never hates; it never hates the beloved.[24]

Spontaneous love can be changed within itself; by spontaneous combustion it can become jealousy; from the greatest happiness it can become the greatest torment. The heat of spontaneous love is so dangerous—no matter how great its passion is—so dangerous that this heat can easily become a fever.[25]

Only when it is a duty to love, only then is love eternally secured against every change, eternally made free in blessed independence, eternally and happily secured against despair.[26]

Can one truly love a friend or a spouse?

Do not give yourself over to the notion that you might compromise, that by loving some men, relatives and friends, you would love your neighbour. . . . No, love your beloved faithfully and tenderly, but let love to your neighbor be the sanctifier in your covenant of union with God; love your friend honestly and devotedly, but let love to your neighbor be what you learn from each other in the intimacy of friendship with God! . . . God is love; therefore we can resemble God only in loving, just as, according to the apostle's words, we can only "be God's co-workers—in love." Insofar as you love your beloved, you are not like unto God, for in God there is no partiality. . . . Insofar as you love your friend, you are not like unto God, because before God there is no distinction. But when you love your neighbour, then you are like unto God.[27]

Worldly wisdom thinks that love is a relationship between man and man. Christianity teaches that it is a relationship between: man—God—man, that is, that God is the middle term. However beautiful the love-relationship has been between two or more people, however complete all their enjoyment and their bliss in mutual devotion and affection have been for them, even if all men have praised this relationship—if God and the relationship to God have been left out, then, Christianly understood, this has not been love but a mutual enchanting illusion of love. For to love God is to love oneself in truth; to help another human being to love God is to love the other man; to be helped by another human being to love God is to be loved.[28]

To be sure, one's wife is to be loved differently than the friend and the friend differently from the neighbor, but this is not an essential difference, for the fundamental equality lies in the category neighbour. The category neighbour is just like the category human being. . . . Thus Christianity has nothing against a man loving his wife in a special way, but he must never love her in a special way that she is an exception to being a neighbor, which every human being is, for then he confuses Christianity—his wife does not become for him his neighbour, and thereby all other men do not become his neighbors, either.[29]

The commandment is that thou shall love, but when you understand life and yourself, then it is as if you should not need to be commanded, because to love human beings is still the only thing worth living for; without this love you really do not live; to love human beings is also the only salutary consolation for both time and eternity, and to love human beings is the only true sign that you are a Christian—truly, a confession of faith is not enough.[30]

Anders Nygren: *Agape* Is Uniquely Christian

Christian love moves in two directions, towards God and towards its neighbor; and in self-love it finds its chief adversary, which must be fought and conquered.

—Anders Nygren, *Agape and Eros*

Kierkegaard's critique of Christian love was the first prominent attempt in the modern era to call Christians to a pure or dramatic form of self-sacrificial love. This issue was brought to the forefront of theological discussions in the 1930s with the publication of Anders Nygren's book, *Agape and Eros*. Nygren lived from 1890 to 1977 and was bishop of Lund, in the Church of Sweden. In this influential book, Nygren argued that the New Testament notion of love, *agape*, is fundamentally different from and thus ought not to be confused with the platonic notion of *eros*. Nygren argued that *agape* is the unique feature of Christianity. He writes, "Without it nothing that is Christian would be Christian. Agape is Christianity's own original basic conception."[31] It is radically different from Eros; indeed the two are "contrary ideals or conceptions of what life means."[32] Nygren summarizes the difference between the two as follows.

> Eros is acquisitive desire and longing. —Agape is sacrificial giving.
>
> Eros is an upward movement. —Agape comes down.
>
> Eros is man's way to God. —Agape is God's way to man.
>
> Eros is man's effort: it assumes that man's salvation is his own work. —Agape is God's grace: salvation is the work of Divine love.
>
> Eros is egocentric love, a form of self-assertion of the highest, noblest, sublimest kind. —Agape is unselfish love, it "seeketh not its own", it gives itself away.
>
> Eros seeks to gain its life, a life divine, immortalised. —Agape lives the life of God, therefore dares to "lose it."
>
> Eros is the will to get and possess which depends on want and need. —Agape is freedom in giving, which depends on wealth and plenty.
>
> Eros is primarily man's love; God is the object of Eros. Even when it is attributed to God, Eros is patterned on human love. —Agape is primarily God's love; "God is Agape." Even when it is attributed to man, Agape is patterned on Divine love.
>
> Eros is determined by the quality, the beauty and worth, of its object; it is not spontaneous, but "evoked", "motivated". —Agape is sovereign in relation to its object, and is directed to both "the evil and the good"; it is spontaneous, "overflowing unmotivated".

> Eros recognises value in its object—and loves it. —Agape loves—and
> creates value in its object.[33]

Nygren's point was not merely one of comparison but one of critique. He held
that the Christian tradition since the early church has distorted Agape by fus-
ing it with Eros. Augustine transformed and indeed deformed the New Testament perspective on love, and most of the Christian tradition followed his lead.[34]
Agape and Eros offered a detailed description of how the Christian theological
tradition, until Martin Luther, held a mistaken view of love. Nygren's reading of
history is that "There are times, like those of primitive Christianity and the
Reformation, when the specifically Christian conception thrust itself powerfully
to the fore; at other times it has to struggle, often against odds, to maintain itself against alien conceptions of love."[35] The "alien" conception of love he refers
to is *caritas*. Nygren's contribution to Christian reflection on love cannot be un-
derestimated. It is largely because of him that Christians today often refer to
the typology of love and agape love as distinct from other forms of love.

Reinhold Niebuhr: Christian Love Is an Impossible Ideal

> The animated purpose of his life is to conform to the agape of God. His
> life culminates in an act of self-abnegation in which the individual will
> cease to be a protagonist of the individual life; and his life ends upon the
> Cross.
>
> —Reinhold Niebuhr, *The Nature and Destiny of Man*

Reinhold Niebuhr was born in 1892 in Missouri. A son of a minister, he followed
his father's calling and in 1915 became pastor of a small parish in Detroit. His time
in Detroit brought him face-to-face with the economic and social conditions of
the working class. This experience afforded him the context in which to consider
issues of social justice as well as the relation of Christianity to the social order.
Harlan Beckley writes, "Niebuhr's thirteen-year parish ministry provided a lab-
oratory for making observations, not a crucible for a sensitizing encounter with
poverty. His observations soon convinced him that the 'mild moral idealism' of
his more youthful liberalism was not sufficient to realize the reform of industrial
relations in America."[36] In 1928 Niebuhr moved to New York to take a teaching
position at Union Seminary where he stayed until his retirement in 1961.

Niebuhr is most remembered for his contribution to a movement or school
of thought known as "Christian Realism." In Niebuhr's words, realism "denotes
the disposition to take all factors in a social and political situation, which offer
resistance to established norms, into account, particularly the factors of self-

interest and power."[37] A dominant theme of realism is the "tension between the ideal and the actual."[38] Robin Lovin comments, "Niebuhr learned to trace the power of ideas, illusions, and self-deceptions in the movement of large historical forces, and so he came to interpret the events of his century for a much wider audience than other theologians could command."[39] Niebuhr's work had an enormous influence. Charles Brown writes, "By energetic teaching and preaching and through a constant flow of books and articles he helped mold the vital center" in U.S. foreign and domestic policy as well as to lead "American Protestantism in recovering its biblical and theological heritage in creative relationship with modern culture."[40] From the 1930s through the 1960s, through the Great Depression, World War II, and the cold war, Niebuhr served as a mentor to "an influential following of clergy, scholars, journalists, and politicians."[41] In March 1948 his picture appeared on the cover of *Time*.

Niebuhr's theology of love sets the frame of reference for his understanding of realism. There is, he held, an irresolvable tension in human life between the ideal and the actual.[42] On one hand there is the ideal, namely the pure love Jesus lived and taught, and on the other hand, we have the actual human condition of living in the world and living among people in society. In Niebuhr's words, "The love commandment stands in juxtaposition to the fact of sin."[43] Love, he says, is the "impossible possibility" in human existence.[44] This plays out in interesting ways in his theology.

In the eyes of the world, Niebuhr writes, the greatest love people can strive for is mutual love. Mutual love by definition is reciprocal love. Each person in a relationship expects to get something out of the relationship. Niebuhr rejects the notion that mutual love is the highest form of love. For if one looks out for one's own interest in love, one does not really love. Niebuhr holds that if mutual love is thought to be the ultimate good, then that necessarily leads one to pursue actions based on self-interest.[45] Yet he does not reject such love outright. Sacrificial love, he suggests, stands in paradoxical relation to mutual love because mutual love can only be initiated by sacrificial love.[46] True love, he writes, may elicit but can never require a reciprocal response.[47]

As an ideal, the love command is not directly applicable to social life. Yet love does require justice in social life. Niebuhr argues for a view of justice as "the best that is possible" given a particular situation. Justice is never then absolute; it always stands in relation to higher levels of justice that more adequately reflect the ideal of love. He writes,

> The dream of perpetual peace and brotherhood for human society is one which will never be fully realized. It is a vision prompted by the conscience and insight of individual man, but incapable of fulfillment by collective

man. It is like all true religious visions, possible of approximation but not of realization in actual history. . . . [Our] concern for some centuries to come is not the creation of an ideal society in which there will be unco-erced and perfect peace and justice, but a society in which there will be enough justice, and in which coercion will be sufficiently non-violent to prevent . . . disaster.[48]

The first set of excerpts is taken from an essay Niebuhr published in 1932 titled "The Ethic of Jesus and the Social Problem." They highlight Niebuhr's notion of true love and actual life. They also introduce his view of justice.

There is indeed a very rigorous ethical ideal in the gospel of Jesus, but there is no social ethic in the ordinary sense of the word in it, precisely because the ethical ideal is too rigorous and perfect to lend itself to application in the economic and political problems of our day. This does not mean that the ethic of Jesus has no light to give to a modern Christian who faces the perplexing economic and political issues of a technological civilization. It means only that confusion will be avoided if a rigorous distinction is made between a perfectionist and absolute ethic and the necessities of a social situation.

The ethic of Jesus was, to begin with, a personal ethic. . . . His ethic was an ethic of love, and it therefore implied social relationships. But it was an individual ethic in the sense that his chief interest was in the quality of life of an individual. . . . He was not particularly interested in the Jewish people's aspirations toward freedom from Rome, and skillfully evaded the effort to make him take sides in that political problem. He accepted monar-chy on the one hand and slavery on the other, though he called attention to the difference between the ideal of his Kingdom, which measured great-ness by service, and the kind of greatness which the "kings of the Gentiles" attained.[49]

But this very emphasis upon religious motives lifts the ethic of Jesus above the area of social ethics. We are asked to love our enemies, not because the social consequences of such love will be to make friends of the enemies, but because God loves with that kind of impartiality. We are demanded to for-give those who have wronged us, not because a forgiving spirit will prove redemptive in the lives of the fallen, but because God forgives his sins. Here we have an ethic, in other words, which we can neither disavow nor per-fectly achieve.[50]

In practical terms it means a combination of anarchism and communism dominated by the spirit of love. Such perfect love as he demands would obviate the necessity of coercion on the one hand because men would refrain from transgressing upon their neighbor's rights, and on the other hand because such transgression would be accepted and forgiven if it did occur. That is anarchism, in other words. It would mean communism because the privileges of each would be potentially the privileges of all. Where love is perfect the distinctions between mine and thine disappear. The social ideal of Jesus is as perfect and as impossible of attainment as is his personal ideal. But again it is an ideal that cannot be renounced completely.[51]

Whether we view the ethical teachings of Jesus from the perspective of the individual or of society we discover an unattainable ideal, but a very useful one. It is an ideal never attained in history or in life, but one that gives us an absolute standard by which to judge both personal and social righteousness.[52]

The struggle for social justice in the present economic order involves the assertion of rights, the rights of the disinherited, and the use of coercion. Both are incompatible with the pure love ethic found in the Gospels. . . . Whatever may be possible for individuals, we see no possibility of a group voluntarily divesting itself of its special privileges in society. Nor do we see a possibility of pure disinterestedness and the spirit of forgiveness on the part of an underprivileged group shaming a dominant group into an attitude of social justice. Such a strategy might possibly work in intimate personal relationships but it does not work in the larger group relations.[53]

The social struggle involves a violation of a pure ethic of love, not only in the assertion of rights, but in the inevitable use of coercion. Here again one need but state the obvious; but the obvious is usually not recognized by academic moralists. No society can exist without the use of coercion, though every intelligent society will try to reduce coercion to a minimum and rely upon the factor of mutual consent to give stability to its institutions. Yet it can never trust all of its citizens to accept necessary social arrangements voluntarily. It will use police force against recalcitrant and antisocial minorities, and it will use the threat of political force against a complacent and indifferent group of citizens which could never be relied upon to initiate adequate social policies upon its own accord. No government can wait upon voluntary action on the part of the privileged.[54]

The love ideal which Jesus incarnates may be too pure to be realized in life, but it offers us nevertheless an ideal toward which the religious spirit may strive. . . . The fact that in Jesus the spirit of love flowed out in emulation of God's love, without regard to social consequences, cannot blind the eye to the social consequences of a religiously inspired love. If modern religion were really producing it, it would mitigate the evils of the social struggle. It would, to emphasize the obvious once more, not abolish the social struggle, because it would not approximate perfection in sufficiently numerous instances. The fight for justice in society will always be a fight. But wherever the spirit of justice grows imaginative and is transmuted into love, a love in which the interests of the other are espoused, the struggle is transcended by just that much.[55]

The second set of excerpts is from his 1932 book *Moral Man and Immoral Society*. These selections reaffirm the impossibility of the love command.

The transcendent perspective of religion makes all men our brothers and nullifies the divisions, by which nature, climate, geography and the accidents of history divide the human family. By this insight many religiously inspired idealists have transcended nation, racial and class distinctions.[56]

The great seers and saints of religion have always placed their hope for the redemption of society in the possibility of making the love-universalism, implicit in religious morality, effective in the whole human society. . . . It was a natural and inevitable hope in the early Christian community that the spirit of love, which pervaded the life of its own group, would eventually inform the moral life of the whole human race. That hope has been reborn again and again in the history of the Western world.[57]

Love is most active when the vividness or nearness of the need prompts those whose imagination is weak, and the remoteness of the claim challenges those whose imagination is sensitive.

   Love, which depends upon emotion, whether it expresses itself in transient sentiment or constant goodwill, is baffled by the more intricate social relations in which the highest ethical attitudes are achieved only by careful calculation.[58]

The weaknesses of the spirit of love in solving larger and more complex problems become increasingly apparent as one proceeds from ordinary relations between individuals to the life of social groups. If nations and other social groups find it difficult to approximate the principles of justice, as we have previously noted, they are naturally even less capable of achieving the principle of love, which demands more than justice . . . no nation in history has ever been known to be purely unselfish in its actions. The same may be said of class groups with equal certainty.[59]

The paradox of the moral life consists in this: that the highest mutuality is achieved where mutual advantages are not consciously sought as the fruit of love. For love is purest where it desires no returns for itself; and it is most potent where it is purest. Complete mutuality, with its advantages to each party to the relationship, is therefore more perfectly realized where it is not intended, but love is poured out without seeking returns.[60]

The following excerpts are from his book *An Interpretation of Christian Ethics* published in 1935. Note the contrast between love and the natural tendency of persons and groups to look out for themselves, as well as his discussion of the place of forgiveness in love.

The Christian believes that the ideal of love is real in the will and nature of God, even though he knows of no place in history when the ideal has been realized in its pure form.[61]

The religion of Jesus is prophetic religion in which the moral ideal of love and vicarious suffering, elaborated by the second Isaiah, achieves such a purity that the possibility of its realization in history becomes remote. His Kingdom of God is always a possibility in history, because its heights of pure love are organically related to the expedience of love in all human life, but it is also an impossibility in history and always beyond every historical achievement.[62]

The ethic of Jesus does not deal at all with the immediate moral problem of every human life. . . . It has nothing to say about the relativities of politics and economics, nor of the necessary balances of power which exist and must exist in even the most intimate social relationship. The absolutism and perfectionism of Jesus' love ethic sets itself uncompromisingly not only against the natural self-regarding impulses, but against the necessary prudent defenses of the self, required because of the egoism of others.[63]

The very basis of self-love is the natural will to survive. In man the animal impulse to maintain life becomes an immediate temptation to assert the self against the neighbor. Therefore, in the ethic of Jesus, concern for physical existence is prohibited.[64]

In the thought of Jesus men are to be loved not because they are equally divine, but because God loves them equally; and they are to be forgiven (the highest form of love) because all (the self included) are equally far from God and in need of his grace.[65]

The will of God is defined in terms of all-inclusive love.[66]

The ethical demands made by Jesus are incapable of fulfillment in the present existence of man.[67]

The impossibility of the ideal (the love commandment) must be insisted upon against all those forms of naturalism, liberalism, and radicalism which generate utopian illusion and regard the love commanded as ultimately realizable because history knows no limits of its progressive approximations.[68]

Christ is thus the revelation of the very impossible possibility which the Sermon on the Mount elaborates in ethical terms.[69]

Only a forgiving love, grounded in repentance, is adequate to heal the animosities between nations. But that degree of love is an impossibility for nations. It is a very rare achievement among individuals.[70]

In a struggle between those who enjoy inordinate privileges and those who lack the basic essentials of the good life, it is fairly clear that a religion which holds love to be the final law of life stultifies itself if it does not support equal justice as a political and economic approximation of the ideal of love.[71]

To command love is a paradox; for love cannot be commanded or demanded. To love God with all our hearts and all our souls and all our minds means that every cleavage in human existence is overcome.[72]

The Christian love commanded does not demand love of the fellow-man because he is with us equally divine (Stoicism), or because we ought to have "respect for personality", but because God loves him.[73]

> The crown of Christian Ethics is the doctrine of forgiveness. . . . Love as forgiveness is the most difficult and impossible of moral achievements. Yet it is a possibility if the impossibility of love is recognized and the sin in the self is acknowledged.[74]

> Forgiveness in the absolute sense is therefore an impossibility as much as any other portion of Christ's perfectionism.[75]

Sacrificial love is true love. It transcends both mutual love and justice. The excerpts below are from Niebuhr's *The Nature and Destiny of Man*, published in 1943. Note his brief criticism of the mystical tradition.

> Christ as the norm of human nature defines the final perfection of man in history. This perfection is . . . the perfection of sacrificial love. The same Cross which symbolizes the love of God and reveals the divine perfection to be not incompatible with a suffering involvement in historical tragedy, also indicates that the perfection of man is not attainable in history.[76]

> From the standpoint of history mutual love is the highest good. . . . The sacrifice of the self or others is therefore a violation of natural standards of morals, as limited by historical existence.[77]

> Mutuality is not a possible achievement if it is made the intention and the goal of any action. Sacrificial love is thus paradoxically related to mutual love.[78]

Without the truth of the Cross

> [the ethical life] tends to denigrate either into egoist utilitarianism, which makes self-regarding motives ethically normative; or into a mystical ethics which flees from the tensions and incomplete harmonies of history to an undifferentiated unity of life in eternity.[79]

> Love which seeketh not its own is not able to maintain itself in historical society.[80]

Speaking of Jesus, Niebuhr writes,

> The animated purpose of his life is to conform to the agape of God. His life culminates in an act of self-abnegation in which the individual will cease to be a protagonist of the individual life; and his life ends upon the Cross.[81]

The Cross symbolizes the perfection of love which transcends all particular norms of justice and mutuality in history.[82]

There is always the possibility of sacrificing our life and interest; and this possibility always has the corresponding assurance that to lose our life thus is to gain it. But such a gain cannot be measured in terms of the history which is bound to nature. The gain can only be an integrity of spirit which has validity in "eternity."[83]

Sacrificial love (agape) completes the incompleteness of mutual love (eros), for the latter is always arrested by reason of the fact that it seeks to relate life to life from the standpoint of the self and for the sake of the self's own happiness. But a self which seeks to measure the possible reciprocity which its loves towards another may elicit is obviously not sufficiently free of preoccupation with self to lose itself in the life of the other.[84]

According to the ethic of Jesus the actual motive of agape is always conformity to the will of God.[85]

The God whom Christians worship reveals his majesty and holiness not in eternal disinterestedness but in suffering love. And the moral perfection, which the New Testament regards as normative, transcends history not as thought transcends action but as suffering love transcends mutual love. It is an act rather than a thought which sets the Christ above history, and being an act, it is more indubitably in history than a mere thought.[86]

The following excerpt is from an essay titled "Justice and Love," which appeared in 1950. Note the distinction between a simple Christian moralism and Christian Realism:

"A Christian . . . always considers the common welfare before his own interest." This simple statement reveals a few of the weaknesses of moralistic Christianity in dealing with problems of justice. The statement contains at least two errors, or perhaps one error and one omission.

The first error consists in defining a Christian in terms which assume that consistent selflessness is possible. No Christian, even the most perfect, is able "always" to consider the common interest before his own. . . . Unfortunately there is no such possibility for individual men; and perfect disinterestedness for groups and nations is even more impossible.

The other error is one of omission. To set self-interest and the general welfare in simple opposition is to ignore nine tenths of the ethical issues that confront the consciences of men. . . . A Christian justice will be particularly critical of the claims of the self as against the claims of the other, but it will not dismiss them out of hand. Without this criticism all justice becomes corrupted into a refined form of self-seeking. But if the claims of the self (whether individual or collective) are not entertained, there is no justice at all. There is an ecstatic form of agape which defines the ultimate heroic possibilities of human existence (involving, of course, martyrdom) but not the common possibilities of tolerable harmony of life with life.[87]

A simple Christian moralism counsels men to be unselfish. A profounder Christian faith must encourage men to create systems of justice which will save society and themselves from their own selfishness.[88]

But any illusion of a world of perfect love without these imperfect harmonies of justice must ultimately turn the dream of love into a nightmare of tyranny and injustice.[89]

CHAPTER NINE

Love Activists

This chapter examines three contemporary Christians who call for a level of loving that goes well beyond ordinary expectations: Martin Luther King, Jr., Mother Teresa, and Pope John Paul II. Each of these people has affected the lives of countless others around the world. These leaders, who are among the most important Christians of the twentieth century, were all moved to action by a particular vision of Christian love. With Martin Luther King, Jr., we hear the seemingly impossible command to love our enemies. With Mother Teresa we see another demanding aspect of biblical love lived out. Mother Teresa spent years caring for "the least of these," the poorest of the poor in the world, and advocated treating each as if he or she were Jesus. Pope John Paul II has preached a philosophy of personalism during his papacy. Personalism, he says, is a philosophical translation of the Great Commandment characterized by total self-giving.

Martin Luther King, Jr.

I believe firmly that love is a transforming power that can lift a whole community to new horizons of fair play, good will and justice.
— Martin Luther King, Jr., *Walk for Freedom*

It is not an exaggeration to say that Martin Luther King, Jr. changed the world. To people around the globe, his name evokes cries for freedom and justice. King was born on January 15, 1929, in Atlanta and was murdered, indeed martyred, thirty-nine years later on April 4, 1968, in Memphis. Outstanding leader, social prophet, winner of the 1964 Nobel Peace Prize, King is most often associated with his famous 1963 "I Have a Dream" speech. He made that impassioned speech on the stairs of the Lincoln Memorial in front of 250,000 people. His dream, including that his "four little children will one day live in a nation where they will not be judged by the color of their skin but by the content of their character"[1] continues to inspire us decades later. King is something of an icon, an image of a way of life based on justice, nonviolence, and love. He is a constant reminder and inspiration of individual responsibility to see these values through.

King's legacy is not tied primarily to his dreams. He is revered not only for what he believed America could be but also for how he worked to achieve his dream. King advocated a method of social transformation called "nonviolent direct action." He described nonviolent direct action as "a courageous confrontation of evil by the power of love, in the faith that it is better to be the recipient of violence than the inflicter of it, since the latter only multiplies the existence of violence and bitterness in the universe, while the former may develop a sense of shame in the oppressor and thereby bring about transformation and change of heart."[2] The striking feature of nonviolent direct action is that it not only demands change of the oppressors but also demands that the oppressed, those pursuing justice, must also be transformed. It is at this point that Martin Luther King, Jr. adds to the Christian tradition on love.

In his 1963 "Letter from Birmingham City Jail," King describes four stages of nonviolent direct action. First, he says, we must look at the facts of a situation and see if injustices exist. If indeed they do exist, the second stage is to seek to resolve them through negotiation. If the second stage fails, then steps are taken to prepare for direct action. The third stage, King says, is self-purification. People have to prepare themselves to be faithful participants. Only after these three stages are complete does direct action, such as marches and sitting at segregated lunch counters, begin. The purpose of nonviolent direct action, he argues, "is to create a situation so crisis packed that it will inevitably open the door to negotiation."[3]

Several features of King's philosophy relate to our topic of love. He holds that before one can be involved in direct action, that is to say, before one can appropriately face the consequences of direct action, that is, brutality, insults, and violence from angry racist mobs, one must be solidly grounded with a sense of purpose. Note how King describes the year-long Montgomery bus boycott.

> From the beginning, we have insisted on nonviolence. This is a protest—
> a nonviolent protest against injustice. We are depending on moral and spiritual forces. To put it another way, this is a movement of passive resistance, and the great instrument is the instrument of love. We feel that this is our chief weapon, and that no matter how long we are involved in the protest, no matter how tragic the experiences are, no matter what sacrifices we have to make, we will not let anybody drag us so low as to hate them.[4]

King says elsewhere: "In a world depending on force, coercive tyranny, and bloody violence, you are challenged to follow the way of love. You will then discover that unarmed love is the most powerful force in all the world."[5] The Montgomery bus boycott was a practical affirmation of King's intellectual commitment to nonviolent direct action. He became convinced that a commitment to Christian love combined with the nonviolence that he learned from studying the life and teachings of Mahatma Gandhi, "is one of the most potent weapons available to an oppressed people in their struggle for freedom."[6] Such love, he writes, "is a very stern love that would organize itself into collective action to right a wrong by taking on itself suffering."[7] In the epilogue to his important biography on King, David Garrow addresses our tendency to idolize King. Quoting one of King's classmates, Garrow writes, "By exalting the accomplishments of King Luther King, Jr. into a legendary tale that is annually told, we fail to recognize his humanity—his personal and public struggles—that are similar to yours and mine. By idolizing those whom we honor, we fail to realize that we could go and do likewise."[8]

The following excerpt is from an article where King describes the bus boycott and encourages blacks to "walk for freedom."

Love must be at the forefront of our movement if it is to be a successful movement. And when we speak of love, we speak of understanding, good will toward all men. We speak of a creative, a redemptive sort of love, so that as we look at the problem, we see that the real tension is not between the Negro citizens and the white citizens of Montgomery, but it is a conflict between justice and injustice, between the forces of light and the forces of darkness, and if there is a victory—and there will be a victory—the victory will not be merely for the Negro citizens and a defeat for the white citizens, but it will be a victory for justice and a defeat of injustice. It will be a victory for goodness in its long struggle with the forces of evil.

This is a spiritual movement, and we intend to keep these things in the forefront. We know that violence will defeat our purpose. We know that in our struggle in America and in our specific struggle here in Montgomery, violence will not only be impractical but immoral. We are outnumbered; we do not have access to the instruments of violence. Even more than that, not only is violence impractical, but it is immoral; for it is my firm conviction that to seek to retaliate with violence does nothing but intensify the existence of evil and hate in the universe.

Along the way of life, someone must have sense enough and morality enough to cut off the chain of hate and evil. The greatest way to do that is through love. I believe firmly that love is a transforming power that can lift a whole community to new horizons of fair play, good will and justice.[9]

The Montgomery bus boycott was successful but not without incident. King's house was firebombed.

> Love is our great instrument and our great weapon, and that alone. On January 30 my home was bombed. My wife and baby were there; I was attending a meeting. I first heard of the bombing at the meeting, when someone came to me and mentioned it, and I tried to accept it in a very calm manner. I first inquired about my wife and daughter; then after I found out that they were all right, I stopped in the midst of the meeting and spoke to the group, and urged them not to be panicky and not to do anything about it because that was not the way.
>
> I immediately came home and, on entering the front of the house, I noticed there were some five hundred to a thousand persons. I came in the house and looked it over and went back to see my wife and to see if the baby was all right, but as I stood in the back of the house, hundreds and hundreds of people were still gathering, and I saw that violence was a possibility. It was at that time that I went to the porch and tried to say to the people that we could not allow ourselves to be panicky. We could not allow ourselves to retaliate with any type of violence, but that we were still to confront the problem with love.[10]

King's view of love, inspired by the Sermon on the Mount, has a very particular focus, namely, love of enemies. He offers four reasons why we ought to love our enemies. The first is that only love can destroy hate. Hate creates more hate; violence begets violence. He writes, "The chain reaction of evil—hate begetting hate, wars producing more wars—must be broken, or we shall be plunged into the dark abyss of annihilation."[11] It is clear that the product of hate is destruction and death, but King notes that hate also harms the hater. His second argument is that hate "scars the soul and distorts the personality" of the one who hates.[12] In his 1967 Christmas sermon he preached, "I've seen too much hate to want to hate, myself, and I've seen hate on the faces of too many sheriffs, too many white citizens' councilors, and too many Klansmen of the South to want to hate, myself, and every time I see it, I say to myself, hate is too great a burden to bear."[13] In his article on enemy love he wrote, "Like an unchecked cancer, hate corrodes the personality and eats away its vital unity. Hate destroys a man's sense of values and his objectivity. It causes him to describe the beautiful as ugly and the ugly as beautiful, and to confuse the true with the false and the false with the true."[14]

Love transforms. This idea underlies King's third reason why we ought to love our enemies. King preached reconciliation and the creation of the beloved community, and in order for these to happen the enemy must become a friend. This is done only through love. "We never get rid of an enemy by meeting hate with hate; we get rid of an enemy by getting rid of enmity. By its very nature, hate destroys and tears down; by its very nature, love creates and builds up. Love transforms with redemptive power."[15]

The final reason why we should love our enemies is that Jesus commands us to love. "We are called to this difficult task in order to realize a unique relationship with God. We are potential sons of God. Through love that potentiality becomes actuality. We must love our enemies, because only by loving them can we know God and experience the beauty of his holiness."[16] In another sermon King writes, "I have discovered that the highest good is love. This principle is at the center of the cosmos. It is the great unifying force of life. God is love. He who loves has discovered the clue to the meaning of ultimate reality; he who hates stands in immediate candidacy for nonbeing."[17]

> Probably no admonition of Jesus has been more difficult to follow than the command to "love your enemies." . . . Far from being the pious injunction of a Utopian dreamer, the command to love one's enemy is an absolute necessity for our survival. Love even for enemies is the key to the solution of the problems of our world.
>
> I am certain that Jesus understood the difficulty inherent in the act of loving one's enemy. He never joined the ranks of those who talk glibly about the easiness of the moral life. He realized that every genuine expression of love grows out of a consistent and total surrender to God. So when Jesus said, "Love your enemy," he was not unmindful of its stringent qualities. Yet he meant every word of it. Our responsibility as Christians is to discover the meaning of this command and seek passionately to live it out in our daily lives.[18]

Loving your enemies includes some practical steps.

> First, we must develop and maintain the capacity to forgive. He who is devoid of the power to forgive is devoid of the power to love. It is impossible even to begin the act of loving one's enemies without the prior acceptance of the necessity, over and over again, of forgiving those who inflict evil and injury upon us. . . . Forgiveness does not mean ignoring what has been done or putting a false label on an evil act. It means, rather, that the evil act no longer remains as a barrier to the relationship.

Second, we must recognize that the evil deed of the enemy-neighbor, the thing that hurts, never quite expresses all that he is. An element of goodness may be found even in our worst enemy. . . . This simply means that there is some good in the worst of us and some evil in the best of us. When we discover this, we are less prone to hate our enemies. When we look beneath the surface, beneath the impulsive evil deed, we see within our enemy-neighbor a measure of goodness and know that the viciousness and evilness of his acts are not quite representative of all that he is. . . . Then we love our enemies by realizing that they are not totally bad and that they are not beyond the reach of God's redemptive love.

Third, we must not seek to defeat or humiliate the enemy but to win his friendship and understanding. At times we are able to humiliate our worst enemy. Inevitably, his weak moments come and we are able to thrust in his side the spear of defeat. But this we must not do. Every word and deed must contribute to an understanding with the enemy and release those vast reservoirs of goodwill, which have been blocked by impenetrable walls of hate.[19]

"The meaning of love," King writes, "is not to be confused with some sentimental outpouring. Love is something much deeper than emotional bosh."[20] It is not friendship love, romantic love, nor does it mean that we have to "like" our enemies.

Now we can see what Jesus meant when he said, "Love your enemies." We should be happy that he did not say, "Like your enemies." It is almost impossible to like some people. "Like" is a sentimental and affectionate word. How can we be affectionate toward a person whose avowed aim is to crush our very being and place innumerable stumbling blocks in our path? How can we like a person who is threatening our children and bombing our homes? This is impossible. But Jesus recognized that love is greater than like. When Jesus bids us to love our enemies, he is speaking neither of *eros* nor *philia*, he is speaking of *agape*, understanding and creative, redemptive goodwill for all men. Only by following this way and responding with this type of love are we able to be children of our Father who is in heaven.[21]

King often spoke of the distinction between *agape* and other sorts of love. In an important article titled "An Experiment in Love," he offers deeper reflections on his understanding of Christian love.

In speaking of love at this point, we are not referring to some sentimental or affectionate emotion. It would be nonsense to urge men to love their oppressors in an affectionate sense. Love in this connection means understanding, redemptive good will. When we speak of loving those who oppose us, we refer to neither *eros* nor *philia*; we speak of a love which is expressed in the Greek word *agape*. Agape means understanding, redeeming good will for all men. It is an overflowing love which is purely spontaneous, unmotivated, groundless, and creative. It is not set in motion by any quality or function of its object. It is the love of God operating in the human heart.

Agape is disinterested love. It is a love in which the individual seeks not his own good, but the good of his neighbor (1 Cor. 10:24). Agape does not begin by discriminating between worthy and unworthy people, or any qualities people possess. It begins by loving others for their sakes. It is an entirely "neighbor-regarding concern for others," which discovers the neighbor in every man it meets. Therefore, agape makes no distinction between friends and enemy; it is directed toward both. If one loves an individual merely on account of his friendliness, he loves him for the sake of the benefits to be gained from the friendship, rather than for the friend's own sake. Consequently, the best way to assure oneself that love is disinterested is to have love for the enemy-neighbor from whom you can expect no good in return, but only hostility and persecution.

Another basic point about agape is that it springs from the need of the other person—his need for belonging to the best in the human family. The Samaritan who helped the Jew on the Jericho Road was "good" because he responded to the human need that he was presented with. God's love is eternal and fails not because man needs his love. Saint Paul assures us that the loving act of redemption was done "while we were yet sinners"—that is, at the point of our greatest need for love. Since the white man's personality is greatly distorted by segregation, and his soul is greatly scarred, he needs the love of the Negro. The Negro must love the white man, because the white man needs his love to remove his tensions, insecurities, and fears.

Agape is not a weak, passive love. It is love in action. Agape is love seeking to preserve and create community. It is insistence on community even when one seeks to break it. Agape is a willingness to go to any length to restore community. It doesn't stop at the first mile, but it goes the second mile to restore community. It is a willingness to forgive, not seven times, but seventy times seven to restore community. The cross is the eternal expression of the length to which God will go in order to restore broken community. The resurrection is a symbol of God's triumph over all the forces that seek to block community. The Holy Spirit is the continuing community creating reality that moves through history. He who works against community is working against the whole of creation. Therefore, if I respond to hate with a reciprocal hate I do nothing but intensify the cleavage in broken community. I can only close the gap in broken community by meeting hate with love. If I meet hate with hate, I become depersonalized, because creation is so designed that my personality can only be fulfilled in the context of community. Booker T. Washington was right: "Let no man pull you so low as to make you hate him." When he pulls you that low he brings you to the point of defying creation, and thereby becoming depersonalized.

In the final analysis, agape means a recognition of the fact that all life is interrelated. All humanity is involved in a single process, and all men are brothers. To the degree that I harm my brother, no matter what he is doing to me, to that extent I am harming myself. For example, white men often refuse federal aid to education in order to avoid giving the Negro his rights; but because all men are brothers they cannot deny Negro children without harming their own. They end, all efforts to the contrary, by hurting themselves. Why is this? Because men are brothers. If you harm me, you harm yourself.[22]

Very few people have communicated the power of love stronger than has Martin Luther King, Jr.

To our most bitter opponents we say: "We shall match your capacity to inflict suffering by our capacity to endure suffering. We shall meet your physical force with soul force. Do to us what you will, and we shall continue to love you. We cannot in all good conscience obey your unjust laws, because non co-operation with evil is as much a moral obligation as is co-operation with good. Throw us in jail, and we shall still love you. Bomb our homes and threaten our children, and we shall still love you. Send your hooded perpetrators of violence into our community at the midnight hour and beat us and leave us half dead, and we shall still love you. But be ye assured that we will wear you down by our capacity to suffer. One day we shall win freedom, but not only for ourselves. We shall so appeal to your heart and conscience that we shall win you in the process, and our victory will be a double victory."

Love is the most durable power in the world. This creative force, so beautifully exemplified in the life of our Christ, is the most potent instrument available in mankind's quest for peace and security.[23]

Mother Teresa

The word 'love' is so misunderstood and so misused.
—Mother Teresa, *Love: A Fruit Always in Season*

Mother Teresa of Calcutta was not a theologian. She was not a philosopher nor was she a particularly "deep" thinker. As the editors of a book about her once wrote, "Mother Teresa speaks little, publishes even less." They describe her thoughts, recorded in letters, interviews, and public addresses, as "generally spontaneous." They note that she was "uninhibited by the fear of repetition."[24] Malcolm Muggeridge wrote that "she is normally economical of words . . . they invariably come from the heart. . . . She never, as far as is known, prepares beforehand what she proposes to say."[25] Yet another commentator, Robert Inchausti, suggested that, "She speaks too simply, uses the traditional language of the church, and often replies to sophisticated questions with platitudes and cliches that normally would be dismissed as trite."[26] Mother Teresa, then, is a different type of contributor to the Christian understanding of love. What makes her words so penetrating is how profound her life was. Intellectually, she does not add much to our conversation. Indeed, her words if read independently from her life do seem trite. What makes her words so powerful is that they are one with her deeds. Inchausti describes this connection as follows.

> Perhaps the reason Mother Teresa seems so banal and yet profound when she speaks is that, like an action painting, her mind has become one with her acts. There is no kernel of meaning to be cracked, only a texture of activity to be experienced in its making. She represents a shift from saintly piety to active love, from product to maker, from artwork to performer, from elaborate delivery systems of the welfare state to small deeds of great love embodied in the concrete touch. We see in her movement from the disinterested pursuit of the good, true, and the beautiful to the selfless actualization of those same virtues through loving service.[27]

Her "platitudes and cliches" are sources of wisdom and inspiration for people because her life gives them an abundance of meaning.

Mother Teresa was born in 1910 in Yugoslavia. At eighteen she joined the Loreto sisters. She spent the next twenty years teaching in her order's schools. In 1946 while on a train, Sister Teresa had a "call within a call." She received a revelation, a message. In her words, "I was to leave the convent and help the poor while living among them. It was an order. To fail it would have been to break the faith."[28] "So, with the permission of her congregation, she left the convent. In place of her traditional religious habit she donned a simple white sari with blue border and went out to seek Jesus in the desperate byways of Calcutta."[29] For fifty years she worked with the poorest of the poor in Calcutta. By the time she died in 1997, her legacy was well known. She cared for an incalculable number of diseased, dying, and abandoned people. She was the recipient of many international awards including the 1979 Nobel Peace Prize. She founded a religious order, the Missionaries of Charity, which now has over 150 communities around the world.

Describing the poor and poverty in Calcutta stretches the imagination of middle-class America. In her biography of Mother Teresa, Kathryn Spink briefly narrates the reality of Calcutta and gives us some small picture of the people Mother Teresa cared for. The context of the excerpt below is to defend Mother Teresa against the criticism that the poor would be better off if she were to give them "fishing rods so they could fish for themselves." Mother Teresa's response was, "Ah, my God, you should see these people. They have not even the strength to lift a fishing rod, let alone use it to fish. Giving them fish, I help them to recover the strength for the fishing tomorrow."[30] Spink affirms Mother Teresa's words.

> Anyone who has touched a person dying in degradation knows this to be true. People with skin hanging in loose folds from their bones, children with stomachs distended with worms, and hollow eyes turning blind for lack of vitamins, lepers with leonine features and open, infected wounds— these are visions that burn the soul and often obscure the political points to be made about the status quo. Inevitably perhaps they change the sense of what is or is not important. Anyone who has nurtured the last residue of human life in a body wasted away by hunger, disease and neglect knows that the mere touch of a warm hand is indeed of immeasurable value. The very poorest of the poor are people who have been deprived even of their humanity. They are often enslaved to the biological needs of hunger and thirst. Their horizons have shrunk to the size of the bowl of rice or crust of bread they so desperately crave. When the concern of another human being, albeit expressed in the smallest and most apparently insignificant way, leads to the request for a clean shirt, for toe nails to be cut, faces to

be shaved, there is no denigrating the miracle of the restoration of humanity, the rediscovery of the sense of what is beautiful and right. A place like Calcutta, precisely because it quickly teaches that its problems are going to endure beyond one's own years, also shows the value of sharing a cup of water, spending time with a handicapped child, visiting a pensioner.[31]

There is a striking and unforgettable moment in Ann and Jeanette Petrie's documentary film *Mother Teresa*. One of the sisters brings a boy, a young boy, perhaps two or three years old, into the infirmary. The boy is sick, malnourished, suffering from physical disabilities. He was abandoned. As she sets the boy down on the bed, his eyes roll back and forth, unable to focus on anything or anyone. The sister spoon-feeds him, talks to him, and touches him. Mother Teresa then rubs his chest and speaks to him. Suddenly, his eyes focus on her. He is loved. He is recognized as a person. It is a striking moment and a testimony to the power of love.

Mother Teresa wrote no systematic treatise on love. To read her insights, we have to gather her thoughts from a variety of places. The best place to start is with the address she gave as she accepted the Nobel Peace Prize. Here are a few paragraphs from that speech.

> And God loved the world so much that he gave his son—it was a giving; it is as much as if to say it hurt God to give, because he loved the world so much that he gave his son. He gave him to the Virgin Mary, and what did she do with him?
>
> As soon as he came in her life, immediately she went in haste to give that good news, and as she came into the house of her cousin, the child—the unborn child—the child in the womb of Elizabeth, leapt with joy. He was, that little unborn child was, the first messenger of peace. He recognized the Prince of Peace, he recognized that Christ had come to bring the good news for you and for me. And as if that was not enough—it was not enough to become a man—he died on the cross to show that greater love, and he died for you and for me and for that leper and for that man dying of hunger and that naked person lying in the street not only of Calcutta, but of Africa, and New York, and London, and Oslo—and insisted that we love one another as he loves each one of us. And we read that in the Gospel very clearly: "Love as I have loved you; as I love you; as the Father has loved me, I love you." And the harder the Father loved him, he gave him to us, and how much we love one another, we too must give to each other until it hurts.

It is not enough for us to say: "I love God, but I do not love my neighbor." St. John says that you are a liar if you say you love God and you don't love your neighbor. How can you love God whom you do not see, if you do not love your neighbor whom you see, whom you touch, with whom you live? And so this is very important for us to realize that love, to be true, has to hurt.

It hurt Jesus to love us. It hurt him. And to make sure we remember his great love, he made himself the bread of life to satisfy our hunger for his love—our hunger for God—because we have been created for that love. We have been created in his image. We have been created to love and be loved, and he has become man to make it possible for us to love as he loved us. He makes himself the hungry one, the naked one, the homeless one, the sick one, the one in prison, the lonely one, the unwanted one, and he says: "You did it to me." He is hungry for our love, and this is the hunger of our poor people. This is the hunger that you and I must find. It may be in our own home.[32]

"Love, to be true," she wrote, "must first be for our neighbour. This love will bring us to God."[33]

St. John says something very strange: how can you love God whom you don't see if you don't love your neighbour—one another—whom you see? And he uses very strange words: "If you say you love God and don't love your neighbour, you are a liar." Because we cannot see Christ we cannot express our love to him, but our neighbours we can always see, and we can do to them what, if we saw him, we would like to do to Christ.

God gives us that great strength and the great joy of loving those he has chosen. Do we use it? Where do we use it first? Jesus said love one another. He didn't say love the world, he said love one another—right here, my brother, my neighbour, my husband, my wife, my child, the old ones. . . . It is easy to love the people far away. It is not always easy to love those close to us. It is easier to give a cup of rice to relieve hunger than to relieve the loneliness and pain of someone unloved in our own home. Bring love into your home for this is where our love for each other must start.[34]

Mother Teresa constantly remarks that love must begin in the home.

I think the world today is upside-down, and is suffering so much, because there is so very little love in the homes and in family life. We have no time

for our children, we have no time for each other; there is no time to enjoy
each other. If we could only bring back into our lives the life that Jesus,
Mary, and Joseph lived in Nazareth, if we could make our homes another
Nazareth, I think that peace and joy would reign in the world.

Love begins at home; love lives in homes, and that is why there is so
much suffering and so much unhappiness in the world today. If we listen
to Jesus he will tell us what he said before: "Love one another, as I have
loved you." He has loved us through suffering, dying on the Cross for us,
and so if we are to love one another, if we are to bring that love into life
again, we have to begin at home.

We must make our homes centers of compassion and forgive endlessly.

Everybody today seems to be in such a terrible rush, anxious for
greater developments and greater riches and so on, so that children have
very little time for their parents. Parents have very little time for each other,
and in the home begins the disruption of the peace of the world.[35]

If Mother Teresa's preaching on love ended there, there would not be much
to report. Family love is not a radical idea; identifying God with the poor, however, is.

If sometimes our poor people have had to die of starvation, it is not because God didn't care for them, but because you and I didn't give, were not
instruments of love in the hands of God, to give them that bread, to give
them that clothing; because we did not recognize him, when once more
Christ came in distressing disguise—in the hungry man, in the lonely man,
in the homeless child, and seeking for shelter.

God has identified himself with the hungry, the sick, the naked, the
homeless; hunger, not only for bread, but for love, for care, to be somebody
to someone; nakedness, not of clothing only, but nakedness of that compassion that very few people give to the unknown; homelessness, not only
just for a shelter made of stone, but that homelessness that comes from having no one to call your own.[36]

"My poor ones in the world's slums are like the suffering Christ. In them
God's Son lives and dies, and through them God shows me his true face."[37] She
offers a proverb linking the essentials of life: prayer, belief, love, and service. "If
we pray we will believe. If we believe we will love. If we love we will serve. Only
then can we put our love for God into living action through service of Christ
in the distressing disguise of the Poor."[38]

Today Christ is in people who are unwanted, unemployed, uncared for, hungry, naked and homeless. They seem useless to the state or to society and nobody has time for them. It is you and I as Christians, worthy of the love of Christ if our love is true, who must find them and help them. They are there for the finding.[39]

Our work . . . calls for us to see Jesus in everyone. He has told us that He is the hungry one. He is the naked one. He is the thirsty one. He is the one without a home. He is the one who is suffering. These are our treasures. . . . They are Jesus. Each one is Jesus in His distressing disguise.[40]

Our purpose is to take God and His love to the poorest of the poor, irrespective of their ethnic origin or the faith that they profess. Our discernment of aid is not the belief but the necessity. We never try to convert those whom we receive to Christianity but in our work we bear witness to the love of God's presence and if Catholics, Protestants, Buddhists or agnostics become for this reason better men—simply better—we will be satisfied. Growing up in love they will be nearer to God and will find Him in His goodness.[41]

Love must be expressed in action to be love, but it is not to be confused with action.

Love does not live on words, nor can it be explained by words—especially that love which serves him, which comes from him and which finds him and touches him. We must reach the heart and to reach the heart as we must do—love is proved in deeds.

In one of the places in Melbourne I visited an old man and nobody ever knew that he existed. I saw his room in a terrible state, and I wanted to clean his house and he kept on saying: "I'm all right." But I repeated the same words: "You will be more all right if you will allow me to clean your place," and in the end he allowed me. There in that room there was a beautiful lamp covered with the dirt of many years, and I asked him, "Why do you not light your lamp?" Then I asked him, "Will you light the lamp if the Sisters come to see you?" And the other day he sent me word: "Tell my friend the light she has lit in my life is still burning."

Simple acts of love and care keep the light of Christ burning.[42]

We must never think any one of us is indispensable. God has ways and means. He may allow everything to go upside down in the hands of a very talented and capable Sister. God sees only her love. She may exhaust herself, even kill herself with work, but unless her work is interwoven with love it is useless. God does not need her work. God will not ask that Sister how many books she has read, how many miracles she has worked, but He will ask her if she has done her best, for her best, for the love of Him.[43]

The principle Mother Teresa repeats over and over again is that true love hurts. In her Nobel Peace Prize speech, for example, she said that it hurt God to send Jesus into the world and it hurt Jesus to love us.

There is so much love in us all, but we are often too shy to express our love and we keep it bottled up inside us. We must learn to love, to love until it hurts, and we will then know how to accept love.

We must be a channel of peace. We must love until it hurts. We must be Christ. We must not be afraid to show our love.[44]

A living love hurts. Jesus, to prove his love for us, died on the Cross. The mother, to give birth to her child, has to suffer. If you really love one another properly, there must be sacrifice.[45]

Love can be misused for selfish motives. I love you, but at the same time I want to take from you as much as I can, even the things that are not for me to take. Then there is no true love any more. True love hurts. It always has to hurt. It must be painful to love someone, painful to leave them, you might have to die for them. When people marry they have to give up everything to love each other. The mother who gives birth to her child suffers much. It is the same in religious life. To belong fully to God we have to give up everything. Only then can we truly love. The word "love" is so misunderstood and so misused.[46]

Mother Teresa practiced this love and experienced this love.

I can never forget how a little child, a Hindu child, taught me how to love the great love. In Calcutta, we didn't have sugar; and a little Hindu child, four years old, he heard Mother Teresa has no sugar. And he went home and he told his parents: "I will not eat sugar for three days. I will give my sugar to Mother Teresa." After three days, the parents brought the child to our house. In his hand he had a little bottle of sugar . . . the sugar of a little child. He could scarcely pronounce my name, but he knew he loved a great love because he loved until it hurt. It hurt him to give up sugar for three days. But that little child taught me that to be able to love a great love, it is not how much we give but how much loving is put in the giving.

Always I will remember the last time I visited Venezuela. A very rich family had given the Sisters land to build a Children's Home, so I went to thank them. And there in the family, I found the first child was terribly disabled. And I asked the mother, "What is the child's name?" And the mother answered me, "Professor of Love. Because this child is teaching us the whole time how to love in action." There was a beautiful, beautiful smile on the mother's face. "Professor of Love" they called their child, so terribly disabled, so disfigured; from that child they were learning how to love.[47]

You and I, being women, we have this tremendous thing in us, understanding love. I see that so beautifully in our people, in our poor women, who day after day, and every day, meet suffering, accept suffering for the sake of their children. I have seen parents, mothers, going without so many things, so many things, even resorting to begging, so that the children may have what they need.

I have seen a mother holding to her handicapped child because that child is her child. She had an understanding love for the suffering of her child. I remember a woman who had twelve children, and the first of them was terribly disabled, terribly handicapped. I cannot describe to you what the child looked like, mentally, physically, and I offered her to take that child into our home where we have so many like that; and she started crying and she said to me, "Mother, don't say that, don't say that. She is the greatest gift of God to me and my family. All our love is centered on this child. Our life would be empty if you took her away from us."[48]

"I believe," she once said, "In person to person contact. Every person is Christ for me and since there is only one Jesus, the person I am meeting is the one person in the world at the moment."[49] As she lived this incredible vision, she was also moved by the suffering of the poor she did not see. This is evident in a letter she sent to George Bush and Saddam Hussein before the Gulf War.

Dear President George Bush and President Saddam Hussein,
I come to you with tears in my eyes and God's love in my heart to plead to you for the poor and those who will become poor if the war that we

all dread and fear happens. I beg you with my whole heart to work for, to labour for God's peace and to be reconciled with one another.

You both have your cases to make and your people to care for but first please listen to the One who came into the world to teach us peace. You have the power and the strength to destroy God's presence and image, his men, his women and his children. Please listen to the will of God. God has created us to be loved by his love and not destroyed by our hatred.

In the short term there may be winners and losers in this war that we all dread, but that never can, nor ever will justify the suffering, pain and loss of life which your weapons will cause.[50]

Spink writes, "The letter went on to explain that she begged on behalf of the innocent ones, the poor of the world and of those who would become poor because of the war. She pleaded for those who would be orphaned and widowed and left alone, and for those who would have 'the most precious thing that God could give us, Life, taken away from them.'"[51] Mother Teresa continues:

I appeal to you—to your love, your love of God and your fellow man. In the name of God and in the name of those you will make poor, do not destroy life and peace. Let the love and peace triumph and let your names be remembered for the good you have done, the joy you have spread and the love you have shared.

Please pray for me and my sisters as we try to love and serve the Poor because they belong to God and are loved in his eyes, as we and our Poor are praying for you. We pray that you will love and nourish what God has so lovingly entrusted to your care.[52]

Pope John Paul II

Love is not something that is learned, and yet there is nothing else as important to learn!

—Pope John Paul II, *Crossing the Threshold of Hope*

The story of Pope John Paul II's life is unparalleled. Born in Poland in 1920, he was given the name Karol Wojtyla. Karol grew up under the Nazi regime during World War II and studied for the priesthood in a secret seminary. After the war, he experienced further repression under the communistic dictatorship. In his words, that war "which should have re-established freedom and restored the right of nations, ended without having attained these goals. Indeed," he writes, "for many peoples, especially those which had suffered the more during the war, it openly contradicted these goals."[53] Karol struggled through these oppressions, was ordained, named bishop, participated in the Second Vatican Council, and eventually became pope. Two remarkable features of his being named pope were his relatively young age, fifty-eight, and the fact that he was the first non-Italian pope in four and a half centuries. As pope he openly endorsed the non-violent movement in Poland that ultimately toppled the communist government. John Paul II has also traveled the globe; he survived an assassination attempt; and wrote an international best selling book. His biographer George Weigel writes,

> John Paul II has also been indisputably the most visible pope in history. In fact, a case can be made that he has been the most visible human being in history. He has almost certainly been seen live by more people than any man who ever lived. When one adds the multiplying impact of television to the equation, the breadth of his reach into the worlds-within-worlds of humanity becomes almost impossible to grasp.[54]

The author of many books and treatises of official Church teaching, the pope has taken a strong interest in the theology of love, particularly married love, from early in his career. "As a young priest," he wrote, "I learned to love human love. This has been one of the fundamental themes of my priesthood, my ministry in the pulpit, in the confessional, and also in my writing."[55] We all have, he believes, a vocation to love and because of this, we need to pay special attention to young people. "As a priest I realized this very early. I felt almost an inner call in this direction. It is necessary to prepare young people for marriage; it is necessary to teach them love. Love is not something that is learned, and yet there is nothing else as important to learn!"[56] So important is love, says the pope, that without it we simply cannot live. In his first encyclical letter, *Redemptor Hominis*, he writes, "Man cannot live without love. He remains a being that is incomprehensible for himself, his life is senseless, if love is not revealed to him, if he does not encounter love, if he does not experience it and make it his own, if he does not participate intimately in it."[57] We know true love by coming to know Jesus. John Paul continues, "The man who wishes to understand himself thoroughly— and not just in accordance with immediate, partial, often superficial, and even illusory standards and measures of his being—he must with his unrest, uncertainty and even his weakness and sinfulness, with his life and death, draw near to Christ."[58]

As we come to know Jesus, we come to know that Jesus is not an individual. Jesus is a person, indeed he is a member of a community of persons we call God. The Trinity, the divine community of love, provides the essential model for Christian love. Richard M. Hogan and John M. LeVoir commentating on the pope's theology write, "We know from revelation, i.e., from the Old Testament and most perfectly from Christ, that God loves through a complete self donation of Himself. This love is perfectly present in the Holy Trinity where each divine Person totally surrenders Himself to the others."[59] The Trinity is the exemplar of true love. "The love of each divine Person is a personal choice, a will-act, made by each based on knowledge of the truth. The self-donation of each divine Person to the others unites all three in a communion of persons. In effect, there is an attitude, a choice, to act as one. This is what love is: an act of the will to do what another wills."[60]

God is a community of love. The persons of the Trinity are social persons, as are we. Note the language of "self donation" used by Hogan and LeVoir. Total giving of the self is the essential, indeed the necessary feature of love for John Paul II. In God's gift of Jesus and indeed Jesus' death on the cross we see and experience this love. Hogan and LeVoir write, "Only on the cross do we see how far the self-surrender of God extends. He gave Himself for our sakes that we might have life. He gave until He had nothing more to give and He did it totally for us. This is love! Since we are made in God's likeness, we are made to love as He did and does: an all-encompassing self-surrender for the sake of others. Only when we mirror the love of the Trinity in our love do we fulfill ourselves as God created us. Only then is life meaningful."[61]

The Cross as the Paradigm of Love

Being a follower of Christ means becoming conformed to him who became a servant even to giving himself on the Cross.

—Pope John Paul II, *Veritatis Splendor*

For John Paul II, the cross of Christ is key to understanding love. The cross gives love meaning and substance. In his encyclical *Dives in Misericordia*, the pope writes, "The events of Good Friday and, even before that, the prayer in Gethsemane, introduce a fundamental change into the whole course of the revelation of love."[62] Jesus gives the gift of his life, a gift that was given through suffering. "Christ, as the man who suffers really and in a terrible way in the Garden of Olives and on Calvary, addresses himself to the Father—that Father whose love he has preached to people, to whose mercy he has borne witness through all of his activity."[63] The pope continues, "The cross on Calvary, the cross upon which Christ conducts his final dialogue with the Father emerges from the very heart of the love that man, created in the image and likeness of God, has been given as a gift, according to God's eternal plan."[64]

The cross testifies to a love that is more powerful than anything else the world does.

> Yet even in this glorification of the Son of God, the cross remains, that cross which—through all the messianic testimony of the Man-the-Son, who suffered death upon it—speaks and never ceases to speak of God-the-Father, who is absolutely faithful to his eternal love for man, since he "so loved the world"—therefore man in the world—that "he gave his only Son, that whoever believes in him should not perish but have eternal life." Believing in the crucified Son means "seeing the Father," means believing that love is present in the world and that this love is more powerful than any kind of evil in which individuals, humanity or the world are involved.[65]

"The cross," the pope says, "is like a touch of eternal love upon the most painful wounds of man's earthly existence; it is the total fulfillment of the messianic program."[66] Thus, "There is no Christian holiness without devotion to the Passion."[67] This truth is not immediately evident to people, indeed the meaning of the cross, the mystery of the cross, is beyond human reason. [68] God's self-giving love, he writes, is "a grand and mysterious truth for the human mind, which finds it inconceivable that suffering and death can express a love which gives itself and seeks nothing in return."[69]

God has given us so much. Jesus gave us his life. We are to respond in kind. John Paul II writes in *Veritatis Splendor*, "The moral life presents itself as the response due to the many gratuitous initiatives taken by God out of love for man. It is a response of love."[70] We are to imitate Jesus, particularly in his cross.

> Jesus asks us to follow him and to imitate him along the path of love, a love which gives itself completely to the brethren out of love for God. . . . Jesus' way of acting and his words, his deeds and his precepts constitute the moral rule of Christian life. Indeed, his actions, and in particular his Passion and Death on the Cross, are the living revelation of his love for the Father and for others. This is exactly the love that Jesus wishes to be imitated by all who follow him. It is the "new" commandment: "A new commandment I give to you, that you love one another; even as I have loved you, that you

also love one another. By this all men will know that you are my disciples, if you have love for one another" (John 13:34–35). The word "as" also indicates the degree of Jesus' love, and of the love with which his disciples are called to love one another. After saying: "This is my commandment, that you love one another as I have loved you" (John 15:12), Jesus continues with words which indicate the sacrificial gift of his life on the Cross, as the witness to a love "to the end" (John 13:1): "Greater love has no man than this, that a man lay down his life for his friends" (John 15:13). . . . This is what Jesus asks of everyone who wishes to follow him: "If any man would come after me, let him deny himself and take up his cross and follow me" (Matt. 16:24). Following Christ is not an outward imitation, since it touches man at the very depths of his being. Being a follower of Christ means becoming conformed to him who became a servant even to giving himself on the Cross (cf. Phil. 2:5–8).[71]

Personalism

> Love is the sincere gift of self. In this sense the person is realized through love.
> —Pope John Paul II, *Crossing the Threshold of Hope*

John Paul II has worn many hats during his long career. Before becoming pope, he served the Church as bishop and teacher. Early in his career, he was deeply engaged in philosophical discourse. During that time, he developed what has become the hallmark of his theology, namely, personalism. Personalism, he says, is an "attempt to translate the commandment of love into the language of philosophical ethics."[72] In his best-selling book, *Crossing the Threshold of Hope*, he writes, "The person is a being for whom the only suitable dimension is love. We are just to a person if we love him. This is as true for God as it is for man. Love for a person excludes the possibility of treating him as an object of pleasure."[73] Moreover, he argues, the commandment of love "requires the affirmation of the person as a person." Although personalism is new expression, it is deeply rooted in Church tradition. John Paul, for example, sees the principles active in the teachings of the Second Vatican Council.

> The true personalistic interpretation of the commandment of love is found in the words of the Council: "When the Lord Jesus prays to the Father so that 'they may be one' (John 17:22), He places before us new horizons impervious to human reason and implies a similarity between the union of divine persons and the union of the children of God in truth and charity.

This similarity shows how man, who is the only creature on earth that God wanted for his own sake, can fully discover himself only by the sincere giving of himself" (*Gaudium et Spes*, 24). Here we truly have an adequate interpretation of the commandment of love. Above all, the principle that a person has value by the simple fact that he is a person finds very clear expression: man, it is said, "is the only creature on earth that God has wanted for his own sake." At the same time the Council emphasizes that the most important thing about love is the sincere gift of self. In this sense the person is realized through love.[74]

The philosophy of personalism can be summarized in two moral norms. The first is that we are to treat all others as persons, with all respect and love that persons by their very nature are due. The second is that in order for us to fulfill our vocation as persons, we must love in a way that we give ourselves to others, like the persons of the Trinity give themselves to each other, like Christ gave himself on the cross to us.

> Therefore, these two aspects—the affirmation of the person as a person and the sincere gift of self—not only do not exclude each other, they mutually confirm and complete each other. Man affirms himself most completely by giving of himself. This is the fulfillment of the commandment of love. This is also the full truth about man, a truth that Christ taught us by His life, and that the tradition of Christian morality, no less than the tradition of saints and of the many heroes of love of neighbor, took up and lived out in the course of history.[75]

John Paul sees humans as essentially free. This freedom, he says, can be used in one of two ways. Either we love, that is, we give of ourselves to others, or we are selfish.

> If we deprive human freedom of this possibility, if man does not commit himself to becoming a gift for others, then this freedom can become dangerous. It will become freedom to do what I myself consider as good, what brings me a profit or pleasure, even a sublimated pleasure. If we cannot accept the prospect of giving ourselves as a gift, then the danger of a selfish freedom will always be present.[76]

If the opposite of love is selfishness, the opposite of personalism is individualism. Personalism is the pope's answer to the distortions of love and selfishness which modern culture seems to promote.

Love, the civilization of love, is bound up with personalism. Why with personalism? And why does individualism threaten the civilization of love? We find a key to answering this in the Council's expression, a "sincere gift". Individualism presupposes a use of freedom in which the subject does what he wants, in which he himself is the one to "establish the truth" of whatever he finds pleasing or useful. He does not tolerate the fact that someone else "wants" or demands something from him in the name of an objective truth. He does not want to "give" to another on the basis of truth; he does not want to become a "sincere gift". Individualism thus remains egocentric and selfish. The real antithesis between individualism and personalism emerges not only on the level of theory, but even more on that of "ethos". The "ethos" of personalism is altruistic: it moves the person to become a gift for others and to discover the joy of giving himself.[77]

Personalism, the philosophical translation of the love commandment, gives a particular direction to the pope's emphasis on love. In this book we have distinguished a Christian love from a point of view that prioritizes the love for God (Augustine, Bernard, and Thomas) and from a point of view that highlights love of neighbor (the presentation of love in the New Testament, Martin Luther, and Mother Teresa). John Paul II's theology of love fits more in this second category than in the first. Clearly, he does not want to separate the love for God from love for neighbor, but his words call people to recognize the commandment to love the neighbor. In *Veritatis Splendor*, he writes,

> These two commandments, on which "depend all the Law and the Prophets" (Matt. 22:40), are profoundly connected and mutually related. Their inseparable unity is attested to by Christ in his words and by his very life: his mission culminates in the Cross of our Redemption (cf. John 3:14–15), the sign of his indivisible love for the Father and for humanity (cf. John 13:1). Both the Old and the New Testaments explicitly affirm that without love of neighbor, made concrete in keeping the commandments, genuine love for God is not possible.[78]

The love John Paul advocates is an "effective" love, an active love for others. In *Dives in Misericordia*, he writes,

> Especially through his lifestyle and through his actions, Jesus revealed that love is present in the world in which we live—an effective love, a love that addresses itself to man and embraces everything that makes up his hu-

manity. This love makes itself particularly noticed in contact with suffering, injustice and poverty—in contact with the whole historical "human
condition," which in various ways manifests man's limitation and frailty,
both physical and moral.[79]

The implications of personalism are far reaching. According to the pope, it demands particular actions in the personal sphere as well as the political sphere.
The following two sections address the pope's ideas on love in society and married life.

Love of Neighbor

We are asked to love and honor the life of every man and woman and to
work with perseverance and courage so that our time, marked by all too
many signs of death, may at last witness the establishment of a new culture
of life, the fruit of the culture of truth and of love.

—Pope John Paul II, *Evangelium Vitae*

In *Sollicitudo Rei Socialis,* Pope John Paul II addresses the social concerns of the
modern world. His approach to these issues is grounded on personalism. Thus
he writes, "One's neighbor must therefore be loved, even if an enemy, with the
same love with which the Lord loves him or her; and for that person's sake one
must be ready for sacrifice, even the ultimate one: to lay down one's life for the
brethren (cf. 1 John 3:16)."[80] *In Evangelium Vitae* he writes,

> A stranger is no longer a stranger for the person who must become a neigh-
> bor to someone in need, to the point of accepting responsibility for his life,
> as the parable of the Good Samaritan shows so clearly (cf. Luke 10:25–37).
> Even an enemy ceases to be an enemy for the person who is obliged to love
> him (cf. Matt. 5:38–48; Luke 6:27–35), to "do good" to him (cf. Luke 6:27,
> 33, 35) and to respond to his immediate needs promptly and with no ex-
> pectation of repayment (cf. Luke 6:34–35). The height of this love is to pray
> for one's enemy.[81]

John Paul II has a particular concern for the poor and marginalized. Service to
the poor, justice for the poor, begins with love. In *Centesimus Annus* he writes,
"Love for others, and in the first place love for the poor, in whom the Church
sees Christ himself, is made concrete in the promotion of justice. Justice will
never be fully attained unless people see in the poor person, who is asking for
help in order to survive, not an annoyance or a burden, but an opportunity for

showing kindness and a chance for greater enrichment."[82] Seeing the poor person as a full person worthy of respect and love is embedded in a basic principle of official Catholic social teaching which the pope refers to as "the option or love of preference for the poor."

> This is an option, or a special form of primacy in the exercise of Christian charity, to which the whole tradition of the Church bears witness. It affects the life of each Christian inasmuch as he or she seeks to imitate the life of Christ, but it applies equally to our social responsibilities and hence to our manner of living, and to the logical decisions to be made concerning the ownership and use of goods. Today, furthermore, given the worldwide dimension which the social question has assumed, this love of the preference for the poor, and the decisions which it inspires in us, cannot but embrace the immense multitudes of the hungry, the needy, the homeless, those without medical care and, above all, those without hope of a better future. It is impossible not to take account of the existence of these realities. To ignore them would mean becoming like the "rich man" who pretended not to know the beggar Lazarus lying at his gate (cf. Luke 16:19–31).[83]

The modern culture, the pope holds, is too often a culture or indeed a civilization of death. We are called, he says, to love and to create a civilization of love.

> It is therefore a service of love which we are all committed to ensure to our neighbor, that his or her life may be always defended and promoted, especially when it is weak or threatened. It is not only a personal but a social concern which we must all foster: a concern to make unconditional respect for human life the foundation of a renewed society. We are asked to love and honor the life of every man and woman and to work with perseverance and courage so that our time, marked by all too many signs of death, may at last witness the establishment of a new culture of life, the fruit of the culture of truth and of love.[84]

True love, the love that imitates the love of the Cross, is demanding. It encompasses the whole person and the total life of the person.

> The love which the Apostle Paul celebrates in the First Letter to the Corinthians—the love which is "patient" and "kind", and "endures all things" (1 Cor. 13:4, 7)—is certainly a demanding love. But this is precisely the source of its beauty: by the very fact that it is demanding, it builds up

the true good of man and allows it to radiate to others. The good, says Saint Thomas, is by its nature "diffusive". Love is true when it creates the good of persons and of communities; it creates that good and gives it to others. Only the one who is able to be demanding with himself in the name of love can also demand love from others. Love is demanding. It makes demands in all human situations; it is even more demanding in the case of those who are open to the Gospel. Is this not what Christ proclaims in "his" commandment? Nowadays people need to rediscover this demanding love, for it is the truly firm foundation of the family, a foundation able to "endure all things".[85]

In this love, there is no room for selfishness, whether of individuals, within families, or indeed within and between societies. Love is total self-giving.

Meditating on the thirteenth chapter of the First Letter of Paul to the Corinthians, we set out on a path which leads us to understand quickly and clearly the full truth about the civilization of love. No other biblical text expresses this truth so simply and so profoundly as the hymn to love. The dangers faced by love are also dangers for the civilization of love, because they promote everything capable of effectively opposing it. Here one thinks first of all of selfishness, not only the selfishness of individuals, but also of couples or, even more broadly, of social selfishness, that for example of a class or nation (nationalism). Selfishness in all its forms is directly and radically opposed to the civilization of love. [86]

John Paul's theology of love is complicated. Love is effective, it must be expressed in action, but it is also of the heart. The following quote notes the interiority of love. This interiority, however, stands in relation to objective standards of love. Emotions alone do not define true love.

The hymn to love in the First Letter to the Corinthians remains the Magna Charta of the civilization of love. In this concept, what is important is not so much individual actions (whether selfish or altruistic), so much as the radical acceptance of the understanding of man as a person who "finds himself" by making a sincere gift of self. A gift is, obviously, "for others": this is the most important dimension of the civilization of love. We thus come to the very heart of the Gospel truth about freedom. The person realizes himself by the exercise of freedom in truth. Freedom cannot be understood as a license to do absolutely anything: it means a gift of self.[87]

Sexual Love

The total physical self-giving would be a lie if it were not the sign and fruit of a total personal self-giving, in which the whole person, including the temporal dimension, is present: if the person were to withhold something or reserve the possibility of deciding otherwise in the future, by this very fact he or she would not be giving totally.

—Pope John Paul II, *Familiaris Consortio*

Throughout his career, the pope has had a particular concern for marriage and the family. In his thinking, he addresses the subjectivity of the man and woman, but such subjectivity must stand in relation to the objective demands of true love. The pope's philosophy of sexual love dramatically differs from that of Abelard and Heloise. For these two, intention was the primary characteristic to consider in the moral life. That is to say, actions are to be judged by considering the intentions of the persons doing the actions. For John Paul II, intention alone is not indicative of true love. Love must conform to the moral order. Some "so called love," then, is clearly not love for the pope. In his "Letter to Families," he writes,

> Opposed to the civilization of love is certainly the phenomenon of so-called "free love"; this is particularly dangerous because it is usually suggested as a way of following one's "real" feelings, but it is in fact destructive of love. How many families have been ruined because of "free love"! To follow in every instance a "real" emotional impulse by invoking a love "liberated" from all conditionings, means nothing more than to make the individual a slave to those human instincts which Saint Thomas calls "passions of the soul". "Free love" exploits human weaknesses; it gives them a certain "veneer" of respectability with the help of seduction and the blessing of public opinion. In this way there is an attempt to "soothe" consciences by creating a "moral alibi".[88]

True love is total love for John Paul II. We are all called to this level of love. Sexual love, if it is to be true and total, must occur in a marriage relationship, the only form of relationship that can provide the conditions necessary for this kind of love.

> God created man in his own image and likeness: calling him to existence through love, he called him at the same time for love. God is love and in himself he lives a mystery of personal loving communion. Creating the

human race in his own image and continually keeping it in being, God in-
scribed in the humanity of man and woman the vocation, and thus the capacity and responsibility, of love and communion. Love is therefore the
fundamental and innate vocation of every human being. As an incarnate
spirit, that is a soul which expresses itself in a body and a body informed
by an immortal spirit, man is called to love in his unified totality. Love includes the human body, and the body is made a sharer in spiritual love.[89]

Sex is both a personal and physical reality and true love does not withhold anything in these areas.

> Consequently, sexuality, by means of which man and woman give them-
> selves to one another through the acts which are proper and exclusive to
> spouses, is by no means something purely biological, but concerns the in-
> nermost being of the human person as such. It is realized in a truly human
> way only if it is an integral part of the love by which a man and a woman
> commit themselves totally to one another until death. The total physical
> self-giving would be a lie if it were not the sign and fruit of a total personal
> self-giving, in which the whole person, including the temporal dimension,
> is present: if the person were to withhold something or reserve the possi-
> bility of deciding otherwise in the future, by this very fact he or she would
> not be giving totally.[90]

Having children "is the fruit and the sign of conjugal love, the living testimony of the full reciprocal self-giving of the spouses."[91] This love, moreover,
points to something greater than itself. It becomes a symbol of God's love for us.
Indeed married love, for the pope, is an icon, an expression of the interior life of
God.[92]

> Being rooted in the personal and total self-giving of the couple, and being
> required by the good of children, the indissolubility of marriage finds its
> ultimate truth in the plan that God has manifested in his revelation: he
> wills and he communicates the indissolubility of marriage as a fruit, a sign
> and a requirement of the absolutely faithful love that God has for man and
> that the Lord Jesus has for the Church.[93]

Weigel comments that John Paul II's theology of sexual love, the total self-
gift of spouses, is "a way to sanctify the world." Indeed, for the pope, sexual love
"is an act of worship . . . an experience of the sacred."[94] For sexual love to be true,

the couple must follow the objective standards described by Church. Namely, "the inseparable connection, willed by God and unable to be broken by man on his own initiative, between the two meanings of the conjugal act: the unitive meaning and the procreative meaning."[95] The mere intention to love the other through the sexual act is not enough to make the act of sex a true act of love. The procreative aspect must be present. He writes, "every action which, either in anticipation of the conjugal act or in its accomplishment, or in the development of its natural consequences, proposes, whether as an end or as a means, to render procreation impossible" is "intrinsically immoral."[96] John Paul continues,

> When couples, by means of recourse to contraception, separate these two meanings that God the Creator has inscribed in the being of man and woman and in the dynamism of their sexual communion, they act as "arbiters" of the divine plan and they "manipulate" and degrade human sexuality—and with it themselves and their married partner—by altering its value of "total" self giving. Thus the innate language that expresses the total reciprocal self-giving of husband and wife is overlaid, through contraception by an objectively contradictory language, namely that of not giving oneself totally to the other. This leads not only to a positive refusal to be open to life but also to a falsification of the inner truth of conjugal love, which is called upon to give itself in personal totality. [97]

The pope recognizes the strong demands of this teaching. Like the cross of Christ, it involves sacrifice. It is nonetheless the law and not merely an ideal,[98] and one that is to be "wholeheartedly accepted" by the couple.

> Accordingly, the function of transmitting life must be integrated into the overall mission of Christian life as a whole, which without the Cross cannot reach the Resurrection. In such a context it is understandable that sacrifice cannot be removed from family life, but must in fact be wholeheartedly accepted if the love between husband and wife is to be deepened and become a source of intimate joy.[99]

The Christian tradition has had many exemplars of this demanding love and Pope John Paul reminds us of the martyrs. Their lives are testaments to this love that provide motivation and inspiration for us today. The love demanded of Christians, this self-giving love, is, in some senses, unreasonable. The lives of the martyrs illustrate for us the possibilities of this love.

The martyrs know that they have found the truth about life in the encounter with Jesus Christ, and nothing and no one could ever take this certainty from them. Neither suffering nor violent death could ever lead them to abandon the truth which they have discovered in the encounter with Christ. This is why to this day the witness of the martyrs continues to arouse such interest, to draw agreement, to win such a hearing and to invite emulation. This is why their word inspires such confidence: from the moment they speak to us of what we perceive deep down as the truth we have sought for so long, the martyrs provide evidence of a love that has no need of lengthy arguments in order to convince.[100]

CHAPTER TEN

Self-Regard, Other-Regard, and Mutuality

Gene Outka argues that "with a word as common as 'love,' it is unrealistic to suppose that all of the characteristic meanings could be absorbed into some single point of identity, if only because it is extremely unlikely that there is one homogeneous field to which the word always applies."[1] We have seen Outka's point illustrated throughout this book. Some authors focus on the one who loves, others on the nature of love, some on the objects of love. Other points of concern are the source of love, the reason to love, and the possibility of love. To say that our authors have different points of focus is not to deny important substantive differences. Chapter 8 and parts of chapter 9 defined Christian love in a dramatic and exclusive manner. Christian love is self-sacrificial. The authors in this chapter, on the other hand, suggest that while self-sacrifice is a necessary condition of Christian love, it does not fully capture the essence of Christian love. This chapter has three sections. The first part describes the fundamental characteristics of love and loving. Just as we are becoming comfortable understanding love in interpersonal relationships, the second section reminds us of the communal, indeed global, qualities of Christian love. The third part discusses mutuality as the primary characteristic of love.

Radical Love and Equal Regard

Two of the most influential theologians to write on love in the latter part of the twentieth century are Jules Toner and Gene Outka. They present very different views of love, yet views that may not be incompatible. Toner examines the experience of loving. Outka, approaching the topic from analytical philosophy, carefully examines the meaning of Christian love. The difference in their writings is anticipated in the first part of this section with two insightful quotations about love offered some fifty years ago.

Looking at Love from Two Angles

Love is more unitive than knowledge . . . its bent is to a real union.

—Thomas Gilby

By love we mean at least these attitudes and actions: rejoicing in the presence of the beloved, gratitude, reverence and loyalty toward him.

—H. Richard Niebuhr

Two quotations, from two different writers, will be presented below, both of which answer the question, what is love? Both were written in the late 1950s. Together they suggest two different ways to think about love. The first, a commentary on Thomas Aquinas's theology of love, describes the effects of love on the lover. It compares love to knowledge. Knowledge is something one attains, something one has, something one communicates. The author, Thomas Gilby, examines what happens when you truly love another. Your heart melts. You long to be with the other. This view highlights the lover and the transformation of the lover. If you love, you become a different person. The Protestant theologian H. Richard Niebuhr (Reinhold Niebuhr's brother and the author of the famous line, "Though God is love, love is not God"[2]) wrote the second quotation. Drawn to a different focus, Niebuhr describes what love elicits from the lover. It details feelings one has toward the beloved. When you love someone, you rejoice in her presence, you are grateful for her life, you have reverence or respect for her dignity, and you are loyal and faithful to her.

What is love? Gilby writes:

Love is more unitive than knowledge in seeking the thing, not the thing's reason; its bent is to a real union, though this can be constituted only by knowledge. Other effects of love are enumerated: a reciprocal abiding of lover and beloved together; a transport out of the self to the other; an ardent cherishing of another; a melting so that the heart is unfrozen and open to be entered; a longing in absence, heat in pursuit, fervor, and enjoyment in presence. In delight, too, there is an all at once wholeness and timelessness that reflects eternity; an edge of sadness similar to that of Gift of Knowledge, an expansion of spirit, a complete fulfillment of activity without satiety, "for they that drink shall yet thirst."[3]

What is love? Niebuhr writes:

By love we mean at least these attitudes and actions: rejoicing in the presence of the beloved, gratitude, reverence and loyalty toward him.

Love is rejoicing over the existence of the beloved one; it is the desire that he be rather than not be; it is longing for his presence when he is absent; it is happiness in the thought of him; it is profound satisfaction over everything that makes him great and glorious.

Love is gratitude: it is thankfulness for the existence of the beloved; it is the happy acceptance of everything that he gives without the jealous feeling that the self ought to be able to do as much; it is a gratitude that does not seek equality; it is wonder over the other's gift of himself in companionship.

Love is reverence: it keeps its distance even as it draws near; it does not seek to absorb the other in the self or want to be absorbed by it; it rejoices in the otherness of the other; it desires the beloved to be what he is and does not seek to refashion him into a replica of the self or to make him a means to the self's advancement. As reverence, love is and seeks knowledge of the other, not by way of curiosity nor for the sake of gaining power but in rejoicing and in wonder. In all such love there is an element of that "holy fear" which is not a form of flight but rather deep respect for the otherness of the beloved and the profound unwillingness to violate his integrity.

Love is loyalty; it is the willingness to let the self be destroyed rather than that the other cease to be; it is the commitment of the self by self-binding will to make the other great. It is loyalty, too, to the other's cause to his loyalty.[4]

Must we decide which of these is most accurate? Do they not describe the same phenomenon from different angles?

Jules Toner: The Phenomenology of Love

It is because of you . . . the last word is you. I love you because you are you.
—Jules Toner, *The Experience of Love*

In 1968 Jules Toner published the book *The Experience of Love*. A significant feature of the book is its method. Instead of writing on how we ought to love, Toner writes about what one experiences when one loves. He aims to develop an intelligible and concrete description of the human, conscious experience of love. As he does this, he invites the reader to reflect on his or her own experiences of love. This method, which looks to describe the experience of the moral act, is called phenomenology. Toner writes, "In the full concrete experience of love, our whole being, spirit and flesh, is involved: cognitive acts, feelings and affections, freedom, bodily reactions—all these are influencing each other and all are continually fluctuating in such a way as to change the structure and intensity of the experience."[5] The book attempts to describe the true meaning of love, that is to say, the basic love that underlies all particular forms of love. He calls this foundational love "radical love." The word radical means going to the roots or origins of a thing. It suggests an analysis that directs one to the irreducible part of a phenomenon. Toner, then, peels back and works through the layers of love to get to what he refers to as the root of the love experience. Radical love is the core of love on "which all the other elements depend for their meaning."[6] His description focuses on three ideas: response, union, and affirmation. He begins with response.

> Radical love originates in human experience as a response which, if not entirely dependent on the object of love, is so to some extent . . . love is an act immanent to the lover, a response made possible by the object of love which in some way influences the subject of love.[7]

> Love involves passivity and spontaneous activity. . . . The active-passive character of radical love at its origin is evident in two aspects of the response: in this response the lover has the experience of being liberated and of being taken a willing captive, both at once but in different respects and both involving activity and passivity in the lover.[8]

> Love begins at the touch of the loved one upon the lover's affectivity. Wonderfully, at that touch the power of love within the lover's being is energized. It is not as if the beloved created what was not there, but rather as if a deeply hidden energy pressing from within were suddenly released into full conscious life. Whether it comes slowly, almost imperceptibly, or whether it comes in a sudden and dazzling shock, it always gives the sense of liberated life flowing or flashing from the subject's personal center.[9]

> What I am responding to is an actual person who is here and now, incomplete in his actuality to be sure and destined to completeness, but lovable now for what he is actually not merely for what he is potentially or for the destiny he has which I can help him to achieve.[10]

> [Radical love] is a response to the beloved's total reality. It is directly and explicitly a response to his actuality, fundamentally and in every instance to his fundamental actuality as a personal act of being; secondarily, to his qualitative actuality revealed in his acts and partially revealing his act of

being. It is indirectly and implicitly a response to his potentiality, dynamism, and need. This response is experienced as liberation of the subject's energy for love and liberation from the confinement of individual being. It is at the same time experienced as a willing captivity to the beloved.[11]

The most obvious aspect of love, but perhaps hardest to explain, is the union experienced between the lover and the loved.

> The lover is present to the loved one and has the loved one present to himself.[12]

> Radical love is not a tendency affection but a being affection by which I am in union with, am present with the loved one.[13]

> Radical love is experienced as being in accord with the loved one, vibrating as it were, in harmony with the beloved's act of being and so with the whole melody of the beloved's life. It is a welcoming of the loved one into the lover's self and his life-world, as fitting there, making a harmony with the lover's being and life. Because it is consonant, harmonious, the presence constituted by love can reach to depths of presence.[14]

> The lover wants to be in the beloved, to have the beloved in him, to interpenetrate with the other without loss of either self.[15]

Toner makes an important distinction between "giving of self," which does not necessarily indicate radical love, and "giving self" that is essential to radical love. He first discusses giving of self.

> In this sort of giving the giver shares something of what he is: his wisdom, his wit, his strength, his joyfulness. What is shared are the qualities of the lover's own being. . . . But such giving is not giving self simply, and it is not love. That sharing one's wit and wisdom and strength and so on with the other is not itself love is evident from the fact that just as we can give our external possessions with or without love so also we can share in this way with or without radical love for the one with whom we share.[16]

> For the giving which is love is not merely a giving to someone for the other to possess and use. The giving which is an act of radical love is a giving into, so that by it the gift is in the loved. . . . It is giving self; for it is myself who

am in the loved one by my love, not merely my possessions, or even my thoughts, my wit, my joy, my wisdom, my strength. It is I myself.[17]

One who loves another with radical love consciously participates in the life of the loved one in the sense of experiencing the other's life as his own, and this experience is proportioned to the intensity of the love.[18]

The most revealing sign of radical love is the lover's "identification with the loved one."[19]

I refer to the experience of my loved one's life as my own. . . . Note well that I do not affirm him as myself, that is, as an extension or projection of myself, his personal reality absorbed by mine or mine by his. I affirm him as I affirm myself.[20]

The self . . . is only actualized in loving others with a genuinely radical love, an affirmation of the other for the other's own sake.[21]

Loving someone in depth . . . means loving from the lover's most personal self, with sincerity, intensity, endurance . . . to affectively affirm this unique person in a response informed by full, detailed, knowledge which catches the delicate shadings of his profoundest attitudes, moods, likes and dislikes, ideals, fears, hopes, capabilities, weaknesses, etc.[22]

Reducing love to its most irreducible aspect, Toner writes, "The deepest aspect of radical love [is] affective affirmation of the beloved for himself and in himself, in his very act of personal being."[23] He continues, "You are why I love you. If this is not the reason I love you, the affection is not radical love."[24]

Radical love is a response in which the lover affectively affirms the beloved for the beloved's self (as a radical end), in himself (on account of his intrinsic lovable actuality), directly and explicitly in his personal act of being, implicitly in his total reality, by which affirmation the lover's personal being is constantly present to and in the beloved and the beloved present to and in him, by which the lover affectively identifies with the loved one's personal being, by which in some sense the lover is the beloved affectively.[25]

It is because of you . . . the last word is you. I love you because you are you. And I would be you by love without ceasing to be myself because I must be I in order that you may be you in the way that I alone can make you be you. If in so doing I become I in the way that only you can make me be, that is love's reward but not love's motive.[26]

Gene Outka: Agape *Means Equal Regard*

Agape enjoins one to identify with the neighbor's point of view, to try imaginatively to see what it is for him to live the life he does, to occupy the position he holds.

—Gene Outka, *Agape*

The standard reference among theologians for the analytical study of Christian love is Gene Outka's *Agape: An Ethical Analysis*. Although published some thirty years ago, the book remains a significant resource on the study of love in the Christian theological tradition. Outka notes from the outset that his task is not to construct a theory of love but rather to bring clarity to the literature he describes as "confused as well as rich."[27] Even though his task is analytical, Outka is most often quoted for his description of *agape* as "equal regard."

Agape, argues Outka, is "the active concern for the neighbor's well-being."[28] That phrase alone, however, does not capture the full meaning of the term. The basis of *agape* is an "agent-commitment" and a "neighbor-evaluation."[29] By "neighbor-evaluation" Outka means that for a person to love with *agape*, she must see the neighbor in a specific way. *Agape* means that we see the other for her own sake. We do not first look at her uniqueness or her special characteristics but rather we recognize in each person her fundamental humanness. There are two related points here. First, *agape* rejects outright the consideration of seeing any person as simply a means to my personal goals or for my personal benefit. Second, *agape* is impartial and universal. *Agape* applies to all people. It is to be prior to any judgment made about another's general appearance or social utility. *Agape* is the "attribution to everyone alike of an irreducible worth and dignity."[30] Outka writes, "At the most basic level there ought to be no exclusiveness, no partiality, no elitism. . . . It is universal in that not a single person is to be excluded."[31] *Agape*, Outka argues, is equal regard for all people.

"Agent-commitment" and "neighbor-evaluation" are closely linked. Agent-commitment means that for a person to love with *agape*, she must put the neighbor's basic well-being on the same level as her own basic well-being, and she must do so with a "permanent stability." Outka argues that this "permanence involves persistence in the face of obstacles and continued concern for another's welfare despite lack of personal benefit."[32] It is this permanence that distinguishes *agape* from friendship. He writes, "Equal regard is unalterable; to abandon it would never be appropriate. Alternatively, friendship may fluctuate; it depends at least in part on mutual liking, and usually on admiration and esteem as well."[33]

Outka continues:

> In part, the principle of equal regard enjoins man not to let his basic attitudes toward others be determined by the disparities in talent and achievement and the inequalities in attractiveness and social rank which differentiate men. He is not, for example, to value his neighbor in accordance with the value of that neighbor's social position. He is to attempt to get behind social, political, and technical titles which are the all-too-evident tokens of inequality. He is not to confuse the differences in instrumental value which various titles doubtless often reflect with the irreducible value of the well-being of the holders of these titles. He is enjoined to identity with the neighbor's point of view, to try to image what it is for him to live the life he does, to occupy the position he holds.[34]

What does it mean then to say we love our neighbor? What is the content of that love? Outka holds that within the Christian theological tradition there have been three dominant features of love. He suggests, "A major reason why people disagree about what is the most loving action in a given situation is that they often attach different priorities" to these three features. His own view is that there is a complex interaction among the three. The first is the essential equality we all have in relation to God. The second is our basic human interests and the "need of the neighbor to have his basic interests considered and his welfare accounted as valuable as another's."[35] The third is basic human freedom. Outka rejects the notion that loving actions can restrict the neighbor's moral capacity. "If the human agent is to conform to grace, then whatever he does for others he ought not to take their own initiative and ability to act from them."[36] He continues, "Loving the neighbor means fostering his subjective identity and integrity. The conditions which avoid exterior constraints and impositions and enhance personal freedom are *eo ipso* [by that itself] what love requires."[37]

Outka notes restrictions to the scope of *agape* in everyday life. We have limited ability. Thus he argues, "the most that can be required is equal consideration but not identical treatment."[38] We are involved in special obligations. Thus he argues, "at the very least special obligations ought to presuppose and never require less than *agape* requires. *Agape* is the guardian in rather than the direct inspiration of every special relation. It sets the boundaries."[39]

Equal regard moderates both self-sacrifice and self-love. In a perceptive statement he declares, "One need not assume even in this life that neighbor-regard and self-sacrifice are automatically correlative."[40] The value of self-sacrifice is instrumental; it is not necessarily a good in itself. He continues, "Self-sacrifice must always be purposive in promoting the welfare of others and never simply expressive of something resident in the agent."[41] Equal regard commends a basic love of self. He writes, "No love-relationship is ever devoid of *epithymia* [the normal drive toward self-fulfillment]: love would be impoverished without it."[42] Indeed, "Those who actually love their neighbors will be found on examination always to love themselves as well."[43] *Agape* then is equal regard for oneself and all one's neighbors.

Outka concludes:

> *Agape* enjoins one to identify with the neighbor's point of view, to try imaginatively to see what it is for him to live the life he does, to occupy the position he holds. . . . He is never merely a means or instrument. To ignore him completely or treat him as a pure social functionary, for example, is not permitted on any grounds. . . . If through no fault of his own an individual ceases to be a public asset, he should still receive equal consideration. . . . One is enjoined to honor from first to last the space he occupies and the time he has.[44]

Political Consequences of Christian Love

> When we thus assert the universality of Christian love . . . [i]t is not possible to remain neutral in the face of poverty and the resulting just claims of the poor; a posture of neutrality would, moreover, mean siding with the injustice and oppression in our midst."
>
> —Gustavo Gutierrez, *A Theology of Liberation*

In 1971, the Peruvian priest Gustavo Gutierrez published what was to become one of the most influential books of theology in the latter part of the twentieth century, *A Theology of Liberation*. Since the publication of that book, liberation theologies have developed in contexts throughout the world. Gutierrez's theology began from the underside of history, that is to say, from the experience of the poor and oppressed. Liberation theology entails action to critique and indeed change the social conditions that cause poverty. The excerpts below suggest how opposite are God's love and the situations people find themselves in.

> The human person is destined to total communion with God and to the fullest fellowship with all other persons. . . . This was Christ's revelation.

To be saved is to reach the fullness of love; it is to enter into the circle of charity which unites the three Persons of the Trinity; it is to love as God loves. . . . Acceptance is the foundation of all communion among human persons. To sin is to refuse to love, to reject communion and fellowship, to reject even now the very meaning of human existence. Matthew's text is demanding: "Anything you did not do for one of these, however humble, you did not do for me" (25:45). To abstain from serving is to refuse to love; to fail to act for another is as culpable as expressly refusing to do it. . . . The parable of the Good Samaritan ends with the famous inversion which Christ makes of the original question. They asked him, "Who is my neighbor?" and when everything seemed to point to the wounded man in the ditch on the side of the road, Christ asked, "Which of these three do you think was neighbor to the man who fell into the hands of the robbers?" (Luke 10:29, 36). The neighbor was the Samaritan who approached the wounded man and made him his neighbor. The neighbor, as has been said, is not the one whom I find in my path, but rather the one in whose path I place myself, the one whom I approach and actively seek. . . . This is why Matthew's text says we will be definitively judged by our love for others, by our capacity to create comradely conditions of life.[45]

But this charity exists only in concrete actions (feeding the hungry, giving drink to the thirsty, etc.); it occurs of necessity in the fabric of relationships among persons. . . . But charity does not exist alongside or above human loves; it is not "the most sublime" human achievement like a grace super-imposed upon human love. Charity is God's love in us and does not exist outside our human capabilities to love and to build a just and friendly world.[46]

Loving us as a human, Christ reveals to us the Father's love. Charity, the love of God for human beings, is found incarnated in human love—of parents, spouses, children, friends—and it leads to its fullness. The Samaritan approached the injured man on the side of the road not because of some cold religious obligation, but because "his heart was melting" because his love for that man was made flesh in him.[47]

[We] will find the authentic love of God only by means of a real, concrete approach to human persons. It is not enough to say that love of God is inseparable from the love of one's neighbor. It must be added that love for God is unavoidably expressed through love of one's neighbor. Moreover,

God is loved in the neighbor. . . . To love one's brother, to love all persons, is a necessary and indispensable mediation of the love of God; it is to love God.[48]

We find the Lord in our encounters with others, especially the poor, marginated, and exploited ones. An act of love towards them is an act of love towards God. This is why Congar speaks of "the sacrament of our neighbor," who as a visible reality reveals to us and allows us to welcome the Lord.[49]

Nevertheless, the neighbor is not an occasion, an instrument, for becoming closer to God. We are dealing with a real love of persons for their own sake and not "for the love of God," as the well-intended but ambiguous and ill-used cliche would have it—ambiguous and ill-used because many seem to interpret it in a sense which forgets that the love for God is expressed in a true love for persons themselves. This is the only way to have a true encounter with God. That my action towards another is at the same time an action towards God does not detract from its truth and concreteness, but rather gives it even greater meaning and import.

It is also necessary to avoid the pitfalls of an individualistic charity. As it has been insisted in recent years, the neighbor is not only a person viewed individually. The term refers also to a person considered in the fabric of social relationships, to a person situated in economic, social, cultural, and racial coordinates. It likewise refers to the exploited social class, the dominated people, marginated. The masses are also our neighbor. . . . Indeed, to offer food or drink in our day is a political action; it means the transformation of a society structured to benefit a few who appropriate to themselves the value of the work of others. This transformation ought to be directed toward a radical change in the foundation of society, that is, the private ownership of the means of production.[50]

The gospel proclaims God's love for every human being and calls us to love as God loves. Yet recognition of the fact of class struggle means taking a position, opposing certain groups of persons, rejecting certain activities, and facing hostilities. For if we are convinced that peace indeed supposes the establishment of justice, we cannot remain passive or indifferent when the most basic human rights are at risk. That kind of behavior would not be ethical or Christian. Conversely, our active participation on the side of justice and in defense of the weakest members of society does not mean that we are encouraging conflict; it means rather that we are trying to eliminate its deepest root, which is the absence of love.[51]

When we thus assert the universality of Christian love, we are not taking a stand at an abstract level, for this universality must become a vital energy at work in the concrete institutions within which we live. . . . It is not possible to remain neutral in the face of poverty and the resulting just claims of the poor; a posture of neutrality would, moreover, mean siding with the injustice and oppression in our midst. The position we take under the inspiration of the gospel must be real and effective.[52]

Gutierrez maintains that God's love is universal, yet at the same time, God has a "predilection for those on the lowest rung of the ladder."[53] That is to say, God has a partiality or preference toward the poor.

The universality of Christian love is, I repeat, incompatible with the exclusion of any persons, but it is not incompatible with a preferential option for the poorest and most oppressed. When I speak of taking into account social conflict, including the existence of the class struggle, I am not denying that God's love embraces all without exception. Nor is anyone excluded from our love, for the gospel requires that we love even our enemies; a situation that causes us to regard others as our adversaries does not excuse us from loving them. There are oppositions and social conflicts between diverse factions, classes, cultures, and racial groupings, but they do not exclude respect for persons, for as human beings they are loved by God and are constantly being called to conversion.[54]

Material poverty, writes Gutierrez, is a "scandalous condition inimical to human dignity and therefore contrary to the will of God."[55] It "is an expression of a sin, that is, of a negation of love."[56] Thus he argues that out of love we must eliminate poverty.[57] Gutierrez distinguishes material poverty from spiritual poverty, defining the latter as having "no other sustenance than the will of God."[58] In a discussion of spiritual poverty he writes:

The Incarnation is an act of love. Christ became human, died, and rose from the dead to set us free so that we might enjoy freedom. . . . But [Jesus does not take on the human, servile] condition and its consequences to idealize it. It is rather because of love for and solidarity with others who suffer in it. It is to redeem them from their sin and to enrich them with his poverty. It is to struggle against human selfishness and everything that divides persons and allows that there be rich and poor, possessors and dispossessed, oppressors and oppressed.

Poverty is an act of love and liberation. It has a redemptive value. If the ultimate cause of human exploitation and alienation is selfishness, the deepest reason for voluntary poverty is love of neighbor. Christian poverty has meaning only as a commitment of solidarity with the poor, with those who suffer misery and injustice. The commitment is to witness to the evil which has resulted from sin and is a breach of communion. It is not a question of idealizing poverty, but rather of taking it on as it is, an evil, to protest against it and to struggle to abolish it. . . . Christian poverty, an expression of love, is solidarity with the poor and is a protest against poverty. This is the concrete, contemporary meaning of the witness of poverty. It is a poverty lived not for its own sake, but rather as an authentic imitation of Christ; it is a poverty which means taking on the sinful human condition to liberate humankind from sin and all its consequences.[59]

Underlying Gutierrez's words we can hear the themes of both Toner and Outka. True Christian love is active and responsive; it is giving self where one identifies with the other. Christian love cares for the well-being and the moral integrity of the other.

Christian Love Is Mutual Love

The final section of this chapter captures the conversations of some contemporary Christian theologians. The four selections all argue for the priority of mutuality in Christian love.

Martin D'Arcy: The Circuit of Love

It is at the poignant moments when we realize this that we are most tempted to do a forbidden thing—to hand ourselves over utterly and to go into the dark that we may be lost to ourselves and fused with the other.
　　　　　　　　　　　—Martin D'Arcy, *The Mind and Heart of Love*

Several years after the publication of *Agape and Eros*, the Catholic theologian Martin D'Arcy responded to Nygren's argument. D'Arcy challenged Nygren on several methodological grounds. He argued that Nygren's reading of the ancient and medieval theologians was problematic and that Nygren selectively used the

Bible. D'Arcy's primary critique of Nygren was that by eliminating *eros* from the human condition, Nygren essentially eliminated basic human nature. Human desire and choice and ultimately the possibility of our personal response to God come from *eros*. D'Arcy agrees with Nygren that God's love is a gift, but he maintains that humans have the power to cooperate with or to reject this gift. A person, writes D'Arcy, has the ability to form a friendship with God.

> Man is the highest in the animal world and the lowest in the world of spirit. But because he is spiritual he has a far-off kinship with God in that with his mind he meets truth and with his love he desires goodness—and God is truth and goodness and knows and loves perfectly. This means that friendship, and exchange of love, is possible between man and God. But as man's mind is so feeble and his will so contrary to have any close friendship with God would be impossible if he had to rely on his own strength.[60]

> Nygren so exalts Agape that no place is left for any properly human response and co-operation, the great Scholastic thinkers held on to the principle that in all friendships two are concerned and not one. Even though man's love in the new covenant of friendship with God is supernatural, that is to say, beyond his natural capacity, he does not become an automaton; he is not forced, not taken hold of willy nilly and made to love. The whole purpose of God's action is to give and not to take away, to restore and increase the dignity of the human person. This means that man must be left his freedom, his power to accept or refuse, and his power, consequently, to merit by cooperation with Divine love.[61]

> It is in this reciprocal love that losing one's life is saving it, that to give is to receive, that death is swallowed up in victory. . . . Persons do not die when the love is mutual; they live more fully each in the other's love. But when it comes to the infinite love of God for man, man, so far from having anything subtracted from his being, has the personal joy of giving back to God something of that infinite love which has taken possession of him. It is this mystery of love which the Christian sacrifice figures forth.[62]

D'Arcy's argument is not merely with Nygren. It is rather with the development in the Christian theological tradition that equates true love with self-sacrifice. D'Arcy offers an alternative position to that of Kierkegaard, Nygren, and Niebuhr. If these three writers were worried about excessive self-interest, D'Arcy worried about excessive self-surrender. Gene Outka refers to this as the

question of the "blank check." Does true love mean that you must write a blank
check to the other and they can expect anything from you? Outka writes, "The
feature of self-sacrifice in itself would appear to provide no way of distinguish-
ing between attention to another's needs and submission to his exploitation and
no warrant for resisting the latter."[63] D'Arcy rejected "blank check" conceptions
of self-sacrifice. While there is no simple formula or rule to decide appropriate
love in every relationship, D'Arcy argued, "what no one can neglect is a sense
of personal dignity"[64] in any relationship.

> I do not and cannot ask the question whether I am ultimately loving my-
> self first for the simple reason that when loving another I cannot get any
> benefit unless I give my love to that other. The less I consider any gain to
> self and the more I give freely and without second thoughts, the better for
> me and my love. I live by another's bounty as he lives by mine. This is per-
> fect love on earth between persons, but, alas! a word of caution is needed.
> There are two impediments at least to its perfect fruition. The first is that,
> however much lovers in the act of loving deny it, there is no certainty of
> equality of giving and taking, no surety that love will be returned; and sec-
> ondly, there is a barrier which no human person can cross. The fine point
> in personality must always remain untouched. We share but in part, and
> we are left lonely. It is at the poignant moments when we realize this that
> we are most tempted to do a forbidden thing—to hand ourselves over ut-
> terly and to go into the dark that we may be lost to ourselves and fused with
> the other. Many times we have seen the menace of this temptation and the
> disasters which follow on total surrender.[65]

In a model of love that praises excessive self-surrender, "The lover becomes like
a moth which dashes itself against the hot lamp."[66]

> The self-regarding love preserves the integrity of the self and prevents the
> other love from getting out of hand and being too prodigal. There is a con-
> stant threat against the rights and independence of man in modern society;
> he is with difficulty able to call his body and his soul his own. . . . In human
> affairs, therefore, the self-regarding love, which stands for reason and
> judgement and watches over and commands progress in self-perfection,
> must ever be active and even take precedence over the love of self-efface-
> ment. We have to say, what doth it profit to save the whole world and suffer
> the loss of our souls?[67]

But it is not until the searchlight of truth has played upon the many shapes which hold our attention and the many loves which beckon to us, that we can give ourselves wholeheartedly to another in personal friendship. The law of personal friendship is, as has been said, that we give what we are and we receive from the other. The law holds and does distinguish this relation from all other relations, whether of gain or loss. A person is such that he would, while remaining himself and having a never-dry fount to draw from, give himself to another. The other likewise because he is a person gives and has no thought of gain. Thus each makes up to the other in abundance the sacrifice and the apparent loss. A new circuit of love begins where two complete one another and live together in one.[68]

Margaret Farley: Just Love

[We have] a moral obligation not to relate to another person in a way that is truly destructive of ourselves as persons.

—Margaret Farley, *Personal Commitments*

The theologians of the Christian Church have primarily been men. This book illustrates that fact. The writings of men take up a disproportionate amount of space, given the fact that women make up at least half of the Christian population. Does the fact that men write theology, specifically in this case, the theology of love, give their work a particular slant? Do women have a different experience of love? If they do, would this experience then translate into distinctive theological reflection? This question was first asked and indeed answered in academic theological circles in 1960 by Valerie Saiving. Saiving questioned whether Nygren and Niebuhr, and indeed contemporary theology, tended to describe the human condition from a male experience to the exclusion of women's experience. What if the meanings of sin and love were not universal to the extent suggested by Nygren and Niebuhr? What if pride and self-aggression were not so much the universal description of sin but more of a reflection on sin by men. If love, expressed primarily through self-denial and self-sacrifice, were the antidote for such sin, would the same hold true for women?

Some women writers have suggested that there is a lingering problem involved in defining love primarily in terms of self-sacrifice. Throughout history, they suggest, there has been a double standard. Women have always been expected to give more of themselves in relationships than have men. Indeed, it is argued, can this disproportionate emphasis have a destructive effect on women? Barbara Hilkert Andolsen, for example, writes, "women (by nature and/or as a result of cultural conditioning) are often prone to destructive self-abnegation. Many women live for others to a damaging degree. Largely focused upon others, such women are unable to establish a satisfying self-definition."[69] If for men, love as self-sacrifice is an ideal, and for women it is the expectation, can that not lead to repressive and exploitative relationships? Perhaps then for women "excessive self-regard is not the sole root of human evil." Perhaps, as Andolsen suggests, for many "women the problem is too little self-assertion rather than too much."[70] Andolsen, in conversation with several women theologians concludes, "neither self-sacrifice nor other regard captures the total meaning of *agape*. The full expression of the Christian ideal is mutuality."[71]

Margaret Farley offers an interesting development in this conversation. Building on Jules Toner's work, she describes love as "affective affirmation which is responsive and unitive."[72] She argues, however, that this description is not sufficient. It can justify not only true and good loves, but it might also describe distorted, foolish, or even destructive loves. She suggests, "A love is right and good insofar as it aims to affirm truthfully the concrete reality of the beloved."[73] In her words, such a love is a just love (a love characterized by justice). We do not use the other for our advantage. We do not love the other for what she or he provides us. Indeed we do not love the other for what they do. We love them for who they are in their uniqueness and their particularity, for their basic humanness. We love them for who they were and who they will be.

A just love not only affirms the concrete reality of the other, it also is in itself an affirmation of the lover.

> A just love of persons will . . . affirm their essential equality as human persons, but it will also attend to the differences among them in terms of capabilities and needs. It will take account of and respect the essential autonomy of persons and the meaning and value that they themselves give to their lives (though it will not thereby abdicate its own responsibility for discerning meaning and values in the concrete lives of the ones loved). It will also take account of and respect the relationships that are as essential to persons as is their freedom or autonomy.[74]

> When I love another person, I place my own self in affirmation of the other. Because of this, there is no love for another that does not entail some affirmation (whether true or false, adequate or inadequate) of myself. . . . If love of another person is to be just, it must of necessity be also just in terms of its affirmation of myself. If as a way of loving it falsifies or distorts my concrete reality, it cannot be a just way of loving another.[75]

Mutual affirmation, while part of love, does not express the fullness of love. When one truly loves, one makes sacrifices.

> Central to our personhood is the capacity to come into union by knowledge and love with all reality and especially with other persons, other centers of consciousness and freedom. . . . As we cease to exist only within and for ourselves (move beyond self-preoccupation), we come paradoxically to fuller possession of ourselves. . . .To love another with a just and faithful love turns out to mean that we affirm both the other's good and our own, though what we intentionally seek and ultimately choose may be only the good of the other.[76]

> Commitment involves, even requires, self-sacrifice. But it also follows that self-love and love of another are not necessarily incompatible. And that self-sacrifice is not necessarily incompatible with self-love. And, finally, that, self-fulfillment not only need not be in opposition to the faithful love of another but may, in fact, be realized through it.
>
> But if commitment obviously includes self-sacrifice, it is just as obvious that there are limits to the sacrifice that is required or even morally allowed. Self-sacrifice can destroy as well as contribute to true relationship.[77]

Farley adds an important qualifier to the notion of the obligation of self-sacrifice in a relationship. Self-sacrifice, she notes, is a required element of love, but not all self-sacrifice is love.

> [We have] a moral obligation not to relate to another person in a way that is truly destructive of ourselves as persons. It does not mean that we ought never to sacrifice our own welfare—sacrifice even our home, our health, our security, our reputation, our professional future, our very life.[78]

> What it does mean (to say that we must not relate to others in ways destructive of ourselves as persons) is that while we may sacrifice everything we have, we may not sacrifice everything we are. We may not sacrifice in a final sense our autonomy. We may not sacrifice our capability for union and communion with God and human persons.[79]

Edward Vacek: The Most Complete Christian Love Is Philia

> Philia corrects the temptation to think that life is nothing more than individuals walking next to, or behind or in front of others, but not with others.
> —Edward Vacek, *Love, Human and Divine*

Edward Vacek's *Love, Human and Divine: The Heart of Christian Ethics* is a
lengthy, detailed, and insightful reflection on contemporary Christian theology
of love. Like Toner's, Vacek's method is phenomenological; that is, he relies heav-
ily on human experience, particularly "the experience of those who have been
informed by Christianity," to understand love.[80] In his words, "I appeal to contemporary experience as a criterion of what is true in the tradition, even as that
experience is mightily formed and challenged by the tradition."[81] Vacek defines
love as follows: "Love is an affective, affirming participation in the goodness of
a being (or Being)."[82] Later he notes, "Love is an emotional, affirming participation in the dynamic tendency of an object to realize its fullness."[83] Any full
description of love, he suggests, will contain two aspects. It will "account for our
experiences of wanting to be with or have those we love, and delighting when
we do so. Love unites." Second it "also must account for our experience of wanting the best for the beloved."[84] Love is a complex reality made up of unity and
interaction between the one who loves, the act of love, and the object of love.
Each affects the particular love we are talking about.

Vacek describes the theology of love in seven steps.

> (1) God affirms us; (2) God receives us; (3) we accept God's love; (4)
> we affirm God; (5) God forms community with us; (6) we cooperate
> with God in loving God and the world; and finally (7) we grow in a
> limited coresponsibility with God.[85]

We will focus on Vacek's understanding of the relationship between love for
God and neighbor love. He argues that

> within our covenant with God, our love of neighbor and, indeed, of the
> world is our way of cooperating with God's love for them and thus is a way
> of being further united with God. This position might be put in two sets
> of three theses, the first set dealing with our love of God, the second set
> with our love of neighbor: (1) Our love of God is not identical with love
> of neighbor. (2) We can love God and not (yet) love our neighbor. (3) Our
> love of God leads to love of neighbor. (4) Our love of neighbor is not iden-
> tical with love of God. (5) We can love our neighbor and not (yet) love
> God. (6) Our love of neighbor leads to the love of God.[86]

Indeed, he argues, "It is perilous to insist that love of God necessarily includes
love of neighbor."[87] It is "idolatry to makes these two identical."[88] How then
are we to think about love of God and love of neighbor?

A Christian loves, within limits, what God loves. What then does God love? In brief, God loves God, the world, other persons, and me. Within our limits, what then should we love? The answer is the same: God, the world, other human beings, and myself. But whether we go to worship or to the soup kitchen, all should be done in response to and as part of our relation with God. This is not a matter of God first, after that others, and then perhaps one's self. God asks our whole heart all the time, and our love for creatures should increasingly be part of the way we cooperate with God. The Christian moral life is a love relationship with God. The mystery of our lives is that we come to share in the life of the One who loves the universe.[89]

We can distinguish three different types of love.

Let me begin by setting down a crucial distinction. . . . We may love the beloved (1) for the sake of the beloved, (2) for our own sake, or (3) for the sake of a relationship we have with the beloved. I call these love relations (1) agape, (2) eros, and (3) philia. Thus, I distinguish agape, eros, and philia by the phrase "for the sake of." The one for whose sake we love determines the kind of love we have. This distinction lies in our intention, in the meaning the act has for us, not in any results of the act. Thus, it may well be that in loving others we do the greatest good for ourselves. But if we love others in order to do the best for ourselves, we are not loving them for their sakes. If another act that was better for ourselves was available, we might abandon them and pursue that act. When we love others as a way of fulfilling ourselves, this love of others is eros, not agape. If, as some argue, God loves only in order to express God's nature, then God does not love us for our own sakes; that is, God does not, in my terms, love us agapically.[90]

While Vacek presents rich descriptions of the three types of love, the main element of his argument is that *philia* "is the most complete Christian love."[91]

Most Christian authors praise a self-sacrificing love or a love that works for the other; some praise a love by which we live from others; unfortunately, only a few argue at length on behalf of a love that means being with others. When the Church thinks of saints, it thinks mostly of those who sacrifice themselves and not of those who nourish friendships such as marriages. . . . [My central thesis], however, is that communion or philia is the foundation and goal of Christian life. This love is a "power that cre-

ates unity and forms the human community ever more extensively and in-
tensively." Indeed, all human love finds its culmination and ultimate goal
in a community of solidarity with and in God.[92]

In philia we love them not for their own sake, as separate individuals, not
for our sake (nor for the sake of yet another party), but for the sake of the
mutual relationship we share with them.[93]

There are two aspects of philia. We love others for the sake of the mutual
relationship we share with them, and we love them as partners in that relationship. This love involves a cherishing of the joint experience which is
one's life with another as well as a cherishing of the particular person who
has lived through it with us. Thus, our "reason" for loving them is the special relationship we share with them; they are loved not just for themselves
nor as someone "good for us," but rather as those with whom we want to
share a mutual relation. In philia, unlike pure agape and eros, there is a
communal life which, so to speak, circulates between the members. The
members love and are loved in terms of their special relationship. Their love
flows from the relationship and is directed back to it.[94]

Mutuality is (1) a form of sharing life (2) through interaction of free persons (3) who communicate themselves to one another (4) in a way that is
progressively involving.[95]

In a mutual love, we want to make a difference in how our partners live.
And when we are touched (physically or emotionally) by our beloved, we
welcome that touch and respond to it as part of our relationship.[96]

Through philia we transcend our individual, private needs and interests.
We join ourselves to something beyond ourselves when we make friends,
form a family, or join a church. . . . Contrary to what agapists often claim,
partners in our special relationships are not prized simply for what they
contribute to us. That is, philia is not simply eros. To the contrary, the "infinite value" of persons is often first learned in special relationships.[97]

Philia relationships are themselves great goods, and therefore they are worth
the time and energy invested in them. Most of us spend countless hours in
creating, maintaining, and fostering our relationships. We play with one
another, go for walks with one another, talk on the phone just to keep up.

We "waste time" together that could be more profitably spent were it not for the fact that the relationships we thereby maintain and build are among the highest goods of our lives.[98]

Thus philia creatively promotes a life that is fuller than we could achieve by ourselves. This is above all true of that most unequal of relationships, our relation to God. We can never be God's equal, but through God's creative love we can be God's friends and children.[99]

Vacek argues for a unity of love and a proportionate interaction among the three loves:

Each of the three loves we have discussed counteracts basic human disorders. First agape corrects for selfishness, which is ever ready to mask itself as healthy self-love. . . . when the problem is overweening pride, agape enables us to appreciate the value of others in and for themselves. Or when the problem is that our philia relations tend to become exclusive not simply in the sense that we form "friendships" only with some, but in the sense that we exclude some human beings altogether from our love, perhaps even harming them, then agape insists that we must value the welfare of all human beings, whether they are community members or not. Special relationships ought not contravene an openness to all persons.[100]

When, second, the problem is that we have little appreciation for ourselves, the remedy is self-love or eros. When the problem is depression or self-hate, eros for the world may enliven us. . . . Self-love increases our sense of our own goodness, and since goodness tends to overflow, those who love themselves may in fact love others more.

Third . . . self-love or an agapic love will not of themselves overcome this basic loneliness [that many people feel]. "Sin is the turning-away . . . from interdependencies with all other beings, including the matrix of being from whom all life comes." Philia corrects the temptation to think that life is nothing more than individuals walking next to, or behind or in front of others, but not with others.[101]

Both eros and agape are necessary for human flourishing. . . . But more is needed than these two loves. We also need that form of love by which we belong in a community. We not only give and take; we also share. That is, we exist in special relationships.[102]

Human life typically includes all three loves in rhythmically occurring ways. Philia can transform agape and eros, making them a part of the ongoing mutual relation it creates.[103]

Agape, eros, and philia each have their own goodness. In this book I have frequently sought a set of priority rules that could solve practical questions about whom or what we should love first and about which kind of love is most important in Christian life. I have found none other than that we should love God above all else. I cannot say we should always or never love our neighbor or ourselves or even other creatures first or last. And there is no lexical rule that says philia always or never trumps either agape or eros. There is a time and place for each love.[104]

D'Arcy writes, "The perfection of love . . . is to be found in personal friendship, whether between a man and a woman, between man and man, or between man and God." Christians envision the eschatological victory of God as a unity of all things, where God is all in all.[105]

Don Browning et al.: The Intersubjectivity of True Love

Love as equal regard is not something that one individual expresses unilaterally toward another. It is something that people create together . . . through successive attempts to communicate needs and desires, to listen and understand, to empathize with, hold, and accept, and then to live their mutual agreements."

—Don Browning et al., *From Culture Wars to Common Ground*

The past several years there has been a renewed interest in marriage within Christian theology. Evidence of this is the popularity and influence of the book *From Culture Wars to Common Ground: Religion and the American Family Debate*, co-written by five theologians. The authors suggest that there are three primary models of love that guide married couples today. They argue that these models parallel classic models of love in the Western tradition. "The first defines love as mutuality or equal regard ('giving your spouse and children the same respect, affection, and help as you expect from them'). The second depicts marital love as self-sacrifice ('putting the needs and goals of your spouse and children ahead of your own'). The third model understands love as serving self-fulfillment ('fulfilling your personal needs and life goals')."[106] The authors hold that the appropriate Christian model of love is mutuality. They do not reject the other three models but rather subsume them under the organizing principle of mutuality or equal regard. The following paragraphs discuss their views of individual fulfill-ment, self-sacrifice, and mutuality.

While some theologians are deeply suspicious of self-regard and individu-alism, the authors of *From Culture Wars to Common Ground* affirm the neces-sity of a limited or, in their words, "ordinate" self-concern (note the Augustin-ian language here). Individualism, they hold, does not necessarily lead to selfishness. They affirm "legitimate and energetic" self-regard.[107] "Love as equal regard," they write, "does not exclude self-love, self-regard, or an ordinate con-cern with one's own self-fulfillment. It simply requires that we take the other's self-fulfillment as seriously as our own, just as it requires the other to give equal consideration to our fulfillment."[108] The authors interpret the "as" in the great commandment, "Love your neighbor as yourself" to mean equal.[109] Thus they defend appropriate and proportionate self-love.

Their position seems to reflect common experience. For example, we find good relationships enriching. We enjoy and take pleasure from our loves. In a marriage you probably do not want to feel like you are the only one giving in the relationship. While you do not want to be the only one who gives, you prob-ably realize that a relationship requires work and sacrifice. The authors make it clear that sacrificial love, "by either husbands or wives, fathers or mothers, can-not be eliminated from Christian understandings of love. The cross has an un-avoidable role in the Christian life and in Christian families."[110] As they did when they affirmed but limited self-fulfillment in true love, the authors argue that self-sacrifice is an element of love, but not the end of love.[111] Even in the New Testament, they suggest, self-sacrifice "is a moment within a love ethic of mutuality."[112] Self-sacrifice has limits. "When a partner no longer has the ca-pacity or freedom to respond to enduring love or when evil is so deep that fi-nite human love cannot hope to transform it, then the vulnerable and defense-less need to acknowledge the limits of their love."[113] Self-sacrifice, they argue, is required in a relationship, but it is to be subordinate and in service of mutual-ity. "The Christian believes that expansive and enduring marital love is finally a reflection of the outpouring and overflowing of God's love, indeed, the divine passion. The additional capacity for sacrificial self-giving inspired by the suffer-ing and grace of God is what turns love as equal regard into a distinctively Chris-tian reality."[114]

The theory of equal regard love invites two practical questions. How does one measure mutuality? How long in a relationship does one go before evaluat-ing the totality of the relationship? Here the authors suggest a novel point. They suggest that outsiders cannot judge this. Equal regard love needs to be deter-mined by the couple within the concrete conditions of their relationship. It cannot be done from those outside the relationship nor can only one of the partners in a relationship do it. "No one person alone can determine adequately what equal regard means for another person."[115] This love must be described "inter-subjectively" through communication and within the concrete demands of the relationship. "Rhythms of equality and self-sacrifice are necessarily spread out over time."[116] Partners ought to sense and anticipate the needs of the other but also must dialogue and converse with the other and to arrive at common decisions. "Love as equal regard is not something that one individual expresses unilaterally toward another. It is something that people create together . . . through successive attempts to communicate needs and desires, to listen and understand, to empathize with, hold, and accept, and then to live their mutual agreements."[117] True love is mutual. It is based on deep respect for the partner and an attitude that is willing to work for the good of the other as well as for oneself. How this plays out in particular relationships is contingent on the honest, open, and continuous dialogue between the lovers.

CHAPTER ELEVEN

Reflections on Christian Love

The fundamental purpose of this book has been to have the reader encounter the wealth of reflection on love in the Christian tradition. If the reader experienced only a fraction of the joy while reading these texts that I felt as I worked on them, the book's purpose would have been fulfilled. To come up with a systematic theory of Christian love that addresses the themes and concerns of all the authors presented in these pages is probably an impossible task. Yet, I cannot end without giving some sense of my reaction to the content. What follows is an overview of the understanding of Christian love I learned during this project. My conclusion is like a quilt. I have liberally borrowed sections from our authors and sewn them together in what I hope to be a coherent form covering most of the pressing issues. My remarks are in three sections. In the first I discuss three statements I think to be essential to a Christian understanding of love. The second section describes what I understand to be the substance of Christian love. In the final section I recognize the limits of this love but reject the notion that *agape* is an impossible ideal.

General Propositions

A Christian view of love begins with three propositions: God is love, humans love, and the full meaning of human love is found through participation in God's love.

God is love and God loves. (This is not to say that the word love is full enough to describe the totality of God's being. "God is love" is a basic statement of faith, biblically supported and confirmed in experience.) This God of love is a Trinity, a unity of persons. The proposition "God is love" has two meanings. The first refers to the inner nature of God, the relationship of love between the persons of the Trinity. The second refers to the reality of God's relation to creation. God loves creation and all that is within creation.

Humans love. We can consider this statement in two ways. First, it is within the very nature of humans to love. Humans, created in the image and likeness of the God of love, have a natural inclination to love and a natural desire to be loved. To paraphrase Thomas Aquinas on natural law, the human inclination to love is nothing else than an imprint on us of the divine love.[1] When we love, when we appropriately pursue and develop this inclination, we participate in God's love in an active way.

If human love is a matter of inclination, it is also a matter of choice. Because we are inclined to do something does not necessarily mean we will actually follow through and do it. Love is a matter of the will; it is a matter of the head as well as the heart. We choose what we love, how we love, and when we love. The challenge of the moral life, in Augustinian terms, is to develop and nurture our loves. We must love the right things in the right way.

When someone becomes a Christian, however, she chooses to answer the fundamental question of whether I want to be loving or not in a distinctive way. An essential element of being a Christian is to be loving. Love is a vocational expectation for the Christian. 1 John captures the many reasons why this is so. The author notes that Christians are commanded, in both Testaments of the Bible, to love. Yet there is more to it than simply the rule of law. We are to love because through loving we come to know God. We are to love, moreover, because God loves us and loving others is the appropriate response to God's love for us. Indeed, if we do not love, John declares, we live in a state of "death." That is to say, if we do not love, we do not really live.

The full meaning of human love is found through participation in God's love. This proposition must be understood in at least two ways. The first is that our capacity to love is strengthened by our acceptance of God's love for us and our recognition of God's love for others. We become better lovers when we admit and appreciate God's love. Second, we become better lovers when we understand the characteristics of God's love and try to live these characteristics. The most direct answer to these questions for the Christian is found in the narratives of the life, teachings, death, and resurrection of Jesus. The dominant word for love in the New Testament is *agape*. (*Agape* was also the word chosen for the words for love in the Hebrew Scriptures when the text was first translated into Greek.) *Agape* is used to describe the broad range of loves and relationships in the Bible. I will use it in the biblical sense here. This is a departure from the more common use of the word, popularized by Nygren, which defines it exclusively and contrasts it to mutual loves.

The Substance of Love

The content of human love is found in the commands from the Old Testament and the New Testament. Christians are to love God and love their neighbors as they love themselves. Yet what is the "substance" of that love? How do we know love? I found phenomenological discussions from Toner and Farley to be helpful here. Their description of the experience of love as an affective affirmation of another that is responsive and unitive reflects the general characteristics of love in the Bible. I would add to those four characteristics a fifth. *Agape* is steadfast and enduring.

Affective

Our most common understanding of love is that it is an emotion. When one loves another something happens inside the person. Love is a stirring of one's heart. Aquinas and D'Arcy capture this aspect of love when they write that "love melts the soul and softens the heart." H. R. Niebuhr notes that love rejoices and is satisfied in the other. Love can bring delight and fulfillment to the soul as well as pain and sadness. Love is an emotion. It is a movement from one's heart, one's soul, that is to say, from within one's inner self. Thus the mystics suggest that love is prior to reason and indeed transcends reason. Talking about love is for them best done in poetic terms.

Love, however, is more than emotion. One might say that it is the directive and dominant center of emotions. When you truly love it changes your life. When you are truly loved and you accept that love you are never the same. Love transforms people and their ideas of happiness, fulfillment, and meaning.

Nygren exaggerates the division between *agape* and *eros*. *Eros* is part of the human condition. We are lovers. *Agape* does not reject, deny or destroy eros or indeed *philia*, it informs them. The affections, the inclinations, are to be developed and nurtured. Augustine's insight that we become like what we love is accurate; *agape* must direct our loves.

The affective element of *agape* is illustrated in numerous occasions in the Bible. In Hosea we read how God was moved and did not punish the people for their sins. "My heart recoils within me; my compassion grows warm and tender. I will not execute my fierce anger" (Hos. 11:8–9). In the New Testament we see the affections of Jesus. He was moved to tears when his friend died. When he encountered the suffering, the tormented, and the hungry, he was moved to help them. He felt the agony of the separation of God's love for him as he hung on the cross.

Without the soul being stirred, without emotion, there is no *agape*. When the soul is stirred by *agape* it is, to use Thomas's analogy, like a furnace; it radiates and loves all around it. The stronger the fire, the deeper the love, the more able it is to love others.

Affirming

Agape affirms the other. It says "yes" to the other and to the self. You and I have dignity. *Agape* is the simple yet profound recognition of the worthiness of and goodness in persons.

This affirmation happens on two levels. First, when one loves another she affirms the basic human dignity of the other. This notion has been a constant theme throughout this book. Augustine, Aquinas, Mother Teresa, and Outka all advocate this element of *agape*. Indeed this is the basis of love of neighbor. Note that there are different warrants or reasons to assert this "neighbor-evaluation" or the fundamental equality of people. In Outka's words, we ought to have an equal regard for our neighbors. Augustine speaks of the fact that each and every other has an intrinsic aspect that enables him or her to love God. For Aquinas we are united to others in charity and the potential we share with others for happiness with God. Mother Teresa sees Jesus in everyone she meets. Martin Luther argues for a more "agent-committed" view, that is to say, he argues that we are to be Jesus to everyone. Martin Luther King's refusal to hate his opponents was at the same time a determination to affirm his opponents while condemning their actions and attitudes. *Agape*, in its most fundamental expression, is egalitarian and universal. It compels Thomas to say, "Love the sinner and hate the sin."

People who are loved are also affirmed for their uniqueness. To love another is to acknowledge her gifts, her beauty. Love recognizes particular bonds and relationships. When someone truly loves she sees the other as a person. Toner says, "I love you because you are you." H. R. Niebuhr notes that love is reverent. It is deep respect for the other. It is gratitude toward, a happy acceptance of, the other. The readings of this book have only a few examples of bad love. One is the story of Abelard and Heloise. In reading the letters we hear Heloise continuing to love Abelard because he is Abelard. Their relationship, though part of her distant past, still moves her and causes her to see Abelard in a special way. Abelard seems to erase Heloise and his relationship with her from his mind. She is now his "sister in Christ," as, it appears, is every other woman. The reader is forced to wonder if he ever really loved her or if he was denying his love for fear of its power.

Unless we love people for who they are in both their uniqueness (as best we can) and their humanness, we do not truly love. Turn that statement around: We do not want to be loved merely because we are a person (no one wants to be generically loved) nor do we want to be loved because of a particular character or physical trait (what if my full head of dark hair is no longer full nor dark). We want to be loved in our totality.

God loves us as individuals. God loves us in our unique particularity. God "calls us each by name." The New Testament stories of Jesus show him reaching out to all he met. The list is long and includes sinners, Samaritans, men, women, rich, poor, religious leaders, people who have fallen away from religious practice, those in good health, those who were very sick, Roman soldiers, Zealots, and "ordinary" people. Jesus addressed people in their basic humanness and in their particular situations. He did not live on a mountaintop nor did he preach an abstract love.

Agape affirms the other's basic humanness and the other's unique personhood. There is a mutual relationship between the two. You cannot truly and fully love your child or your spouse unless you recognize their basic human dignity and their basic relationship to God. You cannot truly love the neighbor unless you know something about her as a person. On another level, we learn the basic affirmation of strangers through loving individuals who are close to us. The loves that command our most direct attention are the loves we have for friends and family. Love for neighbors, close and far, can develop intentionally when we acknowledge that they are like our loved ones and indeed like us at an essential level. This step of recognition may not be easy. It depends on the knowledge and experience of God's love for others. The concrete love for others ought to inform our particular loves. It ought to cause a greater awareness of God's love around us and invite us to love our family and friends in a deeper way.

We affirm God in at least two ways. We affirm God by acknowledging God's love for us, God's dominion over us. Vacek is correct when he notes that loving God and loving neighbor are related but distinct. Yet the second way we affirm God is to affirm the things that God loves, that is to say, we affirm God through affirming others in their uniqueness and basic humanity.

Responsive

Love is an active response for the well-being, the development of, the other. Love means participating in the promotion of the other's full humanness. It helps to create and foster the conditions for the possibility of the other to flourish. 1 John demands, "Let us love, not in word or speech, but in truth and action" (1 John 3:18). When Jesus pressed Peter on Peter's love for him, Jesus repeatedly told him to "Feed my sheep." Jesus himself fed, cured, and relieved the suffering of countless persons. Agape includes, as a necessary condition, the direct service to the other. Mother Teresa's life is a beautiful expression of this love. Martin Luther's sermons are dramatic assertions of this love. This service will include self-sacrifice. This being said, with Outka we must admit that *agape* and self-sacrifice are not necessarily correlative. Love includes sacrifice but love is not fully defined by sacrifice.

One way to get at the question of the role of sacrifice in *agape* is to describe the relationship between love of self and neighbor love. It is clear from even a cursory reading of the New Testament that love demands service, that is, placing concern for the other over self-concern. Does this necessarily mean self-destruction and self-abrogation? Garth Hallett convincingly argues that the most appropriate phrase to describe relationship between love of self and neighbor love in the New Testament is "self-subordination." Self-subordination means that "one should give independent consideration of one's own benefit, but only on the condition that maximum benefit to others is first assured."[2] "Overall," he writes, "it seems that when there is no question of conflict with God's call or others' good, the New Testament has no quarrel with benefit to self."[3] He continues, "the verdict of the New Testament would therefore seem to be that Christians, or people generally, should give precedence to others' good, and only seek their own when it does not conflict with others'."[4] In reading the gospels, Hallett writes, we do not hear of Jesus

> serving his own good in a way unrelated to others' good: not when he rested by the well, nor when he drank his hosts' wine, nor when he accepted their invitation to dine, nor when he rode into Jerusalem instead of entering on foot. However, neither do we find him denying his own good in a way unrelated to others' good.[5]

Agape is characterized by service to others, by "going the extra mile," by self-giving and self-sacrifice. "In all of this, however, there is no question of sacrifice simply for sacrifice's sake."[6]

A dominant feature of *agape* is then a readiness and willingness to subordinate the fulfillment of my needs so as to be able to help the other fulfill her needs. This subordination may, in extreme conditions, call for my life. It can never demand, however, that I violate my deepest values and my fundamental relationship to God. In Farley's shorthand terms, I can sacrifice what I have but never who I am.

Agape includes an active response to the other. It demands paying attention to the other's situation as well as to what God expects of us in concrete situations. Our response toward God is analogous to our response to others. We must seek God, spend time with God, talk with God, and subordinate our interests to God's expectations.

Unitive

The fruit of love is unity. Love unites. It is within the very nature of love to bring together. One cannot read the Bible without noticing this. In the creation stories, people are united with God. They sin and break the relationship. God then makes a series of covenants with people. God initiates relationships, unions, with people. In the New Testament, Jesus calls people to unite with him, to follow him, to be with him. Love unites.

When you love, you step out of yourself and experience the other. This experience has the potential to bring people together. When one loves the stranger or enemy, one experiences that the other is like me, on a fundamental level. In friendship we see the other as "another self" and experience her beauty and uniqueness. In romantic committed love, we are united with the other on both levels and we add a third. Such lovers unite temporally, sharing their daily lives, and physically, sharing their bodies. The consummation of this is the sharing of their souls. The mystics describe yet another sort of unity, unity with God. It is in the nature of *agape* to call the persons to union with others and with God.

To say that the fruit of love is unity is not to say that *agape* necessarily leads to intimacy or even mutuality. I may feel a unity with others unbeknownst to them. Great lovers can experience solidarity with others even if the others are across the globe. If a person loves agapically she cannot but be moved by the sufferings of others in war, poverty, and oppression. *Agape* opens the soul to be moved by the lives of strangers. It forces us to recognize that those who suffer are our brothers and sisters. It pushes us to find out more about them. Who are these people? Why do they suffer? *Agape* demands that we respond on some level to their needs. The fruit of this is solidarity. If we love agapically, our lives will be changed.

Steadfast

God's love endures. If there is a simple lesson about God learned from the Bible and known from human experience, both communal and individual, it is that God's love lasts. Psalm 136, for example, sings the praises of God's enduring love through the ages. *Agape* is *hesed;* it remains even in the face of human unfaithfulness. It is not surprising then that a constant theme of the authors in this book is that God's love is steadfast.

To say love endures is not to say that love never changes. The mystics describe steps in the development of love. There are stages in its maturity. Thomas claims that *caritas* has a beginning, a middle, and a perfection. To say that love is loyal, with H. R. Niebuhr, is to say that love can have a history. This point was made to me clearly on two separate occasions while writing this book. Two friends, both married for a long time, responded from the riches of their experience and said to me, "The meaning of love! It has changed so much for me. When I think of what it means for me to say 'I love you' to my wife today, it is so different from what I thought love meant when I was first married her."

To say love endures is not to say that it must always be reciprocal or mutual. A primary theme in the scriptural narrative is that while God's love endures, our love for God and indeed each other often does not. Thomas notes God does not turn from people; it is people who turn from God.

In reading and preparing the material for this book I was struck on a number of occasions by our authors' ability to capture an essential element of love in a short phrase. Of all the texts, one in particular caught my attention—Martin Luther King's words to his opponents.

> We shall match your capacity to inflict suffering by our capacity to endure suffering. We shall meet your physical force with soul force. Do to us what you will, and we shall continue to love you. . . . Throw us in jail, and we shall still love you. Bomb our homes and threaten our children, and we shall still love you. Send your hooded perpetrators of violence into our community at the midnight hour and beat us and leave us half dead, and we shall still love you.

Agape is steadfast, enduring, loyal, and faithful.

An Impossible Ideal?

Agape is the acknowledgment that God is love and God loves my neighbors and me. It is the response of Christians to the command to love, the desire to return God's love, and the desire to know God. That is to say, to live fully, to live as Jesus lived. We love with *agape* when we love God, our neighbors, and our self with love that moves from our affections, that affirms, is responsive, unitive, and steadfast. *Agape* is the fundamental love that is to inform our particular loves.

Is it an "impossible ideal?" An ideal is a goal, something we seek to achieve. Ideals are different than rules. We are judged responsible and indeed moral on particular actions in relation to rules. In relation to ideals, we are thought responsible in terms of how well we try to achieve them. Ideals inform not only our actions, but also our attitudes. In this sense *agape* is more like an ideal than a rule. Is this ideal impossible? I take the phrase "impossible ideal" not to be redundant. That is to say, if there are impossible ideals there must be possible ideals and if there are possible ideals there must be a range of probability in the possibilities. The probabilities would depend on the ideal and the context of the ideal. *Agape*, I think, is a possible ideal that is not achieved nearly enough in life. For the Christian, *agape* informs all loves. It transforms our relationships with strangers, enemies, parents, children, spouses, and significant others. Many people experience times or moments in a specific relationship where *agape* is very present. They sense that they are participating in something beyond their own doing. They bring to life the imprint of divine love on their soul. It happens. The ideal can be achieved in that time in that relationship. The probability lessens greatly if we hold that we have to achieve this in all our relations, all of the time. Sin is the great antagonist to love. Sin, described simply here as turning away from God or turning into ourselves, has dramatic consequences. Because of sin:

—We may not be moved by love or to love. Our hearts may be hardened.

—We do not affirm others. We put them down. We seek to dominate or belittle them, even those whom we "love."

—We turn in on ourselves and away from God and become numb to the needs of neighbor, whether spouse or stranger. We can love the wrong things and become caught up in a life that closes us off from others.

—We often do not want to unite or wish to take the emotional risk entailed in a relationship. To love another is to make oneself vulnerable. This can be risky business. We can get hurt; we can suffer by trying to love; we can be dropped, or ignored. We do not reach out.

The death of love is often preceded by neglecting affections. Love dies not because of hate but because of apathy. The death of love is often preceded by the denial of the basic dignity of the other. The death of love happens when we reject instead of affirm the other's special, personal, and unique goodness. The death of love is encouraged when we ignore the other's needs and wants while prioritizing our own wants. The death of love occurs when we pursue discord, division, disassociation, and distance in the place of unity.

Agape is not a once-and-for-all thing. It is a vocation, a life choice. Sin and failure are not the last words, for the last words are not left to us. Jesus told the story we call "The Prodigal Son" about sin and *agape* and the last words therein, that is to say, God's love. In the middle of the story, the humbled, unfaithful young man decides to head home. His father catches sight of him in the distance, and the father's love (affective, affirming, responsive, unitive, enduring) is so overpowering that he does not let his son get the words of confession out of his mouth. Jesus says, "But while he was still far off, his father saw him and was filled with compassion. He ran and put his arms around him and kissed him" (Luke 15:20). Christian love, in the beginning and to the end, takes its meaning from God's love.

Notes

Preface

1. David Tracy, *The Analogical Imagination: Christian Theology and the Culture of Pluralism* (New York: Crossroad, 1981), 68.
2. Bernard of Clairvaux, Sermon 70:1, quoted in M. Corneille Halflant, "Introduction," to *Song of Songs I*, by Bernard of Clairvaux, trans. Kilian Walsh, vol. 2 of *The Works of Bernard of Clairvaux* (Kalamazoo, MI: Cistercian Publications, 1971), x.

Chapter One

1. Gerhard Wallis, "*'ahabh*," in *Theological Dictionary of the Old Testament*, eds. G. Johannes Botterweck and Helmer Ringgren (Grand Rapids, MI: Eerdmans, 1974), 4:107.
2. Ibid., 105.
3. Katherine Doob Sakenfeld, "Love: Old Testament," in *The Anchor Bible Dictionary*, ed. David Freedmon (New York: Doubleday, 1992), 4:377, and E. M. Good, "Love in the Old Testament," in *The Interpreter's Dictionary of the Bible*, ed. George Buttrick (Nashville: Abingdon Press, 1989), 8:166.
4. Sakenfeld, "Love: Old Testament," 4:378, and H. J. Zobel, "*hesed*," in *Theological Dictionary of the Old Testament*, eds. G. Johannes Botterweck and Helmer Ringgren (Grand Rapids, MI: Eerdmans, 1974), 5:44–64.
5. Zobel, "*hesed*," 5:51.
6. Sakenfeld, "Love: Old Testament," 4:377.
7. Ibid., 4:378.
8. Ibid., 4:380.
9. Zobel, "*hesed*," 5:63.
10. Alice Laffey, "Ruth," in *The New Jerome Biblical Commentary*, eds. Raymond Brown, Joseph Fitzmeyer, Roland Murphy (Englewood Cliffs, NJ: Prentice Hall, 1990), 554.
11. Dennis McCarthy and Roland Murphy, "Hosea," in *The New Jerome Biblical Commentary*, eds. Raymond Brown, Joseph Fitzmeyer, Roland Murphy (Englewood Cliffs, NJ: Prentice Hall, 1990), 218.
12. Ibid., 219.
13. Ibid., 226.
14. Anthony Ceresko, "Jonah," in *The New Jerome Biblical Commentary*, 581.

15. John Collins, "Jonah," in *The New Oxford Annotated Bible*, eds. Bruce Metzger and Roland Murphy (New York: Oxford University Press, 1991), 1189 OT.

16. Corrine Carvalho, "Jonathan and David: Monarchy Mediated Through Sonship" (master's thesis, Graduate Theological Union, 1984), 86.

17. Edward Vacek, *Love, Human and Divine: The Heart of Christian Ethics* (Washington, DC: Georgetown University Press, 1994), 295.

18. Sakenfeld, "Love: Old Testament," 4:378.

19. David Penchansky, "Proverbs," in *Mercer Commentary on the Bible*, eds. Watson Mills and Richard Wilson (Macon, GA: Mercer University Press, 1995), 527.

20. Roland Murphy, "Introduction to Wisdom Literature," in *The New Jerome Biblical Commentary*, 447.

21. Alexandra DiLella, "Sirach," in *The New Jerome Biblical Commentary*, 497.

22. R. MacKenzie and Roland Murphy, "Job," in *The New Jerome Biblical Commentary*, 472.

23. Wesley Fuerst, *The Books of Ruth, Esther, Ecclesiastes, The Song of Songs, Lamentations* (Cambridge: Cambridge University Press, 1975), 159–60.

24. Roland Murphy, *The Song of Songs: A Commentary on the Book of Canticles or the Song of Songs* (Minneapolis: Fortress Press, 1990), 98.

25. Othmar Keel, *The Song of Songs: A Continental Commentary* (Minneapolis: Fortress Press, 1994), 31.

26. Murphy, *Song of Songs*, 103.

27. Marcia Falk, *The Song of Songs: A New Translation* (San Francisco: HarperCollins, 1993), xvi.

28. Irene Nowell, "Tobit," in *The New Jerome Biblical Commentary*, eds. Raymond Brown, Joseph Fitzmeyer, Roland Murphy (Englewood Cliffs, NJ: Prentice Hall, 1990), 568.

29. Ibid., 570.

30. *The Encyclopedia of Judaism*, ed. Geoffrey Wigoder (New York: Macmillan, 1989), 467.

Chapter Two

1. Victor Furnish, in his book *The Love Command in the New Testament* (New York: Abingdon Press, 1972), writes that "it is impossible to hold that the love command always and everywhere has a central place in the ethical teaching of the New Testament" (198). Richard Hays, in *The Moral Vision of the New Testament: A Contemporary Introduction to New Testament Ethics* (San Francisco: Harper Collins, 1996), argues that love is not a unifying theme for New Testament ethics. He cites "the scattered incidental references to love" in Mark, Hebrews, and Revelation. The word love does not even appear in the Acts of the Apostles (see Hays 200–203).

2. See Pheme Perkins, *Love Commands in the New Testament* (New York: Paulist Press, 1982), 2–4.

3. Norman Perrin, *The New Testament: An Introduction* (New York: Harcourt Brace Jovanovich, 1974), 47.

4. Martin Ostwald, "Glossary of Technical Terms," in *Nicomachean Ethics*, by Aristotle, trans. Ostwald (Indianapolis: Bobbs-Merrill Educational Publishing, 1983), 312.

5. William S. Cobb, *The* Symposium *and the* Phaedrus: *Plato's Erotic Dialogues* (Albany: State University of New York Press, 1993), 6.

6. Ibid., 12.

7. Giovanni Reale, *A History of Ancient Philosophy: Plato and Aristotle* (Albany: State University of New York Press, 1990), 171.

8. Ibid.

9. Ibid.

10. Plato, *Symposium*, quoted in *Sexual Love and Western Morality: A Philosophical Anthology*, ed. D. Verene (Boston: Jones and Bartlett Publishers, 1995), 18–19.

11. William Klassen, "Love: New Testament and Early Jewish Literature," in *The Anchor Bible Dictionary*, ed. David Freedmon (New York: Doubleday, 1992), 384.

12. See Klassen, "Love: New Testament and Early Jewish Literature." See also the Liddell, Scott, and Jones *Lexicon of Classical Greek*, s.v. "agapao" and "agape" at www.perseus.tufts.edu.

13. Robert Adams, "Agape," in *The Cambridge Dictionary of Philosophy*, ed. Robert Audi (Cambridge: Cambridge University Press, 1995), 12.

14. G. Johnston, "Love in the New Testament," in *The Interpreter's Dictionary of the Bible*, ed. George Buttrick (Nashville: Abingdon Press, 1989), 169.

15. Edward Vacek, *Love, Human and Divine: The Heart of Christian Ethics* (Washington, DC: Georgetown University Press, 1994), 181.

16. Raymond Brown, *An Introduction to the New Testament* (New York: Doubleday, 1997), 249.

17. Francis Moloney, "Johannine Theology," in *The New Jerome Biblical Commentary*, eds. Raymond Brown, Joseph Fitzmeyer, Roland Murphy (Englewood Cliffs, NJ: Prentice Hall, 1990), 1420.

18. John Piper, *Love Your Enemies* (Cambridge: Cambridge University Press, 1979), 95.

19. Perkins, *Love Commands in the New Testament*, 64.

20. William Klassen, "Love: New Testament and Early Jewish Literature," 386.

21. Furnish, *The Love Command in the New Testament*, 202.

22. Brown, *Introduction to the New Testament*, 241.

23. Pheme Perkins, "The Gospel According to John," in *The New Jerome Biblical Commentary*, eds. Raymond Brown, Joseph Fitzmeyer, Roland Murphy (Englewood Cliffs, NJ: Prentice Hall, 1990), 973.

24. Edward Schillebeeckx, *Jesus: An Experiment in Christology* (New York: Crossroads, 1981), 207.

25. See Robert Karris, "The Gospel According to Luke," in *The New Jerome Biblical Commentary*, eds. Raymond Brown, Joseph Fitzmeyer, Roland Murphy (Englewood Cliffs, NJ: Prentice Hall, 1990), 697.

26. Benedict Vivano, "The Gospel According to Matthew," in *The New Jerome Biblical Commentary*, eds. Raymond Brown, Joseph Fitzmeyer, Roland Murphy (Englewood Cliffs, NJ: Prentice Hall, 1990), 669.

27. Garth Hallett, *Christian Neighbor Love: Six Rival Versions* (Washington, DC: Georgetown University Press, 1989), 113.

28. G. Johnston, "Love in the New Testament," 169.

29. Piper, *Love Your Enemies*, 56.

30. Richard Horsley, "Ethics and Exegesis: 'Love Your Enemies' and the Doctrine of Nonviolence," in *The Love of Enemy and Nonretaliation in the New Testament*, ed. Willard Swartley (Louisville: Westminster John Knox Press, 1992), 93.

31. Piper, *Love Your Enemies*, 56–57.

32. Catherine Cory, "Jesus and the Gospels," in *The Christian Theological Tradition*, eds. Catherine Cory and David Landry (Upper Saddle River, NJ: Prentice Hall, 2000), 76.

33. Hays, *The Moral Vision of the New Testament*, 154.

34. Perkins, "The Gospel According to John," 979.

35. Hays, *The Moral Vision of the New Testament*, 146.

36. Michael Hollerich, "Christianity After the Apostles," in *The Christian Theological Tradition*, eds. Catherine Cory and David Landry (Upper Saddle River, NJ: Prentice Hall, 2000), 116.

37. Hays, *The Moral Vision of the New Testament*, 147.

38. Jerome Murphy-O'Connor, "The First Letter to the Corinthians," in *The New Jerome Biblical Commentary*, eds. Raymond Brown, Joseph Fitzmeyer, Roland Murphy (Englewood Cliffs, NJ: Prentice Hall, 1990), 811.

39. Brown, *An Introduction to the New Testament*, 449.

40. Ibid.

41. Joseph Fitzmeyer, "Pauline Theology," in *The New Jerome Biblical Commentary*, eds. Raymond Brown, Joseph Fitzmeyer, Roland Murphy (Englewood Cliffs, NJ: Prentice Hall, 1990), 1407.

42. Brendan Byrne, "The Letter to the Philippians," in *The New Jerome Biblical Commentary*, eds. Raymond Brown, Joseph Fitzmeyer, Roland Murphy (Englewood Cliffs, NJ: Prentice Hall, 1990), 794.

43. For detailed discussion of these texts see Don Browning, Bonnie Miller-McLemore, Pamela Couture, K. Brynolf Lyon, and Robert Franklin, *From Culture Wars to Common Ground: Religion and the American Family Debate* (Louisville: Westminster / John Knox Press, 1997), 129–54.

44. Ibid., 131.

45. For a discussion of the authorship of Ephesians, see Brown, *An Introduction to the New Testament*, 627–30.

46. G. Johnston, "Love in the New Testament," 172.

47. Furnish, *The Love Command in the New Testament*, 205.

48. G. Johnston, "Love in the New Testament," 170.

49. James Gustafson, *Can Ethics Be Christian?* (Chicago: University of Chicago Press, 1975), 77.

Chapter Three

1. John Mahoney, *The Making of Moral Theology: A Study of the Roman Catholic Tradition* (Oxford: Clarendon Press, 1989), 43.

2. John Noonan, "Intoxicated by God,"review of *Saint Augustine*, by Garry Wills, *The New York Times Book Review*, 25 July 1999, 10.

3. Mahoney, *The Making of Moral Theology*, 43.

4. Daniel Day Williams, *The Spirit and the Forms of Love* (Lanham, MD: University Press of America, 1981), 53.

5. John Rettig, Introduction to *Tractates on the Gospel of John 112–24, Tractates on the First Epistle of John*, by Saint Augustine (Washington, DC: The Catholic University of America Press, 1995), 105–6.

6. Peter Brown, *Augustine of Hippo* (Berkeley: University of California Press, 1969), 123.

7. David Hunter, "Augustine of Hippo," in *The Christian Theological Tradition*, eds. Catherine Cory and David Landry (Upper Saddle River, NJ: Prentice Hall, 2000), 142.

8. L. Hackstaff, "Introduction," in *On the Free Choice of the Will* , by Saint Augustine, eds. Anna Benjamin and L. Hackstaff (Indianapolis: Bobbs-Merrill Educational Publishing, 1964), xxiv.

9. Peter Brown, *Augustine of Hippo*, 95.

10. Hunter, "Augustine of Hippo," 144.

11. See Brown, *Augustine of Hippo*, chapters 9 and 10. See also Gerald Bonner, *St. Augustine of Hippo: Life and Controversies* (Norwich: Canterbury Press, 1986), 201–4.

12. See Philip Merlan, "Neoplatonism," in *The Encyclopedia of Philosophy*, ed. Paul Edwards (New York: Macmillan Publishing Co., 1967), 5:474.

13. George Boas, "Love," in *The Encyclopedia of Philosophy* (New York: Macmillan Publishing Co., 1967), 5:90.

14. Amy Kass and Leon Kass, eds., *Wing to Wing, Oar to Oar: Readings on Courting and Marrying* (Notre Dame, IN: University of Notre Dame Press, 2000), 220.

15. Henry Chadwick, trans., *Confessions* (Oxford: Oxford University Press, 1991), 31 n.13.

16. Allan Bloom, *Love and Friendship* (New York: Simon & Schuster, 1993), 506.

17. Ibid., 521.

18. Plato, *Symposium*, quoted in Kass and Kass, *Wing to Wing, Oar to Oar*, 229.

19. Ibid.

20. Ibid., 230.

21. Ibid.

22. Ibid., 231.

23. Donald Burt, *Friendship and Society: An Introduction to Augustine's Practical Philosophy* (Grand Rapids, MI: William Eerdmans Publishing Company, 1999), 29.

24. Augustine, *The Confessions*, trans. Maria Boulding (New York: New City Press, 1997), book 13, section 9.

25. Henry Chadwick, "Introduction," in *Confessions*, trans. Chadwick (Oxford: Oxford University Press, 1991), xxii.

26. Augustine, *The Confessions,* trans. Boulding, book 13, sec. 9.

27. See Chadwick, "Introduction."

28. Ibid., xxvi.

29. John Collins, *A Primer of Ecclesiastical Latin* (Washington, DC: The Catholic University of America Press, 1985), 131.

30. Rettig, Introduction, 115.

31. Ibid, 115–17.

32. Etienne Gilson, *The Christian Philosophy of St. Augustine* (New York: Octagon Books, 1983), 311.

33. Augustine, *The City of God*, trans. Gerald Walsh and Grace Monahan (New York: Fathers of the Church, 1952), book 14, sec. 7.

34. John Burnaby, *Amor Dei: A Study of the Religion of St. Augustine* (Norwich: The Canterbury Press, 1991), 96.

35. Augustine, *Confessions*, book 1, sec. 1.

36. Augustine, *The City of God against the Pagans*, book 14, sec. 7.

37. David L. Mosher, Introduction to *Eighty-Three Different Questions*, by Augustine, trans. Mosher (Washington, DC: Catholic University of America Press, 1982), 2.

38. Augustine, *Eighty-Three Different Questions*, trans. David L. Mosher (Washington, DC: Catholic University of America Press, 1982), Question 35.

39. Ibid.

40. Ibid.

41. Augustine, *The Confessions*, book 2, sec. 1.

42. Ibid.

43. Ibid., book 2, sec. 6.

44. Ibid., book 2, sec. 7.

45. Ibid., book 2, sec. 9.

46. Ibid., book 2, secs. 9–10.

47. Ibid., book 2, sec. 16.

48. Ibid., book 3, sec. 1.

49. Brown, *Augustine of Hippo*, 32. Ernest Fortin's claim that "friendship does not play that prominent a role in Augustine's thought" is not accurate. See John Muether, "The Story of an Encounter," in *Augustine Today*, ed. Richard John Neuhaus (Grand Rapids, Eerdmans Publishing Company, 1993), 118.

50. Augustine, "Sermon 299D, 1," quoted in Burt, *Friendship and Society*, 57.

51. Augustine, "Letter 27, 1," quoted in Burt, *Friendship and Society*, 61.

52. Brown, *Augustine of Hippo*, 200–201.

53. Ibid., 180.

54. Augustine, *The Confessions,* book 4, sec. 7.

55. Ibid., book 4, secs. 11–12.

56. Ibid., book 4, sec. 13.

57. Ibid., book 4, secs. 13–14.

58. Ibid., book 4, sec. 15.

59. Hunter, "Augustine of Hippo," 150.

60. Augustine, *The City of God: Books XVII–XXII*, trans. Gerald Walsh and Daniel Honan (New York: Fathers of the Church, 1954), Book XIX, 8: 207–08.

61. Ibid.

62. Ibid.

63. Augustine, *The Good of Marriage*, in *St. Augustine on Marriage and Sexuality*, ed. Elizabeth Clark (Washington, DC: The Catholic University of America Press, 1996), ch. 3: 45.

64. Augustine, *Confessions*, book 4, sec. 2.

65. Brown, *Augustine of Hippo*, 62. Garry Wills, *Saint Augustine* (New York: Viking, 1999), xvii, cites the Council of Toledo 400, Canon 17, to defend this point.

66. Augustine, *Confessions*, book 6, sec. 25.

67. Ibid., book 6, sec. 26.

68. Augustine, *Eighty-Three Different Questions*, Q. 71.

69. Ibid., Q. 71.6.

70. Ibid.

71. Ibid.

72. Ibid., Q. 71.7.

73. Brown, *Augustine of Hippo*, 264.

74. Augustine, *On Christian Doctrine*, trans. D. W. Robertson (Indianapolis: The Bobbs-Merrill Company, 1958), book 2, ch. 4.

75. D. W. Robertson, Introduction to *On Christian Doctrine*, by Augustine, trans. Robertson (Indianapolis: The Bobbs-Merrill Company, 1958), ix.

76. Ibid., x.

77. Augustine, *On Christian Doctrine*, book 1, ch. 36.

78. Ibid., book 3, ch. 10.

79. Ibid., book 1, chs. 3–4.

80. Augustine, *Eighty-Three Different Questions*, Q. 30.

81. Augustine, *Faith, Hope, and Charity*, trans. Bernard Peebles, vol. 4 of *Writings of Augustine,* ed. Ludwig Schopp (New York: CIMA Publishing, 1947), 359.

82. Augustine, *Faith, Hope, and Charity*, ch. 31.

83. Augustine, *On Christian Doctrine*, book 1, ch. 5.

84. Ibid., book 1, sec. 22.

85. Augustine, *The Confessions,* book 4, sec. 10.

86. Augustine, *On Christian Doctrine*, book 1, ch. 22.

87. Augustine, "On the Morals of the Catholic Church," trans. Richard Stothert and Albert Newman, in *St. Augustine: The Writing against the Manicheans and against the Donatists*, vol. 4 of *The Nicene and Post-Nicene Fathers of the Christian Church,* ed. Philip Schaff (Grand Rapids, MI: Eerdmans Publishing Company, 1983), ch. 26.

88. Ibid.

89. Ibid.

90. Ibid., ch. 27.

91. Ibid.

92. Ibid.

93. Ibid., ch. 28.

94. Burnaby, *Amor Dei*, 136–37.

95. Ibid., 137.

96. Ibid.

97. Augustine, *On Christian Doctrine*, book 1, ch. 23.

98. Quoted in Burt, *Friendship and Society*, 62.

99. Augustine, *The Trinity*, trans. Stephen McKenna (Washington, DC: The Catholic University Press of America, 1963), book 8, ch. 10.

100. See Michael Hollerich, "John Milbank, Augustine, and the 'Secular,'" in *History, Apocalypse, and the Secular Imagination: New Essays on Augustine's City of God*, ed. Mark Vessey (Bowling Green: Philosophy Documentation Center, 1999).

101. Augustine, *Tractates on the First Epistle of John*, in *Tractates on the Gospel of John 112–24*, trans. in John Rettig (Washington, DC: The Catholic University of America Press, 1995), 7.8.

102. Augustine, *Commentary on Paul's Letter to the Galatians*, quoted in Wills, *Saint Augustine*, 57.

103. P. O'Donovan, "*Usus* and *Fruitio* in Augustine, *De Doctrina Christiana I*," *Journal of Theological Studies* 33.2 (October 1982): 387.

104. Burt, *Friendship and Society*, 39.

105. St. Augustine, *The City of God*, trans. Walsh and Monahan, book 15, sec. 4.

106. Ibid.

107. Augustine, *The Confessions*, book 10, sec. 38.

108. Augustine, *Eighty-Three Different Questions* Question, Q. 36.

109. Augustine, "On the Morals of the Catholic Church," ch. 20.

110. Ibid., ch. 21.

111. Ibid., ch. 21.

112. Augustine, *On Christian Doctrine*, book 1, ch. 33.

113. Augustine, *The Trinity*, book 14, ch. 14.

114. Augustine, *On Christian Doctrine*, book 1, ch. 24, 24.

115. Ibid.

116. Ibid.

117. Ibid., book 1, ch. 26.

118. Ibid.

119. Augustine, *Enchiridian*, ch. 32.

120. Augustine, *On Christian Doctrine*, book 1, ch. 27.

121. Ibid.

122. Ibid., book 1, ch. 28.

123. Ibid., book 1, ch. 29.

124. Ibid., book 3, ch. 10.

125. Ibid.

126. Augustine, "Sermon 344," in *The Works of Saint Augustine: A Translation for the 21st Century, Sermons III/10 (341–400) on Various Subjects*, ed. John Rotelle (Hyde Park, NY: New City Press, 1995), 49.

127. Augustine, *The Confessions*, book 4, 20: 64.

128. St. Augustine, *City of God*, book 19, sec. 14.

129. Mary Sarah Muldowney, Introduction to *Sermons on the Liturgical Seasons*, by Saint Augustine (NY: Fathers of the Church, 1959), ix–xxi.

130. Augustine, "Sermon 344," in Rotelle, *The Works of Saint Augustine*, 49–50.

131. Ibid., 50.

132. Augustine, "Sermon 349," in Rotelle, *The Works of Saint Augustine*, 101.

133. Ibid., 102.
134. Ibid.
135. Ibid., 103.
136. Ibid., 103–04.
137. Ibid., 105.
138. Ibid., book 8, ch. 8.
139. Ibid., book 8, ch. 7.
140. Ibid.
141. Ibid., book 8, ch. 4.
142. Augustine, *Eighty-Three Questions,* Q. 35.
143. Augustine, *The Confessions*, book 10, sec. 8.
144. Ibid.
145. Gilson, *The Christian Philosophy of St. Augustine*, 20.
146. Charles Taylor, *Sources of the Self: The Making of the Modern Identity* (Cambridge, MA: Harvard University Press, 1989), 134.
147. Augustine, *The Confessions*, book 10, sec. 9.
148. Taylor, *Sources of the Self,* 129.
149. Augustine, *The Confessions*, book 10, ch. 7.
150. Augustine, "On the Morals of the Catholic Church," ch. 11.
151. Ibid., ch. 12.
152. Burt, *Friendship and Society,* 5.
153. Augustine, "On the Morals of the Catholic Church," ch. 13.
154. See Augustine, *The City of God*, book 19, sec. 25.
155. Ibid.
156. Albert Newman, trans. "On the Morals of the Catholic Church," by Augustine, in *St. Augustine: The Writing against the Manicheans and against the Donatists,* vol. 4 of *The Nicene and Post-Nicene Fathers of the Christian Church,* ed. Philip Schaff (Grand Rapids, MI: Eerdmans Publishing Company, 1983), 48, n.7.
157. Ibid., ch. 15.
158. Ibid., ch. 19.
159. Ibid., ch. 22.
160. Ibid.
161. Ibid., ch. 24.
162. Ibid.

Chapter Four

1. Richard McBrien, *Catholicism* (San Francisco: Harper, 1994), 1052.
2. William James, "Mysticism," in *Classical and Contemporary Readings in the Philosophy of Religion,* ed. John Hick (Englewood Cliffs, NJ: Prentice Hall, 1970); E. J. Tinsley, "Mysticism," in *The Westminster Dictionary of Christian Theology,* eds. Alan Richardson and John Bowden (Philadelphia: The Westminster Press, 1983); "Mysticism," in *The Oxford Dictionary of the Christian Church*, eds. F. L. Cross and E. A. Livingstone (Oxford: Oxford University Press, 1990).

3. Bruno James, *The Letters of St. Bernard of Clairvaux* (Kalamazoo, MI: Cistercian Publications, 1998), xix.

4. Jean Leclercq, Introduction, to *Bernard of Clairvaux: Selected Works*, trans. Gillian Evans (New York: Paulist Press, 1987), 17.

5. James, *The Letters of St. Bernard of Clairvaux*, xx.

6. According to J. N. D. Kelly, when Pope Honorius II died in 1130 "the powerful chancellor Aimeric, with a minority of cardinals sympathetic to the newer reform tendencies . . . hastily buried the dead pope in a temporary grave and then clandestinely elected Gregorio as Innocent II." The majority of cardinals did not accept this and later in the day elected Pierleoni as Anacletus II. See J. N. D. Kelly, *The Oxford Dictionary of Popes* (Oxford: Oxford University Press, 1986), 167.

7. James, *The Letters of St. Bernard of Clairvaux*, xxi.

8. Gillian Evans, *Bernard of Clairvaux* (Oxford: Oxford University Press, 2000), 72.

9. Ibid.

10. Jean Leclercq, *Bernard of Clairvaux and the Cistercian Spirit* (Kalamazoo, MI: Cistercian Publications, 1976), 60.

11. Ibid.

12. Leclercq, Introduction, 23.

13. Leclercq, *Bernard of Clairvaux and the Cistercian Spirit*, 60. Edward Little argues that before 1139 there is "some slight evidence" that the relationship between Bernard and Abelard was "probably friendly." See Edward Little, "Relations Between St. Bernard and Abelard Before 1139," in *Saint Bernard of Clairvaux: Studies Commemorating the Eighth Centenary of His Canonization*, ed. M. Basil Pennington (Kalamazoo, MI: Cistercian Publications, 1977), 168.

14. Leclercq, "Introduction," 24.

15. Brian McGuire, *The Difficult Saint* (Kalamazoo, MI: Cistercian Publications, 1991), 34.

16. James, *The Letters of St. Bernard of Clairvaux*, xxii.

17. Indeed when McGuire's mentor suggested he write a biography of Bernard, McGuire's response was, "I can't stand the man" (McGuire, *The Difficult Saint*, 34.)

18. Leclercq, Introduction, 30.

19. Leclercq, "The Making of a Masterpiece," introduction to *On the Song of Songs IV*, by Bernard of Clairvaux, trans. Irene Edmonds (Kalamazoo, MI: Cistercian Publications, 1980), xxii.

20. Leclercq, Introduction, 30.

21. Franz Possett, "*Divus Bernhardus*: Saint Bernard as Spiritual and Theological Mentor of the Reformer Martin Luther," in *Bernardus Magister*, ed. John Sommerfeldt (Kalamazoo, MI: Cistercian Publications, 1992), 517.

22. A. Lane, "Bernard of Clairvaux: A Forerunner of John Calvin?" in *Bernardus Magister*, ed. John Sommerfeldt (Kalamazoo, MI: Cistercian Publications, 1992), 533.

23. Evans, *Bernard of Clairvaux*, 25.

24. Gillian Evans, Introduction to *On Loving God*, in *Bernard of Clairvaux: Selected Writings*, trans. Evans (New York: Paulist Press, 1987), 173.

25. See John Sommerfeldt, "Bernard as Contemplative," in *Bernardus Magister*, ed. Sommerfeldt (Kalamazoo, MI: Cistercian Publications, 1992).

26. Roland Murphy, "Canticle of Canticles," in *The New Jerome Biblical Commentary*, eds. Raymond Brown, Joseph Fitzmyer, Roland Murphy (Englewood Cliffs, NY: Prentice Hall, 1990), 463.

27. Bernard of Clairvaux, Sermon 83.II.4 in *Bernard of Clairvaux: Selected Works*, trans. Gillian Evans (New York: Paulist Press, 1987).

28. Ibid., Sermon 83.II.5.

29. Leclercq, Introduction, 47.

30. Bernard of Clairvaux, *Song of Songs I*, trans. Kilian Walsh., vol. 2 of *The Works of Bernard of Clairvaux* (Kalamazoo, MI: Cistercian Publications, 1971), Sermon 2.I.2.

31. Ibid., Sermon 2.II.3.

32. Ibid., Sermon 3.I.1.

33. Evans, *Bernard of Clairvaux*, 132

34. Bernard of Clairvaux, *Song of Songs I*, Sermon 3.II.3–4.

35. Ibid., 3.III.5.

36. M. Chenu, *Nature, Man, and Society in the Twelfth Century* (Chicago: University of Chicago Press, 1968), 283.

37. Bernard of Clairvaux, *Song of Songs I*, Sermon 7.II.1–3.

38. Ibid., 7.III.3–4.

39. Bernard of Clairvaux, *On the Song of Songs IV*, trans. Irene Edmonds (Kalamazoo, MI: Cistercian Publications, 1980), 85.IV.12.

40. Ibid., 85.IV.13.

41. John Sommerfeldt argues that Bernard's enumeration of the degrees of love are "many and varied." See John Sommerfeldt, *The Spiritual Teachings of Bernard of Clairvaux* (Kalamazoo, MI: Cistercian Publications, 1991), 98.

42. John Sommerfeldt, *The Spiritual Teachings of Bernard of Clairvaux*, 116.

43. Bernard of Clairvaux, *On Loving God*, trans. Emero Stiegman (Kalamazoo, MI: Cistercian Publications, 1995), XV.39.

44. Ibid.

45. Ibid., VIII.23.

46. Ibid., VIII.25.

47. Ibid., XV.39.

48. Ibid., IX.26.

49. Ibid., XV.39.

50. Ibid., IX.26.

51. Ibid., XV.39.

52. See Sommerfeldt, *The Spiritual Teachings of Bernard of Clairvaux*, 221; and G. Smerillo, "*Caritas* in the Initial Letters of St. Bernard," in *Saint Bernard of Clairvaux*, ed. Pennington, 135.

53. Bernard of Clairvaux, *On Loving God*, X.27.

54. Ibid., IX.28.

55. Ibid., IX.9.

56. Leclercq, Introduction, 41.

57. Evans, *Bernard of Clairvaux*, 53.

58. Bernard of Clairvaux, *On Loving God*, IX.28.

59. Ibid., XI.33.

60. Ria Vanderauwera, "The Brabant Mystic: Hadewijch," in *Medieval Women Writers*, ed. Katharina M. Wilson (Athens, GA: University of Georgia Press, 1984), 186.

61. Columba Hart, Introduction to *Hadewijch: The Complete Works*, ed. Columba Hart (New York: Paulist Press, 1980), 3.

62. Hart, Introduction, 8.

63. Harvey Egan, *An Anthology of Christian Mysticism* (Collegeville, MN: The Liturgical Press, 1991), 226.

64. Ibid., 19.

65. Ibid.

66. Ibid.

67. Ibid., 225.

68. Paul Mommaers, Preface, in *Hadewijch: The Complete Works*, ed. Columba Hart (New York: Paulist Press, 1980), xiii.

69. Vanderauwera, "The Brabant Mystic: Hadewijch," 188.

70. Mommaers, Preface, xiii.

71. Hart, *Hadewijch*, 8.

72. Thanks to my colleague Anne King for her words here.

73. Hart, Introduction, 38.

74. Ibid., 40.

75. Shawn Madigan, "Hadewijch: I Am All Love's and Love Is All Mine," in *Mystics, Visionaries, and Prophets*, ed. Shawn Madigan (Minneapolis: Fortress Press, 1998), 170.

76. Hadewijch, "Letter 20," quoted in "The Brabant Mystic: Hadewijch," by Vanderauwera, 194–95.

77. Ibid., 195.

78. Ibid., 195–96.

79. Ibid., 196.

80. Hadewijch, "Poems in Stanzas," in Hart, *Hadewijch*, 216.

81. Ibid., 218.

82. Ibid., 219.

83. Ibid., 220.

84. Ibid., 221.

85. Ibid., 224.

86. Ibid., 224–25.

87. Ibid., 236–37.

88. A. C. Spearing, Introduction to *Revelations of Diving Love*, by Julian of Norwich, trans. Elizabeth Spearing (London: Penguin Books, 1998), viii.

89. Ibid., ix.

90. John Jae-Nam Han, "Julian of Norwich," in *Catholic Women Writers: A Bio-Bibliographical Sourcebook*, ed. Mary Reichardt (Westport, CT: Greenwood Publishing Group, 2001), 187.

91. Julian of Norwich, *Showings*, trans. Edmund Colledge and James Walsh (New York: Paulist Press, 1978), ch. 86.

92. Ibid., ch. 7.

93. Ibid., ch. 22.
94. Ibid., ch. 4.
95. Ibid., ch. 7.
96. Ibid., ch. 5.
97. Ibid., ch. 53.
98. Ibid., ch. 27.
99. Ibid.
100. Ibid., ch. 37.
101. Ibid.
102. Ibid., ch. 39.
103. Ibid., ch. 49.
104. Ibid., ch. 54.
105. Ibid., ch. 58.
106. Ibid., ch. 59.
107. Ibid., ch. 60.
108. Ibid.
109. Ibid.
110. Ibid.
111. Ibid.

Chapter Five

1. James Broderick, *Saint Ignatius: The Pilgrim Years, 1491–1538* (San Francisco: Ignatius Press, 1998), 42.
2. The title "courtly love" was given the movement by Gaston Paris in an article published in 1883. See John Parry, Introduction to *The Art of Courtly Love*, by Andreas Capellanus, trans. Parry (New York: Frederick Ungar Publishing Co., 1959), 3. It is a term often used but one that is not without controversy; see F. Newman, ed., *The Meaning of Courtly Love* (Albany: State University of New York Press, 1972). For example, in the essay in that volume titled "Cleo and Venus: An Historical View of Medieval Love," John Benton argues that "'courtly love' has no useful meaning" 37.
3. See Parry, Introduction.
4. See Theodore Silverstein, "Guenevere, or the Uses of Courtly Love," in *The Meaning of Courtly Love*, ed. Newman. Etienne Gilson rejects the notion that Bernard's theology influenced courtly love. He describes Bernard's mystical love and courtly love as "two independent products of the civilization of the twelfth century." He concludes, "St. Bernard may have largely contributed to the decadence of the courtly ideal, but never in him could it have found its inspiration" (Etienne Gilson, *The Mystical Theology of Saint Bernard* [New York: Sheed and Ward, 1940], 197). Brian McGuire agrees with Gilson here but for very different reasons. McGuire writes, "But Bernard's loves were so circumscribed and so male-oriented that they eliminated even interest in what we call courtly love . . . it would be wrong to enmesh Bernard in the poetry of a world which in fact he wanted to transform according to his own vision with the monastery at its cen-

tre, a place where woman had no role to play" (Brian McGuire, *The Difficult Saint* [Kalamazoo, MI: Cistercian Publications, 1991], 33).

5. C. S. Lewis, *The Allegory of Love* (London: Oxford University Press, 1981), 2.

6. Lewis, *The Allegory of Love*, 32–37.

7. F. Newman, Preface, in *The Meaning of Courtly Love*, ed. Newman, vii.

8. Irving Singer, *The Nature of Love: Plato to Luther* (New York: Random House, 1966), 44.

9. Ibid.

10. Diane Ackerman, *A Natural History of Love* (New York: Random House, 1995), 51.

11. Ibid.

12. Lewis, *The Allegory of Love*, 3–4.

13. Capellanus, *The Art of Courtly Love*, 28–29.

14. Ibid., 31.

15. Ibid., 31–32.

16. Ibid., 33.

17. Ibid., 34

18. Ibid.

19. Ibid., 35.

20. Ibid., 81–82.

21. Capellanus, *The Art of Courtly Love*, 184–86.

22. Peter Abelard, *Historica calamitatum*, quoted by Betty Radice in "The French Scholar-Lover: Heloise," in *Medieval Women Writers*, ed. Katharina Wilson (Athens: The University of Georgia Press, 1984), 91.

23. Radice, "The French Scholar-Lover: Heloise," 91.

24. Ackerman, *A Natural History of Love*, 61.

25. See Etienne Gilson, *Heloise and Abelard* (Chicago: Henry Regnery, 1951), 9–19.

26. Abelard, *Historica calamitatum*, 91.

27. Quoted in Ackerman, *A Natural History of Love*, 63.

28. Quoted in Radice, "The French Scholar-Lover: Heloise," 94.

29. Heloise, "First Letter of Heloise to Abelard," in *Mystics, Visionaries, and Prophets: A Historical Anthology of Women's Spiritual Writings*, ed. Shawn Madigan (Minneapolis: Fortress Press, 1998), 113.

30. Ibid.

31. Ibid.

32. Ibid., 114.

33. Ibid., 115.

34. Radice, "The French Scholar-Lover: Heloise," 95.

35. Heloise, "First Letter of Heloise to Abelard," 115–16.

36. Ibid., 117.

37. Ibid.

38. Ibid., 117–18.

39. Heloise, "Letter 1. Heloise to Abelard," in *The Letters of Abelard and Heloise*, trans. Betty Radice (New York: Penguin Books, 1976), 109.

40. Abelard, "Letter 2. Abelard to Heloise," in *The Letters of Abelard and Heloise*, 119.

41. Ibid.

42. Radice, "The French Scholar-Lover: Heloise," 95.
43. Heloise, "Second Letter of Heloise to Abelard," 123.
44. Ibid., 123–24.
45. Abelard, "Letter 4. Abelard to Heloise," in *The Letters of Abelard and Heloise*, 148.
46. Ibid., 153.
47. Ibid., 156.
48. Heloise, "Letter 5. Heloise to Abelard," in *The Letters of Abelard and Heloise*, 159.
49. Ibid.
50. Radice, "The French Scholar-Lover: Heloise," 99.
51. Ackerman, *A Natural History of Love*, 65.

Chapter Six

1. David Smith, "Thomas Aquinas," in *The Christian Theological Tradition*, eds. Catherine Cory and David Landry (Upper Saddle River, NJ: Prentice Hall, 2000), 220.
2. Ibid., 222.
3. Ibid., 223.
4. Thomas Aquinas, *Summa Theologica* (New York: Benziger Brothers, 1947), II–I, Q. 28, Art. 2.
5. Ibid.
6. Ibid., II–I, Q. 28, Art. 3.
7. Ibid., II–II, Q. 25, Art. 7.
8. Ibid., II–I, Q. 28, Art. 5.
9. Ibid.
10. Ibid., II–II, Q. 24, Art. 8.
11. Ibid., II–II, Q. 25, Art. 2.
12. Ibid., II–II, Q. 27, Art. 2.
13. Ibid., II–II, Q. 24, Art. 2.
14. Ibid., II–II, Q. 24, Art. 6.
15. Ibid., II–II, Q. 24, Art. 7.
16. Ibid., II–II, Q. 24, Art. 9.
17. Ibid., II–II, Q. 24, Art. 10.
18. Ibid., II–II, Q. 24, Art. 8.
19. Ibid., II–II, Q. 27, Art. 8.
20. Ibid., II–II, Q. 25, Art. 1.
21. Ibid., II–II, Q. 27, Art. 5.
22. Ibid., II–II, Q. 26, Art. 2.
23. Ibid., II–II, Q. 25, Art. 12.
24. Ibid., II–II, Q. 25, Art. 5.
25. Ibid., II–II, Q. 25, Art. 3.
26. Ibid., II–II, Q. 25, Art. 7.
27. Ibid., II–II, Q. 25, Art. 6.
28. Ibid., II–II, Q. 25, Art. 8.
29. Ibid., II–II, Q. 26, Art. 4.

30. Ibid., II–II, Q. 26, Art. 6.
31. Ibid.
32. Ibid., II–II, Q. 26, Art. 7
33. Ibid.
34. Ibid., II–II, Q. 27, Art. 7.
35. Ibid.
36. Ibid., II–II, Q. 26, Art. 9.
37. Ibid.
38. Ibid., II–II, Q. 26, Art. 10.
39. Ibid., II–II, Q. 27, Art. 1.
40. Ibid., II–II, Q. 26, Art. 11.

Chapter Seven

1. Daniel Day Williams, *The Spirit and Forms of Love* (New York: University Press of America, 1981), 78.
2. Roland Bainton, *Here I Stand: A Life of Martin Luther* (New York: Abingdon Press, 1950), 54.
3. Paul Althaus, *The Theology of Martin Luther* (Philadelphia: Fortress Press, 1966), 117.
4. Shirley Jordon, "Martin Luther," in *The Christian Theological Tradition*, eds. Catherine Cory and David Landry (Upper Saddle River, NJ: Prentice Hall, 2000), 258.
5. Brian Gerrish, *Grace and Reason: A Study in the Theology of Luther* (Chicago: University of Chicago Press, 1979), 95.
6. Ibid.
7. Althaus, *The Theology of Martin Luther*, 134.
8. Quoted in Ibid., 133.
9. Jordon, "Martin Luther," 265.
10. Ibid., 266.
11. Charles Taylor, *Sources of the Self: The Making of Modern Identity* (Cambridge: Harvard University Press, 1989), 217.
12. Ibid., 217–18.
13. Taylor, *Sources of the Self*, 292.
14. Lawrence Stone, "Passionate Attachments in the West in Historical Perspective," in *Perspectives on Marriage: A Reader*, eds. Kieran Scott and Michael Warren (New York: Oxford University Press, 2000), 131.
15. Taylor, *Sources of the Self*, 218.
16. Quoted in Paul Althaus, *The Ethics of Martin Luther* (Philadelphia: Fortress Press, 1982), 88.
17. Althaus, *The Theology of Martin Luther*, 300.
18. Althaus, *The Ethics of Martin Luther*, 88.
19. Ibid.
20. Martin Luther, *Luther's Works*, vol. 27, ed. Jaroslav Pelikan (Saint Louis: Concordia Publishing House, 1964), 38.
21. Ibid., 27: 39.
22. Ibid., 24: 252.

23. Ibid., 51: 104.
24. Ibid., 51: 266–69.
25. Ibid., 51: 269–71.
26. Ibid., 27: 51–51.
27. Ibid., 27: 54–55.
28. Ibid., 27: 56.
29. Ibid., 27: 57–58.
30. Ibid., 27: 58–59.
31. Ibid., 25: 512–14.
32. Ibid., 44: 8–9.
33. Ibid., 21: 87–88.
34. Ibid., 44: 10–11.

Chapter Eight

1. Alastair Hannay and Gordon Marino, "Introduction," in *The Cambridge Companion to Kierkegaard*, eds. Alastair Hannay and Gordon Marino (Cambridge: Cambridge University Press, 1998), 3.

2. Georg Lukacs, "The Foundering of Form against Life: Soren Kierkegaard and Regine Olsen," in *Modern Critical Views: Soren Kierkegaard*, ed. Harold Bloom (New York: Chelsea, 1989), 6–7.

3. Alasdair MacIntyre, "Soren Aabye Kierkegaard," in *The Encyclopedia of Philosophy*, ed. Paul Edwards (New York: Macmillan, 1967), 4: 336.

4. Waldo Beach and H. Richard Niebuhr, "Soren Kierkegaard," in *Christian Ethics: Sources of the Living Tradition*, ed. Waldo Beach and H. Richard Niebuhr (New York: The Ronald Press Company, 1955), 416.

5. Lukacs, "The Foundering of Form against Life," 13.

6. Hugh Kerr, "Soren Kierkegaard," in *Readings in Christian Thought*, ed. Kerr (Nashville: Abingdon Press, 1985), 274.

7. Ibid.

8. MacIntyre, "Soren Aabye Kierkegaard," 336.

9. Howard and Edna Hong, "Translator's Introduction," in *Works of Love*, by Soren Kierkegaard, trans. Howard and Edna Hong (New York: Harper Torchbooks, 1962), 12.

10. M. Holmes Harthorne, *Kierkegaard, Godly Deceiver* (New York: Columbia University Press, 1990), 46.

11. Kierkegaard, *Works of Love*, 69.

12. Ibid., 36.

13. Ibid., 62–63.

14. Ibid., 77.

15. Ibid., 65.

16. Ibid., 67–68.

17. Ibid., 65.

18. Ibid., 66.

19. Ibid., 70.

20. Ibid., 39.

21. Ibid., 64.

22. Ibid., 9.

23. Ibid., 72.

24. Ibid., 49.

25. Ibid.

26. Ibid., 44.

27. Ibid., 74–75.

28. Ibid., 113.

29. Ibid., 142.

30. Ibid., 343.

31. Anders Nygren, *Agape and Eros* (Chicago: University of Chicago Press, 1982), 48.

32. Ibid., 208.

33. Ibid., 210.

34. Ibid., 55.

35. Ibid., 29.

36. Harlan Beckley, *Passion for Justice: Retrieving the Legacies of Walter Rauschenbusch, John A. Ryan, and Reinhold Niebuhr* (Louisville, KY: Westminster/John Knox Press, 1992), 193.

37. Quoted in James Childress, "Realism," in *The Westminster Dictionary of Christian Ethics*, eds. James Childress and John Macquarrie (Philadelphia: The Westminster Press, 1986), 527.

38. Beckley, *Passion for Justice*, 201.

39. Robin Lovin, *Reinhold Niebuhr and Christian Realism* (Cambridge: Cambridge University Press, 1995), 236.

40. Charles Brown, *Niebuhr and His Age: Reinhold Niebuhr's Prophetic Role in the Twentieth Century* (Philadelphia: Trinity Press International, 1992), 2.

41. Ibid., 1.

42. Beckley, *Passion for Justice*, 201.

43. Reinhold Niebuhr, *An Interpretation of Christian Ethics* (San Francisco: Harper & Row), 39.

44. Reinhold Niebuhr, *Human Destiny*, vol. 2 of *The Nature and Destiny of Man*, by Niebuhr (New York: Charles Scribner's Sons, 1964), 76.

45. Franklin Gamwell, "Reinhold Niebuhr's Theistic Ethic," in *The Legacy of Reinhold Niebuhr*, ed. Nathan Scott (Chicago: The University of Chicago Press, 1975), 69.

46. Niebuhr, *Human Destiny*, 247.

47. Ibid.

48. Reinhold Niebuhr, *Moral Man and Immoral Society: A Study in Ethics and Politics* (New York: Charles Scribner's Sons, 1960), 21–22.

49. Reinhold Niebuhr, *Love and Justice*, ed. D. B. Robertson (Cleveland: World Publishing Company, 1967), 30.

50. Ibid., 31–32.

51. Ibid., 32.

52. Ibid., 32–33.

53. Ibid., 34.

54. Ibid., 35.

55. Ibid., 38.

56. Niebuhr, *Moral Man and Immoral Society*, 71–72.

57. Ibid, 72.

58. Ibid., 74.

59. Ibid., 74–75.

60. Ibid., 265–66.

61. Niebuhr, *An Interpretation of Christian Ethics*, 5.

62. Ibid., 19.

63. Ibid., 23.

64. Ibid., 25.

65. Ibid., 30.

66. Ibid., 31.

67. Ibid., 35.

68. Ibid., 71.

69. Ibid., 73.

70. Ibid., 79.

71. Ibid., 80.

72. Ibid., 129.

73. Ibid., 131.

74. Ibid., 137.

75. Ibid., 141.

76. Niebuhr, *Human Destiny*, 68.

77. Ibid., 68–69.

78. Ibid., 69.

79. Ibid., 70.

80. Ibid., 72.

81. Ibid., 74.

82. Ibid.

83. Ibid., 74–75.

84. Ibid., 82.

85. Ibid., 84.

86. Ibid., 92.

87. Niebuhr, *Love and Justice*, 27–28.

88. Ibid., 28.

89. Ibid., 29.

Chapter Nine

1. Martin Luther King, Jr., "I Have a Dream," in *A Testament of Hope: The Essential Writings of Martin Luther King, Jr.*, ed. James Washington (San Francisco: HarperCollins, 1986), 219.

2. Ibid., 26.

3. Ibid., 292.

4. Ibid., 82.

5. Martin Luther King, Jr., *Strength to Love* (Philadelphia: Fortress Press, 1983), 146.

6. Martin Luther King, Jr., *A Testament of Hope: The Essential Writings of Martin Luther King, Jr.*, ed. James Washington (San Francisco: HarperCollins, 1986), 38.

7. Ibid., 26.

8. David Garrow, *Bearing the Cross: King Luther King, Jr., and the Southern Christian Leadership Conference* (New York: Vintage Books, 1988), 625.

9. Ibid., 82–83.

10. Ibid., 83.

11. King, *Strength to Love*, 51.

12. Ibid.

13. King, *A Testament of Hope*, 256.

14. King, *Strength to Love*, 51.

15. Ibid., 52.

16. Ibid., 53.

17. Ibid., 145.

18. Ibid., 47–48.

19. Ibid., 48–50.

20. Ibid., 50.

21. Ibid.

22. King, *A Testament of Hope*, 19–20.

23. Ibid., 54–55.

24. Georges Gorree and Jean Barbier, eds., *The Love of Christ: Spiritual Counsels* (San Francisco: Harper & Row, 1982), vii.

25. Malcolm Muggeridge, "No Slums in Heaven: An Introduction," in *A Gift for God: Prayers and Meditations*, by Mother Teresa of Calcutta (San Francisco: HarperCollins, 1996), 1–2.

26. Robert Inchausti, *The Ignorant Perfection of Ordinary People* (Albany: State University of New York Press, 1991), 63.

27. Ibid., 69.

28. Kathryn Spink, *Mother Teresa: A Complete Authorized Biography* (San Francisco: HarperCollins, 1997), 22.

29. Robert Ellsberg, *All Saints: Daily Reflections on Saints, Prophets, and Witnesses for our Time* (New York: Crossroad Publishing Company, 1997), 393.

30. Mother Teresa, quoted in *Mother Teresa*, by Spink, 246.

31. Spink, *Mother Teresa*, 246.

32. www.tisv.be/mt/nobel.htm.

33. Mother Teresa, quoted in *The Love of Christ*, eds. Gorree and Barbier, 30.

34. Mother Teresa, quoted in *Life in the Spirit: Reflections, Meditations, Prayers, Mother Teresa of Calcutta*, ed. Kathryn Spink (San Francisco: Harper & Row, 1983), 37–39.

35. Mother Teresa of Calcutta, *A Gift for God: Prayers and Meditations* (San Francisco: HarperCollins, 1996), 11–13.

36. Ibid, 24–25.

37. Mother Teresa, quoted in *Life in the Spirit*, ed. Spink, 1.

38. Ibid.

39. Mother Teresa, quoted in *Love: A Fruit Always in Season*, ed. Dorothy Hunt (San Francisco: Ignatius Press, 1987), 43.

40. Ibid., 45.

41. Ibid., 51.

42. Mother Teresa, quoted in *Life in the Spirit*, ed. Spink, 40–41.

43. Mother Teresa, quoted in *The Love of Christ*, eds. Gorree and Barbier, 113–14.

44. Mother Teresa, quoted in *Love*, ed. Hunt, 202.

45. Mother Teresa of Calcutta, *A Gift for God*, 13.

46. Mother Teresa, quoted in *Love*, ed. Hunt, 130–31.

47. Ibid., 219–20.

48. Ibid., 39–40.

49. Mother Teresa, quoted in *Mother Teresa*, by Spink, xi.

50. Ibid., ix.

51. Spink, *Mother Teresa*, ix.

52. Mother Teresa, quoted in *Mother Teresa*, by Spink, x.

53. John Paul II, *Centesimus Annus* (Washington, DC: United States Catholic Conference, 1991), 38–39.

54. George Weigel, *Witness to Hope: The Biography of Pope John Paul II* (New York: HarperCollins, 1999), 4.

55. John Paul II, *Crossing the Threshold of Hope* (New York: Knopf, 1994), 123.

56. Ibid., 122–23.

57. John Paul II, *Redemptor Hominis* (Washington, DC: United States Catholic Conference, 1979), 27.

58. Ibid., 28.

59. Richard Hogan and John LeVoir, "The Family and Sexuality," in *John Paul II and Moral Theology: Readings in Moral Theology No. 10*, by Charles Curran and Richard McCormick (New York: Paulist Press, 1998), 158.

60. Ibid.

61. Ibid., 158–59.

62. John Paul II, *Dives in Misericordia* (Washington, DC: United States Catholic Conference, 1981), 23.

63. Ibid., 24.

64. Ibid., 25.

65. Ibid,. 25–26.

66. Ibid., 27.

67. John Paul II, *Crossing the Threshold of Hope*, 75.

68. John Paul II, *Faith and Reason* (Washington, DC: United States Catholic Conference, 1998), 37.

69. Ibid., 137.

70. John Paul II, *Veritatis Splendor* (Boston: St. Paul Books and Media, 1993), 21.

71. Ibid., 33–34.

72. John Paul II, *Crossing the Threshold of Hope*, 200–1.

73. Ibid., 201.

74. Ibid., 201–02.

75. Ibid., 202.

76. Ibid.

77. John Paul II, *Letter to Families* (Washington, DC: United States Catholic Conference, 1994), 15.

78. John Paul II, *Veritatis Splendor*, 26.

79. John Paul II, *Dives in Misericordia*, 7–8.

80. John Paul II, *Sollicitudo Rei Socialis*, in *Catholic Social Thought: The Documentary Heritage*, eds. David O'Brien and Thomas Shannon (Maryknoll: Orbis press, 1992), 423.

81. John Paul II, *Evangelium Vitae* (St. Paul, MN: The Leaflet Missal Company, 1995), 43.

82. John Paul II, *Centesimus Annus*, 108.

83. John Paul II, *Sollicitudo Rei Socialis*, 425.

84. John Paul II, *Evangelium Vitae*, 86.

85. John Paul II, *Letter to Families*, 15.

86. Ibid.

87. Ibid.

88. Ibid., 16.

89. John Paul II, *Familiaris Consortio* (Washington, DC: United States Catholic Conference, 1983), 9.

90. Ibid.

91. Ibid., 25.

92. See Weigel, *Witness to Hope*, 334, 341, 342.

93. Ibid., 17.

94. Ibid., 341.

95. John Paul II, *Familiaris Consortio*, 29.

96. Ibid.

97. Ibid.

98. Ibid., 32.

99. Ibid., 33.

100. John Paul II, *Faith and Reason*, 48–49.

Chapter Ten

1. Gene Outka, *Agape: An Ethical Analysis* (New Haven, CT: Yale University Press, 1972), 258.

2. H. Richard Niebuhr, *Christ and Culture* (New York: Harper & Row, 1951), 17.

3. Quoted in Allen Mandelbaum, Introduction to *The Inferno*, by Dante, trans. Allen Mandelbaum (New York: Bantam Books, 1982), xvi.

4. H. Richard Niebuhr, *The Purpose of the Church and Its Ministry* (New York: Harper & Row, 1977), 35.

5. Jules Toner, *The Experience of Love* (Washington, DC: Corpus Books, 1968), 65.

6. Ibid., 62.

7. Ibid., 95.

8. Ibid., 95–96.

9. Ibid., 97.
10. Ibid., 100.
11. Ibid., 108–09.
12. Ibid., 117.
13. Ibid., 120.
14. Ibid., 121.
15. Ibid., 123.
16. Ibid., 125.
17. Ibid., 127.
18. Ibid., 130.
19. Ibid., 141.
20. Ibid., 141–42.
21. Ibid., 144.
22. Ibid., 160.
23. Ibid., 166.
24. Ibid., 169.
25. Ibid., 183.
26. Ibid., 198.
27. Outka, *Agape*, 2.
28. Ibid., 260.
29. Ibid., 13.
30. Ibid., 260.
31. Ibid., 12.
32. Ibid., 11.
33. Ibid., 282.
34. Ibid., 262–63.
35. Ibid., 265.
36. Ibid., 266.
37. Ibid., 267.
38. Ibid., 269.
39. Ibid., 274.
40. Ibid., 278.
41. Ibid., 278.
42. Ibid., 288.
43. Ibid., 288.
44. Ibid., 311–12.
45. Gustavo Gutierrez, *A Theology of Liberation: History, Politics, and Salvation* (Maryknoll, NY: Orbis Books, 1988), 113.
46. Ibid.
47. Ibid., 114.
48. Ibid., 114–15.
49. Ibid., 115.
50. Ibid., 116.
51. Ibid., 159.
52. Ibid.

53. Ibid., xxvi.

54. Ibid., 160.

55. Ibid., 165.

56. Ibid., 168.

57. Ibid., 173.

58. Ibid., 170.

59. Ibid., 172.

60. Martin D'Arcy, *The Mind and Heart of Love* (New York: Meridian Books, 1956), 88.

61. Ibid., 90.

62. Ibid., 275–76.

63. Outka, *Agape*, 275

64. D'Arcy, *The Mind and Heart of Love*, 366.

65. Ibid., 364.

66. Ibid., 365.

67. Ibid.

68. Ibid., 367.

69. Barbara Hilkert Andolsen, "Agape in Feminist Ethics," in *On Love and Friendship: Philosophical Readings*, ed. Clifford Williams (Boston: Jones and Bartlett, 1995), 172.

70. Ibid., 177.

71. Ibid.

72. Margaret Farley, *Personal Commitments: Beginning, Keeping, Changing* (San Francisco: Harper & Row, 1986), 80.

73. Ibid., 82.

74. Ibid., 82–83.

75. Ibid., 83.

76. Ibid., 105

77. Ibid.

78. Ibid.

79. Ibid., 106.

80. Edward Vacek, *Love, Human and Divine: The Heart of Christian Ethics* (Washington, DC: Georgetown University Press, 1994), xiv.

81. Ibid.

82. Ibid., 34.

83. Ibid., 44.

84. Ibid., 34.

85. Ibid., 117.

86. Ibid., 141.

87. Ibid., 142.

88. Ibid., 143.

89. Ibid., 149.

90. Ibid., 157–58.

91. Ibid., xvi.

92. Ibid., 280–81.

93. Ibid., 281.

94. Ibid., 286.
95. Ibid., 287.
96. Ibid., 288.
97. Ibid., 295.
98. Ibid., 298.
99. Ibid., 299.
100. Ibid., 308.
101. Ibid., 308–09.
102. Ibid., 309–310.
103. Ibid., 310.
104. Ibid.
105. Ibid., 312.
106. Don Browning, Bonnie Miller-McLemore, Pamela Couture, K. Brynolf Lyon, and Robert Franklin, *From Culture Wars to Common Ground: Religion and the American Family Debate* (Louisville, KY: Westminster John Knox Press, 1997), 18.
107. Ibid., 59.
108. Ibid., 275.
109. Ibid., 273.
110. Ibid., 127.
111. Ibid., 282.
112. Ibid., 127.
113. Ibid.
114. Ibid., 285.
115. Ibid., 153.
116. Ibid., 295.
117. Ibid., 276.

Chapter Eleven

1. Thomas Aquinas, *Summa Theologica* (New York: Benzinger Brothers, 1947), I–II, Q. 91, Art. 2.
2. Garth Hallett, *Christian Neighbor Love: Six Rival Versions* (Washington, DC: Georgetown University Press, 1989), 5.
3. Ibid., 61.
4. Ibid.
5. Ibid., 57.
6. Ibid.

Index

Abelard, Peter: Bernard's challenge to, 126–27, 284n13; Heloise and, 157–63, 268; intention and moral life for, 236; written life story, 159

Abraham, 44–45

Ackerman, Diane, 153, 158, 163

adultery: courtly love and, 152; Luther on married love and, 191–92; in Old Testament, 41–44

agape: affective element of, 267; affirming element of, 268–69; Augustine and, 267, 268; *eros* and, 53–54, 199–200, 252–53, 259, 261–62, 267; Great Commandment and, 65; Greek New Testament and, 52–54, 81–82, 266; as impossible ideal, 272–73; Jesus and meaning of, 54; King on, 215–17, 268; love for enemies and, 215–16, 268; neighbor love, 246–48, 268–69, 270; New Testament, 52–54, 65, 67–69, 73–76, 81–82, 199–200, 266, 267; Niebuhr on, 207–8; Nygren on, 199–200, 252–53, 267; Outka on, 246–48, 268; Paul and, 69; *philia* and, 53, 54, 259, 261–62; responsive element of, 269–70; self-love and, 270; self-sacrifice and, 207–8, 269–70; as service, 269–70; and shifts in early Christian community, 67–68; sin and, 273; steadfast element of, 271–72; substance of, 266–72; summation of, in First Letter of John, 73–76; as unique feature of Christianity, 199–200; unitive element of, 270–71; Vacek on, 259, 261–62; women theologians on, 256

Agape: An Ethical Analysis (Outka), 246–48

Agape and Eros (Nygren), 199–200, 252

'*aheb*, 1, 2

Althaus, Paul, 181

amor, 165–68

Andolsen, Barbara Hilkert, 255–56

Aristotle, 164, 167

The Art of Courtly Love (Capellanus), 151, 155–56

Augustine, St., 77–124; and *agape*, 267, 268; and *caritas*, 81–82, 100, 108, 111–12, 200; concrete examples of loving, 111; and *cupiditas*, 111–12; and divine charity, 116–17; on family love and relationships, 112–17; on friendship, 83, 87–88, 89–99, 101, 102, 280n49; Great Commandment and, 100–106, 110–12; on his family, 85–86; on his youthful sinning, 86–89; influence on Christian tradition of love, 77, 200; on interpreting the Bible, 99–100; and inwardness, 119–22; and Latin Bible, 81–82; on legitimate human love/charity, 114–16; life of, 78, 81, 84, 85–86; on love as binding, 105; love as desiring, 83, 84; love as dominant feature in theology of, 77–78; and love as use/enjoyment, 100–102, 111–12; and love for enemies, 111; and love for God, 100–106, 110–11, 117–24, 171; on loving abstractly, 110–11; and loving the material world, 107–8, 118–19; on lust, 85–86, 88–89; Luther and, 189; on marriage, 95–96; on the mind, 118, 120, 121, 123; on misdirected love, 83–89; on neighbor love, 100–106, 110–13, 117–18, 268; and neoplatonism, 78–81, 122; on ordering/hierarchy of loves, 101–3, 107–10, 189; and priority of intention over act, 105–6; on psychology of love, 84; and self-love, 102–3, 109–10, 189; sermons of, 112–17; theme of movement and rest of the soul, 80–81; Thomas Aquinas and, 165; true love and the will, 84; on two stages of love, 110–11; on unlawful and lawful human loves, 115–17; on virtue and right conduct, 121–24

Bainton, Ronald, 180

Beckley, Harlan, 200

Beloved Disciple, 66

Benton, John, 287n2

Bernard of Clairvaux, 125–40; and Abelard's theology, 126–27, 284n13; and courtly love, 151–52, 287n4; and genre of mystical tradition, 127–28, 287n4; life of, 125–27; and love for God, 136–37; and self-love, 135–40; and Song of Songs, 128, 129–35, 141; on spiritual marriage, 133–35; on stages of love, 135–40, 285n41; writings of, 127–28, 129–40, 141